HILL GUIDES™ SERIES

SANTA BARBARA
& THE CENTRAL COAST

California's Riviera

Fourth Edition

Kathleen Thompson Hill
&
Gerald Hill

INSIDERS' GUIDE®

GUILFORD, CONNECTICUT
AN IMPRINT OF THE GLOBE PEQUOT PRESS

INSIDERS' GUIDE®

Cover and text design by Lana Mullen
Illustrations by Mauro Magellan
Photos by Kathleen and Gerald Hill unless otherwise noted

ISSN 1536-6227
ISBN 978-0-7627-4559-3

Printed in the United States of America
10 9 8 7 6 5 4 3 2 1

CONTENTS

PREFACE

The central coast of California is a treasure trove of discoveries, all too often neglected by travelers who race along the highway between Los Angeles and the San Francisco Bay area. To fully appreciate California's Riviera, we ask you to pause with us long enough to come to know the charming towns, the varied menus, the new wave of wines, and the pleasant and interesting people of this underdiscovered scenic wonderland.

We take you through historic Santa Barbara, which has established a Mediterranean style of architecture and living with a climate to match, beautified and surprisingly sophisticated San Luis Obispo, and the coastal and wine country villages and valleys in both counties. Solvang has managed to create a slice of Denmark-in-America without too much glitz, and Santa Maria has become synonymous with scrumptious barbecue. Paso Robles spiffed itself up masterfully, suffered a devastating earthquake in December 2003, and turned a huge negative into a major positive, adding loads of wine tasting rooms, cheese shops, and new restaurants around the town's central square.

The recently acclaimed wines of the central coast are demonstrating the wisdom shown by pioneering experts who believed San Luis Obispo and Santa Barbara Counties could be some of the world's ideal wine-producing regions. Follow us to the vineyards in the hills above San Luis Obispo, the roads fanning out from Paso Robles, the lanes of Edna Valley, and the old frontier towns of Santa Ynez Valley. Grapes are growing everywhere, and we guide you to tasting rooms of every size and style.

Five sensitively restored missions, the remarkable Hearst Castle, and dozens of tempting restaurants await your visit. The beaches call out to you: Morro Bay, Avila Beach, Pismo Beach, Goleta, Carpinteria, Grover Beach, and Santa Barbara, as well as hidden coves in between, with clear white sand, easy access, pleasant accommodations, and summer sun nearly year-round.

We urge you to explore California's Riviera in depth. You may never leave.

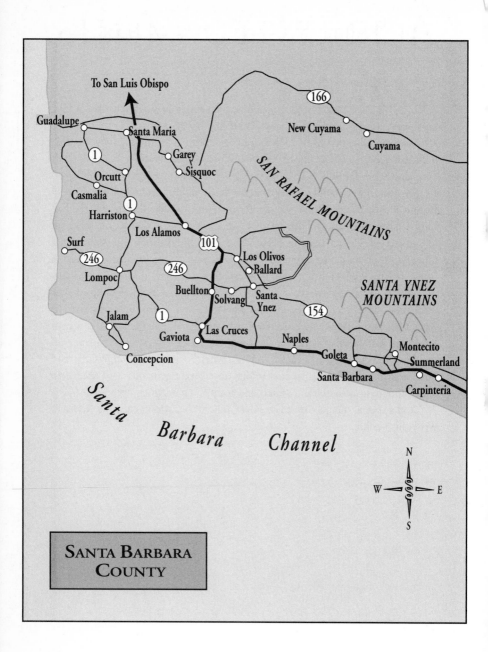

ACKNOWLEDGMENTS

$\mathcal{A}$s is true for all our books, our work was made possible by the assistance and cooperation of many people and organizations.

We would like first to thank Laura Kath of Mariah Marketing (www.mariah marketing.com), a fellow Globe Pequot author, for her especially hot tips, guidance, and super friendly help in Santa Barbara and in the Santa Ynez Valley.

We were given fabulous help by the staffs of the Santa Barbara Visitors Bureau, the San Luis Obispo County Visitors and Conference Bureau, the San Luis Obispo Downtown Association, the San Luis Obispo Chamber of Commerce, the Santa Barbara Historical Society, the Paso Robles Vintners & Growers Association, the Santa Barbara County Vintners' Association, and the Santa Barbara Public Library among others.

Several friends served as reporting scouts, including Gordon Phillips, Marie Hicklin, Gig and Mel Owen, Sue Holman, and Susan Weeks. Karen Kyle of the San Luis Obispo Art Center steered us toward valuable information and contacts. Joni Kelly helped with fact checking.

The store proprietors, chefs, winery owners, winemakers and staffs, and hotel and motel operators we met in our travels were generous with their help and willingness to share their secrets and recipes. Thank you very much.

And a special thanks to the late Julia Child for her strong encouragement to write this book.

INTRODUCTION

he first time we went to Santa Barbara together was on our honeymoon. We were slowly making our way down the Pacific coast from San Francisco, with one criterion for places to stay: We had to be able to hear the ocean's waves from our hotel room. Bliss! Eventually we arrived in Santa Barbara—a gorgeous and welcoming place for singles, couples, partners, and families of all sizes and most income levels.

For this book we treat as central coast everything from Hearst Castle at San Simeon in the north to south of Carpinteria near the Santa Barbara–Ventura County line. Some people would include Monterey County, but you can enjoy that information in our *Hill Guide to Monterey and Carmel,* which provides complete details on everything from natural wonders to galleries, shops, museums, wineries, and restaurants.

Santa Barbara, Santa Barbara County, San Luis Obispo, Paso Robles, and the rest of San Luis Obispo County are all beautiful and rich in California history, with varied climates (coastal to arid), beautiful beaches, waving palm trees, little-known wineries and restaurants, and natural flora.

This is hourse country, with an intensity rarely seen. While many Californians fill their backyards with swimming pools, residents of these two counties fill theirs with horses. Hence, horse or western fans will find great western stores in most towns and cities and will undoubtedly go home with a cool cowboy hat they won't wear.

We almost hesitate to spread the word, but because these areas are well accustomed to visitors from throughout the world, our consciences are clear. So here we go.

SANTA BARBARA

Santa Barbara is one of the most beautiful and romantic places in North America. Plain and simple. It is at once quiet and exciting, flat and mountainous, small-town and big-city, progressive and conservative, and elegant and casual.

You can visit a western guest ranch a la President Ronald Reagan and Fess Parker, or go whale watching, wine tasting, mountain biking, sailing, parasailing, sunbathing, Jet Skiing, surfing, and beachcombing along nine beaches stretching 20 miles; you can play volleyball, try in-line skating, go shopping-shopping-shopping, visit art galleries galore, and enjoy theatrical and musical performances year-round. To say nothing of celebrity spotting.

Hollywood stars flock here to find a unique privacy of togetherness in breathtaking surroundings, and many live here at least part-time, knowing that Santa Barbarans won't reveal their secret hideaways. In the early 1900s Santa Barbara became the film capital of the world before Hollywood developed as movie capital. In a ten-year period, 1,200 movies (lots of Westerns) were made here, and you will recognize the scenery as you visit the wineries throughout Santa Barbara and San Luis Obispo Counties.

Santa Barbara County sits 90 miles north of Los Angeles and borders on Ventura County to the south. It's an easy ninety-minute drive from Los Angeles, but a good eight hours from San Francisco, which is 332 miles north. Traveling from San Francisco, we recommend a luxurious stop in Cambria or in the San Luis Obispo wine country to split the drive into two days and allow for a visit to Hearst Castle at San Simeon. But you can just barrel on down in one day if you wish.

The county includes the cities of Carpinteria, Goleta, Montecito, Summerland, Santa Barbara, and the five Channel Islands. Ballard, Buellton, Lompoc, Los Alamos, Los Olivos, Guadalupe, Santa Maria, Santa Ynez, and Solvang are all in northern Santa Barbara County and have their own interesting and distinct reasons for you to visit.

You will find Santa Barbara's Mediterranean climate to be possibly the best you have ever experienced: sunny 300 days over twelve months of the year. Newscasters refer to drizzle or a temperature drop to about 55° as a "storm." The temperature averages in the 60s and 70s, with surprisingly low humidity, considering Santa Barbara's proximity to the Pacific Ocean.

Santa Barbara's mixed population results in marvelously diverse ethnic foods and markets, with restaurants ranging from local Mexicans' favorite Mexican to northern outposts of some of Los Angeles's finest. Population totals for Santa Barbara reach around 95,000—nearly 422,000 for the county.

SAN LUIS OBISPO

San Luis Obispo may be one of your great West Coast travel discoveries. The county stretches from the Monterey County line south to Santa Barbara

County, with exciting cliffs and beaches along the Pacific Ocean, and interesting towns such as San Simeon (and the Hearst Castle), Cambria, Morro Bay, San Luis Obispo, Pismo Beach, Arroyo Grande, Nipomo, Avila Beach, Atascadero, Templeton, and Paso Robles with its expanding wine country.

Located 200 miles north of Los Angeles and 230 miles south of the San Francisco Bay area, the city of San Luis Obispo feels small and intimate, with tree-lined streets, small boutiques (as well as several large chain coffee shops and bookstores), innovative and comfort-food restaurants, and reasonable prices. In addition to Mission San Luis Obispo de Toloso's library and historic museum, an arts center and galleries, California Polytechnic State University (Cal Poly), a children's museum, and a modern performing arts center, the city also has its own "path of history" walking tour. San Luis Obispo's Thursday evening farmers' market is a classic, with abundant local growers' fruits of labor, entertainment, and shops staying open late.

Paso Robles and its neighbor to the south, tiny Templeton, are both Western movie–style towns where it's hot and dusty in summer, lovely in winter. Both are growing as food and wine centers and are worth rediscovering.

The climate in San Luis Obispo County varies, with mild days (50° to 70°) year-round on the coast to cool 55° nights and hot 109° days in the summer inland near and east of San Luis Obispo.

Lake Nacimiento, Lopez Lake, Laguna Lake, Santa Margarita Lake, and Atascadero Lake afford boating, water sports, and lake fishing. Hiking, kayaking, golf, miniature golf, horseback riding, specialty farms, museums, whale watching, a monarch butterfly grove at Pismo State Beach, sailing, sailboarding, and the Charles Paddock Zoo in Atascadero all offer plenty to do and see for the whole family. And then there are the wonderful wineries.

How to Get Here

Santa Barbara and most of the central coast are easily reachable via U.S. Highway 101 or California Highway 1, which occasionally merge and become one. US 101 is a scenic and relatively peaceful freeway route that runs the length of California slightly inland from the ocean, while Highway 1 runs along the Pacific Ocean, at times seeming to hang over it. You can also ride Amtrak's Coast Starlight to and through this gorgeous terrain, sometimes getting even closer views of the ocean than from the highway. Several airlines land at Santa Barbara Airport just outside of nearby Goleta, and the Santa Barbara Airbus transports visitors to and from Los Angeles area airports.

Santa Barbara's county Air Pollution Control District now offers "Santa

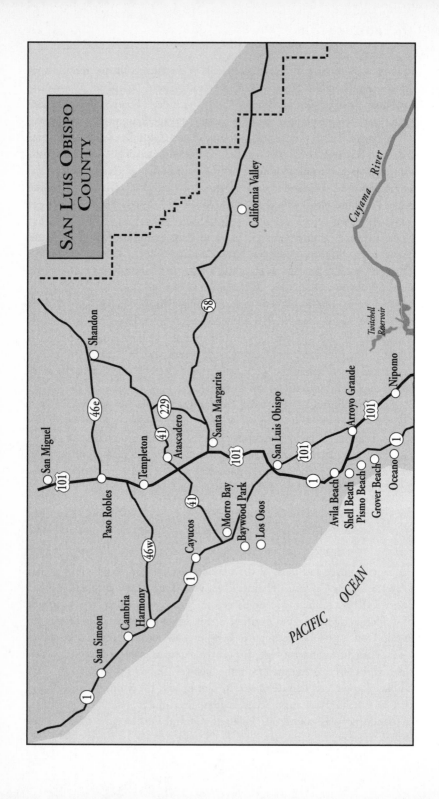

Barbara Car Free!," an ingenious linkage of Amtrak trains, the electric Old Town Trolley, rented bicycles, tour guides, sailboats and kayaks and other boats, pedal cabs, and taxis. We highly recommend taking Amtrak, for which it and Santa Barbara Car Free! offer half-off fares and substantial hotel discounts for Amtrak passengers and anyone else who arrives without a car and commits to the Car Free program. We did it, and it is environmentally sound, easy, and relatively responsibility-free. Amtrak also takes you through sights you can't see from a car, and the food is hugely improved, with healthy offerings both in the dining car and "cafe" downstairs in the Club Car, and electrical outlets near some seats. Highly recommended. For more information write P.O. Box 60436, Santa Barbara 93160; call (805) 696-1100; or log on to www.santabarbaracar free.org.

Getting Here by Car

From Los Angeles, either take the Ventura Freeway (US 101) straight out of town heading north to Santa Barbara through Thousand Oaks, Oxnard, Ventura, and Carpinteria to Summerland, Montecito, and Santa Barbara, or take the scenic route along Highway 1 from Newport Beach or Santa Monica along the coast through Malibu. Highway 1 and US 101 join near Oxnard and run northwestward along the water through Carpinteria, Summerland, and Montecito to Santa Barbara.

To reach San Luis Obispo you basically follow US 101 or Highway 1 when they are one and the same or when they separate and then follow our directions to specific destinations. North of Santa Barbara, Highway 1 splits off from US 101 near Las Cruces and takes you to Lompoc, Vandenberg Air Force Base, Guadalupe, and Grover Beach, and then rejoins US 101 at Arroyo Grande, heading north to Pismo Beach, Avila Beach, and San Luis Obispo. It splits off to the west again at San Luis Obispo and goes to Morro Bay, Cambria, and San Simeon and Hearst Castle.

From Bakersfield and Fresno, take Highway 46 to Paso Robles, and then US 101 south to San Luis Obispo and Santa Barbara.

From San Francisco and San Jose, your two choices are to take US 101 on the east side of the Coast Range and Santa Lucia Mountains (excellent wine tasting along the way) or to take Highway 1 down the Pacific Ocean for the dramatically scenic and occasionally breathtaking route through Carmel, Big Sur, San Simeon and Hearst Castle, Cambria, and Morro Bay, where Highway 1 turns inland to meet US 101 at San Luis Obispo. You can also cross the Santa Lucia Mountains on Highway 46 from Cambria to Paso Robles on US 101, then follow US 101 south from Paso Robles to Templeton, Santa Margarita, and San Luis Obispo, where it joins Highway 1. Proceed southward on Highway 1 to Avila Beach, Pismo Beach, and Arroyo Grande. From here Highway 1 splits oceanward, passing through Guadalupe, Orcutt, Vandenberg Air Force Base, and Lompoc. It rejoins US 101 in Las Cruces and continues to Gaviota, Isla Vista, Goleta, and finally Santa Barbara.

San Luis Obispo is about four hours from Los Angeles and San Francisco (five hours from San Francisco via scenic, winding Highway 1).

Getting Here by Air

Major airlines: American Eagle (800-433-7300); America West and America West Express (800-235-9292); and United Airlines, United Express, and United Shuttle (800-241-6522) all land at Santa Barbara Airport (805-683-4011), the most elegant and charming small airport we have ever seen. The airport's architecture and landscaping give first-time visitors their first glimpse of the agreed-upon architecture and ambience of the Santa Barbara area. The only slight negative is that the car rental offices are a good walk from the landing tarmac, which sometimes presents a problem when wheeling loaded luggage carts.

Super Ride Shuttle (805-683-9636 or 800-977-1123) offers rides from Santa Barbara Airport to your local destination. The fare is approximately $18. Santa Barbara Airbus (805-964-7759 or 800-423-1618; www.sbairbus.com) provides transportation to and from Los Angeles Airport (LAX), picking passengers up close to their airlines if they reserve ahead. Fares are $34 for one person, $56 for two people together, and $74 for three people traveling together for about a two-hour trip. Airbus also offers tours from Santa Barbara to the Los Angeles County Museum, L.A. Dodgers games, and to the J. Paul Getty Museum, as well as limousine service.

American Eagle (800-433-7300) serves San Luis Obispo County Airport, 3 miles from downtown San Luis Obispo, as do Reno Air, United Express, Alaska Airlines, Air Canada, and Hawaiian Airlines, for a total of forty flights a day.

Air charters: The Santa Barbara area's unique residential and visiting populations often prefer to charter their own air transportation. In case you fit into that category, we offer the most prominent of those services. Call them for personalized specifics: Executive Jet (805-692-9921) and Sunwest Aviation (800-293-2437).

Getting Here by Amtrak

Amtrak's Surfliner connects San Diego, Santa Barbara, and San Luis Obispo, and the Coast Starlight stops in Santa Barbara on its daily Los

Angeles–Seattle run. Santa Barbara's train station has recently undergone an earthquake retrofit and renovations, restoring it to its historic glory. Connect to Santa Barbara Car Free! for great discounts and nonpolluting transportation. If you prefer personalized transportation rather than a taxi to your hotel, contact Cycles 4 Rent (805-652-0462; www.cycles4rent.com), and a scooter will be delivered to the station upon your arrival. Taxis, pedi-cabs, and the Old Town Trolley all show up at the train station when trains arrive.

Getting Here by Bus

Greyhound Bus Lines (800-231-2222) stops regularly in both Santa Barbara and San Luis Obispo. The Santa Barbara bus station is modern, well lighted, and centrally located just a block from State Street at 34 West Carrillo Street (805-965-7551). In San Luis Obispo, Greyhound stops at 150 South Street (805-543-2121).

GETTING AROUND ONCE YOU'RE HERE

By Bus in Santa Barbara

Santa Barbara Metropolitan Transit District provides bus transportation in and between Goleta, Santa Barbara, and Carpinteria. Essential for visitors, it also offers an electric downtown/waterfront shuttle up and down State Street, along Cabrillo and the beach, and to Coast Village Road in Montecito (bus 14). Cost: 25 cents. MTD has a service, called the Field Trip, that runs from the waterfront to the top ten highlights of the area, including the mission botanic garden, the museum, county courthouse, and more. Fare is $1. The Santa Barbara Trolley runs between hotels, historic sites, shopping areas, and cultural attractions. Fare is $11 for adults, $7 for children.

Santa Barbara's electric downtown shuttle departs from Stearns Wharf every ten minutes from 10:15 a.m. to 6:00 p.m. It also departs every thirty minutes weekdays from 7:45 to 10:00 a.m., Friday and Saturday from 6:30 to 9:00 p.m., Saturday from 8:15 to 10:00 a.m., and Sunday from 9:30 to 10:00 a.m. There is no evening service in winter. Watch for the turquoise blue signs for shuttle stops. Fare is 25 cents.

Both Santa Barbara and San Luis Obispo have excellent public transportation systems, but in case you need private alternatives, here they are.

By Taxi in Santa Barbara

Several transportation entities offer taxi service in Santa Barbara, some using hybrid cars: American Cab (805-689-0683), Beachside Taxi (805-966-5600), Orange Cab (805-964-2800), Rose Cab (805-564-2600), Santa Barbara Airport Cab (805-895-2422), SuperRide Airport Shuttle (805-683-9636), and Yellow Cab (805-965-5111 or 800-549-TAXI from California phones only).

Limousine Service in Santa Barbara

Limo services that cater to locals, visitors, and celebrities include Ambassador Limousine Service (805-648-7104), Celebrity Limo Service (805-683-1613), Classic Limousine Service (800-243-5466), Executive Limousine Service (805-969-5525 or 800-247-6980), Home James Limousine Service (805-647-1739), Mammoth Limousine Service (805-683-4807), Ocean Cities Limousine Service (805-962-0507), Personal Tours Ltd. (805-685-0552), Santa Barbara Professional Limousine Service and Final Detail (805-967-9831 or 805-964-5466), Santa Ynez Valley Limousine Service (805-688-6532), Sunset Limousine Service (805-963-0419), and Walter's Limo Service (805-964-7759).

Rental Car Agencies in Santa Barbara

The usual are available and generally well kept up: Avis Rent-A-Car (805-965-1079 downtown and 805-964-4848 at the airport), Budget Rent-A-Car & Truck (805-963-6651 downtown or 800-527-0700), Dollar Rent-A-Car (805-683-1468), Enterprise Rent-A-Car (805-966-3097 downtown and 805-683-0067 in Goleta), Hertz Rent-A-Car (805-967-0411 at the airport), National Car Rental (805-967-1202), and U-Save Auto Rental (805-963-3499).

Cycling in Santa Barbara

Santa Barbara County publishes *The Official Santa Barbara County Bike Map,* which shows routes and rates bike lanes and paths in and between Santa Maria, Orcutt, Lompoc, Solvang, Los Alamos, Buellton, Ballard, Los Olivos, Santa Barbara, Carpenteria, and Montecito. For more information contact Traffic Solutions, Santa Barbara Association of Governments, (805) 963-7283; www.sbcag.org or www.trafficsolutions.info.

By Bus in San Luis Obispo

A free and open trolley runs in a loop around San Luis Obispo's downtown area, a wonderful convenience. SLO Transit (which is an abbreviation, not a comment) provides bus service throughout the city of San Luis Obispo and to Cal Poly. Regional Transit Authority (RTA) runs buses outside the city of San Luis Obispo to Cal Poly, Santa Margarita, Atascadero, Templeton, Paso Robles, San Miguel, and many other communities. Fares $1.00 to $2.75; www.slorta .org.

PARKING

Parking in Santa Barbara is easiest if you plant your car before lunchtime in a public parking lot or garage where the rates are reasonable enough to encourage you to come downtown. Ten parking lots and garages are available behind the shops on State Street, with entrances from the cross streets or from Chapala Street on the west side and Anacapa Street on the east. Chapala runs one-way up (north) and Anacapa runs one-way down (south). (See map, page 12.) There is no parking on State Street, which definitely contributes to its visual beauty.

Downtown parking in San Luis Obispo is available on many streets or in several parking lots. (See map, page 129.) Try the lots at Higuera Street between Broad and Garden Streets; Higuera and Morro Streets; a block west of the mission on Nipomo Street between Higuera and Monterey Streets; east of the mission on Chorro Street between Monterey and Palm Streets; behind the post office on Pacific Street; and on Palm Street between Chorro and Morro Streets, just east of the Ah Louie store.

HOW TO BE A VISITOR AND NOT A TOURIST IN CALIFORNIA'S RIVIERA

Both Santa Barbara and San Luis Obispo have wildly contrasting populations, integrating college students and professors and all their support staff with winemakers and winemaking investors, extremely wealthy southern Californians, Latinos who work the vineyards and kitchens and run their own businesses, and retired and still active dignitaries and celebrities. So they're nice to everybody, because, being so close to Hollywood, who knows who you might really be!

Do yourself a favor and don't criticize the slow pace, lack of big-city influences, and minor disdain for smaller cities. It is okay, though, to complain about gas prices, which are high here. You might as well be honest and say you're visiting, because you will never be able to fake it—you have to live here at least a decade to even pretend to be local. If you're from a big city, just make it clear you're only passing through. Locals here want their place to stay just the way it is, thank you very much, and actually fear it becoming more big-cityish even though they like big-city-quality restaurants and amenities.

Try to master correct pronunciation of street names. Restaurant, hotel, and shop staffs are slightly impressed with celebrity and like to mention that Geena Davis or Julia Child "shops/shopped here all the time," but do not ask a movie star or celebrity for an autograph.

Rearrange your perspectives: Think of everything in terms of its distance from Santa Barbara, a place most residents don't want to leave. Everything south of Carpinteria is practically L.A.

Santa Barbara and San Luis Obispo Counties are full of both working ranchers and gentlemen ranchers (who may or may not be gentlemen) who hire others to do the work.

Learn to like tri-tip barbecues. Tri-tip has become a regional source of pride, competition, and celebration. Restaurants specialize in it, individuals and service organizations set up barbecues in parking lots on weekends, and locals kibitz about marinades versus flavored-salt coatings or rubs.

Go in knowing significant dates about Santa Barbara: the 1925 earthquake, the 1970 burning of the Bank of America, and the 1995 floods will do for starters. The seasons all seem to occur later here than in most places, but for Easterners, Northerners, and almost everyone else, it seems to be mild summer here all the time.

If you go out in the (infrequent) rain, you must be a tourist, because locals hide safely at home so they won't dissolve. Take a sweater or light jacket with you in case the temperature drops to 55°—a near freeze in these here parts. But it does cool off at night year-round.

Relax and enjoy one of the most beautiful developed places on earth: California's Riviera.

The prices and rates listed in this book were confirmed at press time. We recommend, however, that you call establishments before traveling to obtain current information.

CHAPTER 1

MONTECITO, SUMMERLAND, CARPINTERIA, AND GOLETA

n the greater Santa Barbara area are these communities to the southeast: luxurious Montecito, the seashore settlement of Summerland, and the town of Carpinteria. Also in Santa Barbara's orbit is Goleta, a peninsula that juts into the ocean northwest of the city, and home to University of California Santa Barbara and the airport.

MONTECITO

Nestled in the lower slopes of the San Ysidro Mountains and adjoining Santa Barbara's southern edge, Montecito ("little mountain") is home or second home to some of the most famous and wealthy stars and families of the world. Is Montecito a suburb of Santa Barbara, or is it the other way around?

Directions: Take U.S. Highway 101 south of Santa Barbara to the San Ysidro Road exit. The Miramar Hotel is on the west side of the highway, and Montecito Village is on the east side. Turn east on San Ysidro to East Valley Road to the village, which will be to your left (north) at the intersection, while the Plaza del Sol is to your right (south). Or take bus 14 from downtown Santa Barbara.

While you see little of Montecito's plushness from the road (except the Montecito Country Club as a backdrop to the Andree Clark Bird Refuge), lush gardens and enormous spend-whatever-it-takes mansions dot the hillside among the trees. Montecito is also home to the fine Music Academy of the West and the Brooks Institute of Photography, the San Ysidro Ranch and Trailhead, La Casa de Maria Immaculate Heart Community, and the Boescke Adobe off San Leandro Lane.

As early as the 1890s, wealthy Easterners flocked here because of the Santa Barbara area's sheer beauty and perfect climate, ideal to cure physical and emotional ills developed on the East Coast and in the Midwest. Since then the rich and famous have flocked to Montecito, bringing with them friends, the ability to spend to create beautiful and dramatic surroundings, and a small community to cater to their tastes.

Charlie Chaplin built the Montecito Inn in the 1920s to attract and cater to Hollywood stars of various kinds, and they have been coming here ever since. For a while actor Ronald Colman owned the San Ysidro Ranch, which then attracted stars such as Jean Harlow and William Powell.

The spectacular Biltmore Hotel (1927) overlooks Butterfly Beach, where monarch and other butterflies make a brief stop in the eucalyptus trees.

Drive into the village of Montecito and walk around. It is small and won't take long (elegant, small strip malls offer interesting shops beyond the community's center). Be sure to check out the legendary Montecito Inn and the Montecito Cafe on Coast Village Road. Montecito's principal newer shopping centers are Montecito Village Shopping Center on the west side of East Valley and San Ysidro Roads, and the Old Village Shopping Center on the east side of East Valley Road.

LOTUSLAND in Montecito is the wild fantasy of the late Madame Ganna Walska, who supposedly created the very special and huge cycad collection by cashing in her vast emerald and diamond jewelry. Such passion! You can only get in by reservation, but it's worth it if you want to see rare plantings of lovely Japanese, aloe, blue, and lotus gardens.

❧ *Lotusland, address given at time of reservation, Montecito 93150; (805) 969-9000. Office open 9:00 a.m.–noon Monday–Friday; tours 10:00 a.m. and 3:00 p.m. Wednesday–Saturday, February–November. Partly wheelchair accessible.*

The extremely popular MONTECITO CAFE in the historic Montecito Inn offers a casually elegant atmosphere right off the small hotel lobby in a dining room whose walls have heard it all. Movie and political romances have matured here, as may yours. And the food is good, featuring imaginative California cuisine based on chicken breasts, lamb, pasta, and that wonderful flank steak, which is definitely okay, all under $15, unusual for the neighborhood and atmosphere.

❧ *Montecito Cafe, 1295 Coast Village Road, Montecito 93150; (805) 969-3392. Open 11:30 a.m.–9:30 p.m. No lunch reservations. Full bar. Visa, MasterCard, American Express. Wheelchair accessible.*

La Marina and The Patio are the more and the less expensive dining rooms of the Santa Barbara Four Seasons Biltmore. LA MARINA is elegant and makes you feel very special, while THE PATIO is more casual and slightly more reasonable. Locals come here for special occasions, and movie stars have been known to request catered lunches from the restaurants. From The Patio you can hang over the beach and enjoy the glorious Thursday through Sunday buffet that changes each evening.

✤ *La Marina and The Patio, 1260 Channel Drive, Montecito 93150; (805) 969-2261. La Marina: open for dinner from 5:30 p.m. Tuesday–Saturday. The Patio: open daily 8:00 a.m.–9:00 p.m. Sunday brunch. Full bar. Visa, MasterCard, American Express. Wheelchair accessible.*

PIERRE LAFOND's superb delicatessen and cafe are a local hangout for the famous and infamous nearby residents. The low-fat muffins balance out the hand-dipped chocolate truffles and cheesecakes and pumpkin breads. Try the open-faced Scottish salmon sandwich, the thick, rich lasagna, the popular vegetarian Montecito burrito, or the veggie or chicken enchiladas. Fresh-off-the-farm produce is interspersed with a fabulous selection of local wines, and the salad bar salves the conscience. You can enjoy all this at outside cafe tables near the sparkling fountain or in the nearby park dubbed "Corner Green."

You will also want to visit the market and the Lafonds' Wendy Foster home shop and dress boutique.

✤ *Pierre Lafond, 516 San Ysidro Road, Montecito 93150; (805) 565-1502. Open 6:30 a.m.–8:00 p.m. daily; the market is open 9:00 a.m.–8:00 p.m. daily. Beer and wine. Visa, MasterCard, American Express. Wheelchair accessible.*

MONTECITO VILLAGE GROCERY is worth finding for gourmet foods and meats, picnic delicacies, fine liquors, and local as well as imported wines. The store also delivers free to your home or hotel Monday through Saturday.

✤ *Montecito Village Grocery, 1482 East Valley Road, Montecito 93150; (805) 969-1112 or for deliveries (805) 969-7845. Full license. Open 8:30 a.m.–7:00 p.m. Monday–Saturday, 9:00 a.m.–7:00 p.m. Sunday. Visa, MasterCard, American Express. Wheelchair accessible.*

If you are looking for a dining experience more formal than your lap and not as formal as the Biltmore, you might try Palazzio with its two-drink bar, Cava for Spanish/Mexican food, or Via Vai and its sister Pane e Vino.

PALAZZIO is decorated with murals of Venice and Tuscany by Irene Roderick, and while it has a full liquor license, it serves only Italian margaritas and Italian martinis (Absolut vodka in which garlic has swum for at least three hours and kept premade in the freezer for you). Its twin (of the same name) is at 1026 State Street, downtown Santa Barbara.

Palazzio Trattoria Italiano, 1151 Coast Village Road, Montecito 93150; (805) 969-8565; www.palazzio.com. Open for lunch 11:30 a.m.–2:30 p.m. Monday–Saturday, dinner 5:30–11:00 p.m. Sunday–Thursday, 5:30 p.m.–midnight Friday and Saturday. Visa, MasterCard, American Express. Wheelchair accessible.

CAVA features regional Latin cuisine and is between the Cabrillo Boulevard and San Ysidro Road exits from US 101 on Coast Village Road, which runs east of and parallel to US 101. Here you can lounge on Cava's patio while tasting tapas, sipping margaritas, and listening to soothing guitars. Cigars are encouraged.

The wide variety of tapas and appetizers ranges from shrimp sautéed with garlic to nachos; grilled pork, chicken, or veggie carnitas; crab cakes with mango coulis; shrimp empanadas; or a tortilla española, a traditional Spanish potato and onion frittata with chimichurri sauce ($8.50–$14.50). But there's much more than tapas.

Besides the usual hamburgers and grilled chicken sandwiches, there are healthy and exciting salads, like the grilled scallop and shrimp salad with mango, jicama, red pepper, mesclun greens, and lime vinaigrette, or the grilled vegetable, chicken, or steak tostada ($7.00–$19.50).

Dinner offers many of the same selections, plus paella Valenciana; spicy baby back ribs with guava chili sauce, chipotle mashed potatoes, and grilled veggies; grilled lamb chops with mango-mint salsa; and grilled fresh salmon with papaya salsa ($14.00–$26.00).

Cava, 1212 Coast Village Road, Montecito 93150; www.cavarestaurant.com. (805) 969-8500. Open 10:00 a.m.–10:00 p.m. Monday–Thursday, 10:00 a.m.–10:30 p.m. Friday, 8:00 a.m.–10:30 p.m. Saturday and Sunday. Full bar. Visa, MasterCard, American Express, Discover. Wheelchair accessible.

VIA VAI TRATTORIA PIZZA is an informal Italian restaurant in the Montecito Village Shopping Center featuring excellent wood-burning oven pizzas under $20, terrific bruschetta con pomodoro (Tuscan garlic bread topped with fresh tomato, basil, and garlic), fried calamari with spicy tomato sauce, and a great roasted chicken salad outdone only by the spinach salad with warm pancetta, egg, and balsamic vinegar and olive oil dressing. But try the antipasto della casa for an assortment of Via Vai's special appetizers ($9.95–$12.95).

Main courses include loads of pastas and lasagnas, all under $10, and an excellent grilled Italian sausage with polenta and spinach, rotisseried game and fowl, and choices of lamb or pork chops and steaks ($10.95–$25.95).
❧ *Via Vai Trattoria Pizza, 1483 East Valley Road, No. 20, Montecito 93150; (805) 565-9393. Open 11:00 a.m.–10:00 p.m. daily. Beer and wine. Visa, MasterCard, American Express. Wheelchair accessible.*

Just across East Valley Road in the Old Village Shopping Center is PANE E VINO, the trattoria offering of the two Italian restaurants with slightly more interesting and complicated food than Via Vai. Antipasti here include vitello tonnato (sliced roasted veal with capers and a lemony tuna sauce), an excellent stuffed cold artichoke, grilled polenta with sautéed scallops, and dry cured beef with arugula, sweet onions, and vinaigrette ($7.95–$9.95).

Pastas range from the usuals to flat, curly, or round noodles with smoked mussels, capers, smoked mozzarella, and eggplant. There is pancetta with fontina and peas, fresh tuna cubes, or porcini mushrooms, as well as a risotto. Large veal chops, grilled rib-eye steak, and an excellent garlicky grilled rack of lamb top the grilled meats list, with grilled polenta, stewed tomatoes, and Italian sausages a real treat ($9.95–$21.95).

Tiramisu and crème caramel fans will be happy, but try the chocolate terrine tort with fresh berries sauce (Valentino con passata di fracole e lamponi) or the almond dipping cookies with aged Trebbiano wine ($6.95–$8.00). Oh my!
❧ *Pane e Vino, 1482 East Valley Road, Montecito 93150; (805) 969-9274. Open 11:30 a.m.–9:30 p.m. Monday–Saturday, 5:00–9:00 p.m. Sunday. Beer and wine. Visa, MasterCard, American Express. Wheelchair accessible.*

Many Montecito locals believe TRATTORIA MOLLIE is the finest restaurant in town, and followed owner Mollie Ahlstrand across the street to her new modern digs. With a definite Italian flavor, Mollie serves breakfast, lunch, and dinner with fabulous soups, salads, antipasti, bruschetta e crostini topped with mushrooms or prosciutto, choices of risotto and pastas, sandwiches, entrees such as veal piccata, osso buco, chicken cacciatore, sea bass, and a seafood mixed grill, and sinful desserts, ranging from $7 to $15 at lunch and $7 to $28 at dinner.
❧ *Trattoria Mollie, 1250 Coast Village Road, Montecito 93108; (805) 565-9381; www.trattoriamollie.com. Open 7:00 a.m.–2:30 p.m. and 5:30–10:00 p.m. Tuesday–Sunday. Beer and wine. Visa, MasterCard, American Express.*

SUMMERLAND

Both Summerland, just south of Montecito, and Carpinteria are antiques collectors' paradises, with antiques shops scattered along the main streets of both small towns. Explore and browse for yourself.

Once known to Santa Barbarans as "Spooksville" for the mind-expanding spiritualistic events that supposedly went on here, Summerland went through a period as surfer heaven, when it was filled with tan blond kids who hung out in the shabby bungalows along the coast. After that it was an oil boomtown; after oil was discovered offshore, rigs were installed to take away the oil—and the natural view. It now enjoys being a slightly offbeat, fashionable attraction for the rich and famous.

Even former President Bill Clinton and Senator Hillary Rodham Clinton have "dined" at the NUGGET, always famous for its juicy hamburgers, crisp fries, and cocktails, and now famous for its famous customers. There's great patio seating for people watching and sunbathing, if you still do that.

Nugget, 2318 Lillie Avenue, Summerland 93067; (805) 969-6135, fax (805) 969-0143. Open 11:00 a.m.–10:00 p.m. daily. Full bar. Visa, MasterCard, American Express. Wheelchair accessible.

CARPINTERIA

Twelve miles south of Santa Barbara is the small, spread-out burg of Carpinteria, whose main draw is the gorgeous 4,000 feet of ocean frontage and the forty-eight acres of Carpinteria State Beach Park. Here you can camp overnight, surf-fish, and observe (but don't you dare disturb) tide pools, rare phenomena in these parts. The visitor center has interesting natural history exhibits. To make camping reservations call (800) 444-PARK. Some of the best surfing in this part of California is off Rincon Point.

Main Street parallels the beach, and Linden Avenue, which leads to and from the beach, is lined with palm trees, rather than lindens. The best hamburgers and milk shakes in town are clearly at The Spot, which has outdoor tables right on Linden Avenue.

For a nostalgic dining experience reminiscent of an era you may not have known, drop in on THE PALMS, in the once famous Palms Hotel building, where you select and cook your own steak, shrimp, scallops, crab, and lobster just 1 block from the ocean. You can just imagine the sticky Manhattans and billows of Lucky Strike smoke of decades ago ($10–$20).

❧ *The Palms, 701 Linden Avenue, Carpinteria 93013; (805) 684-3811. Bar opens 1:00 p.m., dinner 5:00–10:00 p.m. daily. Full bar. Visa, MasterCard, American Express. Wheelchair accessible.*

To continue in the extremely local place theme, you might also want to try out CLEMENTINE'S, another steak place—where *they* cook it and serve you—and where you will never forget the mouthwatering pies, that all-American sweet indulgence. Clementine's claims to be "Santa Barbara's Best Kept Secret," maybe because it's in Carpinteria instead of Santa Barbara! Great local atmosphere and gossip here, too. Reservations are recommended.

❧ *Clementine's, 4631 Carpinteria Avenue, Carpinteria 93013; (805) 684-5119. Open 5:00–9:00 p.m. Tuesday–Sunday. Full bar. Visa, MasterCard, American Express. Wheelchair accessible.*

Carpinteria's name comes from Spanish for "carpenter's shop," a reference to the Chumash Indian practice of using tar (natural asphaltum) that came up out of the ground to hold their canoes and baskets together. Later the Spaniards got the Indians to use the tar to hold the presidio roof together after they had the Indians clear the land. Early arrivals grew crops by trial and error (lima beans worked), and eventually commercial tar companies opened the pits to extract all they could. You can still see the remains of the pits by following Concha Loma Avenue to Calle Ocho. Park at the end of Calle Ocho and walk across the railroad track to the lookout point for fabulous views of the coast and the Channel Islands.

The CARPINTERIA VALLEY MUSEUM OF HISTORY is worth a visit if you're down this way. Exhibits of clothing and furniture contributed by Carpinteria's pioneer families depict turn-of-the-twentieth-century life and create the ambience of the period. Exhibits include Chumash Indian artifacts, the replica of an early school classroom, traditional agricultural tools, and, what do you know, an oil boom, the current industrial artifact of the region.

❧ *Carpinteria Valley Museum of History, 956 Maple Avenue, Carpinteria 93013; (805) 684-3112; www.carpenteriahistoricalmuseum.org. Open 1:00–4:00 p.m. Tuesday–Saturday. Free admission. Wheelchair accessible.*

SANTA BARBARA POLO & RACQUET CLUB is actually here in Carpinteria. The elite group opens its field so visitors can watch polo matches from the grandstands and partake of the snack bar's substantial offerings. You're welcome to watch polo games Sunday afternoons from April to October. If you've never seen polo, it is an amazingly daring game of horse and player wielding what look like golf clubs to hit a ball on the ground toward the goal. The horses work the hardest and suffer the most. Clubhouse, tennis center, swim club, and fitness facility on-site.

ॐ *Santa Barbara Polo & Racquet Club, 3375 Foothill Road, Carpinteria 93013; (805) 684-8668 or (805) 684-6683 for game times; www.sbpolo.com. Mostly wheelchair accessible.*

One mile west of Carpinteria off US 101 is SANTA CLAUS LANE, a rather fun year-round Christmas haven, despite its unabashed commercialism. Loads of stuff with a Christmas theme, ornaments, an art gallery, toy stores, gift and dried fruit specialty shops, a bakery, candy kitchen, rock shop, and a casual restaurant facing the water all make this place attractive to thousands of visitors annually.

ॐ *Santa Claus Lane, off US 101, ½ mile west of Carpinteria. No phone for center; www.carpenteria.com.*

Be sure to make it to Carpinteria's California Avocado Festival the first weekend in October (805-684-0038) and the annual flower show during the festival, as well as the monthly flea market (last Saturday) at the Carpinteria Valley Historical Museum.

And don't miss the farmers' market on Thursday, in the 800 block of Linden Avenue (4:00–7:00 p.m. in spring and summer; 3:00–6:00 p.m. in fall and winter).

GOLETA

The main attraction in Goleta is the University of California, Santa Barbara, which is not actually in Santa Barbara, nor in Goleta, where it is usually thought to be. The university is really in Isla Vista, just west of Santa Barbara and Goleta; although it is in Santa Barbara County. Actually, Goleta and Isla Vista run together and are not really distinguishable.

Locals and visitors all enjoy biking on designated trails, bird-watching on Goleta Beach, golf, picnics, and hiking. Visit Santa Barbara Shores, a county park next to Sandpiper Golf Course. Stow Grove Park and Lake Los Carneros Park are next to Stow House and the South Coast Railroad Museum.

STOW HOUSE was the central Stow family home when they were prominent lemon growers in Goleta, which once produced one-tenth of the nation's lemons. The orchards around the house are still owned by the Stow family's descendants, although the 5,000-square-foot 1872 Victorian home itself was donated to Santa Barbara County in 1967. Today you can walk through and enjoy its antiques and the excellent restoration job overseen by the Goleta Valley Historical Society. If you visit in October, plan to attend the lemon festival at Stow House with lemon foods, games, arts, crafts, and entertainment for the whole family.

Don't miss the Horace Sexton Memorial Museum of farm tools and machinery next door in the old red barn or the South Coast Railroad Museum, which offers miniature steam train rides in this county park to which the train station was moved in 1981. The park surrounding the railroad museum is true California: tall eucalyptus trees, mustard, and grasses. Enjoy the caboose and picnic areas, as well as the old freight office with the oh-so-sensible Morse code equipment, the passenger waiting room, a slide show, railroad films, and a terrific shop and bookstore with nostalgic train posters and rare Santa Barbara books.

❧ *Stow House, 304 North Los Carneros Road, Goleta 93116; (805) 964-4407; www.goletahistory.org. Open 2:00–4:00 p.m. Saturday and Sunday; tours when visitors show up. Partly wheelchair accessible. To get to Stow House, Horace Sexton Museum, and South Coast Railroad Museum, take US 101 north of Santa Barbara and take the Los Carneros Road exit. Turn right (north) on North Los Carneros Road (train station on the right).*

If you fly into Santa Barbara, check out the Air Heritage Museum at Santa Barbara Airport, which is also in Goleta.

Venture beyond Goleta's superficial appearance, which offers little to attract, to find its most natural beauty of beach, cliffs, dunes, and unusual wild birds, all below the plateau that supports UC/Santa Barbara. You will share our amazement at this beauty so close to tract homes and cement-box shopping. Park at the Goleta Beach lot or on the campus, although it's a bit of a walk or bike ride either way.

Goleta is not known for its fine cuisine, but you might try WOODY'S BODACIOUS BARBECUE, which until 1998 was known as Woody's Beach Club & Cantina. Sandwiches and burgers come with fries and beans, slaw, or tossed salad, and range from one-third pound to the One Pound Behemoth! And then there's the Triple Double Burger or a Texas brisket sandwich ($6.25–$7.25). You'll also find oak-roasted rotisserie chicken dinner, smoked half-duckling, big combos of beef and ribs, Santa Maria–style tri-tip, baby backs, half-chicken, hot links, Mother Clucker chicken sandwich, and a BBQ Orgy ($6.95–$42.95). Turkey and grilled tuna burgers also creep onto the lunch menu, along with big, cheap salads. Kathleen likes Woody's Caesar salad with oak-smoked chicken, grilled tuna, or tri-tip ($8.95). Low-carb menu available. Kids will like the special kids' menu, and grown-up kids will enjoy the very local microbrews.

Most local media rate Woody's the best barbecue around.

🌿 *Woody's Bodacious Barbecue, 5112 Hollister Avenue, Goleta 93116; (805) 967-3775; www.woodysbbq.com. Open 11:00 a.m.–9:00 p.m. Monday– Thursday, 11:00 a.m.–11:00 p.m. Friday and Saturday, 11:00 a.m.–10:00 p.m. Sunday. Beer and wine. Visa, MasterCard, American Express, Discover, Diners. Wheelchair accessible.*

CHAPTER 2

SANTA BARBARA ITSELF

We call Santa Barbara "California's Riviera" because it is. The towering Santa Ynez Mountains drop dramatically to sea level and light-colored, sand-covered beaches. Gently swaying palm trees line the beaches, lightly shade joggers and volleyball players, and create a stunning outline against the mountains. Santa Barbara's beach—the only beach between Alaska and Cape Horn to run east to west—faces south, as does France's Riviera, an unusual orientation along the north–south running Pacific Coast. For left-coast folks it is truly odd to wake up in a Santa Barbara coastside hotel room and see the sun rise over the ocean. We usually see it set over the water. There aren't quite as many sidewalk cafes in Santa Barbara as there are on the other Riviera, and beach lovers generally wear bathing suits here.

As you wander around town and explore the rest of Santa Barbara County and its wineries, the scenery might just look familiar to you, and for good reason. Thousands of Western movies were filmed here, which helps us understand why Nancy and Ronald Reagan had a ranch here for decades. We still can visualize former President Reagan in his cowboy boots and hat mending fences—at the ranch, that is.

Other early film stars, including Douglas Fairbanks, Mary Pickford, and Charlie Chaplin, used Santa Barbara as their favorite retreat. Rockefellers, Vanderbilts, Carnegies, and DuPonts used to arrive by private railcar. Now celebrities such as Diane Keaton, Michael Douglas, Sylvester Stallone, Geena Davis, Julia Louis-Dreyfus, Bill Cosby, James Brolin and Barbra Streisand, Kevin Costner, Kenny Loggins, and Jane Seymour spend part of their year here. Well, actually, many of them live in Montecito, Santa Barbara's rarefied suburb to the south. (See chapter 1.)

Besides its historic California architecture, Santa Barbara boasts 900 different plant species, the bases for which were brought here in the late 1880s by the grandfather of horticulture, Francesco Franceschi. Forty-eight public parks and 22,000 public trees, blooming exotic gardens, manicured private gardens, and

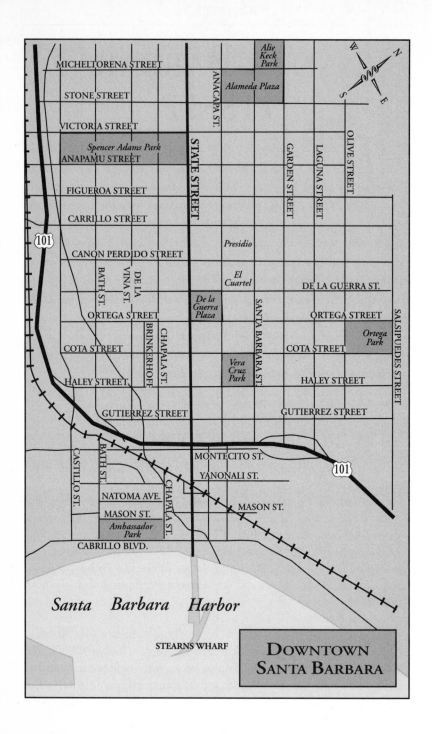

million-dollar estates all contribute to Santa Barbara's once-in-a-lifetime beauty. An orchid lover's paradise, Santa Barbara has 3 million square feet of orchid greenhouses and a spring international orchid show of more than one hundred varieties.

Santa Barbara has had the rare opportunity to redo itself following natural disasters. After the 1925 earthquake destroyed or severely damaged most of the public buildings (including the mission) and private residences, the town took advantage of a miserable situation and established an architectural board of review that developed guidelines for what you now see as Santa Barbara's facade. Floods, fires, and more earthquakes serve to jolt the locals ever so slightly into the reality that all is not always beautiful and perfect. But again and again Santa Barbarans resurrect themselves and their facades (edifices, that is) for all to enjoy.

Santa Barbara's architecture reflects its and California's history from the early days of the Chumash Indians 9,000 years ago, through landings by Spaniards, up to the late-eighteenth-century arrival of Franciscan friars. Residents and architects made a conscious effort to blend and enhance varied design influences—Mediterranean, Spanish, early California/Mexican, Moorish, and English country. As a result, Santa Barbara buildings often have low-pitched, reddish tile roofs, earth-tone plaster walls, arched entryways, enclosed garden courtyards, and occasional wrought-iron gates.

Notice that no cars are parked on downtown State Street, enabling all to enjoy the architecture and celebratory atmosphere. But don't worry; there's plenty of parking in lots behind the shops on State Street.

To help you find your way around Santa Barbara using this Hill Guide, we first take you up and down State Street, Santa Barbara's main shopping paradise, and to highlights on its cross streets. Then we'll go to what we call "significant others," by which we mean attractions and restaurants outside the State Street area that you should try to visit.

STATE STREET

State Street is the ultimate mix of elegant boutiques, upscale ethnic restaurants, funky-to-fine art galleries, local and chain cafes, and strut-your-stuff promenade mixed with historic malls, local offices, and necessary stores like Long's and Rite-Aid. Thus State Street is meant for locals as well as visitors, and both groups mingle comfortably.

We now see more homeless, as well as more storefront vacancies on State Street. Rumored rental rates facing the big promenade are in the

ARLINGTON THEATRE, SANTA
BARBARA, DURING FILM
FESTIVAL, 1999

$40,000–$60,000 per month range, according to local shopkeepers.

We start our walking tour near the top of State Street's core of fine restaurants and shops at the corner of Anapamu and State Streets, across from the Santa Barbara Museum of Art. There is excellent parking in the blocks west and east of this part of State Street. We take you down the west side of the street, and then back up the east side, ending at the museum.

Just 1½ blocks up State Street from the corner of Anapamu Street are two significant must-experiences: Arlington Theatre and Downey's restaurant.

The elegant Arlington Hotel was destroyed by a disastrous 1909 fire, and the second Arlington Hotel was destroyed by the 1925 earthquake. Fox West Coast Theatres subsequently commissioned Santa Barbaran Joseph Plunkett and his partner, William A. Edwards, to design the ARLINGTON THEATRE. This Spanish Revival motion-picture palace, restored in 1976, serves as the Arlington Center for the Performing Arts (where the Santa Barbara Symphony and visiting orchestras perform), and as an outstanding movie theater that is a major venue of the Santa Barbara International Film Festival. Notice the Spanish village feeling to the architecture, as well as the star-studded ceiling, the dramatic arches, and courtyard entry.

On the sidewalk outside the entrance is a sign marking the spot as Old Stage Coach Route I, where stagecoaches stopped from 1861 to 1901. Gasoline-free public transportation!

☙ *Arlington Theatre, 1217 State Street, Santa Barbara 93101; (805) 963-4408; www.thearlingtontheatre.com. Hours vary. Visa and MasterCard for some events. Wheelchair accessible.*

In the same block of State Street as the Arlington are two of Santa Barbara's finest restaurants, Gisella's and Downey's.

GISELLA'S TRATTORIA & PIZZERIA is a friendly, attractive, and reasonably priced Italian bistro right next to the Arlington Theatre with excellent pastas, risotti, and pizzas and panini made in the wood-burning oven. Try the mouthwatering cannelloni della mamma filled with chicken and spinach, gnocchi with your choice of Gorgonzola, butter and sage, tomato, or mozzarella and basil sauces, or chicken, sea bass, and rack of New Zealand lamb in a balsamic vinegar glaze reduction ($8.95–$18.95). Then comes lemon tiramisu, almond chocolate cake, gelati, and ports

❧ *Gisella's Trattoria & Pizzeria, 1311 State Street, Santa Barbara 93101; (805) 963-8219; www.gisellas.com. Open for lunch 11:30 a.m.–2:30 p.m. Monday–Friday, dinner from 5:30 p.m. Monday–Saturday, from 5:00 p.m. Sunday. Beer and wine. Visa, MasterCard, American Express. Wheelchair accessible.*

Santa Barbara's most reviewed and highly rated restaurant is DOWNEY'S, the creation of John and Liz Downey. Since they are not open for lunch, make your dinner reservations in advance to assure a table for this culinary experience.

Downey's received the top rating of "28" from Zagat readers in 2006.

For starters, we highly recommend the white asparagus salad with smoked salmon, and duck and squab lovers will find delicacies as well; the watercress and Belgian endive salad resembles the old Trader Vic's ($8.95–$14.95).

Entrees may include grilled duck, local king salmon, grilled ahi, braised pork loin, local sea bass, Colorado lamb loin, or "natural" rib eye steak ($27.95–$36.95). Desserts and the wine list are impeccable. You are bound to at least see, if not mix with, some of Santa Barbara's most interesting celebrities here.

❧ *Downey's, 1305 State Street, Santa Barbara 93101; (805) 966-5006; www .downeyssb.com. Open for dinner from 5:30 p.m. Tuesday–Sunday. Visa, Master Card, American Express, Discover. Wheelchair accessible.*

The next block has integrated its fast-food joints with a few interesting furniture shops, State and A Bar & Grill, The State Street Antique Mall of vintage clothing and collectibles with about 65 dealers, and the Victoria Court courtyard full of shops. Sushi fans should try Arigato Sushi.

Anapamu Street crosses State Street and sports several establishments worth visiting. On West Anapamu, which means to your left facing up State Street, we take you first to the KARPELES MANUSCRIPT LIBRARY MUSEUM, other branches of which are located in Jacksonville, Florida; Tacoma, Washington; Duluth, Minnesota; Montecito, California; Buffalo, New York; and Charleston, South Carolina. Dedicated to the preservation of the original handwritten letters and documents of the great men and women of the past who have changed and shaped history, this underknown treasure of original manuscripts and documents

DOWNEY'S FRESH APRICOT MOUSSE
from Downey's Restaurant, Santa Barbara

1 ½ lbs. ripe apricots or peaches	*pinch of salt*
3 Tbs. lemon juice	*½ cup granulated sugar*
1 ½ cups heavy cream	*½ cup toasted almonds*
4 egg whites	

Have six 8-oz. wine glasses ready to place in freezer, and a large pastry bag fitted with a large plain tube.

To remove the skin from apricots, plunge them into boiling water for a few seconds, and quickly transfer them into a container of cold water. Remove the flesh from the pit and place flesh in food processor or blender. Add lemon juice to the processor or blender and puree the fruit together. Refrigerate.

Whip the heavy cream until it becomes stiff. Make sure it is cold, as it will whip easier. Transfer to another large bowl. Clean the first bowl thoroughly with soapy water.

Add the salt to the egg whites, and whip until they start to get thick. Add the sugar all at once and continue to whip until stiff peaks form.

Now you must work quickly. Using a large plastic spatula, carefully fold the fruit puree into the whipped cream, and then, even more carefully, fold the egg whites into the cream.

Transfer the mixture to the pastry bag and gently squeeze into the wine glasses. Place in freezer for 45 minutes, then move to the refrigerator for 2 hours.

When ready to serve, clean the sides of the glasses, fill with mousse, and top with toasted almonds. May be made up to 6 hours before serving. Makes 6 mousses.

NOTE: You may substitute blackberries or raspberries, but don't blanch them. After pureeing the berries, pass them through a sieve to remove the seeds.

is a literary and documentary heaven. Together, the Karpeles Manuscript Library Museums constitute the world's largest private holding of important original documents and manuscripts.

The Montecito museum is reserved for scholars to do research, but at the Santa Barbara Karpeles you might see original papers of George Bernard Shaw, Enrico Fermi, former President Harry S Truman, Glenn Seaborg, and former President Dwight D. Eisenhower. The Karpeles holdings—covering history, music, science, literature, and art—rotate through its other museums. Each showing focuses on no more than twenty-five documents at any one time.

Exhibits have included the original proposal draft of the Bill of Rights, the Emancipation Proclamation signed by Abraham Lincoln, the Thanksgiving Proclamation signed by George Washington, and the original autograph drafts of the national constitutions of France, Spain, Mexico, Ireland, and the Confederate States of America. Music manuscripts exhibited have included pages of Beethoven, Mozart, Wagner, Handel, and Puccini; scientific manuscripts have included those of Galileo, Descartes, Kepler, Newton, Einstein, Freud, and Darwin. And you might see the Surrender Agreement of World War II.

Do not miss this. And it's free! One of our favorites.

❧ *Karpeles Manuscript Library Museum, 21 West Anapamu Street, Santa Barbara 93101; (805) 962-5322; www.rain.org/~karpeles/. Open 10:00 a.m.– 4:00 p.m. daily. Free admission. Partly wheelchair accessible.*

Now cross Anapamu to four fun shops, including Crispin Leather, Santa Barbara Hobbies, Pacific Travellers Supply, and Metro Entertainment: Comics, Games & Toys.

CRISPIN LEATHER SHOP smells as if leather scent is sprayed through the air-conditioning! Yum. Crispin has two storefronts offering leather hats, bags, wallets, jewelry, belts, and a few clothes, plus Birkenstocks, Clarks shoes and sandals, Santana boots from Canada, UGG from Australia, Aussi togs and moccasins, and even Dr. Scholl's shoes and Teva sandals.

❧ *Crispin Leather Shop, 18 West Anapamu Street, Santa Barbara 93101; (805) 966-2510; www.crispinleather.com. Open 10:00 a.m.–5:30 p.m. Monday– Saturday, 11:00 a.m.–5:00 p.m. Sunday. Visa, MasterCard, American Express. Wheelchair accessible.*

Vern Morseman's HOBBY CENTRAL is a hobbyist's delight. Here you will find plastic models, airbrush equipment, model rockets, X-ACTO tools, model trains such as Marklin Z, HO and N train supplies, G gauge trains, Screaming/Horizon vinyl figures, how-to books, Dremel tools, finishing supplies, military aircraft models, and a rare kit corner. One of Jerry's favorites.

❧ *Hobby Central, 14 West Anapamu Street, Santa Barbara 93101; (805) 965-2972; www.venturahobbies.com. Open noon–5:00 p.m. Monday, 10:00 a.m.–6:00 p.m. Tuesday–Saturday. Visa, MasterCard, American Express. Wheelchair accessible.*

PACIFIC TRAVELLERS SUPPLY, now owned by Nations Travelstores of L.A., carries Ex-Officio shirts, rain gear, Siena Club note cards, new globes, mapping, loads of guidebooks, software, and Timberland backpacks.

❧

🏵 *Pacific Travellers Supply, 12 West Anapamu Street, Santa Barbara 93101; (805) 963-4438. Open 10:00 a.m.–7:00 p.m. daily. Visa, MasterCard, American Express, Discover. Wheelchair accessible.*

METRO ENTERTAINMENT: COMICS, GAMES & TOYS is a big and little kid's paradise where Pokemon seminars go on at a sidewalk table out front. Often voted Santa Barbara's Best Comic Store, Metro, which occasionally has a free comic day Saturday, is where you get *Star Wars* everythings, Beanie Babies, *South Park* and *X-Files* paraphernalia, magic supplies, games, collectibles, and television and movie memorabilia. One of Jerry's favorites.

🏵 *Metro Entertainment: Comics, Games & Toys, 6 West Anapamu Street, Santa Barbara 93101; (805) 963-2168; www.metro-entertainment.com. Open 10:00 a.m.–7:00 p.m. Sunday and Monday, 10:00 a.m.–8:00 p.m. Tuesday– Saturday. Visa, MasterCard, American Express, Discover. Wheelchair accessible.*

We encourage you to walk across State Street on Anapamu to visit a classic bookstore and cafe, SULLIVAN & GOSS BOOKS & PRINTS LTD., one of the largest art bookstores in the world, and its cafe, the ARTS & LETTERS CAFE. Just walking in here is like walking into a book museum. What a treat to enjoy such reverence!

Sullivan & Goss features elegant rare books, prints, monographs, and paintings and caters to artists, collectors, galleries, and art lovers. Among the artists whose original work is exhibited are Robin Gowen and Don Freeman.

To get to the Arts & Letters Cafe gallery dining room, walk or wheel through Sullivan & Goss and through the exquisite flower-framed patio where you can dine and occasionally listen to live opera and Broadway musicals.

The menu is as appealing as the surroundings. Try their famous pumpkin soup served hot or chilled (even praised by the *New York Times* as well as the Hills), the prosciutto and persimmon topped with arugula and hazelnut vinaigrette, or the charcutière, a plate of duck and truffle pâté, cornichons, black olives, Jarlsberg cheese, mustard, and baguette and rye breads. The salads are all excellent, but standouts include roasted chicken with wild rice, duck breast and prosciutto with baby spinach, and the kasseri spinach pasta salad. Sandwiches, with choice of soup, include the French country with duck and truffle pâté, creamy Brie, cornichons, and Dijon mustard. Memorable!

At lunch the Eastern blue crab cakes are grand treats, particularly for Westerners. Dinner delicacies include pan-roasted salmon with Merlot and fennel and potato hash, and roasted vegetable and polenta lasagna. Or you may want to try the prix fixe Menu des Artistes, which includes a choice of soup and entree, the chef's dessert selection, and coffee or tea ($9.95–$23.95). The "secret" Spanish courtyard dining is especially popular with locals.

☙ *Sullivan & Goss Books & Prints Ltd. and Arts & Letters Cafe, 7 East Anapamu Street, Santa Barbara 93101; (805) 730-1460; www.sullivangoss.com. Bookstore open 10:00 a.m.–5:30 p.m. Sunday–Thursday, 8:00 a.m.–5:30 p.m. Friday and Saturday. Cafe open for lunch 11:00 a.m.–3:30 p.m., breakfast 8:00 a.m.–3:30 p.m., dinner from 5:30 p.m. Tuesday–Sunday. Visa and MasterCard. Wheelchair accessible.*

Walking into TIENDA HO' down State Street, one of Kathleen's favorites, is like walking into another continent. Pressed mud hut–looking dressing rooms, a running waterfall, palms, rugs, sarongs, and soothing and sexy music combine to create an alluring atmosphere few women and brave men can resist. Fabulous leather and brass belts with enormous buckles, flowing scarves, sale racks, masks, and loads of feminine clothes from Morocco, Indonesia, and India render most women weak. Purchasers are now rewarded with eco-friendly reusable Tienda Ho' tote bags. Enjoy!

☙ *Tienda Ho', 1105 State Street, Santa Barbara 93101; (805) 962-3643 or (800) 962-3643, fax (805) 564-7030; www.tiendaho.com. Open 10:00 a.m.– 8:00 p.m. except when they close at 7:00. Visa, MasterCard, American Express. Mostly wheelchair accessible.*

GILLIO buys and sells fine jewelry, rare coins, antiques, and collectibles and helps you connect to Jim O'Mahoney, who appraises all of the above. They even make house calls if you would like to sell or buy art objects, old paintings, vintage photographs, bronze and silver sculptures, Asian works of art, movie memorabilia, Indian artifacts, old Western and cowboy items, and old sterling silver and stock certificates. Se habla español.

☙ *Gillio, 1103 State Street, Santa Barbara 93101; (805) 963-1345. Open for antiques and collectibles 11:00 a.m.–4:00 p.m. Wednesday–Saturday, and for coins and jewelry 9:30 a.m.–5:30 p.m. Monday–Friday. Visa, MasterCard, American Express, Discover. Wheelchair accessible.*

At the corner of Figueroa and State, turn west for a special treat.

LOS ARROYOS is such a hot new Mexican restaurant that it expanded into the storefront next door. Truly a family enterprise, Los Arroyos offers fresh Mex food you can see prepared as you order it. Using family recipes, the food is prepared with "absolutely NO lard." Order at the counter, and your food arrives at your table. All orders can include Caesar salad instead of rice and black beans.

❧

The most expensive item on Los Arroyos's menu is the ensalada de camaron, a shrimp salad with grilled onions, bell peppers, shrimp, and avocado ($8.25). Enjoy plenty of salads, nachos, soft tacos, vegetarian burritos or tacos, as well as many with meat and eggs. There's a children's menu as well. One of our favorites.

❧ *Los Arroyos, 14 West Figueroa Street, Santa Barbara 93101; (805) 962-5541; www.losarroyosrestaurants.com. Open 11:00 a.m.–9:00 p.m. Monday–Friday, 9:00 a.m.–9:00 p.m. Saturday, 9:00 a.m.–8:00 p.m. Sunday. Beer and wine. Visa, MasterCard, Discover, corporate checks. Wheelchair accessible.*

Back toward State Street from Los Arroyos is SANTA BARBARA CIGAR & TOBACCO, an elegant cigar boutique owned by tobacconists Matthew Lanford and Tom Georgouses. Dark and solid looking, the shop has a humidified cigar room and a smoking lounge in the back, where cigar aficionados gather to talk cigars and world problems, puff, and inhale each others' smoke. While we do not encourage any form of smoking, this is an excellent shop for cigars, pipes, tobaccos, and rare imported cigarettes, if you must.

❧ *Santa Barbara Cigar & Tobacco, 10 West Figueroa, Santa Barbara 93101; (805) 963-1979, fax (805) 963-8780. Open 10:00 a.m.–6:00 p.m. Monday– Saturday, 11:00 a.m.–4:00 p.m. Sunday. Visa, MasterCard, American Express. Mostly wheelchair accessible.*

Just down State Street is ALDO'S ITALIAN RESTAURANT, with a highly Italian ambience and outdoor tables and umbrellas under a huge maple tree. Many locals say this is their favorite Italian restaurant in town.

Italian and French posters wind their way around interior poles and arches, and flamenco guitarists set a romantic tone nightly. All of Aldo's entrees cost $1–$2 more at dinner than at lunch, and salads and soups come in small and large servings. Vegetarian entrees are marked with a "v" on the menu.

Antipasti include bruschetta, and baked artichoke hearts, local mussels, and prosciutto and melon ($2.95–$8.95). Salads range from Greek and salmon to seafood spinach salad and Aldo's chicken Caesar ($6.95–$10.95). Lunchtime sandwiches include eggplant parmigiana, BLT, or meatball ($10.95) and come with soup or salad. Yummy pizzas are all under $10.00, and twenty pastas range from $10.95 a plate at lunch to $18.95 at dinner, including soup or salad; additions of meatballs, sausage, or chicken are an extra $1.50–$2.00.

❧ *Aldo's Italian Restaurant, 1031 State Street, Santa Barbara 93101; (805) 963-6687; www.sbaldos.com. Open 11:00 a.m.–9:30 p.m. Monday–Thursday, 11:00 a.m.–10:30 p.m. Friday and Saturday, 10:00 a.m.–9:30 p.m. Sunday. Visa, MasterCard, American Express, Discover. Wheelchair accessible.*

SPICE AVENUE is an attractive Indian eatery that offers a wide-ranging Maharani Indian Buffet ($7.95/$12.95) as well as a regular menu. Sunny and Nancy Bujji, with Sandy Urmil and Nepalese chef W. Sherpa, moved from London to Santa Barbara in 2002 to open a restaurant, and they have done an excellent job.

Reasonably priced menu appetizers and entrees range from vegetable samosas to Aloo Chaat and assorted palcora ($2.00–$9.00); dhal soup ($3.50); and Tandoori specialties such as shrimp tikka masala; chicken, prawns, and lamb curries; as well as Biryani from the House of Nawabs (Princes) in Hyderbad, India (all under $20.00). Plenty of vegetarian delights.

Spice Avenue also sells spices, relishes, lentils, and artwork to take home.

⅊ *Spice Avenue, 1027 State Street, Santa Barbara 93101; (805) 965-6004; www.spiceavenuesb.com. Open 11:00 a.m.–11:00 p.m. daily. Beer and wine. Visa, MasterCard, American Express. Wheelchair accessible.*

RUSS' CAMERA AND VIDEO has often been voted Best Camera Store by Santa Barbara residents, and we agree. Russ' offers everything from postcards to huge telescopes for viewing passing whales and ships from your rancho. Cameras, film, frames, how-to books, and batteries are all available.

⅊ *Russ' Camera and Video, 1025 State Street, Santa Barbara 93101; (805) 963-9558, fax (805) 966-4947; www.russcamera.com. Open 9:00 a.m.– 5:30 p.m. Monday–Saturday, noon– 4:00 p.m. Sunday. Visa and Master Card. Wheelchair accessible.*

One of our favorite restaurants is around the corner and across the street on Carrillo.

We hereby "discover" ROY for the outside world. Roy used to have the extremely popular Espressway Cafe local hangout on Chapala Street and grew to this fabulous funky bistro and bar. Catch the local art exhibit the minute you pass through the door, along with turquoise vinyl banquettes,

---

ROY'S FRENCH DRESSING
from Roy Gandy, Roy, Santa Barbara

2 Tbs. Dijon mustard
pinch of cayenne pepper
2 Tbs. sugar
1 ½ cups cider vinegar
1 Tbs. coarse brown mustard
1 cup corn oil
sugar

Put Dijon mustard, cayenne pepper, and a little sugar into a food processor and turn on machine. Add the cider vinegar and the coarse brown mustard, and then add the corn oil. Add more sugar and vinegar to taste, blending. (Roy cooks by instinct and wrote this recipe in longhand for us. Be sure to taste frequently and add more vinegar, sugar, and oil to suit your palate. Watch those fingers in the food processor!)

swivel chairs, and old diner parts such as tables and lamps.

Roy Gandy, a native of Buffalo, New York, virtually grew up in his parents' and grandparents' fish house, which the family has had for more than sixty-five years. Roy "chased a woman out here" and never went back, although she did. We are all lucky he never left.

This is down-to-earth, creative good food. The menu changes constantly. If you want nouvelle, we will take you to other restaurants. Every prix fixe ($20) entree comes with subtle soup, a house salad of mixed organic greens from the Santa Barbara farmers' market, and warm melt-in-your-mouth homemade organic wheat bread. A la carte entrees may be wildly different from the prix fixe menu (maximum $15), such as a duck confit Gyosa with sautéed spinach and shiitake mushrooms.

We especially recommend the charbroiled king salmon with lemon hollandaise and a fresh fruit salsa, or the Harris ranch filet mignon, perfectly cooked medium rare unless you ask otherwise. You might prefer the free-range chicken marsala with sliced mushrooms, pork tenderloin sautéed with port, ginger, and brown sugar, or

---

FLOURLESS CHOCOLATE CAKE
from Pastry Chef Lisa Inloes, Roy, Santa Barbara

FOR THE CAKE:

1 cup melted butter

¾ cup sugar

10 oz. semisweet chocolate

6 eggs

2 tsp. vanilla

dash of salt

FOR THE GANACHE:

1½ cups heavy cream

16 oz. semisweet chocolate

THE CAKE: In an electric mixer add the butter to the sugar and chocolate. Mix until smooth. Slowly add eggs while continually mixing for 2–3 minutes. Add the vanilla and salt. Pour into lined 9-inch springform pan. Bake at 350°F for 1 hour.

Cool in pan, then press cake onto plate.

THE GANACHE: Whisk heavy cream and chocolate in a saucepan over low heat until smooth.

Cover cake with chocolate ganache and chill.

---

the grilled boneless lamb loin. There is always a vegetarian pasta at $10. For us the portions are perfect: a smallish meat serving with plenty of veggie accompaniments. For a $10 charge, you can split an entree and get an extra bowl of soup and an extra salad. Deal!

Roy's wine list is carefully selected from among the central coast's finest, with Ravenswood Zinfandel and a Trefethen Cabernet Sauvignon thrown in, all under $35. Beer fans can also try local Firestone Ale and San Luis Obispo Brewery's Amberale, in addition to several Irish, British, and German brews.

A local favorite, Roy is an absolute must on your culinary itinerary. Check out Roy's Jolly Tiger music bar next door.

Roy, 7 West Carrillo Street, Santa Barbara 93101; (805) 966-5636. Open for lunch 11:30 a.m.–2:30 p.m. Monday–Friday, dinner 6:00 p.m.–midnight nightly. Full bar (great martinis). Visa, MasterCard, American Express. Wheelchair accessible.

SHOE PHORIA specializes in competitive pricing of ladies' casual comfort and fashion shoes such as Esprit, Zodiac, Sam & Libby, Report, Destroy, Unlisted, and Nicole Griffin. Styles are very with-it, as are the young employees.

Shoe Phoria, 927 State Street, Santa Barbara 93101; (805) 962-6263. Open 10:00 a.m.–7:00 p.m. daily. Visa, MasterCard, American Express, Discover. Wheelchair accessible.

MI CASA IMPORTS offers excellent Mexican, Spanish, and Central American handcrafted folk art and furniture in a cavernous store full of color. One of our favorites.

Mi Casa Imports, 929 State Street, Santa Barbara 93101; (805) 564-8383. Open 10:00 a.m.–6:00 p.m. Sunday–Thursday, 10:00 a.m.–8:00 p.m. Friday and Saturday. Visa, MasterCard, Discover. Mostly wheelchair accessible.

Just south of El Paso, the GREEN AND YELLOW BASKET (where are the tisket and tasket?) is a complex emporium of washable linen clothes, scarves, Panama hats, Stetson and Tilley hats, gifts, collectibles, big Polonaise Christmas ornaments, storybooks, movies, baskets, cookie cutters, Ty stuffed animals and Beanie Babies, postcards, and the deal of the street: colorful Mexican blankets for $9.98 (normally around $20.00 elsewhere). Do not let the pouty young staff deter you.

Green and Yellow Basket, 911 State Street, Santa Barbara 93101; (805) 965-7777. Open 10:00 a.m.–6:00 p.m. Monday–Thursday, 10:00 a.m.–9:00 p.m. Friday and Saturday and daily in summer. Visa, MasterCard, American Express. Wheelchair accessible but tight.

Slightly more elegant than Spice Avenue up the street, the TAJ CAFE boasts "village cuisine from India—award-winning food from Los Angeles." Taj tends to Californiaize Indian food with soups and salads; "lean and healthful" Tandoori entrees; vegetarian curries and entrees, such as Bangain Bhartha and Saag Aloo or Saffron Paneer; and "Bombay Frankies," which are "homemade egg-washed Bombay-style burritos served with vegetable pickle." Great Indian beverages. Almost everything is under $12, as well as an all-you-can-eat buffet.

❧ *Taj Cafe, 905 State Street, Santa Barbara 93101; (805) 564-8280, fax (805) 564-8277. Open 11:30 a.m.–11:00 p.m. daily. Beer and wine. Visa, MasterCard, American Express, Discover. Wheelchair accessible.*

At the southwest corner of State Street and Canon Perdido Street is the PIERRE LAFOND–WENDY FOSTER boutique, one of the offspring of entrepreneur Pierre Lafond and his wife. They also have a Wendy Foster women's clothing shop in Montecito and own the Lafond Winery west of Buellton.

Actually in the Paseo Nuevo complex, this shop specializes in casual, sophisticated clothing of natural fibers and soft colors from designers Lisa Jasso, Diesel, Industry, Curiositees, Oh Boy!, Lucky, Big Star, and allen allen usa.

❧ *Pierre Lafond–Wendy Foster, 833 State Street, Santa Barbara 93101; (805) 996-2276. Open 10:00 a.m.–6:00 p.m. Monday–Thursday, 10:00 a.m.–8:00 p.m. Friday–Saturday, 11:00 a.m.–6:00 p.m. Sunday. Visa, MasterCard, American Express. Wheelchair accessible.*

BARNES & NOBLE bookstore is a comfort zone for some people, with bestsellers discounted (which is why they remain best-sellers?) and a Starbucks cafe inside. The store offers a wide range of books and has excellent hours for late-night browsing.

❧ *Barnes & Noble, 829 State Street, Santa Barbara 93101; (805) 962-8509. Open 9:00 a.m.–11:00 p.m. daily. Visa, MasterCard, American Express, Discover, Diners. Wheelchair accessible with elevator to upper floors.*

Take the next walkway to the massive PASEO NUEVO mall, which is lined with fifty light- and medium-fast-food restaurants and small shops, such as California Pasta and a Häagen-Dazs ice cream shop. Heavens! You will also find People's Pottery, Rudy's Mexican Restaurant, Nine West, Banana Republic, Chico's, Victoria's Secret, Nordstrom, Macy's, Lucky Brand Dungarees, Limited, Gap, Enlightened Sights, Montana Mercantile, Eddie Bauer Home Collection, and the Center State Theater. If familiar shopping is your thing, this is where you find the shops you will recognize from home.

As you enter the Paseo Nuevo complex and mall, you may well start to salivate. La Piccola Mollie and Cafe Orleans both tempt. Give in.

La Piccola Mollie serves inexpensive Italian specialties, including house-made or dried pasta, colorful salads, pizza, and panini. At Cafe Orleans you order New Orleans, Cajun, and Creole favorites at the counter and seat yourself. These restaurants all offer great people-watching and outdoor seating.

The Paseo Nuevo Cinemas offer a curious assortment of movies convenient to all.

Paseo Nuevo offers ninety minutes' free parking in its garage, which you reach from Chapala Street.

☙ *Paseo Nuevo, State and De la Guerra Streets, Santa Barbara 93101; (805) 963-2202. Open 10:00 a.m.–9:00 p.m. Monday–Friday, 10:00 a.m.–8:00 p.m. Saturday, 11:00 a.m.–6:00 p.m. Sunday. Visa, MasterCard, American Express. Wheelchair accessible.*

Back on State Street at the entrance to Paseo Nuevo is the COFFEE BEAN AND TEA LEAF, a favorite tea and coffee stop for locals. The only problem here is limited seating, but you can sit at tables in the Nuevo Paseo walkway. Feast your eyes and salivary glands on their fruit cheesecakes, carrot cake, and Death by Chocolate cake, and be sure to take home one of their handsome black glass jars filled with their own teas.

☙ *Coffee Bean and Tea Leaf, 811A State Street, Santa Barbara 93101; (805) 966-2442. Open 7:00 a.m.–10:00 p.m. Sunday–Thursday, 7:00 a.m.–11:00 p.m. Friday–Saturday. Visa and MasterCard. Wheelchair accessible.*

ROCKS RESTAURANT & LOUNGE is a two-level restaurant with a cafe/bar atmosphere downstairs that includes computer plug-ins and window tables, great-viewing metal tables on the sidewalk facing State Street, and a big entrance to Paseo Nuevo.

Rocks has great prices—salads and burgers (including tuna carpaccio or sashimi) at lunch are $6.95, with offerings ranging from a warm spinach scallop salad with pesto, pine nuts, and goat cheese to Rocks' half-pound burger that comes with choice of french fries, green salad, or pasta salad and a mere 50 cents extra for cheddar or blue cheese. We like the blackened mahimahi sandwich or grilled salmon sandwich ($6.95–$9.95).

Evening selections are both similar and more extensive, with additions including seared tuna tataki, pepper-crusted filet mignon with baby bok choy and crispy polenta, braised lamb shank with scalloped potatoes and root veggies, and spicy Korean-style ribs ($14–$23).

Rocks' wine list is short but good, offering Domaine Chandon, Schramsberg, Veuve Cliquot, and Moet & Chandon sparkling wines, as well as excellent Santa Barbara, Monterey, Napa, and Sonoma Chardonnays, Sauvignon Blancs, and Cabernet Sauvignons.

☙ *Rocks Restaurant & Lounge, 801 State Street, Santa Barbara 93101; (805) 884-1190. Open 11:30 a.m.–10:00 p.m. Monday–Thursday, 11:30 a.m.–11:00 p.m. Friday–Saturday. Full bar. Visa, MasterCard, American Express, Discover. Downstairs and sidewalk are wheelchair accessible.*

We are about to do another disservice to Santa Barbarans. We hereby "discover" PASCUCCI for the outside world. When you ask almost anyone working on State Street what their favorite restaurant is, they say "Pascucci's." The name combines parts of "pasta and cappuccino," with some good wine poured in.

Think about this: mosaic and iron tables in front, opera playing in the background, brick and mustard walls, large colorful paintings, an open curved kitchen, a big tiled fireplace, and fabulous garlic smells wafting throughout the restaurant at all times of the day—even when the restaurant is closed!

Pascucci's is a happening hangout where you can enjoy extremely tasty local food at reasonable prices. All meats come from the local and elegant Shalhoob Meat Company. For antipasti, try the *carciofi tre formaggio,* which is artichoke hearts and prosciutto baked with fontina, Gorgonzola, and Parmesan cheeses, or the bruschetta of fresh Roma tomatoes, fresh basil, roasted garlic, herbs, and balsamic vinegar on toasted rosemary bread. Oh yes, be sure to sample the breads brought to your table along with the halibut salad or the sourdough cheeseburger.

The soups of the day are excellent, as are the salads, which come in small or large. We often share a large Caesar and one of the thick and aromatic pizzas. At lunch the panini (sandwiches) are mostly $8.95 and are made on garlic-cheese bread and served with mixed green or Caesar salad. The Amalfi includes prosciutto, herbed mushrooms, and smoked mozzarella; the San Remo features grilled garlic and herb marinated tri-tip steak, spicy marinara, and avocado; the Como is grilled shrimp, marinated artichoke hearts, and pesto; and children's pizza or spaghetti can be had for under $5.00.

The pastas are equally exciting and even more varied, and range from $6.75 to $8.75 at lunch and up to $12.00 at dinner. Head for the "specialita" at the end of the menu for grilled vegetable plates, tiger shrimp stuffed with pesto and wrapped in prosciutto, grilled salmon fillet with capellini, and boneless chicken breasts several inventive ways.

❧ *Pascucci, 729 State Street, Santa Barbara 93101; (805) 963-8123; www .pascuccirestaurant.com. Open 11:30 a.m.–9:00 p.m. Monday–Friday, 11:30 a.m.–10:00 p.m. Saturday and Sunday. Full bar. Visa, MasterCard, American Express. Wheelchair accessible.*

It's worth crossing Ortega Street to go to the TRAILHEAD, known to be the friendliest outfitting store in town. We agree. In a building originally the site of the Gutierrez Drug Store (1855), the Trailhead now offers lots of information, as well as active clothing and shoes by Osprey, Arcteryx, Siena Design, Woolrich, La Sportiva, Ecco, and Timberland, as well as Swiss army knives,

Walrus tents, hiking accessories, a great selection of pertinent books, and back-packs of all sizes and shapes.

❧ *Trailhead, 635 State Street, Santa Barbara 93101; (805) 963-9308. Open 10:00 a.m.–6:00 p.m. Monday–Saturday, 10:00 a.m.–5:00 p.m. Sunday. Visa, MasterCard, American Express, ATM, no personal checks. Wheelchair accessible.*

Cyclists will want to be sure to drop in at Velo Pro Bicycles, either for repairs or new equipment and bikes. Two mechanics work full-time behind the counter, while you check out the bike parts, mountain bikes, cruisers, and helmets. Bike brands include Raleigh, GT, Kona, Gary Fisher, Klein, Santa Cruz, Redline, Mongoose, Powerlite, Haro, Robinson, and Bontrager, and Velo Pro is the exclusive Marin bike dealer for Santa Barbara. Rentals vary by bike, and helmets are extra.

Velo Pro sponsors the Santa Barbara Bike Fest (early June).

❧ *Velo Pro Bicycles, 633 State Street, Santa Barbara 93101; (805) 963-7775; www.velopro.com. Open 10:00 a.m.–6:00 p.m. Monday–Thursday and Saturday, 10:00 a.m.–7:00 p.m. Friday, 11:00 a.m.–4:00 p.m. Sunday. Visa, MasterCard, American Express, Discover, ATM. Wheelchair accessible.*

There are lots more shops farther down State Street, but the truly interesting ones are spread out over several blocks. You may want to venture down to Santa Barbara Brewing Company brewery and pub, Hotel Santa Barbara (includes a Starbucks) on the corner, and James Joyce Pub with live Celtic music.

Cross State Street right here and work your way back up the east side to complete your shop walk.

Pierre Lafond Bistro is part of Lafond's small empire and is surprisingly hip and healthy, with equally good local artists' work displayed. At breakfast the omelettes were decent, made with "only natural organic eggs" and filled with multiple choices ranging from spinach and feta to cilantro chicken, salmon, or steak Benedict, and just plain two eggs any style, all with choices of potato styles and toast ($6.00–$12.50), bagel sandwiches, breakfast burritos, pancakes, and the works, plus organic coffees and teas.

Lunch may involve panini, loads of salads from ahi tuna to steak, grilled portobello with black truffles, Cobb, and a Zaca Taco salad ($7.95–$13.95), imaginative sandwiches with vegetarian selections (all under $15.00), gourmet pizzas, vegetarian entrees or organic free-range chicken, Kahuna grilled tri-tip, banana shrimp tamales, grilled salmon, and many pastas at dinner ($14.95–$19.95).

❧ *Pierre Lafond Bistro,* 516 State Street, Santa Barbara 93101; (805) 962-1455; www.pierrelafond.com. Open 7:00 a.m.–10:00 p.m. daily.

Just north of Pierre Lafond Bistro is an open-air Indian market with scads of glass and metal bangle bracelets, pillows, rugs, bedspreads, men's and women's clothing, masks, and tons of imported bargains for home and body.

ZELO RESTAURANT presents an enticing ambience with the grill right in front of the dining room, brick walls, stepped terraces inside, large bright paintings, and a substantial bar. At lunch Zelo offers quesadillas with chicken or shrimp, and pastas including salmon capellini, mustard chicken fettuccine, and Thai beef with side salads for $1.50 extra. Easterners can enjoy a Philly steak sandwich, Zelo's Killer Pastrami, and half-sandwich specials with soup or salad. All sandwiches come with salad, soup, or fries. It's a deal at $6.95–$8.95.

At dinner you might try sautéed garlic oysters, Zelo vera pasta with veggies, sun-dried tomatoes, garlic, and olive oil, spicy Thai beef noodles, or curried sea scallops. Specialties range from sesame seared ahi tuna to grilled filet mignon with caramelized shallots in pink peppercorn brandy and crab-stuffed salmon with dill beurre blanc ($10–$23).

Zelo boasts a list of special vodkas, rums, tequilas, and liqueurs, and a short wine list of Napa, Monterey, and central coast wines, and there's live music on Saturday.

❧ *Zelo Restaurant,* 630 State Street, Santa Barbara 93101; (805) 966-5792, fax (805) 966-5034. Open for lunch noon–3:00 p.m. Friday–Sunday, happy hour 5:30–8:00 p.m., dinner from 5:30 p.m. Tuesday–Sunday; nightclub from 10:00 p.m. nightly. Visa and MasterCard. Not wheelchair accessible.

Don't miss the ITALIAN GREEK MARKET at the corner of State Street and Ortega. A local favorite for decades, this place has been voted Best Deli & Sandwiches for many years in a row by Santa Barbarans. Pay attention!

As you walk in, the deli case on the right makes it clear that this is the place for light lunches and sandwiches: huge marinated artichoke salad, macaroni salads like you've never seen, a large selection of meats, and comics taped to the deli counter's glass. You can sit on stools along the Ortega Street side window or at red-and-white-checked tableclothed tables in the back room. Italian soccer matches play on the television, and Italian basketball team photos line the walls. This is a great place to collect your picnic if you're heading off to the wineries.

The store area sells everything from the *Complete Armenian Cookbook* and Italian vinegars and oils to Genova tonno (tuna), Indo-European grains, Medaglia D'Oro Instant Espresso, Nonno Mario's pizza, small to large tins of

anchovies and sardines, and even halvah at $5.40 per pound. Cafe Bustelo, Lavazza, and Kimbo coffees are all available next to blue bottles of Brioschi for upset stomachs! This is the place if you are looking for Greek wines and retsina.
➢ *Italian Greek Market, 636 State Street, Santa Barbara 93101; (805) 962-6815. Open 8:00 a.m.–6:00 p.m. daily. Beer and wine. No credit cards, but ATM in store. Wheelchair accessible.*

LEFT AT ALBUQUERQUE, truly one of our favorites, has both terrific New Mexican food and a wildly fun ambience. Enjoy a lunch of lime chicken fajitas with sensational beans and piles of fresh condiments ($12.99–$14.99), and the full bar atmosphere, music, and people meeting people.

This Mobil Travel Guide–recommended restaurant has the longest list of gourmet tequilas we have ever seen, red and white corn tortilla chips with fresh, fresh salsas, enormous nachos, and a variety of meat, seafood, and vegetarian dishes. Of the quesadillas, try the tequila lime rock shrimp ($7.99). Prices are the same for both lunch and dinner.

House favorites include "hot-off-the-griddle" corn cakes with tequila lime butter and sun-dried tomato corn salsa; chopped chicken salad with feta cheese and a basil pesto dressing; an unbelievable towering tostada that varies in price for vegetarian, chicken, or steak; cowboy mixed grill; ribs; grilled New York steak; and a green monster enchilada with poblano chicken topped with roasted green chili sauce, jack and cheddar cheeses, sour cream, and green rice, with everything under $20.

The pan-roasted barbecue salmon served with tequila lime butter sauce, sun-dried tomato corn salsa, and green rice and the roadhouse fajitas (price also varies by choice) are also fun. Out of sight burgers and burritos as well.
➢ *Left at Albuquerque, 803 State Street, Santa Barbara 93101; (805) 564-5040; www.leftatalb.com. Open 11:00 a.m.–11:00 p.m. Full bar. Visa, MasterCard, American Express. Wheelchair accessible.*

Just up State Street from Ma Dolce Vita is one of our favorite shops to check into whenever we visit. We love to browse at ANTIQUE ALLEY for little pieces of Santa Barbara history. Its fifteen dealers sell well-selected antiques and collectibles. Alan Howard personally selects his dealers and oversees the whole place, willing to bargain within limits set by each dealer. We have found prize kitchen utensils, rare Viewmaster reels, and other gems we and our twentysomething kids collect at the moment.
➢ *Antique Alley, 706 State Street, Santa Barbara 93101; (805) 962-3944. Open 11:00 a.m.–6:00 p.m. Monday–Thursday, 11:00 a.m.–10:00 p.m. Friday and Saturday, noon–5:00 p.m. Sunday. Visa and MasterCard. Wheelchair accessible.*

For healthy refreshment, you might want to stop into PIRANHA RESTAURANT AND SUSHI BAR for sushi or robata-grilled beef, eggplant, Chilean sea bass, or Norwegian salmon ($17.75). And, of course, teriyaki galore.

➣ *Piranha Restaurant and Sushi Bar, 714 State Street, Santa Barbara 93101; (805) 965-2980. Open for lunch 11:30 a.m.–2:00 p.m. Tuesday–Sunday, dinner 5:30–10:00 p.m. Tuesday–Sunday, until 11:00 p.m. Friday. Beer, wine, and sake. MasterCard, Visa, American Express. Wheelchair accessible.*

MINGEI ORIENTAL IMPORTS has gorgeous Japanese chests, pottery, and wall hangings. Mingei specializes in Edo and Meiji furniture, art, and "objects of merit." A must-see.

➣ *Mingei Oriental Imports, 736 State Street, Santa Barbara 93101; (805) 963-3257. Open 11:00 a.m.–5:00 p.m. Monday–Saturday, noon–6:00 p.m. Sunday. Visa, MasterCard, American Express. Wheelchair accessible.*

KAI SISHI–SHABU SHABU offers fresh sushi and hot-pot meals in a charming Japanese ambience.

➣ *Kai Sishi–Shabu Shabu, 738 State Street, Santa Barbara 93101; (805) 560-8777. Open for lunch 11:30 a.m.–2:30 p.m. Monday–Friday, dinner 5:30–11:00 p.m. Monday–Saturday. Visa and MasterCard. Wheelchair accessible.*

Coach leather accessory fans will enjoy the Coach Factory Outlet, right next to the Starbucks at 800 State Street.

BRYANT & SONS JEWELERS LTD. deals in the finest jewelry there is, including Piaget, Cartier, Ebel, and Baume & Mercier diamonds, Mikimoto pearls, and colored gemstones. Bryant & Sons is also a Tiffany & Company authorized jeweler and has full-time gemologists, appraisers, and a master goldsmith on the premises. This exquisite shop bends around the corner into El Paseo, one of Santa Barbara's older courtyards.

➣ *Bryant & Sons Jewelers Ltd., 812 State Street, Santa Barbara 93101; (805) 966-9187; www.sbweb.com/bryants. Open 10:00 a.m.–5:30 p.m. Monday–Saturday. Visa, MasterCard, American Express. Wheelchair accessible.*

EL PASEO itself is worth exploring, particularly if you wander into El Cuartel and make it all the way to the back at Anacapa Street to one of our favorite restaurants anywhere, the WINE CASK RESTAURANT AND WINE STORE. Owner Doug Margerum, who with his crew used to prepare lunches for Santa Barbara's most prestigious private clubs, has sold the restaurant to health-care mogul Bernard Rosenson. There are plans to reopen the restaurant, but at press time it was still closed.

Within El Paseo's courtyard, wander also to Europa Antiques, which aren't all from Europe; the charming Gentlemen Antiquarians; the Santa Barbara Gallery of the Solvang Antique Center; and Ruby's Copy Jewels.

Parking alert! There's an excellent parking lot just north of El Paseo. Its entrance is on Anacapa Street, which is one-way (toward the ocean).

BORDERS BOOKS, with its high-columned entryway, fills the northwest corner of the intersection. Borders Cafe is just to your left as you walk in, and excellent discounts on best-sellers or well-financed wanna-bes are close to the door. The staff is very friendly here, and this particular Borders borders on the pleasant funk of an independent bookstore. In good weather, you can sit at round tables in front, reading and sipping your Borders coffee.

ᵇ⌀ *Borders Books, Music & Cafe, 900 State Street, Santa Barbara 93101; (805) 899-3668. Open 9:00 a.m.–11:00 p.m. Monday–Thursday, 9:00 a.m.–midnight Friday and Saturday, 9:00 a.m.–10:00 p.m. Sunday. Visa, MasterCard, American Express. Wheelchair accessible.*

FIESTA FIVE THEATRE, a multiscreen movie house with papers blowing around even during the Santa Barbara Film Festival, shows five films at a time for downtown moviegoers.

ᵇ⌀ *Fiesta Five Theatre, 916 State Street, Santa Barbara 93101; (805) 963-0454. Open 1:00–11:00 p.m. Monday–Thursday, 2:15 p.m.–midnight Friday–Sunday. No credit cards. Not wheelchair accessible.*

At the corner of State and Cabrillo, SHOOZ is a wonderful true shoe boutique with staff to actually serve you and help you try on shoes, the old-fashioned way! Owner Elie Entezari offers Anne Klein, Charles David, Martines Valro, Moda Spana, Seychelles, and Misa, as well as gorgeous Dalya Collection sweaters. Worth a look, anyway, just for service nostalgia sake.

ᵇ⌀ *Shooz, 936 State Street, Santa Barbara 93101; (805) 962-3121. Open 10:00 a.m.–7:00 p.m. Sunday–Thursday, 10:00 a.m.–8:00 p.m. Friday and Saturday. Visa, MasterCard, American Express, Discover. Wheelchair accessible.*

The huge attractive building on the northeast corner of State and Carrillo is Montecito Bank and Trust, beyond which you will find the always crowded CHASE BAR & GRILL, which boasts that here "locals are celebrities." Lots of yellow Christmas lights brighten this cavernous burgundy bistro.

For lunch there are Italian sandwiches, and dinner starters include yummy pesto bread, steamed clams, or large Caesar salad ($6.95–$12.95). All dinner entrees include soup, such as housemade minestrone, Venetian fish chowder, or the soup of the day, or salad with choice of dressings. Pastas range from spaghetti with meatballs or sausage to handmade ravioli with choice of sauces and fettuccine Alfredo with chicken ($8.95–$12.95).

All house specialties come with fettuccine or spaghetti, and you get sauce choices—piccata (lemon, wine, and capers) and Provençal (sherry and garlic)—for your chicken, red snapper, halibut, calamari, jumbo shrimp, or hand-trimmed veal. Of course there are steak choices, too, and cioppino, and scampi ($12.95–$21.95). Don't miss the "straight from Brooklyn" rice pudding or the cannoli. You can also drop in for breakfast omelettes, steak and eggs, or French toast. Chase also sponsors the Chase Classic Golf Tournament at Rancho San Marcos to benefit the Police Activities League.

❧ *Chase Bar & Grill, 1012 State Street, Santa Barbara 93101; (805) 965-4351. Open for breakfast 7:00–10:30 a.m. Monday–Saturday, lunch 11:00 a.m.–2:30 p.m. Monday–Friday, dinner 5:00 p.m.–midnight daily. Full bar. Visa, MasterCard, American Express, Discover. Wheelchair accessible.*

To complete the Italian dining choices in this block of State Street, PALAZZIO TRATTORIA ITALIANA is interesting as well as good. While the trattoria's accurate motto is "People generally don't leave here hungry," it also shows its dedication to and appreciation for the arts. Besides, locals voted Palazzio Best Service and Best Italian Restaurant in Santa Barbara repeatedly. Palazzio boasts that its food is ready for takeout in fifteen minutes or less.

Be sure to check out Palazzio's "Sistine Chapel ceiling," begun by local artist Irene Roderick March 2, 1998, and completed January 11, 1999. Read placards on the wall as you enter to get the full impression of this very different restaurant.

All menu selections are available in half-order/full-order portions and prices. An excellent pizza lunch combo with salad or soup is $8.75, and half orders of pastas at lunch are only $6.00.

Antipasti include spinach and artichoke dip; fried calamari; Caprese fresh Italian mozzarella, fresh Roma tomato, and sweet basil; antipasti Palazzio of sun-dried tomatoes, artichoke hearts, mozzarella, prosciutto, roasted peppers, and mushrooms ($10.50/$13.95); and mussels steamed in white wine with Roma tomatoes ($6.75/$9.75).

Spinach, Caesar, and green salads are available.

This is the only Italian restaurant we have ever seen that translates pastas to plain English for guests who are unfamiliar with pasta shapes and sizes—for example, *penne,* thin short tubes; *fettuccine,* long flat; *fusilli,* corkscrew. A real plus!

The oven-roasted rosemary chicken is excellent, as are the roasted eggplant lasagna and penne alla bella Gina with prosciutto, sun-dried tomatoes, shallots, cream sauce, and parmigiano Italiano ($12.95–$19.95).

❧ *Palazzio Trattoria Italiana, 1026 State Street, Santa Barbara 93101; (805) 564-1985; www.palazzio.com. Open for lunch 11:30 a.m.–3:00 p.m., dinner 5:30–11:00 p.m. Sunday–Thursday, 1:30 p.m.–midnight Friday and Saturday. Full bar. Visa, MasterCard, American Express. Wheelchair accessible. Also located at 1151 Coast Village Road, Montecito; (805) 969-8565.*

Ever-present Kinko's completes this block to State Street's intersection with Figueroa Street.

What you are about to encounter is the beautifully preserved and developed LA ARCADA complex, which was restored with storefronts on State Street as integral parts of the project, with the Santa Barbara Museum of Art up the street at the other end of the block.

But first at the northeast corner of State and Figueroa you come to P.S. LTD., an elegant home-accessories boutique that features the Santa Barbara lap robe, Nicholas Mosse pottery from Ireland, French Heritage pottery from Brittany, Rochard Limoges, Churchill weavers, Les Etains pewter, Nancy Thomas folk art, Simon Pearce glass, Woodbury Woodenware, and Gien faience. You will also find Vera Bradley bags, elegant cards, and the best of Beanie Babies, which the owner's husband, Hugh Petersen, La Arcada restorer and developer, collects.

What is a Santa Barbara lap robe? It is really a quilt designed by Seddon Ryan Wylde, who has filled commissions for private label designs from the Boston Symphony Orchestra to the Historic Charleston Foundation and the Metropolitan Museum of Art in New York. She also creates private-label lap robes for the Boston Museum of Fine Arts, resorts, and cities from Nantucket to Catalina.

❧ *P.S. Ltd., 1100 State Street, Santa Barbara 93101; (805) 963-6808. Open 10:00 a.m.–5:30 p.m. Monday–Saturday. Visa, MasterCard, American Express, Discover. Downstairs is wheelchair accessible.*

Before you reach the actual entrance to La Arcada, two tempting restaurant/cafes present themselves. ANDERSEN'S DANISH BAKERY & RESTAURANT produces remarkably large and refreshing fruit plates served with Havarti cheese, Danish bread, ice cream, and a "surprise" all for $10.95. You will also enjoy their salads, "crispy" omelettes, sandwiches, smoked Scottish salmon with dill sauce, capers, Havarti cheese, cream cheese, bread, and "surprise" ($11.95, $13.95 with a side of eggs). All of the seafood salads are good and under $16.00.

Daily hot specials may include pork schnitzel, Hungarian goulash, or New York steak. Andersen's Good Morning Breakfast includes bacon, eggs, ham, cheese, fruit, and potatoes for a whopping $7.95, with no deductions for subtracting the meats or the eggs. Steak and eggs is $19.95. You also may want to check out the smorrebrod, an open-face decorated sandwich on pumpernickel served with fresh fruit and the day's salad, or the mini smorgasbord ($2.00–$29.95).

Andersen's bakery always has warm Danish, strudels, croissants, and wonderful marzipan pastries, éclairs, napoleons, Sarah Bernhardts, Danish layer cake, Danish marzipan layer cake, and butter cookies. Just a sample. And then there's the homemade vanilla ice cream with whipped cream, fruit, and meringue ($4.95)!

❧ *Andersen's Danish Bakery & Restaurant, 1106 State Street, Santa Barbara 93101; (805) 962-5085; www.andersenssantabarbara.com. Open 8:00 a.m.– 8:00 p.m. daily. Visa and MasterCard. Wheelchair accessible.*

Assuming you haven't enlarged yourself by a full size, you might check out SOCORRO, a relaxed resort-clothing store with the lovely, loose, natural-fiber dresses of Mishi, Kiko, and M.A.C. A few hats to protect you from the summer sun, too.

❧ *Socorro, 1106A State Street, Santa Barbara 93101; (805) 966-5779. Open 10:00 a.m.–6:00 p.m. daily. Visa and MasterCard. Wheelchair accessible.*

Right at the corner of State Street and the entrance to La Arcada is BARCLIFF & BAIR, a favorite of locals, and a favorite of ours, too. We love to sit at the sidewalk tables, which face both State Street and the occasionally cooler La Arcada pathway, and enjoy a sumptuous salad and excellent iced tea. The people-watching is primo Santa Barbara. So is the food. And so is the ambience in the dining room to your right as you enter, if you can pass the pastry counter.

Barcliff & Bair makes a point of offering interesting vegetarian alternatives as well as a grilled lamb sandwich ($13) and a roast beef tri-tip sandwich with cheddar cheese ($8/$10), all of which are available by the half or whole. The grilled eggplant and roasted bell pepper with mozzarella and feta cheeses, tomato, fresh basil, and Bermuda onion ($8/$10) melts in your mouth, soups and chicken chili ditto, and Kathleen loves the salads of the day, which are always excellent. The children's menu is just right, with peanut butter and jelly or ham and cheese, tuna, turkey, and tri-tip sandwiches with sliced apple and chips for $4.50. Don't miss the espresso drinks.

Because tea service is unusual for Santa Barbara, we highly recommend a relaxing Friday Afternoon Tea from 2:30 to 4:30 p.m. Reservations are a must. Barcliff & Bair also serves an excellent breakfast special of two pancakes, two eggs, and two sausages or strips of bacon ($6.99).

❧ *Barcliff & Bair, 1114 State Street, Santa Barbara 93101; (805) 965-5742. Open 8:00 a.m.–3:00 p.m. Monday–Thursday, 8:00 a.m.–5:00 p.m. Friday and Saturday, 9:00 a.m.–5:00 p.m. Sunday. Beer and wine. Visa, MasterCard, and personal checks. Wheelchair accessible.*

Now we enter LA ARCADA for a rare experience, both cultural and commercial. On the site of a Catholic church demolished during the 1925 earthquake, La Arcada was designed and constructed in 1926 under the supervision of Myron Hunt. Hunt also designed several other important buildings in southern California, including Pasadena's Rose Bowl, San Marino's Huntington Library and Huntington Hotel, Occidental College in Los Angeles, and Pomona College in Claremont.

Hugh Petersen rescued the slightly dilapidated complex and restored it slowly and accurately, with a handworking wood shop and full-time wood-workers still practicing their craft in the basement. Petersen took Kathleen and a friend into the third-floor men's room to see the green marble fixtures and the mural of Hawaii's Kunai Peninsula. What a treat!

Petersen has peppered this marvelous development with humorous and rare sculpture and his varied collections, so pay attention to labels as you go. Individual local shops are even adorned with his treasures, including an eighteenth-century mission bell, and it's worth browsing just to see them. Petersen is a particular fan of J. Seward Johnson Jr., who created the whimsical "Nice to See You" window washer (known locally as "Bob") in front of the Lewis & Clark shop, as well as "Who's In Charge." You will also find sculptured fountains by famed James "Bud" Bottoms, who did the 8-foot bronze dolphins in the court and the sea lion in the main lobby. The Mozart Trio Fountain in front of the Joseph Bottoms Fine Arts Gallery was designed by Bonifatius Stirnberg, Germany's foremost sculptor of interactive public art.

Farther into La Arcada, be sure to check out Gallery 113, a cooperative of the Santa Barbara Art Association, and Waterhouse Gallery, featuring quality local talent. Restaurants include the colorful and lively Bogart's Cafe and wine bar with a Bogey theme, and the Whale Tail

LA ARCADA, STATE STREET,
SANTA BARBARA

Deli, whose jolly hosts serve terrific breakfasts and lunches wolfed down by locals. Browse at In Stitches for fabulous yarns and classes, Santa Barbara Baggage Company for high-quality leather goods and a mouthwatering scent, and Patagonia. Check out The Barbershop with its classic chairs and clocks.

🥬 *La Arcada, 1100 block of State Street at Figueroa, Santa Barbara 93101; no general phone; www.laarcadasantabarbara.com. Credit cards vary by store. Wheelchair accessible.*

LEWIS & CLARK ANTIQUES AND FINE THINGS does not reflect the American Northwest as Westerners might expect. It actually presents the elegant best from estate sales; French prints; imports from India, Thailand, Morocco, and France; and Spode china from England. Notice the lovely table in the middle of the store and the pillows in tapestry (from $20) and needlepoint ($60–$200). Mother and daughter Elizabeth and Lisa Reifel moved their shop here from Victoria Court in 1997. Don't miss.

🥬 *Lewis & Clark Antiques and Fine Things, 1116 State Street, Santa Barbara 93101; (805) 962-6034. Open 10:00 a.m.–5:30 p.m. Monday–Saturday, noon–5:00 p.m. Sunday. Visa and MasterCard. Wheelchair accessible.*

Just down State Street next to the Museum of Art, Straight Down Clothing chain store offers its standard casual resort and street wear, depending upon your lifestyle.

At the corner of State Street and Anapamu Street is the renowned SANTA BARBARA MUSEUM OF ART in all its glory. From its transformation from an empty post office into a major regional museum, the Santa Barbara Museum has always emphasized renewal and expansion of services to the community. Hence it now offers audio tours of the permanent collection, an exciting children's gallery to encourage family visits, an ongoing youth mural project, a large store, and excellent snacks and refreshments at the new Fresco Museum Cafe. The galleries are arranged so that visitors can view the museum's collection in chronological order to show the exchange of ideas and influences among period artists.

The museum's Ridley-Tree Education Center at McCormick House, 1600 Santa Barbara Street (805-962-1661), is a remarkable center for hands-on art education, offering studio art classes for children, teens, and adults in painting, drawing, ceramics, sculpture, puppetry, mask making, and cartooning. There are also educational exhibitions, including special Rainy Day Saturdays of fun-filled classes and drop-in sessions. The museum also offers bus tours to significant showings in Los Angeles, extremely popular worldwide tours, and even culinary classes, most of which are open to the public for a fee.

Santa Barbara Museum benefits from the area's wealthy and generous residents, such as Lord and Lady Ridley-Tree, Mr. and (the late) Mrs. Austin H. Peck Jr., and the late Suzette Morton Davidson. The museum's ten galleries showcase 4,500 years of art from classic Greco-Roman figures to modernism's masterpieces. The Asian collection fills a whole floor.

Permanent-collection pieces include works of Raoul Dufy, John Singleton Copley, Hans Hofmann, Javier Marin, Auguste Rodin, Henri Matisse, Georges Braque, Frederic Lord Leighton, Marc Chagall, Joaquin Torres-Garcia, Childe Hassam, and Lan Ying.

Fresco at the Beach opened a new cafe in the museum, which is behind the museum store, in June 2007. The menu, abbreviated from that of Fresco at the Beach in the Santa Barbara Inn, offers good-looking salads with scoops of tuna and chicken salad extra, soups, and sandwiches with a wide range of choices of healthy breads and cheeses to accompany roasted turkey, tuna, or chicken salad, "very veggie" and pannini.

The Mushroom Combo panini includes shiitake, portobello, and button mushrooms with Brie cheese, and The Beach is made with grilled chicken breast, Vermont cheddar, avocado, tomato, and chipotle aioli ($4.50–$13.00).

❧ *Santa Barbara Museum of Art, 1130 State Street, Santa Barbara 93101; (805) 963-4364, fax (805) 966-6840; www.sbmuseart.org. Museum open 11:00 a.m.–5:00 p.m. Tuesday–Saturday, 11:00 a.m.–9:00 p.m. Friday, noon–5:00 p.m. Sunday. Cafe open 11:00 a.m.–5:00 p.m. Tuesday–Saturday (until 8:00 p.m. Friday), noon–4:00 p.m. Sunday. Admission: adults $9, seniors (age 65-plus) $6, students with ID and ages six to seventeen $6, under six and members free. Admission is free every Sunday. Visa, MasterCard, American Express. Wheelchair accessible.*

STATE STREET ANTIQUE MALL is one of our favorite shops, with eighty dealers and a lot of stuff. You have to look very carefully here to not miss some goodies, and you have to go back and back if you are looking for something specific.

❧ *State Street Antique Mall, 1219 State Street, Santa Barbara 93101; (805) 965-2575. Open 10:00 a.m.–6:00 p.m. Monday–Thursday and Sunday, 10:00 a.m.–10:00 p.m. Friday and Saturday. Visa and MasterCard. Wheelchair accessible but tight.*

SIGNIFICANT OTHERS

Significant Others, in this case, refers to restaurants and other places of interest not located on State Street that we highly recommend you check out. We save really important historical stops for *Things You Really Should See,* which follows immediately after this section.

BOUCHON Santa Barbara continues to be one of the town's hottest restaurants and is not related to Thomas Keller's Bouchon in Yountville.

Proprietor Mitchell Sjerven graduated from UC/Santa Barbara in international relations and political science, perfect training for opening and running a fine restaurant on Bastille Day (July 14) in 1998.

While opening chef Charles Frederick graduated from the Culinary Institute of America-Hyde Park, current chef Josh Brown graduated from the culinary program at Santa Barbara City College, cooked with passion at several local restaurants, joined Bouchon at its beginning, and has rapidly worked his way up to chef. Brown shops regularly at the Santa Barbara farmers' market and loves to greet guests while doing his "kitchen ballet" at the open kitchen's window.

Brown's Dungeness crab cakes are divine, as are cold and hot soups including a yellowtail carpaccio, seared wild Pacific salmon, bourbon and maple-glazed duck breast, pomegranate-marinated rack of lamb, pan-seared rack of venison, steaks, and fab desserts from a warm Santa Barbara chocolate "molten lava" cake to Meyer lemon curd tarts, vanilla crème brûlée, and an apple Tarte Tatin.

The cheese plate ($15) is to die for and includes the best from Cypress Grove, Redwood Hill Farm, Cowgirl Creamery, Point Reyes Farmstead Cheese Co., Matos Farms St. George, and Fiscalini Farms, all of which the restaurant obtains from Santa Barbara cheese shop C'est Cheese. Entrees $25–$35.

Forty Santa Barbara wines by the glass.

Bouchon, 9 West Victoria Street near State Street, Santa Barbara 93101; (805) 730-1160; www.bouchonsantabarbara.com. Open from 5:30 p.m. daily. Beer and wine. Visa, MasterCard, American Express. Wheelchair accessible.

RODNEY'S STEAKHOUSE is located at Fess Parker's Doubletree Resort and is a superb mecca for steak and lobster lovers. In a fabulously dramatic room named for their late son-in-law, Rodney Shull, in which Marcy and Fess Parker entertain their friends—Hollywood and otherwise—you can enjoy perfect crab cakes ($12), Rodney's chopped salad (tastes like your grandmother's salad) ($9), superb yellowfin tartare ($12), USDA prime steaks displayed at your table for your selection ($22–$65), or broiled lobster tails ($58). We sometimes like to

STUFFED SQUASH BLOSSOMS
from Chef Michael Boyce, Bouchon, Santa Barbara

FOR THE FILLING:
- 8 oz. goat cheese
- zest of 2 lemons
- 2 Tbs. fresh basil, chopped
- vegetable oil
- touch of cream
- salt and pepper to taste

FOR THE TEMPURA BATTER:
- 1 cup crushed ice
- 8 oz. beer
- 1 cup flour

Blend goat cheese and cream in a food processor or in a stand mixer with a paddle attachment until soft. While blending, use spatula to blend cream and goat cheese. Add chopped basil and lemon zest, and salt and pepper to taste.

Using pastry bag, fill 12 squash blossoms with goat cheese mixture, twisting ends together to seal blossom. Chill for 1 hour before frying.

Make tempura batter by combining crushed ice, beer, and flour. Dip blossoms in tempura batter and fry in oil. Blossoms do not need to be submerged in oil but will float when they are done. Serves 6–12 as a side dish.

order all of the "sides," which make a meal in themselves. Excellent Santa Barbara and California wine list and martinis. Don't miss the waterfall wave sculpture near the entrance to Rodney's. Free valet parking at the hotel entrance. ❧ *Rodney's Steakhouse, 633 East Cabrillo Boulevard, Santa Barbara 93103; (805) 884-8581, resort (805) 564-4333, ext. 4381; www.rodneyssteakhouse.com. Open for dinner from 5:30 p.m. nightly. Full bar. Visa, MasterCard, American Express. Wheelchair accessible.*

LOUIE'S CALIFORNIA BISTRO is at The Upham Hotel, Santa Barbara's oldest hotel that was recently and lovingly restored. Louie's is small and worth the trip, with terrific food and extremely reasonable prices. Lunch offers meat loaf with sautéed mushrooms and onions ($12.00), a great tuna Caesar salad ($9.50), and chicken in puff pastry with broccoli and toasted almonds ($12.00). Also try the pastas and pizzas, the seared ahi tuna with tomatoes, or the perfect potato-crusted sea bass, a melt-in-your-mouth experience. Dinner adds chops, steaks, gumbo, and grilled Scottish salmon ($18.50–$26.00). Lots of locals enjoy lunch or dinner here, and The Upham has lots of convenient meeting or party rooms to suit your needs.

❧ *Louie's California Bistro, 1404 de la Vina Street, Santa Barbara 93101; (805) 963-7003; www.louiessb.com. Open for lunch 11:30 a.m.–3:00 p.m. Monday–Friday, dinner from 5:30 p.m. daily. Full bar. Visa, MasterCard, American Express. Wheelchair accessible.*

Sage & Onion and Olio e Limone are two of Santa Barbara's favorite restaurants.

SAGE & ONION offers interesting urban decor, a lovely cozy patio, and truly California eclectic cuisine. Chef and proprietor Steve Giles trained in England under renowned French chef Albert Roux. Starters range from asparagus, lemongrass, and ginger broth soup and red beet tartare with cucumber noodles to lobster salad with fava beans and an English Stilton soufflé with pinot noir sauce or cornbread-stuffed quail with roasted yam ($10–$16).

Main courses are divided into "From the Surf," "To the Turf," and "Vegetarian" and include rainbow trout, striper sea bass, Nantucket Day Boat scallops, free-range chicken breast, braised rabbit, Peking duck breast and natural American Kobe ribeye, or the chef's daily vegetarian special ($22–$39). Tasting menus also available ($60–$80, or $90–$125 with wine pairings).

❧ *Sage & Onion, 38 East Ortega Street, Santa Barbara 93101; (805) 963-1012; www.sageandonion.com. Open from 5:30 p.m. nightly. Beer and wine. Visa, MasterCard, American Express. Wheelchair accessible.*

OLIO E LIMONE is a true local favorite for modern Italian cuisine with an almost homey ambience just steps from Bouchon. Chef Alberto Morello and wife Elaine offer classic Italian dishes, ranging from first courses of spinach ribbon pasta with grilled chicken and corkscrew pasta with tomato sauce and eggplant to lobster-filled half-moon-shaped ravioli with lobster sauce, a small tube pasta with spicy tomato sauce, and daily risotto specials ($9.95–$15.95).

Main courses at lunch include several panini under $13.00, thin-pounded sliced chicken breast with prosciutto and Fontina cheese, Italian sausage with polenta and broccoli, squid with Swiss chard, beef tenderloin medallions, Italian-style eggs with fresh roasted artichoke hearts and asparagus, or a platter of roasted seasonal vegetables ($11.95–$17.95).

Dinner adds more risotto, several meat selections including rib eye steak, grilled veal chop, and New Zealand lamb chops, more Italian specialties, and $12.00–$15.00 to lunchtime prices. Don't miss the warm chocolate banana bread pudding! Absolutely mouthwatering! Select from a long list of Italian and Santa Barbara wines.

❧ *Olio e Limone, 17 West Victoria Street, Santa Barbara 93101; (805) 899-2699; www.olioelimone.com. Open for lunch Monday–Saturday 11:30 a.m.–2:00*

English Pea, Fennel, and Watercress Soup
from Chef Steven Giles, Sage & Onion, Santa Barbara

2 medium onions, diced

2 fennel bulbs, diced with tops removed

2 Tbs. fresh thyme, chopped

2 cups English peas, blanched

4 cloves garlic, chopped coarsely

2 Tbs. butter or oil, canola or olive

2 cups white wine

2 potatoes, peeled and diced

3 qts. chicken or vegetable stock

1 qt. cream

2 bunches watercress

salt and pepper to taste

fresh mint leaves

SPECIAL TOOLS NEEDED: 5-quart soup pot, blender, fine mesh strainer

Sauté onions, fennel, thyme, peas (save a few for garnish), and garlic in butter or oil until translucent (2–3 minutes). Add white wine and potatoes to mixture, bring to a boil, and simmer, reducing by half. Add chicken or vegetable stock, cream, and watercress. Bring back to a boil and then simmer for 18 minutes. Remove from heat.

Puree whole mixture in a blender. Pass through fine mesh strainer. Salt and pepper to taste. Garnish with fresh mint leaves and English peas and serve. Serves 8.

p.m., and nightly from 5:00 p.m. Beer and wine. Visa, MasterCard, American Express. Wheelchair accessible.

PARADISE CAFE is one of most Santa Barbarans' favorite restaurants, although hardly anyone from out of town has even heard of it. We're almost hesitant to tell you about it because it's such an unspoiled prize.

Located 1 block east of State Street at the corner of Anacapa and Ortega Streets, Paradise Cafe occupies what looks like a former bar/storefront on the corner, as well as a houselike building next door.

Lunchtime appetizers include grilled mussels with basil vinaigrette ($9.50), and the salads are large and fresh and range from Cobb to rock shrimp and

spinach ($6.95–$12.95). Omelettes are served through the lunch hour. Jerry loves
the half-pound bacon burger with crispy shoestring potatoes and pasta or green
salad. Drooling good. A tender calamari steak sandwich completes our favorites.
Vegetarian selections are always available.

The dinner menu expands to include oak-grill specialties that come with
soup or salad, and rice or shoestring or roasted potatoes; sautéed mushrooms are
75 cents extra. Try the mouthwatering Colorado chops, the large or small New
York steaks, or the oak-grilled shark, swordfish, ahi tuna, or salmon ($14.95–
$29.95). Several burgers and pastas ($8.95–$13.95) are available, too.
Wonderful fresh berries and cream ($4.25), and espresso drinks. Good local
wine list. Birthday kids love to come here for their free slice of Paradise Pie. One
of our favorites.

❧ *Paradise Cafe, 702 Anacapa Street, Santa Barbara 93101; (805) 962-4416;
www.paradisecafe.com. Open 11:00 a.m.–11:00 p.m. Monday–Saturday, Sunday
brunch 9:00 a.m.–3:00 p.m. Full bar. Visa, MasterCard, American Express.
Wheelchair accessible.*

We encourage you to stroll east on Cota Street from State Street for what
might be Santa Barbara's version of a gourmet ghetto. Here you can taste several
cultures, including New Orleans/Cajun at the Palace Grill, and French at Mousse
Odile. Excellent parking is available in the lot across from the restaurants.

Movie stars and local residents all stand in line on the sidewalk outside the
PALACE GRILL, a self-described Cajun-Creole-Italian restaurant called Best on
the West Coast by *Los Angeles Magazine.* You have to come here several times to
get the full experience. It's simply impossible to try all the goodies (or even a
few) in one visit. Everyone must order the Cajun crawfish popcorn—Louisiana
crawfish tails dipped in cornmeal buttermilk batter and flash-fried to a mouthwatering crispiness (price varies with availability).

Lunch salads include plantation fried chicken salad ($6.95)—fried like the
"popcorn"—and a fresh crab and asparagus salad ($8.95). Then there's the salad
with fresh grilled Norwegian salmon with Creole vinaigrette ($10.95). If you
want to go to heaven right on the spot, try the soft-shelled crab po'boy with garlic mayonnaise ($9.25). The Creole crawfish crab cakes are $9.95 at lunch and
$15.95 at dinner.

Dinner also offers the Palace's signature steaks, thick thick thick and served
from the grill or blackened with a side of browned garlic butter. Étouffées and
chicken marsala, piccata, or Atchafalaya are all intriguing, but be sure to save
room for the Palace's famous Louisiana bread pudding soufflé ($3.95 at lunch,
$6.00 at dinner). Order it anyway, even if you have indulged in one of the bar's
wild martinis.

The Palace Grill is full all the time, and the neon lights in the back proclaiming THE RAJIN CAJUN CATERING CO. set the upbeat tempo. Service at the Palace Grill is surprisingly impeccable, and locals have voted it Best Service in Santa Barbara every year since 1988.

✤✣ *Palace Grill, 8 East Cota Street, Santa Barbara 93101; (805) 963-5000; www.palacegrill.com. Open for lunch 11:00 a.m.–3:00 p.m., dinner from 5:30 p.m. daily. Limited reservations are available Friday and Saturday. Full bar with creative Creole martinis. Visa, MasterCard, American Express. Wheelchair accessible.*

Another door along Cota is the BLUE AGAVE cafe/bar, a pleasantly relaxing restaurant and bar that also sells fine cigars and has a smoking balcony on the second floor facing Cota Street from which rocking music blasts weekend nights. It's casual enough that you can come in alone and feel good about it. Blue Agave uses organic produce when possible, their eggs come from free-range chickens, and their meats and poultry are naturally fed and hormone-, preservative-, and nitrate-free. Slow Food Nation!

Try the black tiger shrimp sautéed in garlic and butter or the tortilla soup as appetizers ($9.50), or the great organic Caesar salads with chopped filet mignon or chicken breast ($8.95–$15.95), the grilled lamb or buffalo burgers with homemade mint mayonnaise and roasted potatoes or salad, or a Lingurian fish stew. A bargain Cowboy Plate features natural turkey sausage poached in Sierra Nevada ale and then grilled, with mashed yams, poblano chili rice, black beans, and butterleaf salad. Kathleen likes the slightly sexist Cowgirl Plate of mashed yams instead of the Cowboy's sausage, plus the other yummies ($9.50–$21.95). Chicken molé, steak au poivre, and almond-crusted fresh salmon are all under $20.

Don't miss the whiskey bread pudding with comfort sauce or the Mexican wedding cake cookies ($3.50–$8.00). Reservations for six or more.

✤✣ *Blue Agave, 20 East Cota Street, Santa Barbara 93101; (805) 899-4694; www.blueagavesb.com. Open 4:30 p.m.–2:00 a.m., happy hour 4:30–6:30 p.m. nightly, dinner 5:00–10:30 p.m., light menu until 11:30 p.m. daily. Full bar. Visa and MasterCard. Partly wheelchair accessible.*

A little farther away but worth the trip (in alphabetical order):

CA'DARIO RISTORANTE ITALIANO is a true Italian restaurant, not the California-ized version we are used to. Some of the menu selections may seem downright exotic, particularly in Italian. Thankfully, the translations are simple.

For instance, the *carpaccio con capperi e grana* ($8.75) is thinly sliced raw beef topped with horseradish sauce and lemon juice, and *grigiata d'asparagi* ($9.50) is grilled asparagus wrapped with pancetta, Parmesan cheese, and balsamic vinegar.

Yum. Or try the *lamelle di spada,* thin slices of smoked swordfish with fennel, radicchio, and arugula ($10.50). For a different taste experience we suggest the *bocconcini trevisani,* a gratin of homemade crepes filled with ricotta cheese and radicchio ($14.95). The osso buco with saffron arborio rice ($26.95) and the daily specials are usually excellent.

Lunch is equally good, although selections are slightly lighter, including lots of salads, pastas, polenta, and steaks and chicken. Ca'Dario is related to Bucatini Trattoria & Pizzeria at 436 State Street, Santa Barbara; (805) 957-4177.

❧ *Ca'Dario Ristorante Italiano, 37 East Victoria Street, Santa Barbara 93101; (805) 884-9419; www.cadario.net. Open for lunch 11:30 a.m.–2:00 p.m. Monday–Friday, dinner 5:30–10:00 p.m. Monday–Friday, and 5:00–10:00 p.m. Saturday and Sunday. Wine and beer. Visa, MasterCard, American Express. Wheelchair accessible.*

CHAD'S REGIONAL AMERICAN CUISINE is the pride and joy of Michelle and Chad Stevens. Chad also owns the first and last Sambo's on Cabrillo and is the grandson of Sambo's founder.

Chad's menu is brief and well planned, adhering to the adage "Do a few things and do them well." For a different experience try the blackened halibut salad, in which the fresh halibut is dusted in Cajun spices, blackened, and placed atop a bed of organic lettuces and tossed with tomatoes, Cajun pecans, sweet red onions, and feta cheese in the house vinaigrette ($12.75). The chicken Brie pasta is Jerry's undoing, with mouthwatering fettuccine tossed with tender pieces of chicken breast, tomatoes, onions, garlic, toasted almonds, melted Brie, and a touch of cream ($14.95).

You can enjoy fresh salmon mahimahi, or ahi tuna either broiled or blackened; Texas-barbecued shrimp wrapped in hickory-smoked bacon and cooked over an open flame; or a regional-pride favorite, pan-seared tri-tip crusted in coarse ground pepper, plus Chad's sinfully delicious chocolate Jack Daniel's soufflé ($4.95). In any case, you must try the soufflé!

❧ *Chad's Regional American Cuisine, 625 Chapala Street, Santa Barbara 93101; (805) 568-1876; www.chads.biz. Open from 5:30 p.m. Monday–Saturday; happy hour 4:30–6:30 p.m. Full bar. Visa, MasterCard, American Express, Discover. Wheelchair accessible.*

FRESCO AT THE BEACH replaced the famous Citronelle in the Santa Barbara Inn in June 2007, bringing new proprietors Jill and Mark Brouillard full circle back to where they both worked in 1991 before starting their own popular Fresco Café. The busy Brouillards also opened the Fresco Café at the Santa Barbara Museum of Art the same month.

Located on the mezzanine of the Santa Barbara Inn (free valet parking available), the restaurant's vast windows offer fabulous views of the south-facing beach.

Emphasizing "European comfort food," Chef de Cuisine Jason Banks makes everything from good salads, soups and sandwiches to coq au vin, risotto, bouillabaisse, and a weekly paella ($20–$24). Piano and jazz Friday and Saturday nights.

❧ *Fresco at the Beach in the Santa Barbara Inn, 901 East Cabrillo Boulevard, Santa Barbara 93103; (805) 963-0111; www.santabarbarainn.com/dining. Open for lunch 11:30 a.m.–2:30 p.m. Monday–Saturday; for dinner 5:00–9:00 p.m. daily; Sunday brunch 10:00 a.m.–2:30 p.m. Full bar. Visa, MasterCard, American Express.*

The SAMBO'S on Cabrillo Boulevard is the first and last Sambo's restaurant in the world. This Sambo's opened on June 17, 1957, and still has some of the original wooden walls and counter and loads of Sambo's memorabilia.

In the 1960s many of us boycotted Sambo's for its apparent belittling of African Americans. Little did we know that the name Sambo was actually a combination of its founders' names, "Sam" from Italian-American Sam Battistone, and "Bo" from his partner, Newell F. Bohnett. At

SAMBO'S FIRST AND LAST
RESTAURANT, SANTA BARBARA

one time there were thirty-nine Sambo "stores" (when did they cease to be "restaurants"?), but boycotts and mismanagement eventually destroyed the empire.

Two generations later, grandson Chad Stevens bought back the original at this site and now also owns Chad's on Chapala Street.

Much to our surprise, Sambo's still serves one of the best breakfasts in town, especially for the money, although the service can be slow. Try to get a sidewalk table to view passersby and the gorgeous beach. The minute you sit down, a basket of mini muffins arrives (Kathleen's favorite is chocolate chip and Jerry's is peanut butter) with soft butter. Coffee follows almost immediately, and soon you wonder if you ought to order anything else!

All egg selections arrive with real potatoes, choice of toast, and strawberries and wedges of melon; a larger serving of fruit can be substituted for potatoes. A real waker-upper is the Polish sausage and eggs, and the imitation crab and real avocado omelette is better than we expected. True carnivores can indulge in pork chops and eggs, which ought to load one up for a day or two. The grilled halibut is light, and the grilled veggie sandwich is quite good and refreshing. Of course there are hamburgers, chicken, and fish strips, and all the other deep-fried favorites ($6.49–$12.95).

❧ *Sambo's, 216 West Cabrillo Boulevard, Santa Barbara 93101; (805) 965-3269; www.sambosrestaurant.com. Open 6:00 a.m.–2:30 p.m. daily. Beer and wine. Visa, MasterCard, American Express, Discover. Wheelchair accessible.*

If you want to explore truly Mexican restaurants, drive along Milpas Street and choose the one that appeals to you. The Mexican bakeries along here are also authentic and tempting.

LA SUPER-RICA TAQUERIA may be California's most famous taco stand, ever since part-time Santa Barbara resident Julia Child proclaimed her affection for it. It's in a simple white building with seafoam green trim and a canvas patio cover on Milpas Street. Just getting out of your car and inhaling on Milpas Street is a treat. You'll salivate as you smell fragrances of beans and tortillas from the many Mexican restaurants along this broad boulevard.

You order at the counter as you walk in, with selections above eye level on a board, with most items in the $3–$5 range. We highly recommend that you try one of the daily specials to best enjoy the cooks' talents.

❧ *La Super-Rica Taqueria, 622 North Milpas Street, Santa Barbara; (805) 963-4940. Open for lunch and dinner daily. Beer and wine. No credit cards. Wheelchair accessible on east side.*

THINGS YOU REALLY SHOULD SEE

Here we tell you about all the important historic sites and museums that are not on State Street and which we think you should see to complete your cultural experience of Santa Barbara. For us the purpose of traveling is to experience the sites, sights, cultures, and languages of a new place. To us the culture includes the foods grown, cooked, and served in a region, as well as the wines, history, art, and architecture.

Tours

Santa Barbara has three kinds of tours that provide an overview of the city. The SANTA BARBARA OLD TOWN TROLLEY offers a ninety-minute open-air guided trolley tour, which is well worth the price. We picked it up at Santa Barbara Mission, which we highly recommend because there is lots of parking in its lot.

Santa Barbara Old Town Trolley starts at the mission at 11:00 a.m. and at 12:30 and 2:00 p.m. and provides a variety of colorful history and current gossip. It takes you by the Crocker cottages, the Atcheson House (as in the Atcheson, Topeka & Santa Fe), down Anacapa Street past the five-star Simpson House Inn bed-and-breakfast, the Ellis Keck Memorial Gardens with their South American blooms, Alameda Park, the Santa Barbara County Courthouse, the Orena Adobe, and Casa de la Guerra. It stops at the beach for a ten-minute stretch near Stearns Wharf, then continues on to Chase Palm Park, Cabrillo Arts Center and the East Beach Grill, and along Coast Villages Road, where many of Hollywood's stars have homes or at least frequent other peoples'. Take in the Biltmore Hotel, Montecito and the Montecito Inn and Cafe, Butterfly Beach, Santa Barbara Zoo, Santa Barbara Zoological Gardens, the first Motel 6, Santa Barbara Harbor, and State Street.

❧ *Santa Barbara Old Town Trolley, (805) 965-0353 or www.sbtrolley.com for information and charters. Web site also offers discounts to other locations. Tickets: $16, two adults $31 if ordered online; otherwise, $18–$36, $9 under twelve years. Not wheelchair accessible.*

The RED TILE TOUR enables you to walk or wheel your way through 12 blocks of downtown to view some of Santa Barbara's most important historical buildings. Begin at the Santa Barbara County Courthouse and cross Anacapa Street to the elegant Spanish-style public library. Go west on Anapamu Street to the Santa Barbara Museum of Art, then down State Street and turn east on Carrillo Street to the Hill-Carillo Adobe. Head back to State Street and go south 2 blocks to El Paseo's arcade or keep going to De la Guerra Street, turn left and visit Casa de la Guerra. Now go across De la Guerra to De la Guerra Plaza, the setting for several movie scenes. The Orena Adobes are in the same block of De la Guerra.

Cross Anacapa Street to Presidio Avenue, the oldest street in Santa Barbara, and then into the Presidio Gardens where the Presidio parade grounds used to be. Back on De la Guerra Street, visit the Santiago de la Guerra Adobe and the Lugo Adobe/Meridian Studios next door. Continue on De la Guerra to the next intersection, Santa Barbara Street, and visit the Santa Barbara Historical

Museum. Heading up Santa Barbara Street, you come to the Casa Covarrubias Adobe and then the Rochin Adobe. Continuing up Santa Barbara to the corner of Canon Perdido, you arrive at El Presidio de Santa Barbara State Historic Park. Head west on Canon Perdido and check out the Presidio Chapel, the Caneda Adobe, and El Cuartel next door to the Spanish deco–style main post office at the corner of Anacapa Street. Notice the Lobero Theatre diagonally across Anacapa Street. Now walk up Anacapa to the courthouse to complete the Red Tile Tour, take a rest, and take the courthouse tour!

SANTA BARBARA'S SCENIC DRIVE takes you to sixteen points of interest in a continuous loop that requires about one hour by car. Great way to get oriented!

Begin, of course, at the Santa Barbara County Courthouse on Anacapa Street (one-way heading toward the water) between Anapamu and Figueroa Streets. Just follow the turquoise Scenic Drive signs with an ocean wave and an arrow, and they will lead you (hopefully) to El Presidio de Santa Barbara State Historic Park, Santa Barbara Historical Museum, El Paseo, Santa Barbara Museum of Art, La Arcada, Mission Santa Barbara, Santa Barbara Museum of Natural History, Santa Barbara Botanic Garden, Andree Clark Bird Refuge, Santa Barbara Zoological Gardens, Stearns Wharf, Moreton Bay Fig Tree, Fernald Mansion and Trussell-Winchester Adobe, the Yacht Harbor and Breakwater, and the luxurious Hope Ranch residential community.

Details

Once you've experienced an overview via a tour, you may want to visit some of the sites in detail. They are presented here in alphabetical order.

ANDREE CLARK BIRD REFUGE near Cabrillo Boulevard. Directions: Exit from US 101 to parking lot on Los Patos Way. Go west toward the water to this scenic lagoon with hundreds of waterbirds, fabulous gardens, a lake, footpath, and bikeway. Or take Cabrillo Boulevard along the beach to it. Ms. Clark still has servants turn down the beds and set the dinner table every night in her twenty-six-room mansion even though she's never there—she's lived in Hawaii for years. (**Santa Barbara Zoo and Zoological Gardens** are right next door. See page 56.)

ARTS & CRAFTS SHOW, along a 1-mile stretch of Cabrillo Boulevard east of Stearns Wharf, is reputedly the longest-running (more than forty years) weekly outdoor art show in the United States, a rather finite claim. Everything is created and made in Santa Barbara.

🌿 *Arts & Crafts Show, Cabrillo Boulevard east of Stearns Wharf, Santa Barbara 93101; (805) 962-8956. Open 10:00 a.m.–sunset every Sunday, Memorial Day, July Fourth, Saturday of Fiesta Week, and Labor Day. Free admission. Credit cards vary by artist. Wheelchair accessible.*

BRINKERHOFF AVENUE off Cota Street between De la Vina and Chapala Streets has a rare collection of unique Victorian homes all in one block. Imagine living here in classic nineteenth-century Santa Barbara. Now you can enter many of them and browse among the antiques, collectibles, and art galleries. Most of the shops are open 11:00 a.m.–5:00 p.m. Tuesday–Sunday.

CABRILLO PAVILION ARTS CENTER, above the East Beach bathhouse across from the Radisson Hotel, features rotating exhibits of local artists' work, providing a bright and energetic insight into Santa Barbara's artistic community. The arts center was built and given to the city by Mr. and Mrs. David Gray Sr. in 1925. Stop for lunch at the East Beach Grill, right here on the beach in the same building. Excellent views and food.

❧ *Cabrillo Pavilion Arts Center, 1118 East Cabrillo Boulevard, Santa Barbara 93101; (805) 897-1982; www.sbparksandrecreation.com. Open 9:00 a.m.–5:00 p.m. Monday–Friday. Wheelchair accessible.*

CARRIAGE AND WESTERN ARTS MUSEUM has a unique collection of horse-drawn vehicles and stagecoaches used by early Santa Barbara families and those just arriving. Check out the army wagons, a fire truck (a bright red steam pumper), and an electric hearse (we should have paid attention to these gasoline-free vehicles!). Kathleen loves the display of historic saddles and bridles, which, along with the artwork and other memorabilia, take you back to the original Western life the movies depicted. Many of these carriages come out for August Fiesta Week.

❧ *Carriage and Western Arts Museum, 129 Castillo Street, Santa Barbara 93101; (805) 962-2353; www.sbva.org/museum.html. Open 8:00 a.m.–3:00 p.m. Monday–Friday, 1:00–4:00 p.m. Sunday. Admission by donation. Wheelchair accessible.*

CASA DE LA GUERRA is the home Jose de la Guerra y Noriega, the fifth comandante of the Santa Barbara Presidio, began building for his family in 1818. Don Jose and his wife, Dona Maria Antonia, had twelve (yes, a full dozen) children. Their home became the social and commercial center in Santa Barbara and even Alta (upper, as opposed to Baja) California. Richard Henry Dana made the home famous in his *Two Years Before the Mast* (1840). Be sure to visit Plaza de la Guerra, right across De la Guerra Street, where the first city council met in 1850 and where the first city hall was built in 1875. It was torn down in 1924 after the current city hall was built. Fiesta Week brings wildly colorful celebrations here in August.

❧ *Casa de la Guerra, 15 East De la Guerra Street, Santa Barbara 93101; (805)*

965-0093; www.sbtfhp.org. Open noon–4:00 p.m. Thursday–Sunday. Wheelchair accessible.

CHASE PALM PARK refers to a 2-mile stretch of Santa Barbara's beach that is lined with palm trees. Pearl Chase (who had a B.A. and an honorary doctorate from the University of California, Berkeley) planted the palms as just one of her efforts to preserve, protect, and beautify Santa Barbara.

Through Chase Palm Park you will find a well-maintained paved recreation path for wheeling, skating, walking, running, or whatever you can think of, as well as a view of some large metal objects sticking up out of the water offshore. Those are oil well drilling rigs, folks, and what we in California call "offshore oil drilling." In 1969 a huge oil spill occurred on one of the oil platforms 5 miles offshore, and the oil drifted for miles. Chase sued the oil companies, which resulted in safety tanks being added to the rigs to prevent such spillage. Thank you, Pearl! You definitely left the world a better place.

Along this part of the beach, you will see volleyball net after volleyball net. This is where many of the televised beach volleyball tournaments in Southern California take place, with sponsors such as Jose Cuervo, Big Bud, and Bud Light. Play ball!

CONTEMPORARY ARTS FORUM in Paseo Nuevo mall off State Street is a terrific gallery of contemporary local art. Get their schedule for year-round exhibits, performances, and lectures.

Contemporary Arts Forum, 653 Paseo Nuevo, second floor, Santa Barbara 93101; (805) 966-5373. Open 11:00 a.m.–5:00 p.m. Tuesday–Saturday, noon–5:00 p.m. Sunday. Free admission. Wheelchair accessible.

DOLPHIN FOUNTAIN, the creation of local sculptor Bud Bottoms, is more formally known as the Bicentennial Friendship Fountain. It's located at the entrance to Stearns Wharf at Cabrillo Boulevard at the bottom of State Street. Through the cosponsorship of the Santa Barbara/Puerto Vallarta Sister City Committee (what a pairing!), dolphins were also installed on Puerto Vallarta's waterfront and in Toba, Japan; Yalta, Ukraine; and Santa Barbara's other sister cities.

EL PRESIDIO DE SANTA BARBARA STATE HISTORIC PARK is where the first forty-two Spanish soldiers and their families arrived in April 1782 and built this large permanent presidio (fort). The presidio's military function ceased with the American invasion, and much of it fell down due to earthquakes and neglect, all to be rescued in 1974 by the Santa Barbara Trust for Historic Preservation,

EL PRESIDIO DE SANTA BARBARA, SANTA BARBARA

which began reconstruction of the presidio as a state historic park. You can now visit the chapel, tour the padres' and comandante's quarters, and watch a fifteen-minute slide show.

❧ *El Presidio de Santa Barbara, 123 East Canon Perdido Street, Santa Barbara 93101; (805) 965-0093; www.sbthp.org. Open 10:30 a.m.–4:30 p.m. daily. Free admission, donations accepted. Wheelchair accessible.*

FERNALD MANSION and TRUSSELL-WINCHESTER ADOBE are must-sees for antiques aficionados. The Fernald Mansion is a fourteen-room 1862 Queen Anne–style Victorian with a carved wood stairway and luxurious wood decoration. Next door, walk through the 1854 Trussell-Winchester Adobe, a "Yankee adobe" typical of Santa Barbara architecture, a hybrid somewhere between American and Mexican styles and covered with wood siding and a roof made of timbers from a ship wrecked off Anacapa Island.

❧ *Fernald Mansion* and *Trussell-Winchester Adobe, 414 West Montecito Street, Santa Barbara 93101; (805) 966-1601; www.sbtfh.org. Open 2:00–4:00 p.m. Sunday. Admission $3. Tours available. Partly wheelchair accessible.*

HOPE RANCH is one of the United States's most luxurious and expensive residential communities, with miles of bridle trails; polo, soccer, and baseball fields; a golf course and tennis courts; and huge, wistful old palm trees, many of which line the main street, Las Palmas Drive (funny thing!). It's fun to drive through and see how some people live. Don't if it will make you cry.

LOBERO THEATRE is in a wonderful old building opened originally as an opera house in 1873 by Jose Lobero, an Italian entertainer. Lobero's original theater was demolished in 1923, and local citizens built the current Spanish-style building designed by George Washington Smith and Lutah Maria Riggs. It now houses the Santa Barbara Chamber Orchestra, the Santa Barbara Grand Opera, the Sings Like Hell concert series, concerts by the faculty (including Marilyn Horne) and students of the Music Academy of the West, and the Mind/Supermind lecture series. Call ahead for Lobero's schedule if you are coming to visit.

❧ *Lobero Theatre, 33 East Canon Perdido, Santa Barbara 93101; (805) 963-0761; www.lobero.com. Box office open 10:00 a.m.–6:00 p.m. Monday–Saturday and two hours prior to performances. Visa, MasterCard, American Express. Wheelchair accessible.*

MISSION SANTA BARBARA, the tenth of the California missions, is known throughout California as the "Queen of the Missions," even though it's not in its original form. The first Mission Santa Barbara was built by Chumash Indians for the Franciscan friars and formally established here on December 4, 1786. The original adobe buildings were badly damaged by the 1812 earthquake. The current stone church was begun in 1815 and completed with a second tower in 1833, but it was damaged again by the 1925 earthquake. A citizens committee raised funds to repair and rebuild the main facade in the 1950s.

Now a Catholic parish, the church is open to the public, and you can visit the mission on a self-guided tour for $4. We highly recommend the tour of the mission, its lovely gardens, historic cemetery (respect the hundreds of unmarked Chumash Indian graves here, please), and the historically accurate exhibits. The museum shop is small and packed with great books and church and historic memorabilia. Restrooms and beverage machines are down the ramp to the left of the tour/shop entrance. Excellent parking lot.

❧ *Mission Santa Barbara, 2201 Laguna Street, Santa Barbara 93105; (805) 682-4713; www.sbmission.org. Open 9:00 a.m.–5:00 p.m. daily except major holidays. Masses at 7:30, 9:00, 10:30 a.m., and noon Sunday; 7:30 a.m. Monday–Saturday. Self-guided tour $4, children under fifteen free; gift shop admission free. Visa and MasterCard. Mostly wheelchair accessible.*

MORETON BAY FIG TREE is the famous Australian fig tree replanted here in 1877 and reputed to be the largest tree of its kind in the United States. Its 160-foot arm span offers approximately 21,000 square feet of shade. It is huge! Dr. Pearl Chase prevented Standard Oil from taking the tree down. It's located at

MISSION SANTA BARBARA

the bottom of Chapala Street on the south side of US 101. You have to take State Street under US 101 to reach it.

RAINBOW ARCH and FESS PARKER'S DOUBLETREE INN (Cabrillo Boulevard at Calle Puerto Vallarta) have a curious story attached. Fess Parker wanted to build another hotel across a side street from his Doubletree Inn. As a 1981 requirement of the California Coastal Commission, Parker dedicated five acres to the City of Santa Barbara for the city to develop as a park, along with an adjacent five-acre parcel. The city then spent $6 million developing the park and importing the carousel. Local artist Herbert Bayer designed a sculpture, called *The Chromatic Gate,* and known to some as the "Rainbow Arch."

SANTA BARBARA BOTANIC GARDEN features more than 1,000 species of rare and indigenous native California plants. You can walk or wheel along 5.5 miles of paths through sixty-five acres of landscaped meadows, canyons, and a redwood forest, across historic Mission Dam, and along the ridge. You'll get spectacular views, on good days, of the central coast and the Channel Islands.

Directions: Take State Street to Mission Street, go up (east) on Mission, left on Garden Street, right on Los Olivos past Santa Barbara Mission, the Museum of Natural History, and Rocky Nook Park. Turn right on Foothill Road (Highway 192), follow signs to the Botanic Garden, take the first left up Mission Canyon Road, bear right at a fork and continue .5 mile to the garden entrance on the left.

The botanic garden is a private, nonprofit institution dedicated to increasing the public's awareness of plant life, with active research and education programs going on all the time. Gardeners, don't miss the garden growers nursery selling native California and Mediterranean plants, or the garden shop with great books, crafts, cards, gifts, and posters.

❧ *Santa Barbara Botanic Garden, 1212 Mission Canyon Road, Santa Barbara 93105; (805) 682-4726; www.sbbg.org. Open November–February weekdays 9:00 a.m.–5:00 p.m.; March–October weekdays 9:00 a.m.–6:00 p.m. Retail nursery open during garden hours. Admission: adults $8, seniors and students $6, children two to twelve $4, under two are free. Visa and MasterCard. Partly wheelchair accessible.*

SANTA BARBARA COUNTY COURTHOUSE is an absolute don't-miss in your visit to Santa Barbara. After the 1925 earthquake, Santa Barbara turned an intense negative to a positive and took the opportunity to rebuild and reinvent itself. The city built a bold new courthouse designed by William Mooser III after he had lived in Spain for many years. The steel frame building was completed in two years at a cost of $1.5 million. Today it is priceless.

Be sure to check out the bell tower as well as the ceiling, inspired by the fourteenth-century El Transito synagogue in Toledo, Spain; the Moorish mosaic tiled stairway to the second floor; the rose window; the board of supervisors' assembly room with murals by Dan Sayre Groesbeck depicting Santa Barbara County history; the

SANTA BARBARA COUNTY COURTHOUSE, SANTA BARBARA

jail wing; the bridge of sighs connecting the jail at the third floor with the main building; the leather-covered brass-studded doors; the great doors; and the law library with its sculptured sword of justice over the entrance.

Outside the Santa Barbara Street exit, look up at the sheriff's tower, the tall wooden gates at the jail entrance, the stage, and the sunken garden where the 1873 courthouse stood. Live concerts and Fiesta Week performances are held here. Don't miss the relief map in the main entrance lobby, and the fountain, *Spirit of the Ocean.*

At the docent desk, pick up a brochure describing the botanical richness of the sunken garden.

♣❦ *Santa Barbara County Courthouse, 1100 Anacapa Street between Anapamu and Figueroa Streets, Santa Barbara 93101; (805) 962-6464. Open 8:30 a.m.–4:30 p.m. daily. Tours 10:30 a.m. Monday, Tuesday, Friday; 2:00 p.m. Monday–Saturday; or by reservation. Partly wheelchair accessible.*

SANTA BARBARA HISTORICAL MUSEUM is a modern adobe constructed in 1965 next to the 1817 Casa Covarrubias and the 1836 Historic Adobe by the Santa Barbara Historical Society. It has exhibited artifacts from Santa Barbara's rich multicultural heritage of the Chumash, Spanish, Mexican, "Yankee," and Chinese cultures. You can see photos, furniture, and the Gledhill Library with rare literary and visual documents, including 30,000 historic photographs. Don't miss the fabulously interesting museum shop with handcrafted artifacts and a great selection of books, cards, and jewelry.

♣❦ *Santa Barbara Historical Museum, 136 East De la Guerra Street, Santa Barbara 93101; (805) 966-1601, fax (805) 966-1603; www.santabarbara museum.com. Open 10:00 a.m.–4:00 p.m. Tuesday–Friday; 10:00 a.m.–4:00 p.m. first Saturday of each month. Guided tours at 1:30 p.m. Wednesday, Saturday, and Sunday. Free admission, donations appreciated.*

SANTA BARBARA MARITIME MUSEUM is at the entrance to the harbor right on Cabrillo Boulevard at the west end of the beach (which seems like the north end of the beach). Here you can almost experience the Santa Barbara area's rich maritime history with exhibits including Chumash culture and navigation, submarine periscopes (they're not Chumash), a radio-controlled boat, and a flying submarine. Browse around the pier. This is where whale-watching boats take off from, too.

♣❦ *Santa Barbara Maritime Museum, 132 Harbor Way, Santa Barbara 93101; (805) 962-8404; www.sbmm.org. Open 10:00 a.m.–5:00 p.m. Thursday– Tuesday June–early September; 10:00 a.m.–6:00 p.m. Thursday–Tuesday September–May. Admission: adults $7, active duty military $4, in uniform free; seniors and students $4; children one to five $2. Wheelchair accessible.*

SANTA BARBARA MUSEUM OF NATURAL HISTORY is a nationally respected center for education and research in California and North American West Coast natural history. Visit Chumash Hall with its diorama of prehistoric native life in the Santa Barbara area, and see a blue whale's giant skeleton; the area's only planetarium; regional and marine exhibits; bird, mammal, and insect habitat displays; and enjoy interactive computers and hands-on displays, a space lab and observatory, fossils, American Indian artifacts, Ty Warner Sea Center, and an intriguing museum store.

Directions: From State Street take Los Olivos or Mission Street to Mission Santa Barbara and turn right up Mission Canyon Road. The Museum of Natural History will be on the left. Pass Puesta del Sol and enter via Las Encinas Road to the parking lot.

❧ *Santa Barbara Museum of Natural History, 2559 Puesta del Sol Road, Santa Barbara 93105; (805) 682-4711; www.sbnature.org. Open 10:00 a.m.– 5:00 p.m. daily. Closed major holidays. Admission free; $4–$7 for Sea Center. Visa and MasterCard. Mostly wheelchair accessible.*

SANTA BARBARA ORCHID ESTATE is sheer heaven to orchid lovers, home gardeners, and general lovers of colors. Although we have never succeeded in getting an orchid to bloom after it came to live with us, we know many people are perfectly capable of nurturing and cajoling them. But we do promise that you will enjoy a visit to this orchid farm, where the Gripp family has grown classic prized orchids since 1957.

You can stroll through greenhouses to see more than 2,000 varieties of orchids and visit the shop to take home houseplants anywhere or have them shipped.

The best times to visit are from February to May in normal weather years, whatever those are, and during the orchid fair the third week of July. Real devotees might want to tie in a trip to the annual orchid show (March or April) with a special event at the orchid estate the same weekend.

❧ *Santa Barbara Orchid Estate, 1250 Orchid Drive, Santa Barbara 93101; (805) 967-1284 or (800) 553-3387; www.sborchid.com. Open 8:00 a.m.–4:30 p.m. Monday–Saturday, 11:00 a.m.–4:00 p.m. Sunday. Visa, MasterCard, American Express, Discover. Mostly wheelchair accessible.*

SANTA BARBARA YACHT HARBOR & BREAKWATER combine for one of our favorite sunrise strolls among more than 1,000 work and pleasure craft, rowing and canoeing teams practicing, whale-watching boats, and supply stores. Launch facilities, boats for rent, and charters are all at the north end of the harbor.

❧ *Santa Barbara Yacht Harbor, Breakwater, Santa Barbara 93101; (805) 965-8112. Wheelchair accessible.*

SANTA BARBARA ZOO AND ZOOLOGICAL GARDENS occupy the former Child Estate (not Julia) and offer 700 animals living in imitation natural habitats plus thirty teemingly lush acres of botanical gardens atop a knoll with the Santa Ynez Mountains as a backdrop and the blue Pacific Ocean as a view. Can't beat it. Bring your picnic or book. Kids of all ages will enjoy the narrow-gauge miniature railroad, barnyard, stage shows, carousel, and snack bar. The Santa Barbara Zoo is about conservation, species survival, and education. The Ridley-Treehouse Restaurant overlooks Swan Lake and offers excellent menu selections for discerning palates and kids. The gift stores are something else! The Andree Clark Bird Refuge is practically next door. Directions: Take Cabrillo Boulevard along the beach and turn north on Ninos Drive, or take bus 14 or the downtown-waterfront shuttle.

❧ *Santa Barbara Zoo and Zoological Gardens, 500 Ninos Drive, Santa Barbara 93103; (805) 962-5339; www.santabarbarazoo.org. Open 10:00 a.m.–5:00 p.m. daily except Thanksgiving and Christmas; tickets sold until 4:00 p.m. Admission: adults (thirteen to fifty-nine) $10, children and seniors $8, children under two free; parking $3. Visa, MasterCard, American Express, Discover. Wheelchair accessible; stroller and wheelchair rentals available.*

SANTA BARBARA'S FARMERS' MARKET is one of the most beautiful we have seen, but then so is Santa Barbara. Local restaurateurs and home cooks come to gather their organic foods and socialize, as is true in every good market in the world. Plan to visit, even if you can't cook in your hotel room.

❧ *Farmers' Market, corner of Cota and Santa Barbara Streets, Santa Barbara 93101; (805) 962-5354; www.sbfarmersmarket.org. Open 8:30 a.m.–12:30 p.m. Saturday, rain or shine. At the 500–600 blocks of State Street, open 4:00–7:30 p.m. on Tuesday in summer, 3:00–6:30 p.m. in winter.*

STEARNS WHARF is supposedly the oldest operating wooden wharf on the West Coast. Built in 1872 by John Peck Stearns, the wharf was partly owned by Jimmy Cagney and his brothers in the 1940s. Here you can visit the Sea Center; the Harbor Restaurant with fresh fish, prime rib, steak, chicken, and Sunday brunch; or Longboard's Grill, a real beach bar and grill with casual food and attire, exotic drinks with umbrellas, outdoor dining where you can smell the fresh air and water, a large-screen television in case you're afraid to miss the game, and breakfast Saturday and Sunday. Souvenir shops, art galleries, wine tasting, and espresso bars are available.

One of the best reasons to visit Stearns Wharf is to look back at Santa Barbara from the pier. Unbelievable view!

TY WARNER SEA CENTER on Stearns Wharf, which is operated by the Santa Barbara Museum of Natural History and the Channel Islands National Marine

SANTA BARBARA FROM STEARNS WHARF

Sanctuary, majors in touchy-feely learning about living marine creatures. It has a touch tank that you can dip your arm into to touch live sea creatures, loads of aquariums of native local sea species, historic Indian peoples displays, life-size models of dolphins and whales, shipwreck artifacts, special Santa Barbara Channel ecological exhibits, a marine art gallery, and, of course, a museum gift shop to take home some of those treasures from the deep blue.

❧ *Ty Warner Sea Center, 211 Stearns Wharf, Santa Barbara 93101; (805) 962-0885; www.sbnature2.org. Open 10:00 a.m.–5:00 p.m. daily, June–Labor Day; noon–5:00 p.m. Monday–Friday and 10:00 a.m.–5:00 p.m. Saturday and Sunday, September–May; touch tanks, noon–5:00 p.m. daily. Visa and MasterCard. Wheelchair accessible.*

CHAPTER 3

SANTA YNEZ VALLEY TOWNS

he Santa Ynez Valley and the Foxen Canyon area north of Santa Barbara hold most of Santa Barbara County's best wineries and some charming small towns. Buellton, Solvang, Santa Ynez, Ballard, and Los Olivos are all in this section of Santa Barbara County. There's also Lompoc to the west and Los Alamos, just north of Buellton and Solvang.

First we tell you about the towns and their individual assets, and believe us, they all truly have something to offer. Then in chapter 4 we take you on a tour of the wineries, working our way northward toward Santa Maria.

The wineries in this area have formed a new appellation, the "Santa Rita Hills American Viticulture Area" (AVA). Member wineries include Sanford Winery, Babcock Winery, Richard Longoria Wines, and Lafond Winery. We lead you to these wineries in this section. The appellation runs west of U.S. Highway 101.

LOMPOC

Most Californians would wonder why anyone would want to go to Lompoc (LAHM poke). The six reasons we can think of are experiencing the spectacular flower fields (seas of sweet peas, asters, lavender, marigolds, larkspur, lobelia, and calendula) in bloom from early June to mid-July; touring the forty-one colorful historical and cultural murals on building walls depicting the vastly diverse cultures of the Lompoc Valley; visiting a prisoner at the Lompoc Federal Penitentiary, known as the country club of prisons (Watergate conspirators served their time here); visiting Jalama Beach; visiting La Purisima Mission State Historic Park; and touring Vandenberg Air Force Base.

Lompoc is actually becoming slightly fashionable because it offers some of the most reasonable new housing on the central coast in a mild and seductive climate.

You can get maps of the murals and a 19-mile tour of hundreds of acres of flowers from the Lompoc Valley Chamber of Commerce (805-736-4567).

There are clusters of murals on blocks near the intersection of Ocean Avenue and North Street. You might plan your visit around the annual Lompoc Flower Festival the last weekend in June, which features a two-hour downtown parade with floral floats, marching bands, and equestrian units from all over California. The festival also offers bus tours of the flower fields, a carnival, flower show (duh!), arts and crafts fair, food booths, and entertainment.

Take Highway 1 or Highway 246 west to Lompoc from US 101 at Buellton. If you approach Lompoc on Highway 246, 3 miles northeast of town you can visit one of California's best restored and preserved missions, LA PURISIMA CONCEPCION in La Purisima Mission State Historic Park. La Purisima is one of only three missions preserved within the state park system and was the eleventh of the twenty-one Spanish missions in California.

All major buildings have been rebuilt and furnished as they were in 1820, and the grounds have been planted to reflect the period, including livestock of the correct genetic types, such as four-horn churro sheep, horses, longhorn cattle, goats, swine, turkeys, and geese. Founded by Franciscan Padre Presidente Fermin Francisco Lasuen, the original aqueduct and pond system are maintained, and more than 900 surrounding acres provide a buffer against modern developments and intrusions. Kathleen particularly likes the weaving room and kitchen, as well as the *lavanderias* in the garden, where Chumash Indians washed the missionaries' clothes.

❧ *La Purisima Mission State Historic Park, 2295 Purisima Road, Lompoc 93436; (805) 733-3713; www.lapurisimamission.org. Open 9:00 a.m.–5:00 p.m., tours daily from the kiosk at 10:00 a.m. and 1:00 p.m., but call ahead to make sure the mission is open. Docent-guided tours for ten or more with two weeks' notice. Admission: $2 per vehicle. Mostly wheelchair accessible.*

The turnoff from Highway 1 to Jalama Beach is 4 miles south of Lompoc on Highway 1. Follow Jalama Road for 15 miles through lush forest and ranches to the twenty-eight-acre park donated to Santa Barbara County in 1943 by Richfield Oil Company. World-famous for sailboarding, Jalama Beach is wildly gorgeous but somewhat dangerous for swimmers because of a strong undertow. Be careful! Campsites have picnic tables and barbecue pits, and RV travelers will appreciate the hookup facilities. If you forgot the essentials, you can get them and fishing tackle and bait (possibly in the essential category). You'll also find a survivable snack bar. Call (805) 736-6316 for campsite availability.

Ocean Park's rugged shoreline is fifteen minutes from downtown and is great for blustery walks and surf fishing, but officials warn against swimming due to the swiftly swirling currents.

VANDENBERG AIR FORCE BASE occupies only 2 percent of its 99,000 acres of gorgeous California coastal terrain. It is occasionally praised for its ecological efforts to maintain a physical buffer between its rocket launchers and the outside world with undeveloped land that harbors 270 endangered species of flora and fauna as well as a wildlife sanctuary.

From Vandenberg the Air Force launches toward the South Pacific both government and commercial unarmed test missiles that pass 4,200 miles in twenty-five minutes. Many launches are announced forty-eight hours ahead so visitors can watch, but weather conditions can force delays or postponements. Tours available second Wednesday of each month. For launch and Wednesday tour information, call (805) 606-3595; www.vanderberg.af.mil. No walk-ons.

If you are hungry, make your way to H Street, where there's a plethora of Thai, Mexican, seafood, and Italian restaurants; steak houses with bars; and coffeehouses.

To get to Buellton, Solvang, Santa Ynez, Ballard, and Los Olivos, take Highway 246 east from Lompoc.

BUELLTON

Twenty miles north of Santa Barbara on US 101 you come to exits to El Capitan State Beach and then Refugio State Beach, with its romantic palm trees and turquoise water, and Lake Cachuma County Park (805-688-4658), full of bass, catfish, trout, bluegill, and crappie. Impulse fishers or potential fishers can get licenses at the local bait and tackle shop, and you can even rent boats if you wish. Enjoy the snack bar, general store, service station, camping sites, and picnic sites galore.

Another 7 miles north is San Onofre Beach, with two ugly oil well drilling platforms besmirching the ocean. Another couple of miles brings you into the city limits of Gaviota, best known for its flower farms. If you travel by Amtrak, the tracks follow the water even more closely than the road does at this point. Gaviota Beach State Park is a highly accessible, right-down-to-the-beach campground and parking lot. Watch for the speed bumps on the road.

Three miles north of Gaviota Beach at Las Cruces, US 101 turns northeast, while Highway 1 heads northwest to Lompoc. Buellton is just 3 miles north of the intersection if you stick with US 101.

If you are coming from the north, you will first pass through Santa Maria on US 101, or Lompoc via Highways 1 and 246.

West of Buellton (which is on US 101 and not actually in the Santa Ynez Valley), several wineries and growers applied and were granted a new wine appellation, Santa Rita Hills. Included within that appellation are Lafond, Sanford, Babcock, and Melville. Mosby is not part of the designation, although it is just west of US 101 and you go right by it on your way to Lafond.

GINNY'S TUSCAN-STYLE RABBIT
from Mosby Winery, Buellton

1 rabbit, cut into 5 pieces

¼ cup olive oil

1 yellow onion, thinly sliced

3 cloves garlic, minced

2 bay leaves

1 large sprig rosemary

1 Tbs. fresh thyme, chopped

2 Tbs. sugar

1 Tbs. flour

⅓ cup white wine vinegar

1 can beef broth

½ cup dried cherries or raisins

1 cup pearl onions, blanched and skinned (or frozen and thawed)

Salt and freshly ground pepper

⅓ cup toasted pine nuts

Italian parsley, chopped

Season rabbit pieces with salt and pepper. Brown rabbit pieces in olive oil in a heavy skillet or Dutch oven. Remove rabbit as it becomes brown. When all rabbit pieces are browned and removed, sauté the sliced onion in the juices until softened (about 6 minutes) and add garlic. Saute for 1 more minute.

Put rabbit back into pan with all juices. Add bay leaves, rosemary sprig, and thyme. Add sugar, flour, vinegar, beef broth, and dried cherries. Stir to coat the rabbit pieces. Cover skillet tightly and place in a 350°F oven.

Braise the rabbit for 1 hour, stirring once after a half hour and checking liquid level. If the rabbit is getting too dry, add a splash of red wine. Check rabbit for tenderness. It may need to cook up to 20 minutes more, depending on size and age of rabbit. If you can guess 10 minutes before it is finished, add pearl onions and salt and pepper to taste. Remove sprig of rosemary and rabbit bones. Serve over soft polenta or rice. Garnish each serving with toasted pine nuts and chopped Italian parsley. Serves 2–4.

To get there, take Highway 246 west from US 101 and turn left onto Avenue of the Flags, which becomes Santa Rosa Road. Mosby comes first on your left.

The property on which the MOSBY WINERY stands was originally the de la Cuesta land grant (until the 1950s) and was then owned by Hollywood playwright Vince Evans. Bill and Jeri Mosby bought the property in 1979.

In 1999 Bill retired after forty-two years as a dentist in Lompoc. A native of Klamath Falls, Oregon, he was high school state wrestling champion and at Oregon State University twice prevailed as Pacific Coast wrestling champion before going to dental school. Jeri says Bill's winemaking fascination "began as a hobby, but by the early eighties our wine was winning serious awards and Bill was expanding the vineyards to include more of the Italian varietals."

Many locals discouraged Bill from trying to grow Italian varietals here; fortunately, he ignored them. Now he is adding two Rhone blends, Syrah and Mourvedre, from son Mike's Monterey County vineyards and Chimere Winery in Santa Maria.

Fine points: Featured wines: Pinot Grigio, Cortese (Gavi), Traminer, Rosato di Sangiovese, Sangiovese, Nebbiolo, Dolcetto, Teroldego, Grappa di Traminer, Roc Michel (Rhone blend). Owners: Bill and Jeri Mosby. Winemaker: Bill Mosby. Cases: 10,000. Acres: 45.

❧ *Mosby Winery, 9496 Santa Rosa Road, P.O. Box 1849, Buellton 93427; (805) 688-2415 or (800) 70-MOSBY, fax (805) 686-4288; www.mosbywines.com. Open 10:00 a.m.–4:00 p.m. Monday–Friday, 10:00 a.m.–5:00 p.m. Saturday and Sunday. Tasting fee: $7, includes glass. Visa, MasterCard, American Express, Discover. Wheelchair accessible.*

Vineyardists Richard and Thekla Sanford established SANFORD WINERY in 1981 in what had been a dairy farm. They remodeled the original dairy building into their offices and tasting room, so enjoy the rural feeling. This is a great place to picnic undisturbed just south of the Santa Ynez River.

Now part of The Terlato Group, which also markets Markham, Alderbrook, and Chimney Rock.

Fine points: Featured wines: Chardonnay, Sauvignon Blanc, Pinot Noir Vin Gris, Pinot Noir. Owners: Richard and Thekla Sanford. Winemaker: Bruno D'Alfonso. Cases: 50,000. Acres: 372 certified organic.

❧ *Sanford Winery, 7250 Santa Rosa Road, Buellton 93427; (805) 688-3300, fax (805) 688-7381; www.sanfordwinery.com. Open 11:00 a.m.–4:00 p.m. daily.*

Bright Lime Avocado Salad
from Chef Shirley Sarvis, Sanford Winery, Buellton

4 Tbs. olive oil

1½ Tbs. fresh lime juice

½ tsp. salt

grinding of white pepper

1 cup tender frisée, separated into single-stem short leaves, loosely packed

1 small avocado

2 small ripe tomatoes, halved from top to bottom and thinly sliced crosswise

2 Tbs. cilantro (fresh coriander), leaves only

2 Tbs. fresh pecans, finely chopped

3 limes, quartered

FOR THE DRESSING: Whisk together olive oil, fresh lime juice, salt, and white pepper.

FOR THE SALAD MAKINGS: Turn frisée with a small amount of dressing and arrange loosely on two large plates. Arrange avocado slices, slightly overlapping, over frisée. Arrange tomato slices similarly. Sprinkle both lightly with salt. Spoon dressing over salad generously. Sprinkle cilantro leaves and chopped pecans over all, and garnish with limes. Serves 2. Serve with Sanford Pinot Noir or Vin Gris.

Tasting fee: $5. Visa, MasterCard, American Express, Discover. Wheelchair accessible via back door.

About 5.5 miles farther out Santa Rosa Road, LAFOND WINERY AND VINEYARDS is the newest enterprise of Pierre Lafond, who owns many businesses, including Santa Barbara Winery in downtown Santa Barbara. Lafond spares no expense in any of his endeavors, so visitors are in for an elegant treat based on the wine alone. The tasting room and hallway walls are lined with historic photos and newspaper stories of Lafond and other winemakers in the early days of local winemaking.

Fine points: Featured wines: Chardonnay, Pinot Noir, Syrah. Owner: Pierre Lafond. Winemaker: Bruce McGuire. Cases: 5,000. Acres: won't reveal.

❧ *Lafond Winery and Vineyards, 6855 Santa Rosa Road, Buellton 93427; (805) 688-7921, fax (805) 693-1524; www.lafondwinery.com. Open 10:00 a.m.–5:00 p.m. daily. Tasting fee: $5 includes 18-oz. crystal glass. Visa, MasterCard, American Express. Wheelchair accessible.*

Right on Highway 246, wine lovers must stop at **BABCOCK VINEYARDS**, whose owner/winemaker Bryan Babcock was rated in 1995 by the James Beard Foundation as one of the "ten best small production winemakers in the world." The other nine were in Europe.

Babcock Vineyards and its owners are modest, and their winery is grossly underhyped, which is definitely a blessing and possibly results in their ability to concentrate on making some of the country's best wines. And it is right here between Lompoc and Buellton, and not in the Napa Valley!

Bryan Babcock has quickly risen to quiet prominence and respect in the winemaking business by simply producing excellent wines. First Bryan earned his B.S. in biology and chemistry from Occidental College in 1982, and then got his M.S. in food science, specializing in enology at the University of California, Davis. In 1984 his very first harvest brought a double gold medal for Babcock's estate Sauvignon Blanc.

Using only estate-grown or Santa Barbara County fruit, Bryan has made some daring moves. When his estate Riesling "wasn't hitting the benchmark he was aiming for," he pulled out the vines and planted Pinot Gris. He produced Sauvignon Blanc when it was out of fashion and criticized for its "herbal character" and converted it to a highly acclaimed wine that sells out every year under Babcock's Eleven Oaks label. And now he's trying to make Gewürztraminer "as good as the best Alsatians."

Bryan Babcock is also helping to spearhead introductions of Spanish Albarino and Tempranillo varieties and Italian Pignolo, which he predicts "will be California's next frontier in winemaking."

Babcock is truly a family operation. Bryan serves as vice president, general manager, and winemaker; his parents, Mona and Walt, are co-owners; his wife, Lisa, handles marketing (and their son, Sean); his sister, Brenda Via, is the financial officer; and her husband, Mikael, is company lawyer.

Fine points: Featured wines: Babcock, Mt. Carmel, Grand Cuvée, Fathom, and Eleven Oaks labels, including Grand Cuvée Chardonnay and Pinot Noir, Mt. Carmel Pinot Noir, Eleven Oaks Sauvignon Blanc and Sangiovese, and Babcock Chardonnay, Gewürztraminer, Pinot Gris, and Pinot Noir; Black Label Cuvée Syrah. Owners: Mona, Walt, and Bryan Babcock. Winemaker: Bryan Babcock. Cases: 25,000. Acres: 70.

🍇 *Babcock Vineyards, 5175 East Highway 246, Lompoc 93436; (805) 736-1455, fax (805) 736-3886; www.babcockwinery.com. Open 10:30 a.m.–4:00 p.m. daily. Tasting fee: $10. Visa, MasterCard, American Express. Wheelchair accessible.*

Pea Soup Andersen's, Buellton

Buellton's primary attraction is Andersen's Pea Soup, which has renamed itself **Pea Soup Andersen's**, based on people's main goal in getting there. And is it worth it! Anton and Juliette Andersen opened the restaurant in 1924 as Andersen's Electric Cafe, a name they chose to celebrate their prized new electric stove! Since then, Juliette's pea soup has attracted millions of comfort-food fans who want to sample the original.

The building's trim is pea-soup green, the doors are pea-soup green, and even the Best Western motel next door has pea-soup green trim. There seems to be a theme here.

Here you can buy Pea Soup Andersen's cookbook, flatish mugs for soup, soup bowls, canned pea soup (surprise!), preserves, soup and fried chicken spices, and Solvang Bakery's breads and pastries. Sample the local cheeses cut in cubes and placed in trays on a wine barrel. The restaurant also has a doll and curio shop, where you will also find fabulous historic photos of the Andersen family and the restaurant.

Despite local rumor, Andersen's insists the pea soup served here is made fresh on-site every morning.

Pea Soup Andersen's, 376 Avenue of the Flags, Buellton 93427; (805) 688-5581; www.peasoupandersens.net. Open 7:00 a.m.–10:00 p.m. daily. Full bar. Visa and MasterCard. Wheelchair accessible.

Pea Soup Andersen's has spawned some good nearby motels, golf courses, special events, a magic-show theater, and a farmers' market, so you can actually stay there if you wish. Another choice is the Danish village of Solvang on the other side of US 101.

Nojoqui Park, on Alisal Road between US 101 and Solvang, has the only waterfall in Santa Barbara County. This is a true community park for day use only and features great picnic areas, softball diamonds, volleyball courts, horseshoe pitches, and playgrounds among California live oaks and birds worth watching. A short but steep trail leads to the waterfall.

From US 101 take the Highway 246 east exit (toward Solvang). In less than a mile you come to a shopping center with Long's Drugs and other familiar large stores, plus a delightful local espresso joint cleverly called Thanks a Latte.

Within the next half mile you have arrived! That is, at two of the central coast's most renowned steak houses: A.J. Spurs, a small chain, and the locally famous and infamous Hitching Post.

The HITCHING POST, which looks like an Old West bar and hangout—which it is—is a must-try if you eat meat or just want to experience what the locals look like or like to eat on occasion.

Nothing has changed since scenes for *Sideways* were filmed here. Along with good, stiff drinks, great oak-fire barbecued steaks, and french fries, you can indulge in fabulous grilled artichokes and mushrooms, seafood and chicken, lamb, turkey, ostrich, pork, ribs, and smoked duck, and a big bite of humor from the servers. The *New York Times* has called it "a must stop for beef and Pinot lovers"; the *Los Angeles Times* says, "perfect steaks and fries and a daring Pinot Noir"; and *Gourmet* said, "We'd drive anywhere for steaks like these." Got the message?

Steaks range from $22 to $44 for a complete dinner. Lots of seafood and children's selections. The Hitching Post also has a wine tasting room for its own label wines. The secret to these great Pinot Noirs is that in 1984, Gray Hartley and Hitching Post proprieter and chef Frank Ostini began making wines for the Hitching Post, and in 1991 they moved on to Qupe/Au Bon Climat, where they make limited bottlings of Pinot Noir and Syrah and an even better reputation for themselves. Here you can taste both.

You can even order cooked steaks and ribs by phone and have them shipped around California. The meat is seasoned and grilled (rare is recommended so you can reheat according to instructions), chilled, packed, and shipped overnight. Be sure to have them include their special artichokes and smoked tomato mayo. Steaks are $15 to $30 for two, artichokes are $20 for four, plus sales tax and $14 shipping. Order two days ahead at (888) 429-6300.

Sideways film and book author Alexander Payne wrote right here at the bar. **Hitching Post,** *406 East Highway 246, Buellton 93427; (805) 688-0676 or (888) 429-6300; www.hitchingpost2.com. Bar opens at 4:00 p.m., dinner 5:00–9:00 p.m. daily. Full bar. Visa, MasterCard, American Express. Wheelchair accessible.*

Knut Siegfried recently bought OSTRICH LAND from Colin and Rosi Cooper, whose first Ostrich Land was in South Africa more than twenty years ago. Now you can visit the unique thirty-three acres of ostriches and emus, a ranch based upon the original 1,000 African black ostrich eggs the Coopers imported to California. Here you can feed the friendly emus, gaze at their green eggs that look like avocados, and see ostrich products such as eggshell lamps, ostrich feather dusters, and leather (highly valued by some people for Western boots). Most of Ostrich Land's eggs and birds are exported to Japan, Korea, China, Taiwan, Ecuador, Brazil, and the Philippines, although you can also buy meat here. Ostrich meat is reputed to be one of the highest-protein, lowest-fat meats available. We have tried ostrich jerky, and while slightly chewy, it is quite tasty. Bon appétit!

Ostrich Land, *610 East Highway 246, P.O. Box 490, Buellton 93427; (805) 686-9696; www.ostrichland.com. Open 9:00 a.m.–5:00 p.m. Saturday and Sunday; more often in summer. Visa and MasterCard. Wheelchair accessible.*

SOLVANG
("MAKE MINE DANISH")

A half mile east of Ostrich Land on Highway 246 you arrive in Solvang. (In Solvang, Highway 246 becomes Mission Drive.)

Solvang is a consciously constructed Danish village plunked down in the Santa Ynez Valley by Danes and Danish Americans who moved here by choice to establish a Danish community in California. It was simply too cold in the Midwest, where most of them came from.

As you drive along Highway 246, you'll suddenly find you have been transported to an eighteenth-century Danish village, authentic except for such modern touches as cement curbs, a neon sign here and there, and automobiles. How did this seeming miracle come about?

Back in 1910, not far from the then-crumbling Santa Ines Mission, this area was a bean field owned by the Santa Ynez Valley Development Company. The only building was the one-room Ynez School, which served the children of the valley farms.

Meanwhile, in Michigan, the Danish Lutheran Church Convention adopted a proposal to develop a Danish colony and a Danish "folk school," patterned after the Grundtvigian folk school movement in Denmark, in a suitable location in the west. In 1911 a committee of two Lutheran ministers (Benedict Nordenstoft and J. M. Gregersen) and Professor P. P. Hornsyld found the valley, bought 9,000 acres of the Rancho San Carlos de Jonata, and named the colony Solvang ("sunny field").

Within a few months the first wave of Danes arrived, including lumber dealer Hans Skytt. Soon there arose the Solvang Hotel, the Bethania Lutheran Church, several homes, a bank, a bakery, and other shops. The folk school, Atterdag ("another day") College, was erected in 1914. Classes on Danish culture and trades for young men were given there until 1937.

The town buildings' only variations on plain were the Spanish arcade on Copenhagen Drive and the one true Danish-style building, the new Bethania Lutheran Church, designed and completed by pioneer Hans Skytt in 1928. Solvang's twenty-fifth anniversary celebration in June 1936 gave birth to "Danish Days," which grew each year until it became overwhelming for the town, which rescheduled it to September after kids return to school to limit attendance at the festival.

Solvang's transformation into an old Danish village began in 1945 after World War II. Home builder Fred Sorensen returned from a visit to Denmark with plans for a home in the Danish provincial style, and he built it, including a windmill—the Mill on the Hill *(Mollenbakken)*. This induced Ray Paaske, himself just home from a German prison camp, to hire Sorensen to design commercial establishments in the Danish style where Copenhagen Drive meets Alisal Drive (now Copenhagen Square).

In the early 1950s a couple of new buildings on Copenhagen Drive were built in the same style (gingerbread along the eaves, visible wood forms like the Tudors, multipaned windows, meticulous attention to detail, sharply peaked roofs, lots of dormers). Then the Spanish arcade went Danish in 1958.

Architect and developer Earl Petersen designed the Royal Copenhagen Motel on Mission Drive (Highway 246) to re-create a street in Hans Christian Andersen's hometown of Odense. Across the street, Petersen developed an entire city block, called Petersen's Village Square, with a hotel, bakery, and several shops, using varied facades, Danish style. Meanwhile more windmills were built, joining the original Paaske Mill on Alisal: the Blue Windmill in Hamlet Square at Second and Copenhagen and one as part of the former Danish Inn on Mission Drive.

The rush was on. Old buildings were converted to Danish provincial by merchants eager to do their part and attract tourist business. The postal service got the message, and the new post office grew up Danish, as did several gas stations and motels. A series of shopping and dining squares in the medieval format and carved signs came into vogue. Among other structures, Earl Petersen designed the 720-seat outdoor Solvang Festival Theater with its old-world stage house, which opened in 1974. Solvangans planted the Hans Christian Andersen Park.

Saleswomen and waitresses wear attractive Danish costumes every day, whether they are of Danish heritage or not. Many women bleach their hair to match someone's notion of female Danes. *Honen*—horse-drawn pre-1900 streetcars (built by local artisans)—clop through town daily in summer and on weekends the rest of the year (adults $3.50, seniors $3.00, children $2.50). The wind harp from the Danish exhibit at the 1915 Pan-Pacific Exposition plays its siren song in the breezy afternoon. There is an imported model of the famed Copenhagen mermaid statue. The mouthwatering aromas of Danish baked goods draw visitors into the multitudinous bakeries and restaurants. Warm hospitality completes the picture.

Local historian Elaine Revelle calls Solvang "a Danish-American jewel set in a wealth of cultures and blessed by the California sun." We agree.

While cranky critics have called Solvang the "Denmark Disneyland" and a town "more Danish than Denmark," we think you should take time to have a look, give it a chance, enjoy it for what it is, and draw your own conclusions. Besides, in the process you can sample more pastries than you will see in the whole rest of your life, try more smorgasbords than you should, and shop till your feet fall off. Everything is close together along a 4-block stretch of Mission Street and within a couple of blocks to the south. Walking maps are available at most hotels, motels, and businesses.

Two restaurants have received raves from Santa Barbara restaurateurs, and we suggest you try them: Brothers Restaurant and the Santa Ynez Feed & Grill, the former a somewhat formal dining room, the latter a casual bistro where Norbert Schulz, former partner in Brigitte's in Santa Barbara, presides as chef. Former Brigitte's owner Bergitta Guehr totally renovated the Meadowlark Inn, and successfully.

Wine lovers should check out the WINE COUNTRY WINE TASTING ROOM, which is actually a wine shop where you can purchase 130 different Central Coast wines from seventy-five wineries. The tasting room specializes in the wines of small boutique wineries, gifts, foods, picnic baskets, and cigars.

❧ *Wine Country Wine Tasting Room, 1539 Mission Drive, Solvang 93463; (805) 686-9699, fax (805) 937-5953; www.syvwine.com. Open 11:00 a.m.–5:00 p.m. daily. Tastes: $8. Visa, MasterCard, American Express, Discover. Wheelchair accessible.*

There are several real tasting rooms easy to visit as you stroll or roll along Copenhagen Drive and Mission Drive. Starting on Mission near Fourth Street, OLD MISSION WINE COMPANY-HOUSE OF HONEYWOOD represents forty Central Coast wineries including Carr, Clayhouse, Huber, Michael Grace, Ovene, and Dierberg Family. www.oldmissionwinecompany.com.

At Mission and First Street, OLIVE HOUSE affords tastes of olives galore along with lots of dining accessories.

A TASTE OF THE VALLEY is the hot new tasting room in Solvang where Bobby Moy carries Au Bon Climat, Arcadian, Qupé, Lane-Tanner, Tantarra, Weddell Cellars, Barrack, Wolf, Clos Mimi, Tolosa, Toucan (two garbage cans), and Kalawashaq' for the Chumash chief whose daughter studies enology at UC/Davis.

Another block east is Alisal Road, where you will find ALISAL CELLARS in the basement of the Paaske Building, conveniently located next door to the yummy Solvang Bakery, where you can enjoy a pause that refreshes for breakfast or lunch.

Opened in 1964, Alisal is Solvang's oldest cellar and tasting room, which also offers beer, champagne, and sake tastings, as well as excellent espresso, in addition to wines from 450 wineries around the world. Here you will also find Avila Wines from Laetitia Winery, including Cabernet Sauvignon, Syrah, Chardonnay, and Grenache, and their blend called Côte d'Avila. www.alisalcellars.com.

Cross the street and head down Copenhagen Drive, where wine tasters may easily get distracted by pastries, buffets, ice cream, and Danish cafes.

BELLISSIMA WINE BAR next to Solvang Restaurant on the south side of Copenhagen is owned and operated by the Sinclair family, which also owns Alisal Cellars. Here you can purchase wines by the glass, gifts, and more of that espresso.

LION'S PEAK and ROYAL OAKS tasting rooms offer their own wines in comfortable settings just west of First Street. www.lionspeakwine.com and www.royaloakswinery.com. MANDOLINA is also on this side of the street and is the tasting room of Lucas & Lewellen Vineyards. www.llwine.com.

Other than the village of Solvang itself, its architecture, and its food, special attractions include the Hans Christian Andersen Museum, the Elverhoj Museum of History and Art, and the Solvang Antique Center.

The HANS CHRISTIAN ANDERSEN MUSEUM is operated by the Ugly Duckling Foundation, dedicated to increasing enjoyment and understanding of Andersen and his work. You get to the museum either through our favorite Solvang bookstore, the Book Loft, or through the adjoining Bulldog Cafe, an excellent espresso and light-food hangout.

❧

Exhibits and displays depict Jenny Lind, a singer beloved throughout the world (and Andersen's unrequited love); a model of Andersen's childhood home; a model of "The Princess and the Pea" by local artist Carl Jacobsen; antique tools for making wooden shoes; hundreds of volumes of Andersen's tales, including many first and early editions, as well as illustrated editions (many in the Danish language); and original letters and photographs. This is a great place for adults and kids, even if they can't read yet.

❧ *Hans Christian Andersen Museum, 1680 Mission Drive, Solvang 93463; (805) 688-2052; www.solvangca.com/museum/h1.htm. Open 10:00 a.m.–5:00 p.m. daily. Free admission. Wheelchair accessible.*

The ELVERHOJ MUSEUM OF HISTORY AND ART specializes in the history of Solvang and the heritage of Denmark. It is one of the few museums outside Denmark devoted solely to Danish culture and the Danish-American experience.

The museum is located in the former residence of one of Solvang's most artistic families, the Viggo Brandt-Erichsens. Built in 1950, the structure was built to mirror the large farmhouses of eighteenth-century Jutland in northern Denmark. The name Elverhoj (pronounced Elverhoy and meaning "elves on a hill") was taken from Denmark's most famous folk play, *Elverhoj,* written in 1828 and still performed. The story involves a king's visit to the night world of dancing female wood spirits.

Don't miss the terrific gift shop and a diorama depicting Solvang before the Danish village was created. As usual, Kathleen is fascinated with the brightly painted kitchen with typical Danish farmhouse folk paintings. Docents in Danish folk costumes take you on personal tours.

❧ *Elverhoj Museum of History and Art, 1624 Elverhoj Way, P.O. Box 769, Solvang 93463; (805) 686-1211; www.elverhoj.org. Open 1:00–4:00 p.m. Wednesday–Sunday. Admission is free, donation box near the door. Visa and MasterCard. Wheelchair accessible.*

SOLVANG ANTIQUE CENTER offers unusually high-quality antiques in sixty-five well-lit galleries and showcases. You will find the most elegant of European carved furniture, porcelain, cut glass, estate jewelry, pianos, Wedgwood, majolica, clocks and music boxes, Japanese antiques, scales and tools, and collectibles. Right off Mission Drive on First Street at the eastern end of town, the antiques center ships anywhere in the world and offers in-house restorations.

❧ *Solvang Antique Center, 486 First Street, Solvang 93463; (805) 686-2322, fax (805) 686-4044; www.solvangantiques.com. Open 10:00 a.m.–6:00 p.m. daily. Visa, MasterCard, American Express. Partly wheelchair accessible.*

The VINTAGE MOTORCYCLE MUSEUM is a surprise find in the middle of this make-believe-Danish town. Motorcycle fans and even just curious passersby will enjoy a stop here to see more than sixty rare motorcycles built between 1904 and 1990. Try to imagine the lives of the people who rode and collected these wild machines of their day. Dr. Virgil Elings's collection includes AJS, BMW, BSA, CZ Ducati, Harleys, Indian, JAWA, Moto Guzzi, Nimbus, Triumph, Thor, and Whizzer, and many more. It's worth the trek of a couple of blocks down Alisal Road.

❧ *Vintage Motorcycle Museum, 320 Alisal Road, Solvang 93463; (805) 686-9522; www.motosolvang.com. Open 11:00 a.m.–5:00 p.m. weekends, by appointment midweek. Admission is $5 adults, children under ten free with adult. Wheelchair accessible.*

Another draw to Solvang is its outstanding PACIFIC CONSERVATORY OF THE PERFORMING ARTS (known in local secret code as PCPA), an outdoor theater designed by Earl Petersen seating 720 guests and featuring rotating repertory. Director Donovan Marley, now in Denver, built the PCPA's reputation. Call (805) 922-8313 or visit www.pcpa.org for the performance schedule (June–October) and information.

Solvang stages festivals throughout the year, among them the Flying Leap Storytelling Festival the third weekend in February (805-688-8823); the Taste of Solvang annual food festival, the theme of which changes each year, the third weekend in March (800-468-6765, ext. 520); the Old Mission Santa Ines Fiesta

OLD MISSION SANTA INES, SOLVANG

the second weekend in August (805-688-4815); Danish Days with folk dancing, music, parades, and food the third weekend in September (805-688-6144); and the giant Winterfest celebration from Thanksgiving to Christmas with millions of white lights, pageantry, and special events (read shopping).

Be sure to visit the wild and crazy SHELBI RANCH, which is really a Movie Cowboy Museum and super discount western clothing store, with the only weekend $1 lunch in town. Shelley and Bill Berman, who made their fortune in clothing manufacture, sell western clothes and fabric dirt cheap here. The $1 lunch, cooked by the Bermans' daughter, includes a Wild Bill Hickory Burger, baked fries, Danish custard ice cream milk shakes, mesquite barbecue chicken breast sandwiches, Albacore tuna sandwich, chili, soup, pizza, or a mixed green salad. Shelley watches the till, and grandma gabs with visitors. All profits go to the Shriners Hospitals for Children, and Shelbi Ranch offers free therapeutic horseback riding for physically challenged children.

❧ *Shelbi Ranch, Hans Christian Andersen Square, 435 First Street, Solvang 93463; (805) 693-5000; www.shelbiranch.com. Open 10:00 a.m.–5:00 p.m. weekends. Partly wheelchair accessible.*

OLD MISSION SANTA INES is one of the gems of the California missions, founded in 1804 by Padre Estevan Tapis and built for the Franciscans by Indians whom the Franciscans planned to colonize and convert to Catholicism. It is currently run by the Capuchin Franciscans. Although much of the mission was destroyed by the 1812 earthquake, half of the original twenty-two arches and more than one-third of the original mission quad still stand. The mission functioned as a self-sustaining village with tanning, threshing, wool pulling, weaving, carpentry, grist and olive milling, winemaking, metal and ironworks, and full-scale farm and ranching operations. Mission Santa Ines was also the first college and seminary in California.

The church, which was rebuilt in 1817, is one of the few chapels of the California missions that has been in continuous use since 1817. In the museum you will see artifacts from the Spanish, Indian, Mexican, and early American civilizations, including arrowheads, adobe bricks and tiles, pestles and mortars, pottery, musical instruments, tools, silver, firearms, and ironwork produced on the mission's grounds, as well as priceless seventeenth- and eighteenth-century European and Indian art.

Don't miss the preserved vestment collection dating from the sixteenth century, including one worn by Padre Junipero Serra, founder of the California missions. Be sure to visit the semiformal garden with its boxwood hedge sculpted in the shape of a Celtic cross, flowers, and a California pepper tree brought by Father Serra—a quiet oasis from rushing society. Mission bells still toll daily to tell the valley what time it is.

The mission cemetery has 1,700 unmarked Indian graves, as well as those of seventy-five early California settlers of Spanish, Portuguese, German, and Irish descent, with engraved gravestones, of course. Please especially respect the unmarked Indian graves.

᠙᠎ *Old Mission Santa Ines, 1760 Mission Drive, P.O. Box 408, Solvang 93463; (805) 688-4815; www.missionsantaines.org. Open 9:00 a.m.–5:30 p.m. daily in winter, 9:00 a.m.–7:00 p.m. in summer. Masses 8:00 a.m. daily, Saturday 5:00 p.m. in English, 7:00 p.m. in Spanish, Sunday 8:00, 9:30, 11:00 a.m. in English, 12:30 p.m. in Spanish. Admission to the museum and gardens: $3 for ages sixteen and older, children under sixteen free. Wheelchair accessible.*

SANTA YNEZ

Possibly the biggest, and most controversial, attraction in Santa Ynez is the CHUMASH INDIAN CASINO, right on Highway 246, with 2,000 slot machines and several vertical acres of parking. How convenient!

This place is about as wild, fun, and exciting as you would expect, taking advantage of U.S. government laws allowing gambling on Indian reservation property that is not allowed elsewhere. You are now on the Santa Ynez Indian Reservation, so please respect it and its territories south and east of here.

If it's your inclination, you can take your chances on a variety of casino thrills, such as slot machines, video gaming, poker, Chumash 21, and boxing.

᠙᠎ *Chumash Indian Casino, 3400 Highway 246 East, Santa Ynez 93464; (805) 686-0855; http://chumash.casinocity.com. Open 10:00 a.m.–2:00 a.m. Monday–Thursday, twenty-four hours Friday–Sunday. Full bar. Visa, MasterCard, American Express. Wheelchair accessible.*

Another popular attraction in Santa Ynez is the SANTA YNEZ VALLEY HISTORICAL MUSEUM and the nearby carriage museum. One of the most interesting exhibits at this charming small museum is the room dedicated to the Chumash Indian culture, including a diorama, Vaquero show, tools, and a fabulous basket collection. The carriage museum has a surprisingly wonderful collection of stagecoaches, wagons, and other horse-drawn vehicles that set the tone for your winery tour into the Santa Ynez Valley, where thousands of Western movies were filmed.

❧ *Santa Ynez Valley Historical Museum, 3596 Sagunto Street, Santa Ynez 93464; (805) 688-7889; www.syvm.org. Open noon–4:00 p.m. Wednesday– Sunday. Free admission.*

ARTISTE IMPRESSIONIST WINERY & TASTING STUDIO is the most different and fun tasting room we have visited in a whole West Coast of wineries.

Owner Bion Rice, second generation winemaker from the family who own Sunstone Winery, has created an art and tasting experience he says is "inspired by Hotel Baudy in Giverny, France, [that] transports us to a working art studio in the 1870s—the height of the Impressionist movement."

And, by golly, he's done it. Artists' works are everywhere, including on wine labels, paint-splattered wine boxes, counters and tables, canvases and sketchbooks around for visitors to leave their impressions, and rooms of fun for adults and kids.

Meanwhile, Price is making some serious blends with plans to open a "studio" in Healdsburg in Sonoma County in late 2007.

❧ *Artiste Impressionist Winery & Tasting Studio, 3569 Sagunto Street, Studio 102, Santa Ynez 93460; (805) 686-2626; www.artiste.com. Open 11:00 a.m.– 5:00 p.m. daily. Visa, MasterCard, American Express.*

Enjoy lots of local eateries next door and nearby.

Christine and Donald Ziegler's luxurious Victorian-style SANTA YNEZ INN recently perked up this lovely little town with fourteen elegantly special rooms, including one with mirrors above the bedposts and one with a huge bathtub right in the room. Many rooms include whirlpool tubs, double steam showers, and fireplaces, and all have DVD and CD entertainment systems in addition to televisions, voice mail, dataports, and fresh flowers. Bicycles, afternoon tea, wine and fabulous hors d'oeuvres at 5:00 p.m., full gourmet breakfasts (from house-made granola full of almonds and macadamia nuts to coffee cakes and high-protein frittatas), sauna, massages (including aromatherapy integrative massage), fitness suite, beauty treatments, facials, and a small library are all available. In the Zieglers' complex you can also explore Coach House Antiques and the popular Vineyard House Restaurant next door.

Santa Ynez Inn now has its own tasting room across the garden. Exceptional wines from local small wineries are available here, including those of Byron, Au Bon Climat, Qupé, Westerlea, and Quelda Ridge.

❧ *Santa Ynez Inn, 3627 Sagunto Street, Box 628, Santa Ynez 93460; (805) 688-5588 or (800) 643-5774, fax (805) 686-4294; www.santaynezinn.com. Rates, $255–$415. Visa, MasterCard, American Express, Discover. Wheelchair accessible, one room with roll-in shower.*

THE VINEYARD HOUSE, SANTA YNEZ

THE VINEYARD HOUSE is one of Santa Ynez's best restaurants, having grown from a small, historic, genuine Victorian house to a substantial establishment with a lovely deck overlooking the lawns it shares with the Santa Ynez Inn. Jim and Debbie Sobell have done wonders here with Chef Gabriel Guzman. Try turkey or beef burgers, protein plate, yummy pastas with Caesar salad, a grilled chicken and Brie sandwich, butternut squash ravioli, rack of lamb, steaks, buttermilk fried chicken, or salmon ($10.50–$26.00). Brunch is terrific, as are the homemade desserts.

The Vineyard House, 3631 Sagunto Street, Box 1930, Santa Ynez 93460; (805) 688-2886, fax (805) 693-1659; www.thevineyardhouse.com. Open 11:30 a.m.–9:00 p.m. Wednesday–Monday, Sunday brunch. Beer and wine. Visa, MasterCard, American Express. Not wheelchair accessible.

For a great hamburger and even more informal dining, try Paula's Burger Barn next door to the Santa Ynez Inn. Locals favor Grappolo beyond this complex at 3687 Sagunto for a combination western-Italian tradition, as well as Chef Rick's. Walk around town, all of 1 block in each direction, to discover The Mole Hole, and Old Adobe Traders for American Indian treasures.

BALLARD

Ballard is one of the smallest and most intensely cute communities anywhere. It's so small that it doesn't have a post office, so the official address is Solvang. All of Ballard is on Baseline Road, an old Wells Fargo stagecoach route

THE BALLARD INN AND RESTAURANT, BALLARD

just east of Alamo Pintado Road. One of the town's most charming buildings is the white-trimmed, red-steepled Ballard School, which is still used for kindergarten classes. Conveniently located near Buttonwood, Rideau, Foley, and Beckmen wineries, Ballard is a perfect stop on your search for perfect wines.

The Ballard Inn and its restaurant serve "creative wine country cuisine." Chef Budi Kazali creates a limited but exquisite menu of appetizers such as truffle turnip soup, honey-tamarind-glazed quail, Hamachi sashimi, pan-seared foie gras, and Caesar salads ($8–$14).

Entrees may include pan-seared scallops, roasted duck breast, herb-crusted tuna, Australian rack of lamb, or a grilled beef tenderloin, all accompanied by creative potato or risotto sides and sauces ($25–$28).

Great local and international wine list.

❧ Ballard Inn and Restaurant, 2436 Baseline Avenue, Ballard 93463; (805) 688-7770 or (800) 638-2466; www.ballardinn.com. Open 6:00–9:00 p.m. Wednesday–Saturday, 5:30–9:00 p.m. Sunday. Beer and wine. Visa, MasterCard, American Express. Wheelchair accessible.

LOS OLIVOS

Los Olivos (the olives) is definitely one of our favorite little places. Surrounded by large ranches and vineyards unabashedly owned by the rich and famous, Los Olivos is a marvelous cross between elegant sophistication and country funk. And besides, the surrounding hills and dales look like scenes in all those Westerns you grew up on—because they are. Los Olivos is ultimate Santa Ynez Valley.

Nancy and the late President Ronald Reagan, Cheryl Ladd, Bo Derek, John Forsythe, Doc Severinsen, Ray Stark, Rona Barrett, James Stewart, Dean Martin, Johnny Mathis, Michael Jackson, Jimmy Connors, Bruce Jenner, Efrem Zimbalist Jr., David Crosby, and Whoopi Goldberg have all called the Los Olivos area of the Santa Ynez Valley their hangout or home. Greta Garbo used to live here, and cowboy movie star residents Leo Carrillo, Gene Autry, Noah Berry Jr., Will Rogers, and Tom Mix first came here on the springtime treks made by Ranchero Visitadores in the 1930s.

Los Olivos itself began in 1860 when a stagecoach stop was established. Several years later, Felix Mattei foresaw that the Pacific Coast Railway would stop here, too, and built a hotel to accommodate rail and stage passengers making connections. Ballard became the railroad's terminus in November 1887, and two expected booming land sales were rained out. Stage service to Los Olivos terminated in 1901, and train service terminated in 1934, so progress and life slowed down tremendously.

The center of town is the Los Olivos flagpole in the middle of the Grand Avenue–Alamo Pintado intersection, the first version of which stood east of this one and had a thirty-gallon Schilling's Best coffee can as a base. The current pole was erected in 1918 to honor World War I veterans.

Most everything you'll want to see is on Grand Avenue or in the first blocks off it on Alamo Pintado, Jonata, or Railway cross streets.

We start a block west of Grand Avenue, on Railway Avenue, at BROTHERS RESTAURANT AT MATTEI'S TAVERN (pronounced "Matty's"). One of the most buzzing restaurants in Los Olivos, it was reopened in 2003 by brothers Jeff and Matt Nichols from Ames, Iowa. Try the cilantro-lime grilled shrimp and sweet red chile cole slaw, vegetable spring rolls, hickory-smoked salmon on bagel crisps, jumbo Mexican white shrimp with cocktail sauce, and Chinese chicken salad for starters.

Main courses include superb 10 oz. eye of the rib eye steak, baked horseradish-dill-crusted organic Irish salmon, grilled pork chop with Firestone-Walker Reserve glaze, roasted chicken breast stuffed with goat cheese, free-range veal chops, and loads of beef goodies, including size choices of prime rib ($18–$45). Perfect martinis; interesting ports and wine list.

❧ *Brothers Restaurant at Mattei's Tavern, 2350 Railway Avenue, Los Olivos 93441; (805) 688-4820, fax (805) 688-8965; www.matteistavern.com. Open for dinner 5:00–9:00 p.m. daily, full bar opens at 4:00 p.m. daily. Visa, MasterCard, American Express. Wheelchair accessible.*

Next, head to the bottom of the east side of Grand at what is now FESS PARKER'S WINE COUNTRY INN & SPA, formerly the Grand Hotel and Remington Restaurant. The hotel was once the Lige Campbell Livery Stable (1910), from which Lige carried mail and passengers to Gaviota in a mud wagon stage until 1914. The west wing occupies what was once the Irv Henning Tent House (1886). An artesian well on the property furnished water for the dairy and a Chinese laundry.

Some travelers might remember the Wine Cask restaurant at Fess Parker's Wine Country Inn & Spa. Then Wine Cask owner Doug Margerum sold both this restaurant and his anchor Wine Cask in Santa Barbara to Bernard Rosenson in 2007. Two months later, Fess Parker took it back, reopened it, and renamed it Restaurant Marcella. At press time the menu and wine list were still being developed.

➳ *Fess Parker's Wine Country Inn & Spa, 2860 Grand Avenue, Los Olivos 93441; (800) 446-2455 or (805) 688-7788; www.fessparker.com. Open for dinner 5:30–9:30 p.m. Wednesday–Saturday, brunch 10:30 a.m.–2:30 p.m. Saturday and Sunday. Visa, MasterCard, American Express. Wheelchair accessible.*

Just up from Fess Parker's is the Cody Gallery, the first art gallery in Los Olivos, and then the Judith Hale Gallery. If the yellow flag is out, Judith Hale is open. This property has been a general store, barber shop, post office, and town library.

Across Alamo Pintado at the corner is perhaps the most familiar site in Los Olivos, the Los Olivos Garage (1903), made famous as Goober's garage in *Return to Mayberry*. Until it closed in 1990 because of a new California contamination law, the garage was the oldest continuously operating gas station in California. Now it houses Wildflower of Los Olivos, which sells dried flowers, home accessories, and garden furniture.

Behind the garage (down the Alamo Pintado side) is an excellent deli, PANINO, the perfect place to select a salad or panino sandwich and dine in front at the round, umbrellaed tables or pick up the perfect picnic to enjoy at a winery. Nineteen meaty sandwich varieties and nine yummy vegetarian kinds make decisions difficult. One of the most popular is a smoked turkey/Genoa salami combo. Or try the Italian combo of layered ham, Genoa salami, and imported provolone cheese and fresh basil, or the smoked turkey with sliced Brie and fresh basil. All on freshly baked bread.

Vegetarian choices include English Cotswold cheese and tomato, English Stilton and Asian pear, mixed veggies, and a kalamata olive tapenade with fresh mozzarella, organic greens, and basil. Several of the sandwiches are made in salad form ($7.95–$9.50). Nine fabulous salads are great on hot days. Specials, and they are, are posted on the slate boards.

You can also get special picnic box lunches with a sandwich, salad, and cookie, as well as smoothies, fabulous carrot cake, and espresso drinks. Check out the attractive splash-painted metal bowls and dishes.

❧ *Panino, 2900 Grand Avenue (around the corner), Los Olivos 93441; (805) 688-9304, fax (805) 688-2552. Open 9:00 a.m.–5:00 p.m. daily. No credit cards. Wheelchair accessible.*

Just up the street from Panino is a charming tasting room for CONSILIENCE, which means "The Unity of Knowledge," as portrayed by Edward Wilson. Good friends Monica and Brett Escalera and Tom and Jodie Daughters make 3,500 cases of vineyard-designate wines only, including Grenache Noir, Pinot Noir, Syrah, and Zinfandel.

❧ *Consilience, 2933 Grand Avenue, Los Olivos 93441; (805) 691-1020; www.consiliencewines.com. Open 11:00 a.m.–5:00 p.m. daily. Visa, Master Card, American Express. Wheelchair accessible.*

Just beyond Panino you will find Persnickity, with vintage linens, soaps, napkin sets, and books.

PATRICK'S SIDE STREET CAFE is in a cozy, historic location that has seen several restaurants come and go. Executive Chef Patrick Rand and Chef Shaun Behrens seem to have it right. Both are graduates of the Culinary Institute of America–Hyde Park, and let's hope they find appreciation here. These purists grow many of their veggies and herbs in the back garden, and they change the menu and ceiling fabric every ninety days.

Lunch runs from $11 to $16 and may include a Winemaker's Lunch with house-made pâté, mussels in ale, great sandwiches, and salads ranging from a lettuce wedge with Green Goddess dressing to a warm duck salad.

Dinner ranges from $17 to $29 for entrees, such as cheese fondue, pepper steak, sand dabs, pork schnitzel, shrimp-shiitake-potato sauté, Muscovy duck breast, baby New Zealand lamb chops, or Malaysian Day Boat scallops.

❧ *Patrick's Side Street Cafe, 2375 Alamo Pintado Avenue, Los Olivos 93441; (805) 686-4004. Open 11:00 a.m.–9:00 p.m. Wednesday–Sunday. Beer and wine. Visa, MasterCard, American Express.*

Just beyond Patrick's Side Street Cafe, turn right (north) on Jonata Street to Wildling Art Museum, which features "the art of wild places" and the plants and animals that live in them.

❧

Retrace your steps and resume your walk up Grand Avenue. Don't miss Corridor Books for cookbooks, travel guides, fiction, and specialized nonfiction.

Check out the John Cody Gallery and the espresso stand next door.

ALEXANDER & WAYNE is owned by Arthur Alexander White and Earl Wayne Brockelsby, who also have Arthur Earl across the street. Alexander & Wayne makes Burgundian and Bordeaux-style varietals including Chardonnay, Pinot Noir, Tempranillo, Sauvignon Blanc, Cabernet Franc, Merlot, Cabernet Sauvignon, Riesling, and a Botrytis Sauvignon Blanc or Port, totaling 2,500 cases. Taste them all here along with Santa Barbara Olive Co. products.

❧ *Alexander & Wayne, 2922 Grand Avenue, Los Olivos 93441; (805) 688-9665; www.alexanderandwayne.com. Open 11:00 a.m.–6:00 p.m. daily. Visa, MasterCard, American Express. Wheelchair accessible.*

On the west side of Grand Avenue, you will find a series of wine tasting rooms representing small, excellent wineries that don't have tasting rooms at their wineries.

At EPIPHANY CELLARS, Eli Parker gets to express himself creatively as a winemaker totally independent of his famous father and namesake, Fess Parker. Eli studied at UC/Davis and apprenticed under many local winemakers before becoming winemaker at Fess Parker Winery & Vineyard, where he continues. Epiphany is an elegant and unpretentious winery and tasting room, planted in an old building the family once used for storage. Here Eli makes wine from single vineyard sources, even from Washington State.

Fine points: Featured wines: Pinot Gris, Syrah, Roussanne, Marsanne, Grenache, Petite Sirah. Owner and winemaker: Eli Parker. Cases: 4,000. Acres: 800 Fess Parker.

❧ *Epiphany Cellars, 2963 Grand Avenue, Los Olivos 93441; (805) 686-2424 or (866) 354-9463, fax (805) 686-2634; www.Epiphany Cellars.com. Open 11:30 a.m.–5:30 p.m. daily. Tasting fee: $5. Visa, MasterCard, American Express. Not wheelchair accessible.*

Daniel Gehrs followed the California/Northwest student wine study route from drinking some of the worst and has grown to making some of the best around. Gehrs eventually served as outstanding winemaker at Zaca Mesa and opening winemaker at Bridlewood, and now he makes his own available at DANIEL GEHRS WINERY in historic Heather Cottage.

Fine points: Featured wines: Chenin Blanc, Pinot Blanc, Barbera, Grenache, Syrah, Cabernet Franc, Merlot, Pinot Noir, Fireside Port. Owner and winemaker: Daniel Gehrs. Cases: 7,000. Acres: purchases fruit from others.

❧ *Daniel Gehrs Winery, Heather Cottage, 2939 Grand Avenue, Los Olivos 93441; (805) 693-9686; www.dgwines.com. Open 11:00 a.m.–6:00 p.m. daily. Tasting fee: from $7. Visa, MasterCard, American Express, Discover. Not wheelchair accessible.*

Walk down the street to the tasting room of RICHARD LONGORIA WINES in the former D. D. Davis' Warehouse and Welding shop, where Davis's brother Bernard ran a steam barley roller.

Rick Longoria served full-time as cellar foreman at Firestone Vineyard, Rancho Sisquoc, J. Carey Cellars, and Gainey Vineyard, until he finally took the plunge in 1997 to make his own label wines full-time. Rick strives for perfection and makes only four wines, to maximize the potential of the character of grapes and vineyards he selects.

Check out Rick's Blues Cuvées, a tribute to his first blues song experience at age seventeen and to the soul of the music and his wines.

Longoria's wines have been highly praised by the *Wine Spectator*, the *Wine Advocate,* and by Dan Berger in the *Los Angeles Times.*

 Fine points: Featured wines: Santa Rita Hills Chardonnay, Albariño Pinot Noir, Cabernet Franc, Blues Cuvée, Syrah, Pinot Grigio Tempranillo. Owners: Rick and Diana Longoria. Winemaker: Rick Longoria. Cases: 3,400. Acres: 8 and buy locally.

❧ *Richard Longoria Wines, 2935 Grand Avenue, Los Olivos 93441; (805) 688-0305, (866) 759-4637, fax (805) 688-2676; www.longoriawine.com. Open noon–4:30 p.m. Monday, Wednesday, and Thursday, 11:00 a.m.–4:30 p.m. Friday–Sunday. Tasting fee: $5, includes logo glass. Visa and MasterCard. Wheelchair accessible.*

WILD HEART WINERY is tucked down a driveway and is an experience in itself. The tasting room is loaded with local jewelry makers' pieces, crosses, and heart gifts. Jim and Suzanne Geist Burens are owners and winemakers and software entrepreneurs from Camarillo. Suzanne "is the wild heart of the bunch," said a staffer.

❧ *Wild Heart Winery, 2933-C Grand Avenue, Los Olivos 93441; (805) 688-7388. Open 11:00 a.m.–5:00 p.m. daily. Visa, MasterCard, American Express. Wheelchair accessible.*

Next door, LOS OLIVOS VINTNERS AND AUSTIN CELLARS specializes in small quantities of a few wines, including Chardonnay, Sauvignon Blanc, Pinot Noir, Cabernet Sauvignon, Merlot, Cabernet Franc, red wine blends, Riesling, Merlot

Port, Zinfandel Port, and Muscat Canelli. (The site once housed the D. D. Davis General Store, the Bucket O' Blood Saloon, and the valley's first theater, the Liberty, which opened in 1916.)

Fine points: Featured wines: see above. Owners: won't reveal. Winemaker: Art White. Cases: 3,000. Acres: None, buy locally.

❧ *Los Olivos Vintners and Austin Cellars, 2923 Grand Avenue, Los Olivos 93441; (805) 688-9665 or (800) 824-8584, fax (805) 686-1690. Open 11:00 a.m.–6:00 p.m. daily. Tasting fee: $2. Visa, MasterCard, American Express. Wheelchair accessible.*

Next is the new tasting room of ARTHUR EARL, which moved here in 1999 from near the crossing of US 101 and Highway 246 in Buellton. Arthur White and Earl Brockelsby converted a warehouse into a full-function winery and tasting room at their "city" winery in Buellton. Focusing on dry whites, dry reds, and sweet wines, Art and Earl are delighted to be able to offer their wines in these pleasant surroundings, honoring the arts of various disciplines.

The owner of the Stonebarger Foundry and shop (1906) in this historic building shaded by a large old oak tree put together Los Olivos's first water system and erected the flagpole (1918).

Fine points: Featured wines: Rousanne, Nebbiolo, Pinot Grigio, Pinot Bianco, Merlot, Syrah, Viognier, Grenache, Mourvedre, and Moscato. Owners: Arthur White and Earl Brockelsby. Winemaker: Art White. Cases: 3,000. Acres: none, buy locally.

❧ *Arthur Earl, 2921 Grand Avenue, Los Olivos 93441; (805) 693-1771 or (800) 646-3275; www.arthurearl.com. Open 11:00 a.m.–6:00 p.m. daily. Tasting fee: $5. Visa, MasterCard, American Express. Wheelchair accessible.*

Chris Benzinger's (not Benziger) LOS OLIVOS TASTING ROOM & WINE SHOP offers tastes, representing small wineries that don't have their own tasting rooms or other wineries Benzinger simply likes. This is a truly fun place where you can learn lots about a variety of wines. This building was first Henry Lewis's barbershop, then "Uncle Tom" Davis ran a small grocery store here until 1935, and then it was used as the post office with combination lockboxes outside.

Here you can sample the finest from Qupé and Vita Nova, whose label reads "Incestuous products from like minds," as well as Claiborne & Churchill (which now has its own tasting room), J. Kerr, Au Bon Climat, Foxen, Fiddlehead, Ken Brown, Talley, dessert wines, and Kalyra (Australia), and enjoy posters from Willi's Wine Bar in Paris.

❧ *Los Olivos Tasting Room & Wine Shop, 2905 Grand Avenue, Los Olivos 93441; (805) 688-7406 or (805) 688-6632. Open 11:00 a.m.–6.00 p.m. daily* *(last tasting 5:30 p.m.). Tasting fee: $8. Visa, MasterCard, Discover. Wheelchair accessible.*

Back at the corner of Grand Avenue and Alamo Pintado, you can enjoy (if you're still sampling) fine ANDREW MURRAY VINEYARDS and Oak Savanna Vineyards wines in a bright and airy, beautifully appointed tasting room in a building called the Corners with a sign that now proclaims Oak Savanna, for which Andrew Murray is also winemaker. The winery itself is above Foxen Canyon Road. Andrew Murray is Santa Barbara County's only exclusively Rhone estate.

Andrew Murray, the person and the winery, are devoted to Rhone varietals and to the production of unfiltered wines from estate-grown grapes. This is a family enterprise with Andrew's parents, Jim and Fran, pitching in at all levels from picking to pouring. Andrew and his wife, Kristen, basically run the winery. Andrew fell in love with Rhones at age fifteen while tasting them with his parents in Condrieu, France, where Viognier is made. He and his father were the first people to plant on hillsides in Santa Barbara County, and on steep hillsides at that, rising quickly from 1,200 feet to more than 1,500 feet.

Kristen is a fabulous cook who loves to entertain (good thing!) in the winery and keeps her cuisine simple so she can enjoy her guests. The winery itself looks like a French country manor, complete with aromatic Provençal gardens and terraces with breathtaking views of the hillside vineyards and surrounding mountains. Kristen's love of food and all things kitchen shows in the books and other gifts available.

Fine points: Featured wines: Syrah, Viognier, Rousanne, Esperance red blend, Grenache, Mourvedre. Owner: Andrew Murray. Winemaker: Andrew Murray. Cases: 9,000. Acres: 45.

❧ *Andrew Murray Vineyards, 2901 Grand Avenue, P.O. Box 718, Los Olivos 93441; (805) 693-9644, fax (805) 693-9664; www.andrew murrayvineyard.com. Open 11:00 a.m.–5:00 p.m. daily. Tasting fee: $10, includes logo glass. Visa, MasterCard, American Express. Wheelchair accessible.*

LOS OLIVOS PARK occupies the southwest corner of Grand and Alamo Pintado, and Los Olivos's version of punks occupy lots of the park in the afternoon. It and they are all interesting to look at. Fear not! They are just enjoying the sunshine as you are. Lavinia Campbell gave the land for a park following its historical uses as a blacksmith shop, garage, drayage, and welding shop.

At the site of Frank and Charlie Whitcher's blacksmith shop, JEDLICKA'S SADDLERY takes you right into the Western movies, old and new. Reminiscent of Los Olivos's role in the older Wild West, Jedlicka's has everything horse fans could need and caters to many of the gorgeous horse ranches in the Santa Ynez Valley. The Whitchers' old ledger listed 77 customers, and Jedlicka's probably has 700 browsers a day in tourist time. Huge red wagons, huge cowboy hats, a wide range of boots for men and women, and gorgeous ranch wear are all sold here. Enjoy!

Jedlicka's Saddlery, 2883 Grand Avenue, Los Olivos 93441; (805) 688-2626. Open 9:00 a.m.–5:30 p.m. Monday–Saturday, 10:00 a.m.–4:30 p.m. Sunday. Visa, MasterCard, American Express, Discover. Wheelchair accessible.

The must-stop restaurant in Los Olivos is the LOS OLIVOS CAFE. The simple decor is also very clever: sponge-painted cement-block walls with functioning pipes hanging from the ceiling, natural cotton fabric swooping between the pipes, and varied Mexican iron light fixtures—all in stark contrast to the original store destroyed here in 1914 when two robbers tried to blow up the safe. Today the deck in front is a superb place to enjoy lunch or dinner after the sun has passed and watch Los Olivos society and visitors stroll by.

The cafe is truly the gathering place in Los Olivos for both locals and *Sideways* movie fans, and for good reasons. Los Olivos Cafe has a wine shop adjoining the restaurant and also offers an afternoon menu of light salads and sandwiches.

Owner, entrepreneur, former stock broker, and Bernat winery owner Sam Marmorstein and Chef Nat Ely offer the complete menu (with choices) devoured by *Sideways* characters during their dinner there for about $33, and it just happens to include some of the restaurant's best dishes. Check out the soup or butternut squash salad; salmon, pot roast, or Florentine ravioli; and the unbelievably lip-smacking Chocolate Scream, which consists of flourless chocolate cake (watch those carbs), home-made ice cream, and caramel sauce.

This is where we often stop when updating guidebooks or visiting family in the area.

Everything here is excellent, and loads of fun. And we have tried almost everything, from spring rolls, artisanal cheese plate, baked Brie, raspberry pecan salad, classic Greek salad, most of the sandwiches, turkey burgers, and ravioli stuffed with spinach, ricotta, and thyme with roasted shallot cream and served with shaved Parmesan and snipped chives. Sandwiches $11–$14, entrees $11–$24.

Lots of Los Olivos Cafe's tapenades and sauces are available online.

Los Olivos Cafe, 2879 Grand Avenue, Los Olivos 93441; (805) 688-7265; www.losoliloscafe.com, www.santabarbarawine.com. Open 11:30 a.m.–9:00 p.m. daily. Beer and wine. Visa, MasterCard, Discover. Wheelchair accessible.

CHAPTER 4

TOURING SANTA BARBARA COUNTY WINERIES

*W*e *first visit Santa Barbara's two downtown wineries before heading to the Santa Ynez Valley and the Foxen Canyon Wine Trail, where most of Santa Barbara County's outstanding wineries are located.*

SANTA BARBARA WINERY is in urban Santa Barbara, not far from the beach. While it's on Anacapa Street, do not try to take Anacapa down to it. There's a freeway in the way, called U.S. Highway 101. Do take State Street all the way down and under US 101. Turn left (east) on Yanonali Street, named for a Chumash Indian chief. The winery's address is on Anacapa, but the winery and tasting room actually face Yanonali. Park at the winery and walk across Yanonali to the tasting room, where'll you find picnic tables and umbrellas—in case you brought along a picnic.

Entrepreneur Pierre Lafond established Santa Barbara Winery in 1962. It was the first commercial winery in Santa Barbara County since Prohibition, and it is now the oldest in the county in continuous operation. You can also visit Lafond Winery and Vineyards west of Buellton and US 101 in the Santa Rita Hills.

Along with some friends known as the "mountain drivers," a community of home winemakers famous for their bacchanalian harvest festivals, Pierre bought grapes from others to make wine and sell it in his shop in the old El Paseo on State Street. A French Canadian by birth and an architect by training, Lafond began by making fruit wines. He has cafes and boutiques on State Street and in Montecito.

Beginning in 1970, Pierre invested in vineyard land along the Santa Ynez River, and he has kept his winemaking operation right here in downtown Santa Barbara. When the Lafond Vineyard matured, Pierre brought in Bruce McGuire to take over winemaking operations.

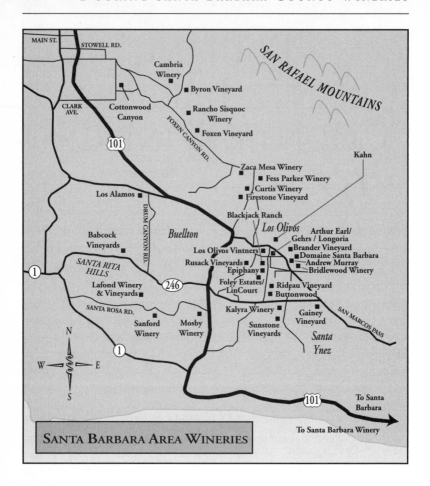

SANTA BARBARA AREA WINERIES

This tasting room is part of the fermentation facility, so you are right in the middle of the action. Here you can indulge in all sorts of taste pleasers, including chocolate Zinfandel sauce, chocolate hazelnut Cabernet fudge, breads and dipping oils, and bread spreads. Be sure to wander around to the right behind the tasting bar to see the photo gallery that leads to the tank room.

 Fine points: Featured wines: Chardonnay, Sauvignon Blanc, Riesling, Cabernet Sauvignon, Pinot Noir, Rosé of Syrah, Grenache, Grenache/Syrah, Syrah, Zinfandel, Late Harvest Sauvignon Blanc. Owner: Pierre Lafond. Winemaker: Bruce McGuire. Cases: 55,000. Acres: 100.

🍇 *Santa Barbara Winery, 202 Anacapa Street, Santa Barbara 93101; (805) 963-3633 or (800) 225-3633, fax (800) 411-9463; www.sbwinery.com. Open*

10:00 a.m.–5:00 p.m. daily. Tasting fee: $5, includes logo glass. Visa, MasterCard, American Express. Wheelchair accessible.

Also in Santa Barbara, JAFFURS WINE CELLARS evolved when Craig Jaffurs and Dave Yates left the aerospace industry and slowly and painstakingly learned the wine biz, first as a hobby, from Chris McGuire at Santa Barbara winery, at UC/Davis, and from other generous winemakers. Buying grapes from growers in the Santa Ynez and Santa Maria Valleys, Jaffurs started making wine at Central Coast Wine Services in Santa Maria, and he now handcrafts his own at his new winery in downtown Santa Barbara. The tasting room is right in the middle of the winery, so visitors experience the smells, temperatures, and noises of winemaking.

Fine points: Featured wines: Rhone varietals Rousanne, Viognier, Grenache, Petite Sirah, and Syrah. Owner and winemaker: Craig Jaffurs. General manager: Dave Yates. Cases: 3,200. Acres: none.

✣ *Jaffurs Wine Cellars, 819 East Montecito Street, Santa Barbara 93103; (805) 962-7003; www.jaffurswine.com. Open 10:00 a.m.–5:00 p.m. Friday–Sunday. Tasting fee: $5 with purchase, $10 without wine purchase, glass included. Visa and MasterCard. Wheelchair accessible.*

SANTA YNEZ VALLEY

The Santa Ynez Valley gets its name from the Santa Ynez River, which runs east to west, south of Highway 246, under US 101, and out to the Pacific Ocean. West of US 101, Highway 246 roughly parallels Santa Rosa Road, and, more accurately, Santa Rosa Road roughly parallels the river.

East of Solvang, turn right (south) on Refugio Road to Kalyra and Sunstone wineries. Do not miss Steve and VitaLoyal's "Corner Farm" at Highway 246 and Refugio Road for herbs, flowers, and organic veggies grown here and served in the valley's best restaurants.

KALYRA WINERY, located where LinCourt used to be before it moved to Foley, is the wildest winery in Santa Barbara County, and well worth the visit for the entertainment factor if nothing else. Foodies will enjoy loads of Australian cookbooks, chutneys, vinegars, olive oils, and dressings. Notice the "Australian rules football" theme.

Don't be fooled by the frat-party atmosphere. *Sideways* producers enlarged the tasting room for the movie, and Kalyra has its serious side—like the wines! Australian owner/winemaker Mike Brown received degrees in microbiology and pharmacology at the University of Adelaide, roamed two continents learning winemaking, and sort of settled down as winemaker for Buttonwood Farm winery, Santa Ynez Winery, Mosby Winery, and Zaca Mesa Winery, some of the best of the area. Mike's younger brother Martin, former barrister and international tour guide, now runs Kalyra's marketing. All wineries hold special events, but try Kalyra's Great Australian BBQ and golf tournament in June, or their Australian Christmas (December) and Great Grape Stomping Party (September), to say nothing of the occasional expedition to Australia.

The Browns' Australian wines, made under the M. Brown label, are also available in the riotous tasting room.

 Fine points: Featured wines: Kalyra Nebbiolo, Merlot, Cabernet Sauvignon, Cabernet Franc, Black Muscat, Orange Muscat, Vintage Port, Tawny Port, M. Brown Barossa Valley Shiraz, Limestone Coast Shiraz, Eden Valley Riesling. Owner and winemaker: Michael Brown. Cases: 8,000. Acres: none, buy from Santa Ynez Valley, Monterey, Amador, and Madera Counties, and Australia.

Kalyra Winery, 343 Refugio Road, Santa Ynez 93460; (805) 693-8864; www.kalyrawinery.com. Open 11:00 a.m.–5:00 p.m. daily. Tasting fee: $7. Visa, MasterCard, American Express. Not wheelchair accessible.

SUNSTONE VINEYARDS & WINERY is just before the bridge over the Santa Ynez River, 1.4 miles south of Highway 246. Take a sharp right onto the dirt road and park to the left.

Designed to create the ambience of a French country winery, and succeeding, Sunstone is one of the most charming wineries you will find anywhere. When you drive onto the grounds, be sure to notice the fabulous multimaterial wall on the eastern end of the building, visible especially when the climbing vines are leafless. The feeling continues in the elegant patio rimmed in rosemary and lavender, in the tasting room, and in the historically accurate Provençal kitchen, complete with wood-burning oven, where elegant meals are prepared and cooking classes are given.

Although grape growing was in Fred Rice's blood (his great-grandfather

SUNSTONE VINEYARDS & WINERY'S KITCHEN

Chicken Potpie with Puff Pastry Dough
from Brittany Rice, Sunstone Vineyards & Winery, Santa Ynez

4 chicken breasts

2 potatoes

1 large yellow onion, diced medium

3 cloves garlic, minced

4 carrots

4 celery stalks

2 fresh ears of corn or 1 cup frozen corn

2 cups sugar snap peas or 1 cup frozen peas

3 cups chicken broth or stock

3 Tbs. flour

fresh dill, Italian parsley, savory, and basil

1 sheet Puff Dough (Trader Joe's or Gelsons)

water

oil or butter for pan

FOR THE FILLING: Fill a large stock pot over halfway with water, placing dill and parsley in water for flavor. Bring to simmer and add chicken breasts. Cook for about 20 minutes.

Meanwhile, peel and dice potatoes, and keep cold. Dice onions and garlic and set aside. In a sauté pan, put oil or butter, the onions, garlic, and oil and sauté for a few minutes. Set aside in bowl. Don't clean the pan. Cook potatoes in sauté pan until soft. Add to bowl with onion and garlic.

Sauté carrots until soft and add celery. In a few minutes, add corn and peas. Combine all veggies with potatoes, onion, and garlic in the bowl.

When chicken is completely cooked, remove from pan and cool. Shred chicken into bite-size pieces.

FOR THE ROUX: Pour broth or stock in a sauté pan with flour and stir constantly while heating, or mixture will become lumpy. Stir until thick. Add veggies to the roux. Salt and pepper to taste. Add chicken, basil, parsley, and savory. Place in 2 large ceramic baking dishes.

FOR THE PUFF DOUGH: Roll out two Puff Dough rounds or squares. Bake at 350°F for 45 minutes or until golden brown. Place on chicken mixture in baking dishes and heat another minute. Serves 4–6. Serve with Sunstone Chardonnay or Sauvignon Blanc.

grew for Inglenook Winery), Fred and Linda had farmed in the Coachella Valley and lived in Santa Barbara before finding this fifty-five-acre property in 1988 to organically farm Merlot, Cabernet Sauvignon, Syrah, Viognier, and Mourvedre varietals. Having only planned to sell grapes to others, they borrowed equipment from friends Marcy and Fess Parker and made their first wines in 1992. The Rices still hand-harvest, hand-sort, and gently crush their fruit.

The Rices' son Bion believes that tasting the wines here at the winery helps the taster experience the *terroir* (soil makeup and surroundings) of this unusual place. Don't miss a chance to explore the 120-foot stone cave dug into the hillside, where wines rest in French oak barrels and elegant dinners are served occasionally. The tasting room offers wines, of course, as well as pasta sauces, grapeseed oils, grape-shape pastas, Merlot wine jelly, Pinot Noir chocolate cherries, and their Eros poster of *The Kiss* by James-Paul Brown.

Bion Rice started his own winery (Artiste) and has an exciting tasting room in Santa Ynez.

 Fine points: Featured wines: Chardonnay, Sauvignon Blanc, Viognier, Merlot, Cabernet Franc, Cabernet Sauvignon, Eros, Syrah. Owners: the Rice family. Consulting winemaker: Daniel Gehrs. Cases: 18,000. Acres: 77 organically farmed.
🍇 *Sunstone Vineyards & Winery, 125 North Refugio Road, Santa Ynez 93460; (805) 688-9463 or (800) 313-9463, fax (805) 686-1881; www.sunstone winery.com. Open 10:00 a.m.–4:30 p.m. daily. Tasting fee: $10, plus $5 for Reserves. Visa, MasterCard, American Express. Wheelchair accessible.*

Turn right (south) from Highway 246 onto the GAINEY VINEYARD road 2.3 miles east of the Refugio Road intersection and continue 0.2 mile to the winery's entrance. Gainey's excellent paved driveway circles a grassy, tree-shaded central court, which seats 700 guests at concerts. The Preservation Hall Jazz Band, Diana Krall, Lucinda Williams, and Randy Newman exemplify the range of entertainers who perform here.

Designed to be an educational forum as well as a lovely place to enjoy wines, the tasting room has white walls (lined with stars' photos), wood-beamed ceilings with skylights, and Mexican tile floors. *Wine Spectator* has called Gainey the "best tasting spot on the Central Coast," and the *Los Angeles Times*'s Robert Lawrence Balzer says, "Gainey Vineyard is one of the most beautiful wineries in the world." Kathleen likes the side table loaded with free recipes and tasting note information.

Unlike other wineries that usually have vineyards close to their winery, Gainey has them both here and in the cooler Santa Barbara zone west of US 101 off Santa Barbara Road within the new Santa Rita Hills appellation. Gainey's Chardonnay has received 98s in a *Wine Spectator* California Chardonnay vs.

GAINEY VINEYARD'S PICNIC AND PERFORMANCE CIRCLE,
SANTA YNEZ

white Burgundy wines blind tasting. Stephen Tanzer calls Gainey's Pinot Noir "sexy juice," and the winery won a four-star gold medal for its 1997 Riesling at the Orange County Fair.

Wine Spectator has also named Gainey one of its Best Wineries to Visit on the California Central Coast. Gainey sells Snapple beverages, Gallo salami, cheeses, and Marcel & Henri's fine pâtés, or bring your own picnic to enjoy in the garden. Ask about cooking classes, winemaker's dinners, concerts, and the unusual harvest crush party, a real hoot and learning experience.

 Fine points: Featured wines: Chardonnay, Sauvignon Blanc, Riesling, Merlot, Pinot Noir, Cabernet Sauvignon, Syrah. Owners: father and son Dan J. Gainey and Dan H. Gainey. Winemaker: Kirby Anderson. Cases: 20,000. Acres 120.

❧ *Gainey Vineyard, 3950 East Highway 246, Santa Ynez 93460; (805) 688-0558, fax (805) 688-5864; www.gaineyvineyard.com. Open 10:00 a.m.–5:00 p.m. daily; tours at 11:00 a.m. and 1:00, 2:00, and 3:00 p.m. Tasting fee: $10, includes glass. Visa, MasterCard, Discover. Wheelchair accessible.*

As you come out of Gainey, turn right (east) on Highway 246 east, and then take a careful left (north) on Highway 154. About 3 miles north on Highway 154, turn right (east) on Roblar Avenue, and turn immediately left on the frontage road to DOMAINE SANTA BARBARA and BRANDER wineries, both of whose wines are available at Brander. Brander is the only winery we have seen that is designed to look like a pink French chateau with turrets. (The chateau is on Brander's labels.)

BRANDER VINEYARD'S CHATEAU
TASTING ROOM, LOS OLIVOS

Brander Vineyard is the baby of Fred Brander, who won his first gold medal in 1978 and thereby became the first Santa Barbara winemaker to win a gold medal anywhere. Fred fell in love with high school chemistry, went to Harvey Mudd College, imported European wines, and then studied enology at UC/Davis. Now Brander mixes great wines with great foods at special events throughout the year.

Enjoy copies of Paul Gauguin's paintings (from $900) on the tasting room walls or picnic under the poplar and cottonwood trees. Flowers and London plane trees combine to create a colorful ambience. Do not miss the Santa Barbara Bouillabaisse Festival, held at Brander the third Sunday in May, at which twenty-five local restaurants compete in a seafood cook-off to showcase dry rosé wines and benefit local charities.

Fine points: Featured wines: Brander label Sauvignon Blanc (four styles), Merlot, Cabernet Sauvignon, Syrah, Merlot, Bouchet, Cuvée Natalie, Cuvée Nicolas, Chateau Neuf de Pink. Owner and winemaker: Fred Brander. Cases: 15,000. Acres: 45.

🍇 *Brander Vineyard and Domaine Santa Barbara, Highway 154 at Roblar Road (frontage road), P.O. Box 92, Los Olivos 93441; (805) 688-2455, fax (805) 688-8010; www.brander.com. Open 10:00 a.m.–5:00 p.m. mid-April to mid-October, 11:00 a.m.– 4:00 p.m. mid-October to mid-April. Tasting fee: $7.50. Visa, MasterCard, American Express. Wheelchair accessible.*

As you leave Brander and Domaine Santa Barbara, turn south on the frontage road, then turn left (east) onto Roblar Avenue to visit the spectacular BRIDLEWOOD WINERY. Cory Holbrook sold his whole-

DOMAINE SANTA BARBARA,
LOS OLIVOS

BRIDLEWOOD WINERY, SANTA YNEZ

sale flower business in Medford, Oregon, to fulfill his twenty-year dream of owning his own winery and of using his successful flower-growing techniques in wine growing.

Bridlewood began with renowned winemaker Daniel Gehrs. The current winemaker is David Hopkins, formerly with Sonoma/Monterey Winery Kendall Jackson.

Cory bought this fabulous property, a former Arabian horse ranch and equestrian rehabilitation center complete with horses, racetrack, ponds, and swans. The new mission-style building and visitor center is surrounded by lush lawns, oak trees, rose gardens, croquet courts, and ponds, with wrought-iron tables and chairs for picnicking. Stop just to experience the splendor.

 Fine points: Featured wines: Arabesque, Sauvignon Blanc, Chardonnay, Viognier, Riesling, Merlot, Cabernet, Sauvignon, Viognier, Syrah, Pinot Noir, Zinfandel. Owner: Cory Holbrook. Winemaker: David Hopkins. Cases: 40,000. Acres: 105.

Bridlewood Winery, 3555 Roblar Avenue, Santa Ynez 93460; (805) 688-9000, fax (805) 688-2443; www.bridlewoodwinery.com. Open 10:00 a.m.–5:00 p.m. daily. Tasting fee: $7, includes glass. Visa, MasterCard, American Express, Discover. Wheelchair accessible.

ROBLAR WINERY & VINEYARDS is across Highway 154 from Brander and Bridlewood and, as the new kid on the block, may also be the most elegant rustic winery.

MEDITERRANEAN-STYLE PENNE
from Cory Holbrook, Bridlewood Winery, Santa Ynez

8 slices prosciutto (or bacon), chopped

1 large onion, chopped

1 small eggplant, cut into 1-inch cubes

2 cups tomatoes, chopped, peeled, and seeded

4 large garlic cloves, chopped

1 Tbs. red wine vinegar

1 tsp. dried thyme, crumbled

1 lb. penne pasta

2 Tbs. olive oil

1½ cups feta cheese (about 7 oz.), crumbled

½ cup pitted Kalamata olives

Italian parsley, chopped

basil, chopped

Cook prosciutto or bacon in large heavy skillet over medium-high heat until crisp. Transfer to paper towels using slotted spoon. Add onion and eggplant to drippings in skillet. Sauté over medium-high heat until eggplant is tender and golden, about 15 minutes. Add tomatoes, garlic, vinegar, and thyme. Reduce heat to medium and cook 5 minutes. Season with sea salt and fresh ground pepper.

Cook pasta in large pot of boiling salted water until just tender but still firm, then drain. Transfer pasta to large bowl. Toss with olive oil. Mix in eggplant sauce, feta, olives, and bacon or prosciutto. Sprinkle with parsley and basil. Serves 4. Serve with Bridlewood Pinot Noir.

Stephen and Denise Adams, who fund chairs in the Stanford School of Business, from which he got his MBA in 1962, also have enjoyed great success in banking, RV dealerships, and outdoor advertising, and also own Adler Fels Winery in Sonoma County.

At Roblar, winemaker Richard Foster produces 5,500 cases of wines, all of which are sold out of the new tasting room, which is adorned with saddles and a huge stone fireplace, excellent cheeses and charcuterie, a huge dining room, and a house chef who makes lunches and packages walk-away salads and panini if you prefer ($9.95–$12.95).

Roblar also has an outstanding cooking school and professional kitchen, where well-known visiting chefs teach classes Saturday evenings that include

SEARED SCALLOPS WITH LEMON AND DILL
from Cory Holbrook, Bridlewood Winery, Santa Ynez

2 Tbs. (¼ stick) butter

12 large sea scallops

¼ cup finely chopped shallots

½ cup Bridlewood Chardonnay

1 Tbs. fresh dill, chopped, plus two sprigs for garnish

1 Tbs. fresh lemon juice

1 tsp. grated lemon peel

2 Tbs. (¼ stick) butter, chilled and cut into ½-inch cubes

salt and pepper

Melt 1 Tbs. butter in large nonstick skillet over medium-high heat. Sprinkle scallops with salt and pepper. Place scallops in hot skillet and cook until golden and just opaque in the center (about 1 minute per side). Transfer scallops to plate and tent with foil to keep warm.

Melt 1 Tbs. butter in the same skillet. Add shallots and sauté 1 minute. Add wine, and boil until reduced by half (about 1 minute). Stir in chopped dill, lemon juice, and lemon peel. Remove pan from heat. Add chilled butter cubes, a few pieces at a time, whisking slowly just until melted. Season with salt and pepper. Divide scallops between 2 plates. Pour sauce over scallops and garnish with dill sprigs. Serves 2. Cory Holbrook suggests serving with couscous with fresh herbs and steamed green beans sprinkled with toasted pine nuts.

preparation, appetizers, and a full-service four-course meal with wine ($125–$150). Check the Web site for more information.

❧ *Roblar Winery and Vineyards, 3010 Roblar Avenue, Santa Ynez 93460; (805) 686-2603; www.roblarwinery.com. Tasting fee: $10, includes two whites and three red wines and glass. Open 10:00 a.m.–5:00 p.m. daily. Visa, MasterCard, American Express. Wheelchair accessible.*

SOMERSET FARMS owner Alexandra Geremia raises Watusi cattle and zebras on her ranch but grows organic vegetables at twenty-acre Somerset Farm at Baseline and Edison, just off Highway 154 not far from the entrance to Roblar Winery and Vineyards, having left her more racing life in Santa Barbara.

Geremia is assisted by her son, Edward, and friend "Sir Gregory," a master florist who migrated from Los Angeles via Santa Barbara and who staffs the sales

PORK LOIN IN PINOT NOIR AND CHERRY REDUCTION SAUCE
from LinCourt Vineyards, Solvang

3½ lbs. boneless pork loin

1 bottle LinCourt Vineyards
    Pinot Noir

8 oz. dried cherries

1 tsp. ground Mexican chili pepper

2 Tbs. fresh garlic

1½ cups shelled walnuts

2 oz. olive oil

1 stick (¼ lb.) butter

sea salt

baking flour (Wondra)

Slice pork loin into ½-inch-thick slices, and pound to ⅛-inch thick between sheets of plastic wrap. Refrigerate until ready to use. Put whole bottle of Pinot Noir, cherries, chili pepper, and fresh garlic in medium saucepan. Simmer on medium heat, stirring frequently to reduce sauce.

Arrange walnuts on baking sheet, sprinkle with olive oil, and dust with ¾ tsp. chili pepper. Place in 300°F oven for 15 to 20 minutes or until toasted brown.

Cool walnuts and add to sauce. Add ⅞ stick of butter, stirring in sauce until butter is melted and mixed in well. Remove sauce from heat when one-quarter of original liquid remains in saucepan. (Cherries will absorb lots of the wine.)

Remove pork from refrigerator, and sprinkle slices with sea salt and flour. Sauté in heavy pan with butter and olive oil, about 2 minutes per side, or until done.

Arrange pork medallions on plate, top with LinCourt Pinot Noir sauce, and serve. Serves 6.

---

stand. Visitors must chat for a while and walk around the pumpkin patch and double-spiral blackberry labyrinth to get to the brilliant sunflowers, squashes, watermelons, assorted green beans and okra, peaches, peppers, and herbs. If you are lucky, you can go out in the fields with Sir Gregory to pick flowers, veggies, and fruits. U-pick blackberries.

❧ *Somerset Farms, 3450 Baseline, Santa Ynez 93460; (805) 682-7800; www.flowersbysirgregory.com. Open 9:00 a.m.–6:00 p.m. Tuesday–Sunday. MasterCard and Visa. Wheelchair accessible.*

After you have lunch in Los Olivos (see chapter 3), simply take Alamo Pintado Road off Grand Avenue to Foley, Blackjack Ranch, Rideau, and

Buttonwood wineries. If you have lunch in Ballard, Baseline Avenue will take you to Alamo Pintado, where you turn left.

On the west side of Alamo Pintado just south of Baseline Avenue is the driveway to FOLEY ESTATES and LINCOURT VINEYARDS. Wind up the road to the charming yellow-and-white 1900s dairy farmhouse that now serves as both Foley's and LinCourt's tasting room. Drive past the house and turn right before the redwood dairy barn, now the functioning winery, into the parking lot. Stroll around the lawn and peacefully take a deep breath and view your surroundings.

The tasting room (in what were the living and dining rooms) has pine floors, ceiling fans, and a brass rail at the bar.

William P. Foley II bought the estate from the Firestone family in 1997 to fulfill his lifelong dream of developing a world-class wine estate. Foley and LinCourt winemaker Alan Phillips has a notable background, beginning with his studies in enology at UC/Davis in 1976, during which time he worked under the amazing André Tchelistcheff at S. Anderson Vineyards in Yountville on weekends and evenings. In 1981 he and Jay Corley formed Monticello Cellars in the Napa Valley, and after ten years helped with start-ups of several wineries, including Vine Cliff Cellars, V & L Eisele Vineyards, and Kates Vineyard & Winery. Then he consulted in New Zealand, Germany, France, Spain, and Portugal. Most recently he served as winemaker at Byington Winery in the Santa Cruz Mountains.

Fine points: Featured wines: Foley Estate Chardonnay, Syrah, Pinot Gris, Pinot Noir, Sauvignon Blanc, Cabernet Sauvignon, and LinCourt Chardonnay, Pinot Noir, Syrah. Owner: William P. Foley II. General Manager and Director of Winemaking: Alan Phillips. Cases: 25,000. Acres: 25.

Foley Estates and LinCourt Vineyards, 1711 Alamo Pintado Road, Solvang 93463; (805) 688-8554, fax (805) 688-9327; www.foleywines.com. Open 10:00 a.m.–5:00 p.m. daily. Tasting fee: $10, includes glass. Visa, MasterCard, American Express, Discover. Wheelchair accessible.

BLACKJACK RANCH WINERY owner Roger Wisted is one of the Santa Ynez Valley's more colorful characters, having worked as a meat cutter, disc jockey, gold broker, and professional poker player. He began to make wine at age fifteen in his parents' supermarket and began collecting wine at seventeen. Wisted now boasts a collection of 5,000 bottles of French and California wines. But his real secret to success, and the reason for his winery's name, is that he invented the only legal form of Blackjack to be played in California, brilliantly copyrighting the special deck of cards and rules.

BLACKJACK RANCH WINERY, SOLVANG

Sideways filmed here for good reason. Stop in for some fun, an authenticated deck of California Blackjack playing cards, and some good wine.

Wisted built his tasting room from the ranch's old wood. The bar wood comes from a bowling lane in the old Solvang Bowling Alley.

 Fine points: Featured wines: Chardonnay, Pinot Noir, Syrah, Merlot, Harmonie. Owner: Roger Wisted. Winemakers: Christian Roguenant (Burgundy native) and Roger Wisted. Cases: 6,500. Acres: 20 and buy from others.

❧ *Blackjack Ranch Winery, 2205 Alamo Pintado Road, Solvang 93463; (805) 686-4492 (tasting room), (805) 686-9922, fax (805) 693-1995; www.black jackranch.com. Open 11:00 a.m.–5:00 p.m. daily in summer, Thursday–Sunday in winter. Tasting fee: $10 for ten wines. Visa, MasterCard, American Express, Discover. Wheelchair accessible.*

A half mile south on Alamo Pintado you will find both Rideau and Buttonwood wineries on the left side of the road. Rideau closes at 4:30 p.m., so be sure to visit it before Buttonwood if you want to get to both.

Nestled in huge oak trees, RIDEAU VINEYARD's tasting room occupies the historic 1884 Alamo Pintado adobe, now beautifully restored. Enjoy the picnic tables on the adobe's porch as well as the tranquil scene. You'll never want to leave.

New Orleans native Iris Rideau used to live up the hill and for ten years drove past the old adobe that had been the Alamo Pintado Stage Coach Inn, which thrived on the overflow from Mattei's Tavern and Inn. Iris just wanted to restore the building, once part of the de la Cuesta land grant, but ended up creating a winery as well in her spare time from her work as a financial planner in Los Angeles.

At many special events you can sample her Creole jambalaya, gumbo, and dips, as well as her fine wines. Check out the French wine tasting glasses. Or picnic at the tables under huge ancient oaks.

 Fine points: Featured wines: Rhône varietals such as Roussanne, Pinot Noir, Chardonnay, Tempranillo, White Riesling, Syrah, Syrah Rosé, Sauvignon Blanc, Nebbiolo, Petite Sirah, Sangiovese, Mourvedre, Viognier. Owner: Iris Rideau. Winemaker: Andrés Ibarra. Cases: 10,000. Acres: 16.

⁂ *Rideau Vineyard, 1562 Alamo Pintado Road, Solvang 93463; (805) 688-0717, fax (805) 688-8048; www.rideauvineyard.com. Open 11:00 a.m.–5:00 p.m. daily. Tasting fee: $15, includes French glass. Visa, MasterCard, American Express, Discover. Wheelchair accessible.*

Another 0.8 mile south of Rideau is homey Buttonwood Farm Winery & Vineyard, a rare spot in any wine country. At Buttonwood there is no pretense, no snootiness, and there is lots of friendliness, interesting artwork, herb and vegetable gardens, and women.

Buttonwood is another name for sycamore, which surround the winery. This is a property of character and characters. Eighty-something Buttonwood founder and owner Betty Williams works and walks her farm, tall, straight, hat on head, Mexican or Indian jewelry around her neck, walking stick in hand, and dog Reggie at her heel. You might chat with her while she arranges her precious flowers in the tasting room.

Betty grew up in Louisiana in the Huey Long era with the superb cooking of her mother, Miss Delphine, whose cookbook you can buy in the tasting room. She graduated from Sarah Lawrence College, did postgraduate work at Tulane University, moved to Southern California, raised three children, got a law degree from the University of Southern California, and taught school. And by that time she was only fifty.

In 1968 Betty bought this property and developed it into a Thoroughbred horse breeding facility, devoting her "spare time" to community activities, including being cofounder of the land trust for Santa Barbara County. In 1983 she began to plant grapes on the mesa portion

Buttonwood Farm Winery & Vineyard Tasting Room, Solvang

of Buttonwood. Twelve acres of organic farm replaced the horses (my, it must be fertile!), and now what is left of that effort is right behind the tasting room.

Betty moved on to reading fiction and nonfiction, investigating the Internet, becoming an e-mail junkie, writing poetry, and caring for her dog.

Don't miss the Japanese (Sumi) pen-and-ink drawings of Seyburn Zorthian, Betty's daughter and partner, which also grace the winery's labels. Originals, prints, and posters are available in the tasting room, as is Betty's charmingly written and photographed book, *The Third Leaf* ($10), on the development of a vineyard.

Summertime visitors get to sample Buttonwood's organic peaches.

Fine points: Featured wines: Marsanne, Sauvignon Blanc, Merlot, Cabernet Sauvignon, Cabernet Franc, Devin, Trevin (Cabernet blend), Syrah, Syrah Rosé, Vintage Port, Tawny Port. Owners: Betty Williams, Seyburn Zorthian, and Bret C. Davenport. Winemaker: Michael Brown. Cases: 9,000. Acres: 106.

❦ *Buttonwood Farm Winery & Vineyard, 1500 Alamo Pintado Road, P.O. Box 1007, Solvang 93464; (805) 688-3032, fax (805) 688-6168; www.button woodwinery.com. Open 11:00 a.m.–5:00 p.m. daily. Tasting fee: $7.50, includes glass. Visa, MasterCard, American Express. Wheelchair accessible.*

While it is not in this natural travel pattern, we don't want you to miss RUSACK VINEYARDS on Ballard Canyon Road. You can get to it two ways: From Solvang, take either Ballard Canyon Road just east of US 101 or Atterdag Road (Chalk Hill Road) northward. When Atterdag intersects with Ballard Canyon Road, follow Ballard Canyon north to Rusack, which will be on the left (west) side of the road.

Nestled in the Ballard Canyon amid lush, wild west green or golden rolling hills, depending on the season, Rusack is the perfect place for a quiet picnic on its redwood deck built around four huge, elegant oak trees.

Alison and Geoff Rusack bought Ballard Canyon Winery in 1992 after successful careers as a Hollywood scriptwriter (Alison) and Santa Monica attorney (Geoff). You can't blame them for choosing this sublime life over Los Angeles traffic.

Rusack is a small, personal winery that produces excellent handcrafted wines and sells only the best in winery gifts. Be sure to notice the beautiful French crystal wine glasses.

Fine points: Featured wines: Chardonnay, Sauvignon Blanc, Rosé, Anacapa (Cabernet Sauvignon, Merlot, and Cabernet Franc blend), Pinot Noir, Sangiovese, Syrah. Owners: Alison and Geoff Rusack. Winemakers: John Falcone and Helen Falcone. Cases: 5,000. Acres: 48.

✢✷ *Rusack Vineyards, 1819 Ballard Canyon Road, Solvang 93463; (805) 688-1278; www.rusackvineyards.com. Open 11:00 a.m.–5:00 p.m. daily in summer, winter hours vary. Tasting fee: $6, includes glass. Visa and MasterCard. Wheelchair accessible.*

FOXEN CANYON WINE TRAIL

The Foxen Canyon Wine Trail basically covers the eleven wineries you can get to via Foxen Canyon Road, which runs from Los Olivos in the Santa Ynez Valley, up the mesa that runs northwestward along the base of the San Rafael Mountains, through the little Santa Maria Valley, and into the city of Santa Maria itself.

You can also start in Santa Maria and get to Foxen Canyon Road by taking the Betteravia Road (east) exit from US 101, following it eastward until it turns right (south). At a fork, take Dominion Road to the right for Cottonwood Canyon Vineyard & Winery, or ease to the left on Foxen Canyon Road, and then leftish again to Cambria and Byron wineries. Tepusquet Road between Byron Winery and Foxen Canyon Road has been washed out, so you should either retrace your tracks to Foxen Canyon Road or approach the rest of the wineries from Los Olivos.

So here we go. There are no restaurants or delis on the Foxen Canyon Wine Trail, so we recommend that you either load up with picnic supplies in Los Olivos or Ballard or make sure that you have had enough to eat before you leave. A few wineries offer some snacks and soft drinks, but nothing very substantial.

We recommend that instead of following Foxen Canyon Road, known on the Ballard side of Highway 154 as Ballard Canyon Road, you go north on Highway 154 or US 101 and turn east on Zaca Station Road up this gorgeous valley and into the hills so you won't miss Firestone Vineyard or Curtis Winery.

As you wind your way through these gorgeous Western movie backdrops, you come to the actual Pacific Gas & Electric Zaca Station. This really does look like Fess Parker (Davy Crockett) country! After 2.6 miles, turn left up the hill and continue 0.6 mile to FIRESTONE VINEYARD, a real treat to visit. The view from this oak-studded knoll overlooking the estate vineyards is truly breathtaking Wild West.

The Firestone family fortune came from tires and rubber, which is why most of us know the name. In the early 1970s Leonard Firestone purchased a parcel of Santa Ynez Valley, and with his son, Brooks, planted 260 acres of grapes. In 1972 Brooks, his wife, Kate, and his father began the winery. Eventually Suntory Ltd. of Japan, the huge wine and spirits company, bought 31 percent of the winery, and in 1994 the Firestones bought out Suntory,

❧

SHRIMP, MANGO, AND GOAT CHEESE SALAD
from Kate C. Anderson, Firestone Vineyard, Los Olivos

FOR THE SALAD:

1 lb. cooked medium shrimp, tails and shells removed

1 16 oz. can black beans, rinsed and drained

1 large ripe mango, peeled and diced into small cubes

1 small red onion, finely chopped

⅓ cup goat cheese, crumbled

8 cups mixed greens

homemade tortilla chips, or crispy store-bought chips

FOR THE DRESSING:

4 Tbs. fresh lime juice

¼ tsp. salt

½ tsp. chili powder

2 Tbs. plus 1 tsp. vegetable oil

Whisk together lime, salt, and chili powder, and then slowly add vegetable oil. Set aside. Combine the first 5 salad ingredients in a bowl and toss lightly with some of the dressing, reserving a portion to toss with the mixed greens. Toss mixed greens with dressing, being careful not to put too much dressing on. Arrange greens on a platter and serve with chips. Serves 6. Serve with Firestone Sauvignon Blanc.

returning the entire winery to a family operation. In 1991 Firestone added its Prosperity label of affordable table wines.

This highly active and connected political (Republican) family has produced Late Harvest Rieslings served by four U.S. presidents: Reagan, Ford, Bush, and Clinton. A framed handwritten note says "Dear Brooks—Thanks so much for the treat of treats—That Riesling was superb—George Bush."

Brooks Firestone has served in the California State Assembly and now on the Santa Barbara County Board of Supervisors. In 1987 the Firestones purchased Carey Cellars, renamed it Curtis, sold it in 1997, and opened a new must-see small facility just up the road. Following Brooks Firestone's election to the California State Assembly, his older son, Adam, left his law practice to become president of Firestone. Since then Firestone continues to be a "multi-generational project," says Brooks Firestone. Hayley Firestone Jessup runs the

VIEW FROM FIRESTONE VINEYARD, LOS OLIVOS

retail operations, Kate C. Anderson (Adam's wife) works with distributors in the Northwest, Polly Firestone Walker works in public relations, and Andrew is a sales manager. Andrew may look familiar to visitors as he was featured in television's *The Bachelor* in 2003. Brooks Firestone recently established a moderate 1.2-mile picturesque footpath visitors can walk between Firestone and Curtis Wineries.

Be sure to check out the second room of this elegant redwood and stone masonry tasting room. Here you can purchase a wide range of condiments (try the Zinfandel orange mustard or the garlic mayonnaise with Sauvignon Blanc), pasta sauces (including artichoke Chardonnay sauce), grapeseed oils, and chocolate sauces with coffee and Merlot or raspberry and Pinot Noir.

 Fine points: Featured wines: Chardonnay, Sauvignon Blanc, Gewürztraminer, Riesling, Syrah, Bordeaux blends, Merlot, Cabernet Sauvignon. Owner: the Firestone family; Adam Firestone, president; Andrew Firestone, general manager. Winemaker: Kevin Willenborg. Cases: 100,000. Acres: 600.

❧ *Firestone Vineyard, 5000 Zaca Station Road, P.O. Box 244, Los Olivos 93441; (805) 688-3940, fax (805) 686-1256; www.firestonewine.com. Open 10:00 a.m.–5:00 p.m. daily. Tours at 11:15 a.m. and 1:15 and 3:15 p.m. Tasting fee: $10, includes glass and tasting at Curtis Winery. Visa, MasterCard, American Express, Discover. Wheelchair accessible, including tours.*

As you leave Firestone, turn left (east) up Zaca Station Road. Almost immediately you'll see oil wells; after 0.6 mile turn left up to Curtis Winery. You can

HEIRLOOM TOMATO SALAD WITH CAPERS, EGGS, AND BACON VINAIGRETTE
from Curtis Winery, Los Olivos

2 Tbs. shallots, finely minced

¼ cup red wine vinegar or Rosé or both

1 lb. thick-cut bacon

¼ cup extra virgin olive oil

4 lbs. heirloom tomatoes, washed

4 eggs, hard boiled

¼ cup capers, rinsed

1 bunch fresh chives, finely chopped

salt and pepper to taste

Macerate shallots in the vinegar or wine mixture and season with salt and pepper.

Render bacon on low-medium heat until crisp. Do not burn or let oil turn dark. Drain bacon well and chop or cut as desired. Reserve bacon cracklings for presentation and save the fat for the vinaigrette.

Combine olive oil and warm fat to equal ¾ cup total. Whisk the fat mixture into the seasoned vinegar solution until thoroughly combined. Keep in warm place prior to serving.

Slice tomatoes ¼ inch thick and arrange on a chilled plate. Cut or chop eggs and arrange on the tomatoes. Season with salt and pepper and dress with vinaigrette.

Garnish the salad with capers, cracklings, and chives immediately prior to serving. Serves 4 to 8. Serve with Curtis Winery Heritage Rosé or Viognier.

also enter or exit from the entrance near Zaca Station's intersection with Foxen Canyon Road.

In contrast to its sister winery, Firestone, CURTIS WINERY is much more rustic, nestled in huge oak trees, with charmingly rough paths to the winery building and interesting old farm machinery and implements displayed under the trees. Curtis is a gravity-flow winery, so be sure to tour the premises to see nature at work.

Winemaker Chuck Carlson graduated from California State University at Fresno, first went to work for Zaca Mesa up the road in 1981 as a lab technician, and soon became assistant winemaker. He joined Firestone Vineyard's winemaking team in 1992 as assistant winemaker and has worked to develop a Rhone program for Curtis, beginning with the 1995 vintage. Chuck has the rare advantage of having worked close to the Foxen Canyon earth for more than twenty years.

ENTRANCE TO CURTIS WINERY, LOS OLIVOS

Curtis was Brooks Firestone's mother's maiden name. Appropriately Curtis's Rhone program began with release of the 1995 Curtis Ambassador's Vineyard Syrah. Chuck and his wife, Kathleen (good name), have two beautiful children, Chas and Emily, and Chuck also enjoys getting his feet wet fly-fishing, spreading his wings and flying, and ruining a good walk by playing golf.

 Fine points: Featured wines: Rhone blends such as Heritage Cuvée, Heritage Rosé, and Heritage Blanc; Syrah, Grenache, Rousssanne, Mourvedre, and Viognier. Owners: the Firestone family. Winemaker: Chuck E. Carlson. Cases: 10,000. Acres: 28.

❧ *Curtis Winery, 5249 Foxen Canyon Road, Los Olivos 93441; (805) 686-8999; www.curtiswinery.com. Open 10:00 a.m.–5:00 p.m. daily. Tasting fee: $10, includes glass and tasting at Firestone. Visa, MasterCard, American Express. Wheelchair accessible.*

KOEHLER WINERY is the creation of Kory Koehler, who bought sixty-seven acres of vineyard in 1997 when all the fruit was being sold to others, who were making highly rated wines.

Koehler decided to make wine herself, hired respected vineyard manager Felipe Hernandez, and then winemaker Chris Stanton. A Napa Valley native and viticulture and enology graduate of UC/Davis, Stanton worked his way up the winemaking ladder via steps at St. Clement north of St. Helena, Guenoc in Lake County, and Mayo Family Winery in Glen Ellen (Sonoma Valley), where his wines drew huge praise and ratings.

Take time to wander the grounds and visit with Koehler's interesting animals.
Fine points: Featured wines: Magia Nera, Grenache, Pinot Noir, Syrah, Chardonnay, Sauvignon Blanc, Viognier, Riesling. Owner: Kory Koehler. Winemaker: Chris Stanton. Cases: 7,000. Acres: 67.
ॐ⁓ *Koehler Winery, 5360 Foxen Canyon Road, Los Olivos 93441; (805) 693-8384; www.koehlerwinery.com. Open 10:00 a.m.–5:00 p.m. daily. Tasting fee: $8. Visa, MasterCard, American Express.*

As you turn left up Zaca Station Road toward Fess Parker's fun winery and vineyard, be sure to enjoy the daffodils along the road (if your timing is right) at the edge of Douglas Vineyards. A mile and a half up Zaca Station, turn right (south) into FESS PARKER WINERY & VINEYARD, paying attention to the speed jumps . . . er, bumps. The parking lot is rimmed with marguerites, lavender, and herbs. Divine!

The winery's stone floors, heavy wood and beams, walk-in (who would want to?) fireplace, soft pink carpet, and antique furniture make visitors never want to go home. Fess's wife, Marcy, created the decor and did an excellent job of making a large facility feel like home. You might enjoy gourmet lunches on Marcella's Veranda, named for Marcy, from April to October. Fess Parker also encourages visitors to visit Fess Parker's Wine Country Inn & Spa in Los Olivos and its Vintage Room restaurant featuring American-Mediterranean–style food.

Davy Crockett and Daniel Boone fans can pick up Daniel Boone and Disney character memorabilia and videos; Davy Crockett videos, magazines, and CDs; coonskin cork toppers; and even the *Cowboy Cookbook,* in which Fess has a recipe. This gift shop has some of the best and most subtle winery clothing we have seen, and it is definitely the only winery where we have seen Daniel Boone coonskin caps for sale! You will also find Fess Parker foods, caviar, cheese sticks, a wide selection of candles, table linens, and a Fess Parker tile clock. If you're lucky, the onetime "King of the Wild Frontier" will wander through and autograph your wine bottle.

The picnic grounds are for use by reservation only, and signs at the grounds entrance also warn "winery beverages only, no smoking, no dogs." July Fourth is always a fun (and crowded) time to visit, when Western American history is reenacted on the vast lawn in full costume. You may also want to inquire about the many Santa Barbara area charity events held here.

Since Fess Parker trademarked the phrase "American Tradition" many years ago, he uses it on some of his labels. His definition of the phrase is: "Any business can succeed with the foundation of hard work, integrity, and a goal of excellence." Eli (Fess Jr.) Parker and his wife, Laureen, were married at the winery in 1995; they have five daughters between them and one son together.

Fine points: Featured wines: Sauvignon Blanc, Chenin Blanc, Chardonnay, Viognier, Mélange (Marsanne and Viognier blend), Pinot Noir, Pinot Blanc, Syrah, White Riesling. Owner: the Fess Parker family. Head Winemaker: Blair Fox. Cases: 45,000. Acres: 714.

❧ *Fess Parker Winery & Vineyard, 6200 Foxen Canyon Road, P.O. Box 908, Los Olivos 93441; (805) 688-1545, fax (805) 686-1130; www.FessParker.com. Open 10:00 a.m.–5:00 p.m. daily. Tasting fee: $8. Visa, MasterCard, American Express. Wheelchair access is at right end of tasting room building.*

To continue on our Foxen Canyon Wine Trail tour, turn right up Foxen Canyon Road as you come out of Fess Parker. (As if created for a Western movie set but actually the real thing, your surroundings include tumbleweeds and enormous oak trees with lichen hanging limp from their branches.) For the next 3 miles you wander up and down and around the lower San Rafael Mountains, *et voilà,* you come down into a surprisingly peaceful hidden valley up on the Zaca Mesa, 1,500 feet high and above the fog line. In the Chumash Indian language, *zaca* means restful place. And guess what: This is where Zaca Mesa Winery is! This is truly the old California we read about.

Exactly 3.2 miles up Foxen Canyon Road from Fess Parker, turn left at the windmill between two stone posts to ZACA MESA WINERY, a place where you can hike on well-maintained nature trails winding through native plants and wildflowers (as long as you hike responsibly), camp, and picnic on the lawn. Play Zaca Mesa's "outdoor sport" of chess on the patio's life-size, 10-by-10-foot chessboard with 3-foot chess pieces.

If you visit in autumn, you can witness the arrival of the winery's gypsy band of dancing scarecrows in the vineyards, wearing its usual mix of baseball caps, long underwear, and hospital gowns.

For 2,000 years the Chumash Indians and then Spanish settlers revered Zaca Mesa's bounties and beauty. More recently, Zaca Mesa was the first winery in Santa Barbara County to plant the now-famous Syrah grape. The winery now almost instantly sells out of its Rhone-style varietals and blends. In 1995 Zaca Mesa's 1993 Syrah placed sixth in the world in *Wine Spectator*'s "Top 100 Wines of 1995."

ZACA MESA'S GIANT CHESSBOARD OUTSIDE THE TASTING ROOM, LOS OLIVOS

Even if you don't like wine, make the trip to Zaca Mesa to enjoy the air and the natural beauty, as well as the delightfully friendly people and the art in the tasting room.

 Fine points: Featured wines: Syrah, Z Cuvée, Viognier, Roussanne, Black Bear Block Syrah, Z Three (blend). Owners: Twin brothers John C. Cushman III and Louis B. Cushman. Winemaker: Clay Brock. Cases: 35,000. Acres: 200 planted of 750.

❧ *Zaca Mesa Winery, 6905 Foxen Canyon Road, Los Olivos 93441; (805) 688-9339 or (800) 350-7972; www.zacamesa.com. Open 10:00 a.m.–4:00 p.m. Tasting fee: $7 for one flight of five tastes, both flights $12. Visa, MasterCard, American Express, Discover. Wheelchair accessible.*

As you leave Zaca Mesa, turn left on Foxen Canyon Road for an exquisite 6.5-mile drive to FOXEN VINEYARD, the pride and joy of Bill Wathen and Richard Doré, great-great-grandson of early Santa Barbara County pioneer Benjamin Foxen (see chapter 8). Today the winery and tasting room occupy the reconstructed 200-year-old, no-frills, big-charm wood buildings of Rancho Tinaquaic. Foxen Canyon is also 2 miles south of Rancho Sisquoc.

Sixth-generation Santa Barbara County resident Dick Doré was born and raised on the family-owned Rancho Tinaquaic right here in Foxen Canyon. Having graduated from UC/Santa Barbara, Dick worked as a banker from the late sixties into the seventies and then gave up his nine-to-five job and moved his family to Europe. For a year and a half, he traveled the back roads of France, Spain, and Italy, a sojourn that led him to his love of great wines.

When Dick and his family moved back to the family ranch in the late seventies, the grape business was just emerging here. He worked odd jobs, including work in local vineyards. His path crossed that of Bill Wathen when he was working as a field hand training grapes and driving a tractor for Bill at what is now part of Cambria Winery's Tepusquet Vineyard. In 1985 Dick and Bill made a hobby wine of Cabernet Sauvignon grapes purchased from Rancho Sisquoc Vineyard, which led to a bonded winery in 1987.

Bill Wathen was born and raised in San Luis Obispo and graduated in

FOXEN VINEYARD,
SANTA MARIA

1975 from California Polytechnic with a degree in fruit science. He then worked with local viticultural pioneers Dale Hampton and Louie Lucas in managing Tepusquet Mesa Vineyard, now part of Cambria's estate vineyard, and at Nielsen Vineyard, now part of Byron (Mondavi). In 1978 he went north to manage vineyards at Chalone Vineyards south of Salinas, where Chalone owner Dick Graff became his mentor. Today Bill and his family live nearby. In his spare time Bill coaches Little League baseball.

Dick and Bill make limited production wines and do an excellent job of it. Be sure to enjoy Foxen's new patio area.

Fine points: Featured wines: Chardonnay, Chenin Blanc, Late Harvest Viognier, Pinot Noir, Syrah, Merlot, Cabernet Franc, Cabernet Sauvignon, Sangiovese. Owners/winemakers: Richard Doré and Bill Wathen. Cases: 12,000. Acres: 10.

❧ *Foxen Vineyard, 7200 Foxen Canyon Road, Santa Maria 93454; (805) 937-4251, fax (805) 937-0415; www.foxenvineyard.com. Open 11:00 a.m.–4:00 p.m. Thursday–Monday in winter, daily in summer. Tasting fee: $3–$5 per glass, and you keep the glass. Visa, MasterCard, American Express. Wheelchair accessible.*

As you follow Foxen Canyon Road northward toward Santa Maria, your next wine-tasting stop is RANCHO SISQUOC WINERY, 15 miles east of Santa Maria. Rancho Sisquoc, part of an old Mexican land grant, shows its historic connections with its unpretentious, environmentally sensitive facilities. The surroundings of this excellent winery on the Sisquoc River include 37,000 acres of green pastures, cattle, and farm purchased in 1952 by San Franciscan James Flood.

Nestled above the Sisquoc River, Rancho Sisquoc's is the only vineyard in the Santa Maria Valley that is frost free. Harold Pfeiffer first made wine here in 1972 for private consumption and as a marketing tool to convince other wineries that quality fruit could be grown in the Santa Maria Valley. The winery opened to the public in 1977 and won many awards in the 1990s. The tasting room is built of heavy, dark, barn siding wood. Terra-cotta pots of colorful flowers are tastefully placed among shade trees. Bring a picnic.

The historic San Ramon Chapel overlooks the entrance to the ranch and adorns every wine label of Rancho Sisquoc. We highly recommend a trek to Rancho Sisquoc, but there's just one problem: You won't want to leave.

Fine points: Featured wines: Chardonnay, Sauvignon Blanc, Sylvaner, Riesling, Malbec, Pinot Noir, Syrah, Cabernet Franc, Merlot, Cabernet Sauvignon, Cellar Select Meritage. Owner: The Flood Ranch Company. Winemaker: Alec Franks. Cases: 10,000. Acres: 320 acres planted of 37,000.

RANCHO SISQUOC WINERY, SANTA MARIA

🍃 *Rancho Sisquoc Winery, 6600 Foxen Canyon Road, Santa Maria 93454; (805) 934-4332, fax (805) 937-6601; www.ranchosisquoc.com. Open 10:00 a.m.–4:00 p.m. daily. Tasting fee: $5, includes a glass. Visa, MasterCard, American Express. Wheelchair accessible.*

As you leave Foxen or Rancho Sisquoc, you have to return to Foxen Canyon Road and head north on it all the way to Santa Maria Mesa Road (Tepusquet Road is washed out). When you get to the intersection, turn sharply back on Santa Maria Mesa Road to Cambria Winery. If you are approaching from Santa Maria, take the Batteravia Road exit east from US 101, follow it around to the right, and visit Cottonwood Canyon before you arrive at the Santa Maria Mesa Road turnoff.

As we continue northward, turn right onto Santa Maria Mesa Road to Cambria. Turn left up Chardonnay Lane when you see the Cambria signs.

CAMBRIA WINERY & VINEYARDS, the hugely advertised and publicized winery, is open only on weekends, so plan accordingly. This part of the Santa Maria Valley was named by native Indians for the natural copper deposits found nearby. Originally called *tepuztli* (later changed accidentally to *tepuzque,* meaning copper coin), the area was renamed Cambria, the Roman word for Wales, by nineteenth-century English and Welsh settlers.

Part of an 1838 Mexican land grant, Rancho Tepusquet was used for raising cattle and row crops through the 1900s. Pioneer grape farmers planted vines here in the 1970s, and Chardonnays from the unique soils of the Santa Maria Bench produced exceptionally flavorful wines. Buyers included Ridge, Acacia, ZD, Beringer, and Kendall-Jackson. In 1987 Jess Jackson of Kendall-Jackson and other wine ventures bought Tepusquet Vineyard, now known as the Cambria Estate Vineyard. Cambria boasts "the longest, coldest wine grape growing season in California, which enables our fruit to develop rich, intense character."

A truly "woman-friendly place," Cambria's owner, winemaker, and tasting-room manager are all women. Owner Barbara Banke named her Chardonnay and Pinot Noir vineyards after her daughters, Katherine and Julia. Winemaker Denise Shurtleff served as winemaker at Corbett Canyon Vineyards prior to joining Cambria.

Fine points: Featured wines: Chardonnay, Viognier, Pinot Noir, Syrah. Owner: Barbara Banke. Winemaker: Denise Shurtleff. Cases: 120,000 9-liter cases. Acres: 1,400.

Cambria Winery & Vineyards, 5475 Chardonnay Lane, Santa Maria 93454; (805) 937-8091, fax (805) 934-3589; www.cambriawines.com. Open 10:00 a.m.–5:00 p.m. daily. Tasting fee: $5, includes glass. Visa, MasterCard, American Express. Wheelchair accessible.

A little farther south on Santa Maria Mesa Road are Byron Vineyard & Winery and IO, which are now only open to the public by appointment. For information call (805) 937-7288.

To get to COTTONWOOD CANYON VINEYARD & WINERY from Cambria Winery, go back on Santa Maria Mesa Road to Foxen Canyon Road and turn right. Then turn a doubling-back left at a little fork onto Dominion Road, and signs will lead you to Cottonwood Canyon's green metal building and 5,600 square feet of caves.

Former computer graphics executive Norman Beko bought this property in 1988 and developed its interesting Burgundy-style wines in the tradition of Montrachet, specializing in Pinot Noir and Chardonnay. Norman likens his winemaking to raising children: "nourishing individual characteristics and developing the natural (but different) qualities of each separately."

Stop by to enjoy the wine, the newly remodeled winery and tasting room with two wine bars, and the lovely lawn, patio, and picnic area.

Fine points: Featured wines: Chardonnay, Pinot Noir, Syrah, Cabernet Franc, Bordeaux blends. Owner and winemaker: Norman Beko. Cases: 4,000. Acres: 50 planted of 78.

Cottonwood Canyon Vineyard & Winery, 3940 Dominion Road, Santa Maria 93454; (805) 937-9063, fax (805) 937-8418; www.cotton

woodcanyon.com. Open 10:30 a.m.–5:30 p.m. daily. Tasting fee: $5 for current releases, $7 for reserves. Visa, MasterCard, American Express. Wheelchair accessible.

SANTA MARIA

One of the main things to do in Santa Maria is eat, particularly if you are here on a weekend. Famous for its tri-tip barbecues, Santa Maria takes its tradition from the Old West days when the rancheros and cowboys would gather under the towering oak trees for Spanish barbecues. The tradition has become a pleasant obsession and weekend ritual. Every Saturday and Sunday, charity volunteers, vendors, and restaurants pull out their barbecues—from hibachis to gas barbies on wheels to huge movable pits—and sizzle succulent tri-tip or top sirloin to join the pinquito beans and salsa, tossed fresh green salad, and toasted sweet French bread to create a mouthwatering festival. The whole town smells like barbecue.

Although it is difficult to find the center of Santa Maria because shopping centers have created several subcenters, you don't have to worry on barbecue days. All the shopping center parking lots along Broadway are full of barbecues and barbecuers.

Santa Maria barbecue consists of prime top sirloin, about 3 inches thick, cooked over a fire of coals from Santa Maria Valley red oak wood. Salt, pepper, and garlic salt are the only seasonings used, but they are used a lot. The steaks are strung on flat steel rods, which are gradually lowered over a bed of red-hot coals for about forty-five minutes. The meat is sliced at the pit and served in large stainless-steel pans by waiters. You get to choose your preferred doneness. The bread is used to "dip up" the juice from the serving pan. This may be heaven, carnivores!

Santa Maria is also well known for its strawberry and flower fields. Plan to attend the annual strawberry festival the fourth weekend in April to enjoy music, carnival, entertainment, and, of course, strawberries in every presentation imaginable (at the Santa Maria Fairgrounds, 805-925-8824). Another worthwhile annual event is the Obon Festival featuring Santa Maria's diverse populations, with Japanese foods, arts, and traditions, also at the fairgrounds.

According to our good friend Gordon Phillips, formerly acting city attorney for Santa Maria, the absolute best place in Santa Maria for coffee, salads, and sandwiches is CAFE MONET, which duplicates itself in Lompoc.

The menu is simple and good. Lots of espresso drinks for every taste, chai, and passion fruit iced tea, along with very special sandwiches available by whole ($4.99) or half ($2.49). They range from the San Pedro Costa Rica with smoked turkey, ham, red onions, tomato, Swiss and cheddar cheese, and sprouts on wheat bread to tri-tip with Swiss cheese, veggie, garlic chicken breast, pastrami, and basil or almond chicken salad. You can also indulge in bagels, cold burrito wraps, and heated filled croissants, plus great soups or soup and half sandwich ($5.85).

❧ *Cafe Monet, 1555 South Broadway, Santa Maria 93454; (805) 928-1912. Open 6:30 a.m.–6:00 p.m. Monday–Friday, 7:00 a.m.–5:00 p.m. Saturday, 8:00 a.m.–5:00 p.m. Sunday. Visa, MasterCard, American Express. Wheelchair accessible.*

The fine Pacific Conservatory of the Performing Arts, which also performs in Solvang, plays here year-round at the Santa Maria Civic Theater in Building D of Alan Hancock College, 800 South College Drive, on the Bradley road side of campus. Call (805) 922-8313 for schedules and reservations.

At the SANTA MARIA HISTORICAL SOCIETY MUSEUM you can enjoy Chumash Indian culture and artifacts of the Mission Rancho and Pioneer periods, and even the Barbecue Hall of Fame!

❧ *Santa Maria Historical Society Museum, 616 South Broadway, Santa Maria 93454; (805) 922-3130. Open noon–5:00 p.m. Tuesday–Saturday. Free admission. Wheelchair accessible.*

There are farmers' markets on Tuesday morning at Oak Knoll South in Orcutt, and on Wednesday afternoon at Heritage Walk at Town Center West shopping center.

Military and air buffs might enjoy visits to the Santa Maria Museum of Flight at the Santa Maria Airport (805-922-8758) or to Vandenberg Air Force Base (805-734-8232, ext. 63595).

LOS ALAMOS

Los Alamos is one of our favorite 1-block western towns and is getting even better. One of many people's favorite wineries, BEDFORD THOMPSON, has moved its tasting room to "downtown" Los Alamos where Nick's Pizza used to bake. Owner/winemaker Stephan Bedford will continue to make wine at his super-natural winery location, surrounded by rows of organic vegetables and vineyards. Stephan has also served as winemaker at Rancho Sisquoc and consults to other wineries.

Fine points: Featured wines: Pinot Gris, Chardonnay, Dry Gewürztraminer, Cabernet Franc, Grenache, Mourvedre, Syrah, Petite Sirah. Owner and winemaker: Stephan Bedford. Cases: 6,000. Acres: all estate and other local fruit.

꙳ ***Bedford Thompson Winery & Vineyard,*** *448 Bell Street, Los Alamos 93440; (805) 344-2107, fax: (805) 344-2047; www.bedfordthompsonwinery.com. Open 11:00 a.m.–5:00 p.m. daily. Tasting fee: $5. Visa and MasterCard. Wheelchair accessible.*

At press time, the Los Alamos landmark Union Hotel was closed for financial and other problems. Never fear, there are at least a couple of worth-the-trip

---

PYRENEES BEAN SOUP
*from Bedford Thompson Winery and Vineyard,
Los Alamos*

½ cup olive oil or duck fat
6 cloves garlic, crushed
1 onion, coarsely chopped
1 Tbs. fresh rosemary, rubbed
1 potato, coarsely chopped
1 piquillo pepper, roasted and finely chopped
1 sweet red pepper, roasted and coarsely chopped
2 cups Buttonwood Farms white beans
8 cups vegetable stock
2 cups Bedford Thompson Cabernet Franc
1 Tbs. sea salt
1 tsp. toasted black pepper
½ cup porcini mushrooms, sliced thin
½ cup black olives, pitted and chopped
hard cheese, crumbled

Heat oil in iron pot over high heat. Add garlic, onion, and rosemary, and sauté a few minutes. Add potato and peppers, and cook a few minutes more. Add beans, vegetable stock, and Cabernet Franc along with the salt and black pepper. Cook on low for 2 hours and add mushrooms. When the beans are just tender (about another 45 minutes), add the olives. Leave on heat for 15 minutes more. Serve with some hard cheese crumbled on top. Serves 6.

eateries in this little town: Café Quackenbush in the small and quaint General Store complex, and American Flatbread/Hearth in the Cottonwoods restaurant, which is only open Friday and Saturday evenings.

CAFÉ QUACKENBUSH makes outstanding sandwiches such as solid white albacore tuna, BLT, roasted peppers with goat cheese, oven-roasted turkey, smoked pork loin, roast beef with Danish blue cheese, and smoked salmon with honey-mustard caper sauce. Carnivores may enjoy the 10-oz. hamburger with sharp Vermont cheddar or blue cheese. Breakfast delights include a unique sweet potato chicken hash and a chicken sausage scramble with goat cheese. ($7.95–$15.95).

The General Store complex and the cafe have loads of art, antiques, and collectible stuff available either for perusal or purchase.

Café Quackenbush, 458 Bell Street, Los Alamos 93440; (805) 344-5181; www.generalstoreca.com. Open 7:00 a.m.–5:00 p.m. Tuesday–Sunday. Visa and MasterCard.

AMERICAN FLATBREAD/HEARTH IN THE COTTONWOODS RESTAURANT only opens Friday and Saturday evenings, which rarity and quality draws folks from Los Angeles who drive up for the organic flatbreads, extensive local wine list, and ales.

Based on traditional flatbreads in New England, American Flatbread tops their flatbreads with whatever is fresh in the local farmers' market, "from local soil into local hands to our hearth."

Two adventurous organic local ingredient salads ($3) start the meal. All flatbreads are made with 100 percent Certified Organic wheat flour. Ten-inch flatbreads easily fill one person, and the 15-incher works well for two.

You will find other healthful ingredients such as grapeseed oil, organic flaxseed, rosemary, Three Sisters raw milk Serena cheese, organic tomatoes, roasted corn and black beans, smoke-dried tomatoes, nitrate-free pepperoni, and fennel sausage. (Flatbreads $4–$19.)

American Flatbread/Hearth in the Cottonwoods, 225 Bell Street, Los Alamos 93440; (805) 344-4400; www.foodremembers.com. Open 5:00–10:00 p.m. Friday and Saturday nights. Beer and wine. Visa, MasterCard, American Express. Wheelchair accessible.

Be sure to walk around Los Alamos to discover its antiques stores, art galleries, and general stores, as well as the Los Alamos Depot Mall and standard Twin Oaks Restaurant.

CHAPTER 5

SAN LUIS OBISPO COUNTY: THE INTERIOR

irst of all, let's get the pronunciation straight: San lou-WISS Obispo, **not** *San lou-EE Obispo. Locals get goose bumps and peg visitors as tourists when they hear the latter.*

San Luis Obispo County runs east from the Pacific Ocean between Los Padres National Forest and Santa Barbara County to the south and the Santa Lucia Mountain range and Monterey County to the north. It has 80 miles of pristine beaches and coastline to die for. The county's northern border is 190 miles south of San Francisco, and its southern border is 190 miles north of Los Angeles, so it is truly the central coast of California.

Its major city is San Luis Obispo, followed by Paso Robles, Templeton, Atascadero, and the coastal towns of Pismo Beach, Morro Bay, Cambria, and San Simeon, near which is Hearst Castle. (We visit the coastal towns in chapter 6.)

San Luis Obispo County is generally much more laid-back and much less Hollywood than Santa Barbara County, and you are much less likely to run into movie stars or glitz here. Dress is always casual. Both the city and county of San Luis Obispo take their name from the 1772 Mission San Luis Obispo de Tolosa, named by the missionaries in honor of fourteenth-century Saint Louis, bishop of Toulouse in France.

Most of San Luis Obispo County's wineries are in the Paso Robles area, although there are excellent ones in the Edna Valley south of San Luis Obispo. In chapter 7 we take you to all those that are open to the public for tasting.

To get to San Luis Obispo, take Highway 1 or U.S. Highway 101 from the north or south, and Highways 46, 41, or 166 from the east. Our travel pattern was from north to south. If you are arriving from south of here, just reverse our order.

As you come from the north, you first see the Camp Roberts California National Guard complex of light green buildings that actually straddle the Monterey/San Luis Obispo county lines.

CAMP ROBERTS HISTORICAL MUSEUM is open to the public, on the military base, which is partly shut down, and partly deserted for the Iraq war. Camp Roberts has been an Army training center since World War II, and the museum itself began life as a home for the American Red Cross. Find collections of uniforms, insignia, weapons, equipment, and yearbooks, and a reference library.

Camp Roberts Historical Museum, Camp Roberts off US 101, Camp Roberts 93451; (805) 238-8288; www.militarymuseum.org/CampRobertsMuseum.html. Open 9:00 a.m.–4:00 p.m. Thursday and Saturday. Free admission. Wheelchair accessible.

Be sure to follow the US 101 exit signs for a brief visit to San Miguel, a ghost town 7 miles north of Paso Robles whose main claim to fame is the well-preserved MISSION SAN MIGUEL ARCANGEL. The mission suffered severe damage in the December 2003 earthquake, but parts of it have already reopened. You can enter San Miguel at one end of "town" and get back on US 101 at the other end, so just make a sweep and stop at the mission most people miss.

Mission San Miguel was founded in 1797 by Father Fermin de Lasuen, father presidente of all the missions of Alta California; Father Buenaventura Sitjar of the Mission San Antonio de Padua; and eight soldiers in the Indian village called Vahca, whose original settlers slaved and sweated to build the mission buildings.

MISSION SAN MIGUEL ARCANGEL, SAN MIGUEL

In August 1806 a huge fire destroyed two rows of buildings and part of the church roof, originally built of straw and rebuilt with tile. The mission's baptismal register shows 2,892 baptisms (of Indians) and 2,249 deaths of those "sleeping in the crowded little cemetery." The stone foundation of the church you see today was laid in 1816, and the interior decorations were designed by Esteban Munras. The mission was secularized in 1836, the Indians ran away, and Governor Pio Pico sold it for $600 to Petronillo Rios and Englishman William Reed, who had married Maria Antonia Vallejo (see page 238). Eventually the mission was confiscated, and after the Civil War it was returned to the Catholic Church.

Since 1928, Mission San Miguel has been run by the founding Franciscan padres, who still run a parish church, novitiate, and retreat house. It stands as one of the best-preserved California missions and has a great loaded gift shop. *Mission San Miguel Arcangel, 775 Mission Street, San Miguel 93451; (805) 467-3256. Open 9:30 a.m.–4:30 p.m. (tour closes 4:15 p.m.). Admission: $2 per person or family. Visa and MasterCard. Mostly wheelchair accessible.*

Now get back on US 101 and take the Twenty-fourth Street exit to Paso Robles. The Twenty-fourth Street exit becomes Nacimiento Lake Road to, you guessed it, Lake Nacimiento, the county's top water sports center for waterskiing, boating, fishing, swimming, camping, and hiking. Call (805) 238-3256 for information.

PASO ROBLES

Paso Robles is much like it used to be when it was a Wild West hot-and-dusty farming town, except now a few fabulous restaurants have sprung up on the east side of City Park and the city has spiffed up quite a bit. Unfortunately, Paso Robles was damaged by a severe earthquake in December 2003 but has made a miraculous recovery, adding loads of convenient winery tasting rooms.

The average temperature here in the summer is 94°F, which means that there are many days over 100°F—in fact several in the 110°F range, with an average of 315 sunny days a year. Unless you really thrive on the heat or have excellent air-conditioning in your car, we suggest you visit this interior part of San Luis Obispo County in any season but summer. Late February and March are ideal: The temperature is 70°F and the speed limit is 70. The rolling hills are even green briefly.

Paso Robles is a Main Street city with wide dusty streets, and just the basics and a few frills available, a central park plaza, and lots of fast foods. But there are some treasures, both historic and culinary.

If you get off US 101 at Twenty-fourth Street, you first come to GOOD OL' BURGERS, a local fixture and hangout for everyone from vintners to mayors to highway patrolmen. It's in a small strip mall along with Starbucks. As you walk inside to order, you see a glass refrigerator with large meatball-like ovals that get squished into being your juicy, delicious hamburger, colorfully called the Coyote, Ranch Hand, or Roundup. The last includes three patties, causing it to be the most expensive thing on the menu. Kathleen prefers the Yardbird, a tasty grilled chicken breast on a wheat bun. You must, absolutely must, indulge in the "tator strips" (fries) and "wagon wheels," huge, hand-dipped onion rings (small of each is plenty to share). The shakes are thick, real, and simple—vanilla, chocolate, and strawberry ($2.50–$5.75). Great for kids, too.

Every winemaker or worker whose dining opinion we asked said, "You gotta try Good Ol' Burgers." We agree. One of our favorites.

Good Ol' Burgers, 1145 Twenty-fourth Street, Paso Robles 93446; (805) 238-0655. Open 10:00 a.m.–9:00 p.m. Monday–Thursday, 10:00 a.m.–10:00 p.m. Friday and Saturday. Beer. No credit cards. Wheelchair accessible.

Paso Robles is truly horse country. Arabian horse ranches and vineyards now surround Paso Robles, replacing the cattle with more lucrative "crops." Every spring, acres of almond orchards explode with whitish-pink blossoms around the town, once the "Almond Capital of the World" and still a true farming center where farmers come into town for supplies. The town center is City Park, even though it is no longer in the center of town. A multiplex movie theater assures the downtown will survive, and we have a few favorite restaurants nearby whose secrets we will share with you. Vine Street is loaded with gorgeous Victorian-era homes worth checking out. Antiques stores show up on every little side street, and there aren't many.

To the east side of the park on Pine Street are Bistro Laurent and Villa Creek restaurants, with Odyssey Culinary Provisions Cafe & Marketplace in the next block. Also check out Alloro and Buona Tavola, also in this area.

Paso Robles folks definitely turned a bad thing into an extremely good thing following their super earthquake, taking advantage of broken storefronts, rebuilding and filling them with tasting rooms for smaller and coastal wineries visitors normally wouldn't reach.

Around Paso Robles's town square, there are twelve tasting rooms for wineries, cheese, and olives, and many local products to explore. You will find local pistachios and almonds; dried apple chips; Pasolivo and all sorts of local and imported extra virgin olive oils; Mill Road wine grape juice, apple cider and vinegars; and local baked goods.

Wineries represented around the square and side streets include Anglim Winery, Arroyo Robles Winery, Bear Cave Cellars, Edward Sellars Winery, Hice Cellars, Midlife Crisis Winery, Orchid Hill Vineyard, Pianetta Winery, Silver Stone Wines, Vinoteca Wine Bar, Vista Creek Cellars, and The Wine Attic.

For your dining pleasure, here are a few restaurants within the same area.

BASIL THAI RESTAURANT brings real variety to downtown Paso Robles with excellent and creative Thai cuisine.

The Basil Platter of appetizers ($10) combines satay, fresh vegetable rolls, fried calamari, "golden bags," and Thai rolls, and is practically a meal for two. Follow it with your favorite noodles, seafood, curry, Volcano Chicken, fried rice, and veggie specials ($5–$16). One of our favorites.

❧ *Basil Thai Restaurant, 828 Eleventh Street (south side of square), Paso Robles 93446; (805) 238-9945. Open 11:00 a.m.–3:00 p.m. and 5:00–10:00 p.m. daily. Beer and wine. Visa, MasterCard, American Express, Discover. Wheelchair accessible.*

VILLA CREEK RESTAURANT & BAR, on Pine Street, is a real center of local fun, umbrella drinks, and good California Mexican food, all with windows opening onto Paso Robles's town square. Enjoy the cool, cavernous, and colorful atmosphere indoors, or dine in back on the patio (shade in the afternoon and evening) on organic or sustainably farmed foods.

Villa Creek's updated menu includes starters of an artisanal cheese plate, shepherds plate, hummus, and grilled vegetables ($7–$13). Chopped chicken salad, hearts of romaine with buttermilk blue cheese and pecans, and a caramelized onion and Gruyere tart fill out the salads ($10).

Lunch includes ample sandwiches that come with house-cut fries or salads, huge burgers and chicken sandwiches, and carnitas (pulled pork) tacos (under $12). Dinner brings additions of lardon salad with a poached quail egg, country pâté, slow-cooked shrimp, veal chops, brick-roasted chicken, buffalo rib eye steak, ahi tuna, and enchiladas ($26–$30).

❧ *Villa Creek Restaurant & Bar, 1144 Pine Street, Paso Robles 93466; (805) 238-3000; www.villacreek.com. Open 11:30 a.m.–2:00 p.m. Tuesday–Friday, 10:00 a.m.–2:00 p.m. Saturday brunch, and 5:00–10:00 p.m. daily; bar opens at 4:00 p.m. Visa, MasterCard, American Express. Wheelchair accessible.*

Another favorite of ours and most winery people is ODYSSEY CULINARY PROVISIONS CAFE & MARKETPLACE at Pine and Twelfth Streets on the northeast corner of the park. This is definitely the best place to pick up picnic supplies in Paso Robles if you plan to enjoy a picnic at a winery or enjoy the cafe ambience right here.

Odyssey prepares deliciously healthy rotisserie take-home chickens by the half ($8.99) or whole ($15.99 with three sides), and salads by the pound ($8.99). Marvelous sandwiches include roasted eggplant, peppers, artichoke hearts, and chèvre on baguette ($8.99), baked Brie or raclette and artichoke on pane pugliese, and roast Brie with chèvre and pesto on Parmesan sourdough ($8.99). All of these come with soup or salad—Greek, Caesar, balsamic potato, penne pasta, Thai pasta, mixed greens, or tabbouleh. Unbelievable! Wrap fans will enjoy choices from Indian curried chicken to Mediterranean veggie ($8.99).

Try pastas or Oriental bowls.

❧ *Odyssey Culinary Provisions Cafe & Marketplace, 1214 Pine Street, Paso Robles 93466; (805) 237-7516, fax (805) 237-7514; www.odysseyworldcafe.com. Open 8:00 a.m.–7:30 p.m. Sunday–Thursday, 8:00 a.m.–9:30 p.m. Friday and Saturday. Beer and wine. Visa, MasterCard, American Express. Wheelchair accessible.*

PAPI'S TACOS & GORDITAS has to be the fine Mexican food find of the year. Although its beer and wine license was suspended briefly, it continues to serve crowds of locals constantly, from $3.95 complete breakfasts to scrumptious fajitas (one order serves two easily), great burgers and sandwiches, burritos, and gorditas (all under $8). This is the place where local Latinos send inquiring Anglos for the best Mexican food. Great salsa bar.

❧ *Papi's Tacos & Gorditas, 840 Thirteenth Street near Pine, Paso Robles 93446. Beer and wine, usually. Visa, MasterCard, American Express, Discover. Wheelchair accessible.*

BISTRO LAURENT, located at the northeast corner of the plaza, was Paso Robles's first French restaurant, and owner/chef Laurent Grangien's country French food still draws in the locals in mobs. Expect blue crab, sweetbreads, roasted quail, and seafood fricassee ($19.00–$34.50). Excellent wine list. Great for lunch or dinner.

❧ *Bistro Laurent, 1202 Pine Street, Paso Robles 93446; (805) 226-8191; www.fp.tcsn.net/bistro/laurent.htm. Open 11:30 a.m.–2:30 p.m. and 5:30–10:30 p.m. daily. Full bar. Visa, MasterCard, American Express. Wheelchair accessible.*

BUONA TAVOLA chef/owner Antonio Varia features northern Italian food at this northern outpost of his fabulous San Luis Obispo restaurant, known there as one of the best in town for antipasti, pasta, exquisite seafood, and wonderful desserts.

❧ *Buona Tavola, 943 Spring Street, Paso Robles 93446; (805) 237-0600. Open 11:30 a.m.–2:30 p.m. Monday–Friday and 5:30–10:00 p.m. daily. Beer and wine. Visa, MasterCard, American Express, Discover. Wheelchair accessible.*

Significant historic buildings in Paso Robles include the recently restored PASO ROBLES INN on the west side of City Park at 1103 Spring Street. The first hotel at this site was built in 1864 and had a wide reputation, attracting movie stars; pianist and Polish Premier Ignace Jan Paderewski, who lived in Paso Robles; and even the Pittsburgh Pirates baseball team. That hotel burned down in 1940. Although the newest incarnation was damaged in the December 2003 earthquake, it has risen again with new buildings, gorgeous gardens and pool, and a great old-fashioned dining room.

The Shell gasoline station next door has "the largest newsstand between San Francisco and Santa Barbara," featuring 1,900 titles!

The PASO ROBLES CARNEGIE HISTORY LIBRARY MUSEUM was designed by W. H. Weeks and completed in 1908 with Andrew Carnegie's $10,000 gift. It now houses a historical museum with rotating exhibits of local and natural history. Also enjoy the Carnegie Western Art Gallery in the basement.

❧ *Paso Robles Carnegie History Library Museum, 1000 Spring Street, Paso Robles 93446; (805) 238-4996. Open 1:00–4:00 p.m. Wednesday–Sunday. Free admission. Not wheelchair accessible.*

The Granary at 1111 Riverside was built in 1890 and sold to the Sperry Milling Company for flour production and storage. Its steam generator served as Paso Robles's first electric power plant. The Granary later served to store grain and in 1992 it was restored and developed by Newlin Hastings as a collection of retail shops, restaurants, and offices.

EL PASO DE ROBLES AREA PIONEER MUSEUM is a fabulous locally curated museum that features displays of farm equipment, including the West's largest display of barbed wire; a school classroom replica; old pay telephones; an historical display of cattlewomen's pariphernalia; carriages; Paderewski memorabilia; Indian artifacts; and unusual household wares depicting life in mid-1880s Paso Robles. The museum hosts "Paso Gathering" the first weekend in November, featuring saddle makers, rawhide braiders, bit and spur makers, horsehair hitchers, silversmiths, and Dutch-oven cooking. (Admission $3.)

❧ *El Paso de Robles Area Pioneer Museum, 2010 Riverside Avenue, Paso Robles 93446; (805) 239-4556; www.pasoroblespioneermuseum.org. Open 1:00–4:00 p.m. Thursday–Sunday. Wheelchair accessible.*

Estrella War Birds Museum displays historic aircraft, vehicles, and memorabilia from World Wars I and II at Paso Robles Municipal Airport. It is also known as the Estrella Squadron of the Confederate Air Force Museum! *Estrella War Birds Museum, 4251 Dry Creek Road, Paso Robles 93446; (805) 227-0440. Open 10:00 a.m.–4:00 p.m. Saturday, noon–3:00 p.m. Sunday. Free admission. Wheelchair accessible.*

A farmers' market is held twice weekly at Twelfth and Park Streets: Tuesday from 9:30 a.m. to 12:30 p.m. and Friday from 4:00 to 7:00 p.m.

TEMPLETON

We strongly encourage you to take the Main Street exit off US 101 just south of Paso Robles to Templeton, a marvelous little relic of the Wild West towns. The current center of activity is across from the granary at McPhee's Grill, the baby of Ian McPhee, creator of Ian's in Cambria, and Dr. Stan Hoffman. A room honors wine guru André Tchelistcheff, the late and revered winemaking consultant to Hoffman's winery.

Ian came to San Luis Obispo County on a football scholarship to California Polytechnic and basically never left. He went home for his first college Thanksgiving and Christmas and then started pleading that his "car broke down" every year after that. Now he is firmly planted in his popular eatery that no one should miss, if only for the fun experience.

Once an 1860s general store, the restaurant still conveys respect for that colorful history, with unique photos toward the back near the restrooms. You can't miss them as you go to the back patio to enjoy your meal at the wrought-iron chairs and tables. The booths have black-and-white checked upholstery, and dark-flowered virgin vinyl tablecloths cover the tables.

The food is exciting, creative, and hearty—vintners, ranchers, and local gossips and historians pack the place every day. We happened in for the Sunday brunch, an ideal way to sample McPhee's wide array of expertise. The antique bar, which serves as a buffet table at brunch, is laden with the finest smoked-here salmon ever, pastas, potatoes, beans green and brown, baby asparagus, and gorgeous salads. After you make however many trips you choose for the salad and appetizer course, you go to the kitchen window to make your selection of hot entree. We enjoyed roasted lamb and even waker-upper chorizo and eggs. All of this with champagne or softer drinks and your choice(s) from the dessert tray. Drop by for lunch for tempura shrimp; Ian's (huge) salad with Point Reyes Blue Cheese; lump crab, bay shrimp, and avocado chopped salad; and an American

DOWNTOWN TEMPLETON

Kobe beef hamburger with grilled onions and perfect, crispy shoestring potatoes ($13.00–$17.00). Lunches are big enough to share ($5.00 charge). Dinner is even better, with entrees priced at $13.95–$48.00. One of our favorites. McPhee's house wines are made by Jim Clendenen of Au Bon Climat.

McPhee's Grill, 416 Main Street, Templeton 93465; (805) 434-3204; www.mcphees.com. Open for lunch 11:30 a.m.–2:00 p.m. daily (buffet brunch Sunday), dinner from 4:30 p.m. Beer and wine. Visa and MasterCard. Wheelchair accessible via back patio and door.

Be sure to walk next door to Hermann's Chocolate Lab for amazing hand-made candies, truffles, and other sweets. Also check out Changala Winery's little tasting bar, which is inside Hermann's, for a tasting of its Viognier, Syrah, Cabernet Sauvignon, and Zinfandel. Try them with the chocolates! Down at the corner is **A. J. Spurs Saloon & Dining Hall**, voted Best North County Restaurant for seven years. Indeed it is popular Wild West, with good drinks, those famous barbecue steaks, ribs, seafood, and pasta, and what they call "fine Western dining" ($16.99–$28.99). Go ahead and ride up on your Harley, and stride right in, boots, spurs, and all.

A. J. Spurs Saloon & Dining Hall, 508 Main Street, Templeton 93465; (805) 434-2700; www.ajspurs.com/templeton.html. Open 4:00–9:30 p.m. daily (also in Buellton at 350 Highway 246 East). Full bar (in both meanings). Visa and MasterCard. Wheelchair accessible.

Both of these restaurants are convenient to wine tasting. We will eventually bring you back here on our wine-tasting loop. Wine barrels at a few Templeton-area wineries broke during the December 2003 earthquake, sending wasted wine down the drain. You should still be sure to visit, however, to try the excellent remaining wines as well as to hear interesting earthquake stories.

ATASCADERO

Best known to the outside world for its state prison, Atascadero is an up-and-coming city attracting loads of Californians because of reasonable real estate prices, good climate, and good shopping at the Atascadero factory outlet stores. Downtown offers sunken gardens and a local museum.

Visitors also enjoy the forty-plus-year-old Charles Paddock Zoo, the only zoo in San Luis Obispo County. Just 1.5 miles west of US 101 on Highway 41, one hundred animals dwell on five acres near Atascadero Lake, where you can hike, bike, picnic, paddleboat, fish, or just feed the ducks and geese. Every Tuesday evening in summer, locals and visitors enjoy free concerts at Lakeside Pavilion.

Just south of Atascadero near the top of Cuesta Grade is the tiny town of Santa Margarita, an antiques devotee's heaven, with loads of shops and a twice-monthly auction at the Santa Margarita Antique Auction Barn.

There's a farmers' market on Wednesday from 3:00 to 6:00 p.m. in the Rite-Aid parking lot at Highway 41 and El Camino Real. For more information on what the area has to offer, contact the Atascadero Chamber of Commerce, 6550 El Camino Real, Atascadero 93422; (805) 466-2044, fax (805) 466-9218; www.atascaderochamber.org.

DOWNTOWN SAN LUIS OBISPO

If we were to move to the central coast, it would probably be to San Luis Obispo. We love it. It seems to have a perfect mix for us: smallish-town atmosphere; big-city conveniences; an excellent, highly reputed university with all the cultural benefits that go with it; a diverse community; a real feeling of community; contained growth; environmental sensitivity; fabulous climate; and good, creative restaurants. When do we go?!

The city of San Luis Obispo began when Father Junipero Serra founded Mission San Luis Obispo de Tolosa in 1772, halfway between what are now Los Angeles and San Francisco. The community evolved into a farming and cattle-raising center in the 1840s, a dairy-farming center in the 1870s, an educational center from 1901, and a military and wine center later. The city began to boom

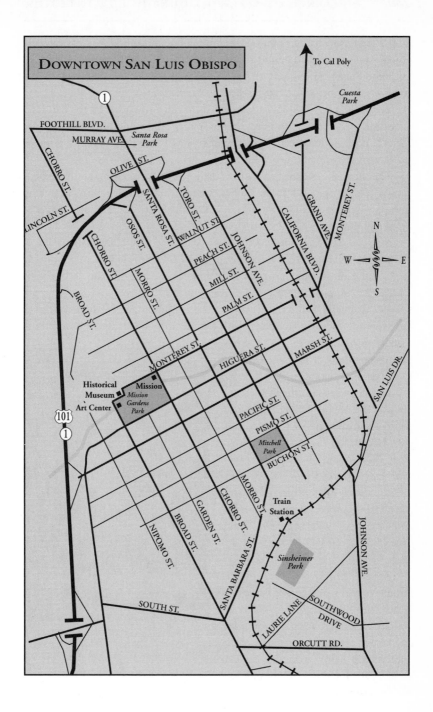

Downtown San Luis Obispo

To Cal Poly

Cuesta Park

FOOTHILL BLVD.

MURRAY AVE.

Santa Rosa Park

OLIVE ST.

CHORRO ST.

LINCOLN ST.

SANTA ROSA ST.

CHORRO ST.

OSOS ST.

MORRO ST.

BROAD ST.

TORO ST.

WALNUT ST.

PEACH ST.

MILL ST.

PALM ST.

JOHNSON AVE.

CALIFORNIA BLVD.

GRAND AVE.

MONTEREY ST.

N
W   E
S

MONTEREY ST.

HIGUERA ST.

MARSH ST.

SAN LUIS DR.

Historical Museum

Art Center

Mission

Mission Gardens Park

101
1

PACIFIC ST.

PISMO ST.

Mitchell Park

BUCHON ST.

NIPOMO ST.

BROAD ST.

GARDEN ST.

CHORRO ST.

MORRO ST.

SANTA BARBARA ST.

Train Station

JOHNSON AVE.

Sinsheimer Park

SOUTH ST.

LAURIE LANE

SOUTHWOOD DRIVE

ORCUTT RD.

in 1894 with the arrival of the Southern Pacific Railroad. In 1901 a vocational school was established, and it grew into the highly respected California Polytechnic State University (Cal Poly). The green lines in the streets guide you to historical points of interest on the Path of History.

Today the mission is still the center of town, surrounded by the San Luis Obispo Art Center, the San Luis Obispo County Historical Museum in the former Carnegie Library, cafes and restaurants, and San Luis Obispo's primary downtown shopping area.

The mission, restored between 1930 and 1934, houses an extensive collection of photos, artifacts, tools, clothes, artwork, and other displays, as well as newspaper clippings about the area's pioneers. The gift shop sells loads of religious and mission history memorabilia and books.

MISSION SAN LUIS OBISPO DE TOLOSA was the fifth built in the chain of twenty-one California missions. Built of adobe bricks made by local Chumash Indians, the mission still functions as a Catholic church at the base of Monterey Street at Chorro Street. Mission Plaza, which is bordered by the San Luis Obispo County Historical Museum and the Murray Adobe, functions as a true community gathering place, with festivals throughout the year and foot-bridges to adjoining cafes and shops.

Restroom alert! There are excellent clean public restrooms right here in Mission Plaza between the mission and the art center, across from the historical museum. Treat them well.

Mission San Luis Obispo de Tolosa, 751 Palm Street at Monterey Street, San Luis Obispo 93401; (805) 543-6850; www.missionsanluisobispo.org. Open 9:00 a.m.–4:00 p.m. in winter, 9:00 a.m.–5:00 p.m. in summer. Mostly wheelchair accessible.

Across from the mission at Monterey and Broad Streets is the SAN LUIS OBISPO ART CENTER, a true community art center where you can view the best of the area's local amateur and professional artists' work. Be sure to drop by for rotating exhibits and class and lecture schedules.

FATHER JUNIPERO SERRA STATUE AT MISSION SAN LUIS OBISPO DE TOLOSA, SAN LUIS OBISPO

❧ *San Luis Obispo Art Center, 1010 Broad Street, P.O. Box 813, San Luis Obispo 93401; (805) 543-8562, fax (805) 543-4518; www.sloartcenter.org. Open 11:00 a.m.–5:00 p.m. Wednesday–Monday, daily in summer. Free admission. Wheelchair accessible.*

The SAN LUIS OBISPO COUNTY HISTORICAL MUSEUM tells local colorful history through changing displays of old photographs and artifacts. The impressive collection displayed in the former Carnegie Library (1904) ranges from Chumash and Salinan Indian artifacts and mission and ranch artifacts from the eighteenth and nineteenth centuries to a Victorian-era parlor, the lens from the lighthouse at Port San Luis, and a postal delivery wagon. We also found more fascinating local history books and booklets here than in any other store.

The building itself was designed by Watsonville, California, architect W. H. Weeks, and built by locals Stephens and Maino with a $10,000 grant from steel tycoon Andrew Carnegie. It is the only building in the county built with local sandstone and granite.

❧ *San Luis Obispo County Historical Museum, 696 Monterey Street, P.O. Box 1391, San Luis Obispo 93401; (805) 543-0638; www.slochs.org. Open 10:00 a.m.–4:00 p.m. Wednesday–Sunday. Free admission. Visa and MasterCard. Not wheelchair accessible.*

If the kids are along, skip right over to the unusual SAN LUIS OBISPO CHILDREN'S MUSEUM a block west and a block south of Mission Plaza at Monterey and Nipomo Streets. This is a hands-on, please-touch place for kids of all ages, with a special family fun day on Tuesday. Kids can race to the scene of a fire on the back of a fire engine, watch themselves on television, or careen down a dinosaur slide. Children under sixteen must be accompanied by an adult, and one adult is required for every four children. Great shop!

❧ *San Luis Obispo Children's Museum, 1010 Nipomo Street, San Luis Obispo 93401; (805) 544-KIDS; www.slokids.org. Open 11:00 a.m.–5:00 p.m. Tuesday– Saturday, noon–4:00 p.m. Sunday. Admission: $8 or sliding, children under two free. Visa and MasterCard. Wheelchair accessible.*

One of San Luis Obispo's most unifying and exciting community events is its somewhat famous FARMERS' MARKET every Thursday, catapulting the town into the weekend one day early! Four blocks of farmers and barbecue pits on wheels stir up delicious experiences and a way to encounter San Luis Obispo's culture.

Massive barbecues crank out grilled ribs, chicken, and even oysters. Local flower growers and cider pressers offer their specialties, along with jugglers, dancers, a one-man puppet show, musical performers, and other variously varied entertainers. Helium balloons appear to tie down booths selling everything from pizza to warm-from-the-oven aromatic cookies. Mascot Downtown Brown, a 7-foot pretend bear, mingles with the crowd, passing out bear hugs everywhere.

Just make your way to Higuera Street (pronounced here *hig-ARE-ah*) downtown. The street is closed off for 4 blocks, so park and walk or roll. Shops stay open until 9:00 p.m., and of course restaurants do, too.

✨ *Farmers' market, 4 blocks of Higuera Street, Business Improvement Association, P.O. Box 1402, San Luis Obispo 93406; (805) 541-0286; www.down townslo.com. Wheelchair accessible.*

The VETERANS MEMORIAL MUSEUM of the Central Coast houses a highly rated collection of military and war memorabilia, both men's and women's, from every American war since World War I, including uniforms and supplies from just-returned Iraq veterans. This is an excellent place to remember war, those who have served and given their lives, and, especially, peace.

✨ *Veterans Memorial Museum, 801 Grand Avenue, San Luis Obispo 93406; (805) 543-1763; www.vetsmuseum.org. Open 10:00 a.m.–3:00 p.m. Wednesday–Saturday. Free admission. Wheelchair accessible.*

We begin our own walking tour right at the mission, as we think you should and will. If you want to walk up the hill (north) 1 block to Palm Street, we encourage you to do so just to see the AH LOUIS STORE, California State Historical Landmark No. 802. If you don't want to hike up there, just join us below.

Ah Louis (Chinese name: Wong On) was the best-known merchant of San Luis Obispo's Chinatown, basically the 800 block of Palm Street. He served as unofficial mayor, postmaster, banker, and community center for the city's 2,000 Chinese laborers who built the railroad and its tunnels around here. Having arrived about 1870 to help his asthma, he first worked as a cook in the French Hotel, then as the foreman and employment agent of all the Chinese who worked for the Pacific Coast Railroad, as well as agent for Chinese quicksilver miners near Cambria. He then sold them all imported and local groceries and everything else they could need.

The Ah Louis Store sold pharmaceuticals, rice, peanut oil, sugar cane, hom don (salted duck eggs), hoy tom (sea cucumber), lop op (dried duck), hom yee (salted fish), dried abalone, oysters, canned fish, and a favorite cooling dessert, leong fun. The store's walls were lined with seventy-two drawers of Chinese herbal remedies, which Ah Louis dispensed after taking his customer's pulse to determine what was wrong. His son Howard continued the operation for many years, and the store is now a gift shop.

❧ *Ah Louis Store, 800 Palm Street, San Luis Obispo 93401; (805) 543-4332. Open "irregular hours." Visa and MasterCard. Not wheelchair accessible.*

If you do not want to make the trek up to Ah Louis, just continue with us from here in front of the mission. Take the new "Old SLO Trolley" around downtown. Signed stops are frequent and obvious.

AH LOUIS STORE, SAN LUIS OBISPO

We begin by heading south from the mission on the same (west) side of Chorro Street.

As you walk or roll, you will enjoy SLO Swim, if you're in the market for small bathing suits and big boards, and Unique Beads & Jewelry, which has great nostalgic beaded curtains and little booths in which to take your selections and create your own necklace. Next comes one of our favorites, and that of many locals, the Cowboy Cookie & Grub Co. for burritos, quiche, hot dogs, and, yes, cookies. Bali Isle Imports is a small emporium of extraordinary exotica, including imported clothes, capes, curtains, incense, and home and personal accessories. The nearby San Luis Obispo Chamber of Commerce has loads of specialized information and can tell you what's playing at the spectacular Performing Arts Center San Luis Obispo, a joint university/city/foundation endeavor at Cal Poly.

Now we are at Chorro and Higuera, the latter being San Luis Obispo's primary shopping street. The Network is a small mall of shops and cafes, including Koffee Klatsch; Flame Bay Cafe, where you can build your own stir-fry; and Lilliput children's clothing. Coverings features super with-it, slightly punk clothes. Ciscos has sandwiches and salads, and there's a great deck with tables looking across the creek and a bridge to the mission.

Mission Mall is an open-air, small mall with upscale shops, including Country Culture yogurt, Just Looking Gallery (caught us!), Up Your Alley women's discount clothing, SLO Country Gourmet Treats, Birkenstock, and Mr. Michael's furs and fine clothing. The Gold Concept is right next to the SLO Coast Surfboards, Frog & Peach Pub (decent pub grub), and Kona's Sandwiches (best cheap treat). Kevin Main's Jewelry Design Studio neighbors with Straight Down Clothing and Ottoman's casual men's clothing.

Restroom alert! There's a public restroom downstairs at the back of this little mall.

At the corner of Higuera and Broad is a wine lover's mecca, CENTRAL COAST WINES, which knowledgeable Laura Miller manages for owner Vaughn Taus. If you don't have time to visit the wineries yourself, this is the place where you can taste and purchase the very best produced on the central coast, as well as some significant imports, including cigars and wine books, such as Running Press's *Wine Spectator Little Book of Wine* and *Little Book of Champagne*. We know of visitors who load up by selecting and ordering cases of wine and having them shipped home, which works if you live in states that don't prohibit such pleasures.

If you are around for the farmers' market Thursday evening, be sure to stop in for the weekly winemakers' pouring and tasting from 6:00 to 9:00 p.m.

❧ *Central Coast Wines, 712 Higuera Street, San Luis Obispo 93401; (805) 784-9463, fax (805) 544-8761; www.ccwines.com. Open 11:00 a.m.–6:00 p.m. Sunday–Wednesday, until 9:00 p.m. Thursday, 11:00 a.m.–8:00 p.m. Friday–Saturday. Tasting fee: $4. Visa and MasterCard. Wheelchair accessible.*

On the south side of Higuera, enjoy independent Novel Experience bookstore; interesting Hands Gallery, with wildly painted furniture and jewelry; Amnesia; and Mother's Tavern.

At LE FANDANGO BISTRO, Michel and Myriam Olaizola bring true French and Basque country food to downtown San Luis Obispo. Local restaurateurs like to hang out in this bar and restaurant, which is relatively free of students. We like the mussels in garlic cream, the Basque sausage and Basque beans, and the croque monsieur ($9.95). The onion soup is the best this side of Les Halles. Try the homemade foie gras "au torchon" or the country pâté ($6.95–$8.95). Entrees include braised rabbit stew, vegetarian casserole gratinée, cassoulet, duck, and frogs' legs ($14.95–$23.95). Twelve local wines by the glass.

❧ *Le Fandango Bistro, 717 Higuera Street, San Luis Obispo 93401; (805) 544-*

5515. Open 11:30 a.m.–2:00 p.m. Tuesday–Saturday, from 5:00 p.m. nightly. Full
bar. Visa, MasterCard, American Express, Discover. Wheelchair accessible.

One of San Luis Obispo's newest popular casual restaurants, Novo features
tapas, small plates with tastes of foods from around the world to share;
interesting salads; and large plates from Thai green curry ($16) to Tandoori or
Malaysian chicken ($16) and North Indian lamb ($18) to artichoke and
Gorgonzola ravioli ($13). Novo is an in-town sequel to Robin's in Cambria, one
of our favorites, where Robin serves a variety of excellent ethnic cuisine. All pastries at Novo are made at its other sister, French Corner Bakery in Cambria.
There's an interesting short wine list from hard-to-get small wineries, as well as
world beers. Lunch sandwiches and burgers come with soup or salad, and light
alternatives abound under $10.

🌿 *Novo, 726 Higuera Street, San Luis Obispo 93401; (805) 543-3986;*
www.novorestaurant.com. Open from 11:00 a.m. daily until people leave. Beer and
wine. Visa, MasterCard, American Express. Wheelchair accessible.

Be sure to go around the corner on Broad Street to a sort of gourmet ghetto.
Our favorite comes first, Big Sky Cafe, followed by Boston Bagel and Tio
Alberto's, a great little place to stop in for gourmet Mexican food.

The *New York Times* calls BIG SKY CAFE "San Luis Obispo's Best
Restaurant," and *Zagat* rates it as "excellent." To say nothing of us: Big Sky is
definitely our favorite restaurant in SLO. But don't tell.

As you might not expect, Big Sky's ceiling is painted like a night sky complete with shining stars. Fake Mexican arches make niches with tile roofing, left-
overs from the place's previous incarnation as a Mexican restaurant. Bloody
Marys are made with sake; the walls are adorned with a revolving art show of
local artists' work. You sit on heavy wooden chairs at heavy wooden tables.

Big Sky serves "analog food for a digital world," meaning sustainable, environmentally sound "modern food," tasty but considerate of your life span. For
instance, the Petit Poulet, the Caribbean Adobo steak, and the Vietnamese shrimp
pasta all come with soup or salad and veggies and are all memorable. When—not
if—you go, do not leave without trying the beignets, fried bread with cinnamon
and sugar, blueberry or chocolate drizzle, and filling ($3.50–$17.95). There's an
excellent free-at-night parking lot across Broad Street.

Do not miss the "killer cornbread" with any meal. Our favorite breakfast
is the Red Flannel turkey hash with basil-Parmesan glazed eggs or the Maytag
blue cheese, bacon, and apple omelette. And then there's the black bean cakes
and eggs, smoked salmon and onion scramble, and fabulous buttermilk pancakes or three-grain journey cakes with choice of banana and toasted walnuts,

cranberries and orange zest, or Swiss cheese fillings ($6.95–$8.95)!

Sandwiches are available at lunch and dinner, as are veggie spring rolls, bowls including gumbo yaya or High Plains turkey chili, the Big Sky noodle bowl with buckwheat soba noodles and semolina pasta in clear veggie broth with add-ons of chicken or seafood, fried chicken salad, goat cheese–stuffed chicken breast salad, vegetable tajone, and pozole ($14.95–$17.95). Our favorite.

❧ *Big Sky Cafe, 1121 Broad Street, San Luis Obispo 93401; (805) 545-5401; www.bigskycafe .com. Open 7:00 a.m.–10:00 p.m. Monday–Saturday, 7:00 a.m.–9:00 p.m. Sunday. Breakfast 8:00 a.m.–2:00 p.m. daily. Beer and wine. Visa, MasterCard, American Express. Wheelchair accessible.*

BIG SKY KILLER CORNBREAD
from Chef Greg Holt, Big Sky Cafe, San Luis Obispo

½ cup butter
1 cup sugar
4 eggs
1 (7 oz.) can diced, roasted green chilies
1¼ cups creamed corn
1 cup grated cheddar cheese
1½ cups flour
1 cup yellow cornmeal
4 tsp. baking powder
¼ tsp. salt

With electric mixer, cream together butter and sugar. When smooth, beat in the eggs, green chilies, creamed corn, and grated cheese. Sift the dry ingredients together and stir into the wet mixture. Bake in a greased cake pan or muffin tins at 350°F for about 25 minutes. [*These are the absolute best cornbread muffins in the world.* —KTH]

Back to Higuera, working our way up the south side from Broad, we come to Penelope's cards and stuffed animals, the Fandango Bistro, and Mother's Tavern, a newish old-looking grill/restaurant with lots of charm and a long dark wood bar with green vinyl stool and chair covers. Cloud Nine carries children's apparel, and Edgeware Cutlery & Gifts sells money clips and Swiss army knives, among other things.

Bubblegum Alley is a major attraction for some people, a narrow walkway from Higuera Street to a parking lot where thousands of people have stuck their gum wads and turned stickiness into an art form, uncensored poetics included.

Atmospheres majors in interior design, and Posies sells Yankee candles, Crabtree & Evelyn products, and Tiffany lamp replicas. Next up the street is a Nannette Keller factory outlet, and the dramatic, gated, white stucco edifice on the corner of Garden Street houses Marshalls Jewelers.

For many people the main attraction on Garden Street is DOWNTOWN BREWING CO., one of the most popular establishments on the central coast. A sign informs visitors on entering that THIS IS AN UNREINFORCED MASONRY BUILDING. UNREINFORCED MASONRY BUILDINGS MAY BE UNSAFE IN THE EVENT OF AN EARTHQUAKE. Duh!

Upstairs is an excellent pub restaurant, loaded with locals at lunchtime, and serving everything from salads to burgers and healthy chicken with huge fries and, guess what, beer. There is lots of made-here beer, such as Extra Pale Ale, Cole Porter, Central Coast Amber Ale, Blueberry Ale, and Earthquake Relief Wheat Beer. A gallery overlooks the tanks, and there's a whole explanation of the brewing process. At least look into the turn-of-the-twentieth-century classic billiard room. Steve Courier is the brewmaster.

❧ *Downtown Brewing Co., 1119 Garden Street, San Luis Obispo 93401; (805) 543-1843; www.downtownbrew.com. Open 10:00 a.m.–midnight daily. Visa, MasterCard, American Express. Not wheelchair accessible.*

Honds Gallery features glass, and SLO Pendleton is a great depot of Pendleton woolens and other casual clothes.

Off Higuera at Morro Street, Gap, Ross, Victoria's Secret, and Starbucks fans will all find their fixes. Jerry likes Nemo Comics nearby. Fans of Cambria's Linn's Main Binn and Restaurant will melt at Linn's Bakery's pastries and goodies (at Chorro and Marsh).

East of Chorro on Higuera near Osos Street, you will run into Woodstock Pizza, a local mainstay; Firestone Grill in an old service station; and Mo's Smokehouse, a casual order-at-the-counter barbecue.

SIGNIFICANT OTHERS

Right downtown in San Luis Obispo, food lovers must check into MUZIO'S GROCERY, a historic (1888) and ever popular, nearly European delicatessen specializing in imported gourmet foods; cheeses from England, France, and Italy; salads; hard-to-get mustards; heaping fabulous sandwiches; and a small but excellent selection of local and European wines. Get a sandwich and sit on a bench outside. One of our favorites.

❧ *Muzio's Grocery, 870 Monterey Street, San Luis Obispo 93401; (805) 543-0800. Open 9:00 a.m.–6:00 p.m. Monday–Saturday. Beer and wine. Visa and MasterCard. Wheelchair accessible.*

TASTE SLO is the most high-tech advanced, twenty-first-century tasting room we have seen. The San Luis Obispo Vintners formed a cooperative tasting room that utilizes an Italian computerized "enomatic" pouring system so that guests can taste opened bottles that do not deteriorate because no oxygen gets to the wine.

Here you can taste seventy-two wines from producers in San Luis Obispo, Edna Valley, Arroyo Grande, Avila Beach, and the Nipomo regions, without leaving SLO, and you pay by the ounce. Two-ounce Tuesday is only $2.50 per ounce. Winemakers show up Wednesday and serve cheese and flights of wines.

❧ *Taste SLO, 1003 Osos Street at Monterey Street in the new Court Street Centre, San Luis Obispo 93401; (805) 269-8278; www.taste-slo.com. Open 11:00 a.m.– 9:00 p.m. Monday–Saturday, 11:00 a.m.–5:00 p.m. Sunday. Visa, MasterCard, American Express. Wheelchair accessible.*

BUONA TAVOLA is a terrific little Italian restaurant right next to the classic Fremont Theatre. Chef/owner Antonio Varia prepares everything from antipasti to pasta, seafood, and Italian desserts. There's garden seating and an excellent local wine list. A favorite of many locals.

❧ *Buona Tavola, 1037 Monterey Street, San Luis Obispo 93401; (805) 545-8000. Open for lunch 11:30 a.m.–2:30 p.m. Monday–Friday, dinner 5:30–10:00 p.m. Monday–Saturday. Beer and wine. Visa, MasterCard, American Express, Discover. Wheelchair accessible.*

APPLE FARM, an actual working gristmill with striking flowers, waterfalls, and a waterwheel grinding wheat, producing apple cider, and churning ice cream, is an all-American, mom's-apple-pie comfort center featuring local agricultural products, sugar, and a large restaurant with hot apple dumplings, fresh-baked cornbread and honey butter, muffins you have to eat with a spoon, warm and runny jam, soups, pies, and a salad bar. Seriously hungry folks might enjoy the roast turkey and dressing, Santa Maria–style tri-tip, country pot roast, or panfried trout. Lunch offers loads of burgers and sandwiches, including a hot meat loaf sandwich to die for, open-faced hot turkey sandwich with mashed potatoes and gravy, and even a Philly cheesesteak or garden burger. Breakfast cooks up apple sausage and almost anything, omelettes, potato pancakes, and enormous country breakfasts ($10–$16).

Be sure to visit the inn, bakery, and cute gift shop where many people get lost enjoying the trinkets.

❧ *Apple Farm, US 101 at Monterey exit, 2015 Monterey Street, San Luis Obispo 93401; (805) 544-6100 or (800) 374-3705. Open 7:00 a.m.–10:00 p.m. daily. Beer and wine. Visa, MasterCard, American Express, Discover. Wheelchair accessible.*

The pink and white, goopily romantic MADONNA INN spells heavenly romance to some people. Alex and Phyllis Madonna put millions into this 2,000-acre resort and created their personal expression of genuine visitor hospitality, with a different fantasy theme in every bedroom, heart-shaped pillows, and lots of red velvet and textured wallpapers. There's even a Caveman Room carved out of solid rock. Are you ready? If you weren't, this might help. You can just visit and have a look, and men must not miss the famous men's room and its more famous waterfall urinal. If you didn't have to go. . . .

Check out the new Classic Gourmet and Wine Shop in what obviously was once a Madonna Inn gasoline station. The restrooms here are worth the stop—especially for a smaller version of the men's waterfall in the inn.

The bakery features French pastries, fruit and cream pies, and their famous Black Forest cakes (slices $5.25–$7.25). Drop in on the ladies' boutique and the men's clothing store.

The Steakhouse dining room glows with thousands of tiny lights to illuminate your steak, seafood, lamb, or chicken cooked over an oak pit barbecue, with great results and entrees ranging from $24.95 to $82.95.

Madonna Inn's house wine is bottled by Castoro, and you can buy many local wines in the Madonna Inn Gourmet Gift Shop, which is a fun place to explore anyway. Enjoy!

❧ *Madonna Inn, 100 Madonna Road right off US 101, San Luis Obispo 93401; (805) 543-3000 or (800) 543-9666; www.madonnainn.com.*

Shoppers, you may want to continue down Madonna Road a wee bit to the Madonna Mall and outlet shopping centers.

CHAPTER 6

SAN LUIS OBISPO COUNTY: THE COAST

his part of central California contains some of the most dramatic coastline of the western United States, beginning at Ragged Point just below Big Sur (Monterey County), where the ocean waves crash into vertical cliffs.

Average temperatures here are much lower than you'll find in the inland wine country, with year-round highs ranging from 61°F to 71°F and lows from 40°F to 54°F. Bring a sweater or jacket and be prepared for spectacular scenery, great walks, and lots of browsing.

SAN SIMEON AND HEARST CASTLE

Once an exciting whaling village, San Simeon is now primarily the historic landmark Sebastian's General Store and San Simeon Pier, built in 1878 by George Hearst, father of William Randolph Hearst, who brought his opulent interior decorations across this pier.

You can get here via Highway 1, U.S. Highway 101, and Highway 46 west, or by taking Central Coast Area Transit (805-541-CCAT or 805-781-4467), which connects San Simeon, Cambria, Cayucos, Morro Bay, Los Osos, Cuesta College, California Polytechnic, and San Luis Obispo.

Hearst Castle (officially Hearst San Simeon State Historical Monument) is about 245 miles south from San Francisco via US 101 and Highway 46 west, and 205 miles via Highway 1 (six to six and a half hours). From Monterey it's about 165 miles on US 101 and 94 miles on Highway 1, and a little more than three hours both routes. From Los Angeles it's 254 miles and six hours either way.

HEARST CASTLE, or La Cuesta Encantada (the Enchanted Hill), is the magnificently opulent dream estate built by William Randolph Hearst north of San Simeon. As a child, Hearst visited San Simeon with his family. After he became an extremely wealthy publisher, he chose this dramatic site on the western slope of the Santa Lucia Mountains to develop his enchanted heaven over nearly thirty years. Hearst's estate was the movie star party mecca in Hollywood's golden age, and today it is a California historical monument visited by nearly a million people each year.

If you choose to join the crowd, it is wise to make reservations, particularly if you want to go on one of the several tours offered. You can explore the castle only on a tour, so we advise booking to see the 165 rooms and 127 acres of gardens, terraces, mosaic pools, and walkways. The whole "house" is furnished with an unusually impressive collection of splendor: Spanish and Italian antiques and art.

From his laborer/miner father Hearst gained his respect and love for the land, and from his mother, Phoebe Apperson Hearst, he acquired his love for European art, Mediterranean architecture, ornamental craftsmanship, and antiques. He built the castle, which he referred to as "the ranch," as a monument to his mother.

Remarkably advanced for its 1919 construction, La Cuesta Encantada was designed by famed architect Julia Morgan and built as a summer home with steel beams and concrete to assure that California earthquakes could not destroy Hearst's dream. (Morgan's plan proved itself during the December 2003 earthquake.) The spectacular Neptune pool was enlarged and rebuilt twice. (Kathleen has a mosaic bench her mother made with tiles given her by one of the original pool mosaicists.) Hearst spared no expense importing European antiques, hand-carved ceilings, marble sculptures, and full-grown cypress trees via the San Simeon pier. The Casa Grande has 115 rooms, and several luxurious guest houses surround the main house.

Something like the famous rambling-forever Winchester House in San Jose in which the creative process became almost more important than the result, the castle still was not finished when Hearst died in 1951, thirty-two years after it was begun.

All tours of the Hearst Castle include a half-mile walk and 150 to 400 stairs (wheelchair tours available by reservation), as well as visits to the Greco-Roman–style outdoor pool, and to an indoor pool lined with Venetian glass and gold. Daytime tours take about one hour and forty-five minutes, including bus tours to and from the visitor center where you park.

First-time visitors will probably enjoy Tour 1 (the only tour available to wheelchairs) for an overall view. Strollers are not permitted on tours. Tours leave the visitor center by bus at the time printed on the ticket, so plan ahead. During the 5-mile, fifteen-minute bus ride to the castle you can listen to an audiotape giving background information, so you can hit the ground running or rolling.

Tours usually sell out in advance, so be sure to call (800) 444-4445 for reservations.

Tour 1 covers La Casa del Sol, an eighteen-room guest cottage, with esplanade and gardens; and La Casa Grande (of which five rooms are shown: the assembly room, the refectory dining room, the morning room, billiard room, and theater).

Tour 2 takes in the upper floors of La Casa Grande, including the doge suite (Italian), the cloister rooms for guests, the library and its 5,000 books and Greek vases, the Gothic suite and Gothic study, and the pantry and kitchen.

Tour 3 includes La Casa del Monte, north wing of La Casa Grande, north terrace and grand entrance, and the video room of photographs and film from the 1920s and 1930s.

Tour 4 (April–October) takes you to the hidden terrace, an overview of the gardens and grounds, La Casa del Mar, Neptune pool dressing rooms, and the wine cellar of La Casa Grande with its 3,000 bottles of rare European vintages and California wines.

Tour 5 is a lovely evening tour (spring and fall) that takes two hours and ten minutes, including bus trips to and from the visitor center, and covers the living history program, illuminated pools and gardens, highlights of La Casa Grande, and La Casa del Mar.

A fun sidelight is the five-story National Geographic Theater showing of *Hearst Castle™: Building the Dream,* which follows the story of the castle from Hearst's inspiration to realization. Enjoy forty minutes of seven-channel Surround Sound and wild aerial scenery.

Hearst San Simeon State Historical Monument, Highway 1, San Simeon 93452; reservations (800) 444-4445, recorded information (805) 927-2000; www.hearstcastle.com. Open 8:00 a.m.–6:00 p.m. March–September, 9:00 a.m.–5:00 p.m. October–February. Admission: adults $20–$30, children six to seventeen $10–$20, depending on season. Visa, MasterCard, Discover. Partly wheelchair accessible.

Besides its historic attractions related to Hearst endeavors, San Simeon has some delightful art galleries, small restaurants, and shops worth exploring. If you are starving for lunch after your castle tour, take a chance on local fare or make your way south to Cambria.

If you visit Hearst Castle, you will probably want to stay in Cambria, which is south on Highway 1, about twenty minutes or 6 miles.

CAMBRIA

Its residents like to boast that Cambria is "where the pines meet the sea," and they are right. A true seaside village once called San Simeon and Santa Rosa,

Cambria today is a well-touristed artists' colony where artists can afford to live (in contrast to Carmel, where few true artists can live or rent a studio). In Cambria you will find local artists' work exhibited everywhere.

The primary business of this onetime farming community now seems to be tourism. Cambria's residents are artists and craftspeople, active retirees, professionals, ranchers, and farmers. Locals and visitors alike indulge in beachcombing, surfing, hiking, biking, fishing, and kayaking, as well as spotting gray whales, seals, sea otters, and elephant seals along the beaches. San Simeon State Beach is just 5 miles north, and Moonstone Beach is right in Cambria. A full range of accommodations faces the beaches in West Cambria. And there's a free Otter Trolley that transports people, not otters, from Moonstone Beach to Cambria's "east and west villages," known to outsiders as East Cambria and West Cambria.

Cambria really has three parts: the restaurants, motels, and inns along Moonstone Drive and beach (great boardwalk); West Cambria; and the older East Cambria.

Cambria is an art and history fan's delight with a load of "cute" shops thrown in. While it has become a little touristy, it also is a very comfortable place in which to be a tourist. So, as Confucius is so often misquoted, just lie back and enjoy it.

Beginning at the north end of West Cambria's Main Street is the Exxon station, which we wouldn't even mention except that it sells an exceptional collection of Beanie Babies for those of you who care, as well as diesel fuel, about which we do care. Right next to the Exxon station (remember the spill, folks) is the Main Street Grill, featuring local (we hope) seafood cooked over the huge barbecue, to eat here or take out, followed by the popular Old Stone Station, which serves fish and chips, prime rib, steaks, and seafood at lunch and dinner.

Caren's Corner, just before the Cambria Fine Arts Gallery, offers an eclectic mix that includes stained glass and crafts, ice cream, and espresso (two plastic tables and a few chairs on the sidewalk, too). The Coffee Den right next to the Chamber of Commerce on Main Street has good coffee and pastries to enjoy here or take away, as well as Van Ryn watercolors.

Artifacts gallery features the work of Bev Doolittle, Charles Wysocki, and Bob Byerly, while the ever-present painting magnate Thomas Kinkade, Animation Art, and Yankee Candle all have outlets in the same building. Simply Angels features everything spiritual and doll-like about angels, New Moon offers personal and home accessories, and the Soldier Factory is a truly rare and interesting emporium of miniatures of all sorts, particularly soldiers and model warplanes. If you are into war, go for it.

On the south side of Main Street in Cambria's west village you will find one of our favorites, the Pewter Plough Playhouse, presenting fabulous local productions and an excellent piano bar facing Main Street for before-, during-, and after-performance stops. Safe at Home majors in collectibles and sports miniatures, and Sergio's Restaurant & Cambria Wine Shop is a primarily Italianate restaurant with Alaskan halibut, Tuscan chicken, crab cakes, sandwiches, and salads, all under $15.

Wearable Images features cotton and natural fabric resort wear for men and women, and the Cargo Company has leather goods, umbrellas, Hawaiian music, knives, cigars, binoculars, and watches. You figure!

Just in time comes the locally popular WEST END BAR & GRILL for lunch or even late dinner with full bar, live music, kids' menu, and food to go, including burgers, fajitas, salads, and tiger shrimp scampi ($8.25).

Don't miss Cynthia Fletcher's Down Under Trading Co., with waxed coats, soaps, boots, and hats from Australia and New Zealand. Next door try the Courtyard Deli, the Melanie Sylvester Gallery, and the Bookery upstairs for antiquarian books. Cambria has a plethora of interesting small used-book stores.

Maison de Marie, next to La Crema Espresso Bar, has an interesting combination of old-world gifts and antiques, and a lovely courtyard full of roses to enjoy while indulging in that coffee and pastry.

In Cambria's east village, the west end of Main Street begins with the favorite Harmony Pasta Factory in the Cambria Village Square shopping center, and Bistro Solé, featuring international cuisine at lunch, dinner, or Sunday brunch.

Restroom alert! Important to most of us is an excellent set of clean public restrooms in the parking lot on Center Street, accessible from Burton Drive and right off Main Street.

Our favorite street in Cambria is Burton Drive, loaded with excellent restaurants, history, art, and wine. We begin with ROBIN'S at the corner of Burton and Center. Robin's really does what it says: present "a melting pot of excellent ethnic cuisine prepared with the freshest of natural ingredients." Lunch includes a soup and Mexican soft chicken tacos, portobello burger, halibut fish tacos, burgers, lumpia, Indian spiced lamb rolls, lobster enchiladas, ribs, and more ($8–$20). Dinner entrees may include American Kobe flank steak, grilled Canadian salmon, herb-roasted free-range chicken, portobello and spinach lasagna, lobster enchiladas, wok-flashed pasta with vegetables and tofu or chicken, pan-seared tofu, and several curries ($14–$29).

Robin's, 4095 Burton Drive, Cambria 93428; (805) 927-5007; www.robins restaurant.com. Open for lunch 11:00 a.m.–4:45 p.m., dinner from 5:00 p.m. Full bar. Visa, MasterCard, American Express. Not wheelchair accessible.

SQUIBB HOUSE, CAMBRIA

Don't miss the SQUIBB HOUSE just down Burton Drive and its Squibb House SHOP NEXT DOOR, a heavenly home to antique primitives, the best of antique kitchen implements, crockery, ceramics, and handcrafted furnishings—all in an 1885 carpentry shop.

Bruce Black has lovingly and accurately restored Squibb House, an 1877 home whose downstairs was used as a classroom while an addition was built to the Cambria school where owner Fred Darke was principal. Darke later served as School Superintendent and County Recorder of San Luis Obispo County. In 1889 Alexander Paterson bought the house, set up his carpentry business next door, and passed the house along to his son Alexander Jr., whose wife, Amy, became Cambria's postmaster.

Earl Van Gordon bought the house in 1919 and operated a general store here, then served as postmaster, school trustee, and justice of the peace, eventually leaving the house vacant. Paul and Louise Squibb took over in 1953 and retired here after founding Midland School in Santa Ynez Valley. The Squibbs began a practice later called "squibbing," in which locals pick litter up off the streets and sidewalks.

Bruce Black now operates the fully restored bed-and-breakfast, as well as the Shop Next Door, with Carol O'Herlihy. Both are among our favorites.

❦ *Squibb House Bed & Breakfast* and *Shop Next Door, 4063 Burton Drive, Cambria 93428; (805) 927-9600; www.squibbhouse.net. Shop open 10:00 a.m.–9:00 p.m. daily. Visa, MasterCard, American Express. Wheelchair accessible.*

Just down this side of Burton from Squibb House is another local institution, BRAMBLES DINNER HOUSE, which has received a *Wine Spectator* Award of Excellence for six years and an International Award of Excellence in 1999. Rotary meets here Friday at noon, locals come in regularly, and early-bird dinners are served from 4:00 to 5:30 or 6:00 p.m. Nick and Debbie Kaperonis and family have owned and operated Bràmbles since 1956.

Try the salmon cooked over seasoned oak wood ($16.95) or prime rib with Yorkshire pudding ($17.95–$19.95) or the Greek and vegetarian specialties. All dinner entrees include soup or salad. Brunch goes slightly Danish with the famous aebleskiver (apple pancakes) with ham or sausage, corned beef hash, omelettes, or shrimp Louie ($11.95–$13.95 with champagne). There's an excellent central coast and California wine list, and the menu specifies recommended wines to accompany entrees.

🍂 *Brambles Dinner House, 4005 Burton Drive, Cambria 93428; (805) 927-4716. Open from 4:00 p.m. nightly, Sunday brunch 9:30 a.m.–2:00 p.m. Full bar. Visa, MasterCard, American Express, Diners, Carte Blanche. Wheelchair accessible.*

Across Burton have a look in Sylvia's Burton Drive Inn and then stroll to Leslie Gainer's FERMENTATIONS, a wonderful wine shop with gourmet delicacies and oils and loads of local wines. Savor tastes of grapeseed oils, mustards, and mango tequila Thai peanut salad dressing, and jalapeño and other sauces. Central coast wines, including Fermentation's own, are available. Enjoy wine-related gifts and glassware, from wine racks to hand-blown glasses and picnic baskets.

🍂 *Fermentations, 4056 Burton Drive, Cambria 93428; (805) 927-7141, fax (805) 927-2289. Open 10:00 a.m.–10:00 p.m. daily. Tasting fee: $5, includes a lovely glass. Visa, MasterCard, Discover. Not wheelchair accessible.*

Kids will enjoy the Rumpelstiltskin Children's Book Gallery for marvelous children's books, storytelling, puppets and puppetry, and local travel guides. Don't miss world-renowned former Mattel doll artist (and local resident) Martha Armstrong-Hand's Rumpelstiltskin in the shop. Seekers American Glass displays some of the best hand-blown glass work we have seen.

Walk or roll and explore the abundance of wide-open shops along Main Street, including the Sow's Ear's Cafe just east of Burton Drive, featuring contemporary and American cuisine from chicken-fried steak and chicken and dumplings to salmon wrapped in parchment—often voted a favorite.

LINN'S MAIN BINN is probably the most popular all-around restaurant and bakery in Cambria. San Luis Obispo locals have voted it Best Desserts in the county. This is where people who come to town to socialize over a cup of coffee and a piece of pie gather. While obsessing over breakfast pastries or fruit pies, be sure to try the potpies for lunch or dinner—some of the best we've had in this country—or the hearty soups and salads. You can also indulge in Linn's pies and gourmet packaged foods at its farm store on Santa Rosa Creek Road. There are fun gift shops at both locations.

❧ *Linn's Main Binn, 2277 Main Street, Cambria 94328; (805) 927-0371. Restaurant open 7:00 a.m.–10:00 p.m. daily, Sunday champagne brunch from 10:30 a.m.; farm store open 10:00 a.m.–4:00 p.m. daily. Beer and wine. Visa, MasterCard, American Express. Wheelchair accessible.*

Worth a trip or perfectly located for motel and inn guests along Moonstone Beach Drive is the SEA CHEST OYSTER BAR AND SEAFOOD RESTAURANT. If you want to go, reservations are absolutely mandatory for this teensy restaurant with great seafaring decor and lines out into the parking lot.

The Sea Chest is right on Moonstone Beach Drive, right across, yes, from the beach and Pacific Ocean. Everything here is good, if you get in. Specialties include broiled halibut ($18.95), Steve's cioppino ($18.95), and calamari ($15.95), as well as fresh oysters at the oyster bar (six for $10.00), mahimahi, and Boston clam chowder. Too bad it isn't open for lunch!

❧ *Sea Chest Oyster Bar and Seafood Restaurant, 6216 Moonstone Beach Drive, Cambria 94328; (805) 927-4514; www.CentralCoast.com. Open from 5:30 p.m. Wednesday–Sunday. Beer and wine. No credit cards. Not wheelchair accessible.*

SEA CHEST OYSTER BAR AND
SEAFOOD RESTAURANT, CAMBRIA

Other restaurants to try here are the Moonstone Beach Bar & Grill, which is conveniently open for breakfast, lunch, dinner, and Sunday brunch (the only restaurant on the beach open for all those hearty meals), or Moonstone Gardens' hamlet restaurant, which serves lunch and dinner from 11:00 a.m. and has three acres of gardens and the Van Gogh's Ear gallery, featuring the work of local and national artists.

Even if you aren't staying there, we encourage you to drop in to visit the OLALLIEBERRY INN right on Main Street, "where time stands still." It's a classic bed-and-breakfast known widely for its fabulous food. Owners Carol Ann and Chef Peter Irsfeld have put together a cookbook of his best recipes, so that you can reproduce their hors d'oeuvres, breakfasts, hash browns, biscuits, soups, and dinner entrees. If you buy the cookbook, you get a coupon entitling you to two nights for the price of one midweek during off-season months.

❧ *Olallieberry Inn, 2476 Main Street, Cambria 94328; (805) 927-3222. Visa and MasterCard. Partly wheelchair accessible.*

Cambria's farmers' market is held on Friday from 2:30 to 5:30 p.m., on Main Street next to Veterans Hall.

HARMONY AND CAYUCOS

The grand metropolis of Harmony (population eighteen) is barely a block long and boasts a post office, wedding chapel, shops and galleries, and the Central Coast Wine Room, an excellent and casual place to taste and select the best of central coast wines, cigars, and gifts.

Moving right along, we come to the tiny beach town and fishing village of CAYUCOS, about 14 miles south of Cambria and 19 miles north of San Luis Obispo. It's heaven for surfers and anglers, who can actually fish off the Cayucos Pier without a license. Antiques fans will find plenty of browsing, and the town's murals depicting local and Old West history entertain everyone. If you're either really tough or really stupid, show up for the annual polar bear dip into the Pacific Ocean's 50°F waters on New Year's Day. At least join the throngs cheering on the troops.

HOPPE'S GARDEN BISTRO & WINE SHOP is definitely a destination restaurant on the coast, with locals traveling several miles to enjoy local abalone, free-range chicken, venison loin, grilled polenta, barbecued sweetbreads, and a shellfish bar. Hoppe's offers a superb wine list of more than 250 wines and has a lovely back patio. You'll know it by its bright colored geraniums outside the yellow historic building.

ᴥ *Hoppe's Garden Bistro & Wine Shop*, *78 North Ocean Avenue, P.O. Box 569, Cayucos 93430; (805) 772-5371. Open 11:00 a.m.–9:00 p.m. Sunday and Wednesday–Thursday, 11:00 a.m.–10:00 p.m. Friday and Saturday. Beer and wine. Visa, MasterCard, American Express, Discover. Wheelchair accessible.*

Just south of Cayucos you come to the entrance to El Chorro Regional Park.

MORRO BAY

Morro Bay is only 14 miles northwest of San Luis Obispo, which makes it a perfect quick jaunt to curl your toes in the sand or sample some fresh abalone dripping with lemon butter. If you happen to enter Morro Bay on Highway 1 from the southeast, you can follow the Boulevard for 10 blocks of delightful shops and small restaurants. Morro Bay's longest street, Main Street, begins at Morro Bay State Park and runs north to Morro Strand State Beach. You will find loads of antiques shops, art galleries, and edible goodies on Main Street.

One of the first things you notice in this bird sanctuary and fishing village is the 576-foot high Morro Rock right off the water's edge. Named "El Moro" for its domelike shape and discovered by Portuguese explorer Juan Rodriguez Cabrillo in 1542, this first of the so-called Nine Sisters volcanic peaks is about twenty-one million years old. The peaks separate the Los Osos and Chorro Valleys and run in a straight line for 12 miles. Original resident Chumash Indians camped at the base of these peaks and ate the berries and roots found growing on the Nine Sisters's slopes. There is an active movement to have the peaks designated historical landmarks to prevent further development in their vicinity.

You can't miss the rock unless the fog's in really badly. Follow Embarcadero north to Coleman Drive, near where the peregrine falcons nest, and you can occasionally see otters rafting down the channel on passing logs and boards. During the summer there are lifeguards on duty at the beach just north of the rock, with public restrooms available.

As a bird sanctuary, Morro Bay provides a nourishing habitat to two dozen threatened and endangered species, including peregrine falcon, brant, brown pelican, black rail, blue heron, and snowy plover. More than 195 migratory bird species make their winter homes at Morro Bay, the last estuary of its kind between Mexico and northern California.

The California Fish and Game Commission designated Morro Rock as an ecological reserve for protection of a peregrine falcon aerie, making access to the rock prohibited and trespassing illegal. Since environmental contamination has made the falcons incapable of producing eggshells thick and durable enough to protect a growing embryo, they are now dependent on men and women to help coddle and raise their young. Pity. So the peregrine fund at Cornell University provides nestlings that Morro Bay adult falcons raise as their own. And this is what we humans have wrought!

Morro Bay is also a major West Coast fishing center, so enjoy the multitude of right-off-the-boat fish markets and restaurants along the Embarcadero. Everyone's local favorites are Hoppe's at Marina Square and Hoppe's Hip Pocket Bistro at 901 Embarcadero.

Sailboarding and sailing are big-time pastimes here, and you can rent kayaks, canoes, and boats along the waterfront or bring your own to the free boat launch ramp and fish-cleaning facilities! Chess lovers should not miss the giant chessboard in Centennial Park 3 blocks from Highway 1 on the Embarcadero. It measures 16 feet square and features giant redwood chess pieces weighing from eighteen to twenty pounds each. Call (805) 772-6278 weekdays for reservations. Use fees range from around $10 for residents to $20 for nonresidents to use the whole board per day, with no hourly time limits.

If your interest in sea ventures is deeper, visit the MORRO BAY AQUARIUM & MARINE REHABILITATION CENTER for a cozy and enlightening experience for kids of all ages.

❧ *Morro Bay Aquarium & Marine Rehabilitation Center, 595 Embarcadero, Morro Bay 93442; (805) 772-7647; www.morrobay.com/morrobayaquarium/. Open 9:30 a.m.–6:00 p.m. daily. Admission: $2 adults, $1 children five to fifteen, under five free. Wheelchair accessible.*

Also be sure to explore the MORRO BAY NATURAL HISTORY MUSEUM and the heron rookery at Morro Bay State Park for a slightly more subdued and educational experience covering flora, fauna, and sea culture of the whole central coast. Black Hill, the second in the Nine Sisters chain of ancient volcanoes, is also in the park.

❧ *Morro Bay Natural History Museum, Morro Bay State Park, Morro Bay 93442; (805) 772-2694. Open 10:00 a.m.–5:00 p.m. daily. Admission $2 adults, free for ages sixteen and under. Wheelchair accessible.*

Within Morro Bay State Park are an excellent golf course and a marina, the latter on State Park Road and open 9:00 a.m.–5:00 p.m. daily, (805) 772-8796. Adventurers and whale fans might also enjoy whale watching (from December 26 until mid-March). Virg's Fish'n (800-762-5263) runs tours daily, weather permitting, which it doesn't always. Virg's will also take you out fishing, or you can take yourself fishing off the pier.

❧

Nearby Cañada de Los Osos (Valley of the Bears), now called Los Osos, is a charming little town worth exploring. It serves as the gateway to Montana de Oro State Park (Mountain of Gold), probably so named because of the wild mustard growing on its slopes. Legend suggests that Junipero Serra, a Franciscan padre and founder of California's missions, scattered mustard seed so he and his pals could find their way back and forth between the missions along El Camino Real. The park itself encompasses more than 8,000 acres of breathtakingly rugged wilderness and dramatically jagged coastline, making it attractive to hikers, cyclists, campers, and surfers.

Check out Elfin Forest for miniature oaks at the end of Fifteenth Street in Los Osos, with tours every third Saturday. Call (805) 528-5279. Kids will also enjoy Tidelands Children's Park on the Embarcadero while parents gaze out at the boats in the marina.

There is a farmers' market on Thursday, 3:00–5:00 p.m., at Young's Giant Food, 2650 Main Street, Morro Bay.

PISMO BEACH

Pismo Beach is between Avila and Shell Beaches on the north and Grover Beach and Oceano on the south, in a 23-mile stretch of glorious, sparkling central coastline. We are not overstating the fact. The water and sky both exhilarate visitors here, at least when the fog isn't in.

If you are coming from the north, Pismo Beach's city hall and the extremely (cannot say that enough) popular F. McLintock's Saloon & Dining House are on the left (up/east side) of Highway 1. The town's business district stretches northward parallel to the highway, as do huge stucco house developments on both sides of the highway, and loads of motels of many price ranges, all emphasizing the ocean view.

Dolliver is Pismo Beach's main street, although its two best local restaurants, Giuseppe's Cucina Italiana and Rosa's Ristorante Italiano, are 1 block up (away from the ocean) on Price Street. Other local food hangouts include the Burger Factory Drive-In, Nick's Place, and Brad's Fish and Chips. And then there are the more touristy spots down closer to the water.

Pismo Beach is best known for its Pismo clam and Pismo Beach Clam Festival, its wide-open (in a couple of ways) sandy beaches, and its 1,200-foot-long pier lined with local and visiting anglers. The beach itself is perfect for crunching through pebbled coves, riding horseback along the waterline (call 805-489-8100), exploring tide pools (do not disturb), and watching migrating butterflies clustered in the eucalyptus grove at the southern entrance to town on

Highway 1. Pismo is a low-key place where dress is casual, as is life in general. (Movie folks are discovering it's a good place to hide out.)

Biking and in-line skating are popular, as are surfing, boogie boarding, and ATV riding year-round on the sand dunes, which are used for many movies and television shows. Rent ATV stuff at BJ's ATV (805-481-5411).

If you arrive hungry, or even if you don't, we suggest you try GIUSEPPE'S CUCINA ITALIANA, which really ought to be a destination restaurant. You will not experience delicately piled nouvelle cuisine of what our friend M. F. K. Fisher used to call "the puddle school" of cooking. Instead, you are in for some of the best Italian food we have ever enjoyed, well served in a fun dining room with white linen tablecloths, elegant Italian ceramics, green walls, and pink rose carpets, chairs, and upholstered booths. There's an old copper espresso machine, along with a striking copper-and-tile, wood-burning pizza oven right at the back of the room. Then there are the green outdoor tables and even a takeout window, serving every part of the community.

Giuseppe's will also deliver to your door anywhere in Pismo Beach or adjoining Shell Beach, a real plus in the right circumstance!

Bottles of olive oil and balsamic vinegar remain on the table for you to use at any time. We shared the best Caesar salad on God's little earth, full of housemade croutons, garlic, and anchovy dressing, as well as one of their imaginative, perfect pizzas. Ours was the daily special pizza with freshly sliced pepperoni, Canadian bacon, tomatoes, and artichokes, along with a Heineken beer and iced tea for a total of $20.22!

Salads may include grilled portobello mushrooms with chopped arugula, tomato, and shaved Parmigiano cheese; Belgian endive, radicchio, sun-dried tomatoes, and Gorgonzola; vine-ripe tomatoes with basil and fresh mozzarella; or sea scallops with lemon, pepper, and virgin olive oil.

The pasta offerings are perfect and include soup, Caesar salad, or butter lettuce with Gorgonzola dressing. Try the tortellini Giuseppe with pancetta, mushrooms, tomatoes, and peas; the butternut squash ravioli in a grana Parmigiana cream sauce; the rigatoni with prosciutto, mascarpone cheese, and portobello mushrooms; or the spaghettini with ahi tuna, tomatoes, and capers in a black olive sauce. Loads of seafood, eggplant, free-range chicken, veal, scampi, and osso buco are available, as well as filet mignon and rack of lamb. Most entrees are in the $15–$25 range.

Pizzas are excellent. Calamari lovers, do not miss the sautéed Monterey squid appetizer!

❧ *Giuseppe's Cucina Italiana, 891 Price Street, Pismo Beach 93449; (805) 773-2873 or (805) 773-2870, fax (805) 773-6768; www.giuseppesrestaurant .com. Open from 11:00 a.m. daily, deliveries 4:30–10:00 p.m. daily. Full bar. Visa, MasterCard, American Express, Discover. Wheelchair accessible.*

❦

Giuseppe's has opened an excellent quickie deli/espresso bar across the street, and a new restaurant in San Luis Obispo.

ROSA'S is Pismo Beach's more traditional, old-style California Italian restaurant, with little decor, excellent food, and lots of local customers. Locals have voted Rosa's the best Italian restaurant and praised it as having the best clam chowder and best Italian cuisine several times.

Enjoy a wide range of antipasti, including the traditional sliced meats and marinated vegetables, calamari fritta with tartar pesto sauce, and an excellent Caesar salad. You will have fifteen pasta choices, most under $15, filet mignon with lobster ravioli, delicious veal or chicken piccata, lamb shank, several choices of shellfish and pasta, pizzas, and Italian desserts ($15.00–$25.95). Cioppino is served Wednesday nights, and Thursday is osso buco night. Great martinis!

🍇 *Rosa's Ristorante Italiano, 491 Price Street, Pismo Beach 93449; (805) 773-0551; www.rosasrestaurant.com. Open for lunch 11:30 a.m.–2:00 p.m. Monday–Friday, for dinner 4:00–9:30 p.m. Sunday–Thursday and 4:00–10:00 p.m. Friday and Saturday. Full bar. Visa, MasterCard, American Express. Wheelchair accessible.*

Steamer's and F. McLintock's Saloon and Dining House are related and offer somewhat similar menus of steak, prime rib, seafood, and shellfish. Prices are a little more expensive at McLintock's, but each dinner includes entree plus onion rings, salsa, salad (spinach, tossed green, or Caesar), Trail Camp Beans, garlic bread, ranch fried potatoes, and either an after-dinner liqueur or ice cream or sherbet. The basic dinner at Steamer's includes soup or salad, and Steamer's offers more seafood and veggie alternatives than does McLintock's. Steamer's is along Highway 1/US 101 on the west side right in Pismo Beach; McLintock's is just north of town on the east side of the highway.

Our favorite place to stay along here is the Cottage Inn, with some rooms practically hanging over the ocean. An excellent continental (read carbohydrate) breakfast is served in the good-size breakfast room off the lobby (see page 264).

AVILA BEACH

As you take the San Luis Bay exit westward off US 101 on the way to Avila Beach, be sure to stop at a couple of interesting places. The John Salisbury's Creekside Farm and Coeur D'Avila/Salisbury Fine Art gallery is an interesting enterprise when it is open, and it's worth a quick turn into the driveway to find out. Salisbury plans a new winery here, too.

Back on San Luis Bay Drive, turn west and then right (north) on See Canyon Road a long mile to KELSEY SEE CANYON VINEYARDS, the labor of love of Dick and Dolores Sylvester Kelsey. Dolores's family ran abalone, fishing, and tugboats out of Morro Bay for decades, and Dick was a tugboat pilot, having several of his boats used in movies. Now they run their winery and several family rental properties in Avila Beach and are rumored to be the developers of a condominium complex there as well. The Kelseys share their tasting counter next to their little winery and their home with Leonard Cohen and his See Canyon winery. This is a great stop on bikes or just to hear local lore.

 Fine points: Featured wines: Chardonnay, Apple Chardonnay, White Zinfandel, Rosé, Cabernet Sauvignon, Merlot, Zinfandel, Syrah. Owners: Dolores and Dick Kelsey. Winemaker for Kelsey, Cohen, and Salisbury: Harold Osborne. Cases: Kelsey, 800; Cohen, 1,700. Acres: Kelsey, 40; Cohen, won't reveal.

Kelsey See Canyon Vineyards and Winery, 1947 See Canyon Road, San Luis Obispo 93405; (805) 595-9700; www.kelseywine.com. Open 11:00 a.m.–5:30 p.m. (when you show up) daily. Tasting fee: none. Visa and MasterCard. Wheelchair accessible.

CYCLISTS AT KELSEY SEE CANYON VINEYARDS,
SAN LUIS OBISPO

Avila Beach, which in the nineteenth century once had been an active port and the second largest city in San Luis Obispo County, was a sleepy tourist town of only 400 permanent residents in 1988 when disaster struck. That year an Avila Beach business owner prepared to expand his building with an excavation for new foundations. Only 7 feet below the surface, the contractor encountered petroleum fuels in the soil.

Further investigation revealed that below most of downtown Avila Beach was a gigantic pool of 400,000 gallons of petroleum fuels, inundating the soil that formed the underpinning of the community's businesses and many homes facing the ocean. For nearly a century crude oil and refined fuels from the central valley oil fields was pumped to tanks on the bluff overlooking the town and then delivered by gravity through pipes laid under the town to a dock where tankers were loaded.

It became obvious that for years these pipes, some more than fifty years old, had been leaking, creating the pool of fuel and saturating underlying sand, which could contaminate all property and, if ignited, could blow the entire village sky high.

Negotiations between Unocal Oil, owner of the suspect pipes, and the county, city, state and federal agencies demanding clean-up dragged along for six years until attorney Saro Rizzo organized a nonprofit organization, Avila Alliance, which sued Unocal on behalf of the citizens and began a public campaign for removal of the danger. Finally all parties sat down to serious settlement, which meant Unocal paying actual costs of $200 million and penalties of $62 million to assist Avila Beach in rehabilitation.

Unocal and Jacobs Engineering in coordination with the U.S. Corps of Engineers, the California Regional Water Control Board, geologist Gerhardt Hubner, and David Church, the chief administrative planner for San Luis Obispo County, developed a plan. The complex solution involved destruction or removal of twenty-one houses and stores, an unpopular but necessary step, excavating 6,700 truckloads of oil-saturated soil and sucking up thousands of gallons of fuels and dirt. There was a constant danger that a spark might set off a devastating explosion, or a break in the draining pipes could contaminate the ocean for miles around. Miraculously, after two years the work was safely completed in 2000.

Equally miraculous is what the City Council of Avila Beach did with its share of the settlement. A waterfront promenade was constructed with attractive walkways providing ocean views, sidewalk furniture, and artworks. Removed buildings were restored, and sites were created for private development of new tourist attractions, including inns, restaurants, and shops, as well as stores to serve the local residents. Today Avila Beach presents a fresh, vibrant image, taking full advantage of its natural location.

To learn more, read David, Goliath and the Beach Cleaning Machine *by Barbara Wolcott.*

Avila Beach is a favorite among families during the summer for the protected beach, great weather, and shallow water for one-wave body boarding. In August 2003 a skilled athletic diver, wearing a wet suit and swimming among dolphins in the "safe" swimming area, was suddenly attacked and killed by a shark. Proceed with caution, but Avila Beach is still a lovely beach to nap and picnic on. The Bob Jones Bike Trail is as beautiful as they get.

Half a block from the beach is the new **ALAPAY CELLARS.** *Alapay* is the Chumash Indian word for "heavenly," which is how owners Rebecca and Scott Remmenga see their winery, Avila Beach, and life. Alapay's whimsical sea and fish decor and fabulous primary-color shirts show how much fun they have, as you might following them on Princess Cruises to Mexico. Scott used to have a wine-label printing business and decided to make what goes into the bottle instead of what goes on it.

Fine points: Featured wines: Chardonnay, Bien Nacido Pinot Noir, Paso Robles Rebekah, Zinfandel, Blush, Viognier, Savignon Blanc, Moscato. Owners: Scott and Rebecca Remmenga. Winemaker: Scott Remmenga. Cases: 3,000. Acres: buy central coast grapes.

❧ *Alapay Cellars, 491 First Street, Avila Beach 93424; (805) 595-2632; www.alapaycellars.com. Open 10:00 a.m.–5:00 p.m. daily. Tasting fee: $3 for ten tastes. Visa and MasterCard. Wheelchair accessible.*

The John Salisbury family recently and lovingly restored the old Santa Fe (or Avila) Schoolhouse on the way to Avila Beach. Seventh-generation farmer's daughter Jennifer and Kevin Rucks manage the tasting room and run the fine-arts gallery with mostly local artists' work. A very cool spot to take a break. Inquire about weekend evening barbecues and concerts on the lawn.

Fine points: Featured wines: Pinot Noir, Chardonnay, Syrah, Zinfandel. Owner and winemaker: John Salisbury. Cases: 3,000.

❧ *Salisbury Vineyards, 6985 Ontario Road, San Luis Obispo in Avila Valley west of SLO, 93405; (805) 595-9463; www.salisbury vineyards.com. Open 11:00 a.m.–6:00 p.m. daily. Visa and MasterCard. Wheelchair accessible.*

For lunch or dinner in Avila Beach, we suggest the CUSTOM HOUSE for seafood sandwiches, fish and shrimp tacos, prime rib, loads of salads, veggie burgers, and avocado, lettuce, and tomato sandwiches, all under $12. Dinner features Custom House cioppino with garlic bread, loads of steaks, some with prawns, ribs, scampi, and sautéed local scallops, cod, and calamari. Great breakfasts. Deli with gelato next door, as well as Mr. Rick's nightclub.

❧

❧ *Custom House,* *404 Front Street, Avila Beach 93424; (805) 595-7555;*
www.oldcustomhouse.com. Open 8:00 a.m.–9:00 p.m. daily. Full bar. Visa,
MasterCard, American Express, Discover. Wheelchair accessible.

The grocery store up the street also makes good sandwiches to take to the
beach.

NIPOMO

Between Pismo Beach and Santa Maria on the east side of US 101 is the
town of Nipomo, and you must make a special trip there to JOCKO'S, a wonderful funky old-fashioned steak house with a historic, Wild West role in the
history of the Santa Maria area. Take the Nipomo exit off US 101 and go east
on Tefft Street to Thompson Avenue. Jocko's is right around the corner on
Thompson just north of Tefft. While Santa Maria is known for its barbecue,
Jocko's is the restaurant where you can try it at its best any day of the week.

In 1886 Emery Knotts opened a saloon on Tefft Street, but after a fire
burned most of the block in 1888, the saloon was moved to the Thompson
Street block, just south of the current Jocko's restaurant. Emery had eight sons
who helped run the saloon or tend bar, including Ralph "Jocko" Knotts, who
was the second licensed driver and a justice of the peace in Nipomo. Jocko's
wife, Millie, was the first telephone operator and a local postmaster.

During Prohibition (1920–33), Jocko ran a garage and service station here,
selling car parts and even a little booze—white lightning and homemade
brew—out of the trunk of a car. In 1926 Jocko and "Bull" Tognazzini opened
a saloon and watering hole called Jocko's Cage at one end of the garage. During
the forties, slot machines, poker games, and card rooms appeared and disappeared quickly in sync with the arrivals and departures of authorities.

Jocko's sons Fred and George ran Jocko's Cage through the fifties and
started serving barbecue on Saturday and Sunday, with horseshoe pits under the
surrounding pepper trees. To expand their seating, they took over a lunch
counter in a renovated streetcar next door.

In 1962 George and Fred opened this "new" restaurant and saloon across the
street at Tefft and Thompson. The walls are "branded" with the cattle brands of
Nipomo ranches, including that of Capt. William C. Dana, original owner of the
38,000-acre Nipomo rancho land grant and distant relative of the Knotts family.

Fans really do drive hundreds of miles to experience the best steak dinner
they ever had, and it is well worth a slight deviation from an almost vegetarian

regime just for the taste. The steaks are about 3 inches thick and coated with that salty, garlicky mixture famous in the area. All dinners come with here-baked beans, salad, potato of choice, and ice cream. The spareribs, chops, chicken, deep-fried rainbow trout, pastas, sandwiches, and salads are equally good. The bar between the two dining rooms is so much fun that you won't mind waiting for your table, which you should plan to do. The martini glass is part of their logo for good reason. Unless you have a place to take your left-overs or have a huge appetite, we suggest you share a steak.

❧ *Jocko's, 125 North Thompson Avenue, Nipomo 93444; (805) 929-3686 or (805) 929-3565. Open 8:00 a.m.–10:00 p.m. Sunday–Thursday, 8:00 a.m.–11:00 p.m. Friday and Saturday. Full bar. Visa and MasterCard. Wheelchair accessible.*

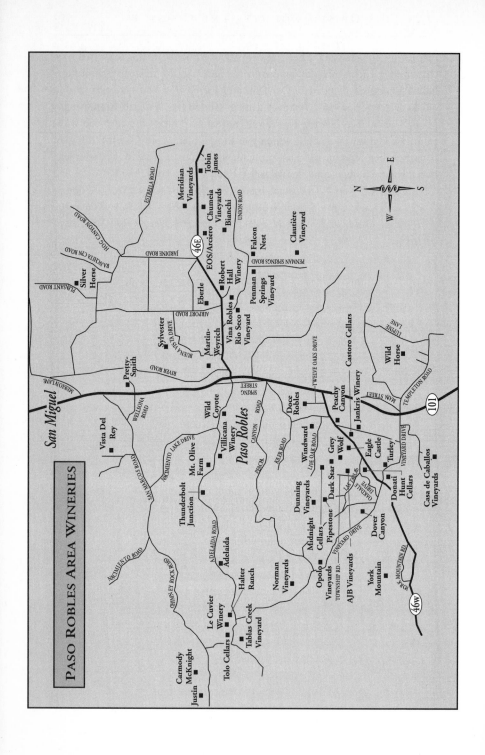

PASO ROBLES AREA WINERIES

CHAPTER 7

TOURING SAN LUIS OBISPO COUNTY WINERIES

ost of San Luis Obispo County's wineries are in the Paso Robles area, which is where we will start and which will take up most of this chapter. But there are also excellent ones in the Edna Valley south of San Luis Obispo, so we go there, too. We take you to all the wineries that are open to the public for tasting.

PASO ROBLES AREA

Paso Robles area wineries, of which there are now more than seventy, cluster on and off Highway 46 East and Highway 46 West and some of the latter's side roads. (Please note that Highway 46 West is not the western extension of Highway 46 East. Highway 46 East is Twenty-fourth Street on the west side of U.S. Highway 101 and becomes Nacimiento Lake Drive. You will notice that wineries on the east side of US 101 resemble Napa Valley's more commercial appearance, while the west side has more intimate, family wineries set amid rolling hills covered with oak trees.) Pretty-Smith Vinyards in San Miguel is the exception to the rule (there has to be one, right?). So we take you to it first, particularly convenient if you are approaching Paso Robles from the north. To get here, take the Mission exit from US 101 in San Miguel to Fourteenth Street, take a right on Fourteenth, cross the railroad tracks, and turn right (south) on River Road to the winery. High-tech executives Lisa Pretty and Victor Smith bought Mission View Estate and have completely redefined it as PRETTY-SMITH VINEYARDS.

Pretty-Smith is a small, friendly boutique winery where the enthusiastic staff does a little of everything. Here you can easily see the whole operation.

Be sure to ask questions. While visiting Pretty-Smith, take the opportunity to walk through Mission San Miguel and its shop. (See page 120 for Mission San Miguel.)

 Fine points: Featured wines: Chardonnay, Fumé Blanc, Merlot, Zinfandel, Cabernet Sauvignon, Late Harvest Muscat Canelli. Owners: Lisa Pretty and Victor Smith. Winemaker: Philip Curnow. Cases: 5,500. Acres: 45 planted.

⤷ *Pretty-Smith Vineyards, 13350 North River Road, San Miguel 93451; mailing address: P.O. Box 3407, Paso Robles 93447; (805) 467-3104, fax (805) 457-3719; www.prettysmith.com. Open 10:00 a.m.–5:00 p.m. Friday–Monday. Tasting fee: none. Visa, MasterCard, American Express. Wheelchair accessible.*

To get to SILVER HORSE WINERY from Pretty-Smith Vineyards on River Road, you can either go north to Mission Lane and eventually right (south) on Pleasant Road, or you can head south on River Road and turn left (east) on Estrella Road, then turn left (north) on Pleasant Road.

You can stroll through Silver Horse's ranch and vineyards and enjoy your picnic on the patio next to the vineyard.

 Fine points: Featured wines: Cabernet Sauvignon, Malbec, Petit Viognier, Tempranillo, Garnacha, Syrah, Sauvignon Blanc, Albarino, Merlot, Zinfandel, Dessert Zinfandel. Owners: Jim and Suzanne Kroener. Winemaker: Steve Kroener. Cases: 2,000. Acres: 43 planted of 88.

⤷ *Silver Horse Winery, 2995 Pleasant Road, San Miguel 93451; (805) 467-WINE; www.silverhorse.com. Open 11:00 a.m.–5:00 p.m. Friday–Monday; call for appointment at other times. Tasting fee: $5 for six wines, $10 with glass. Visa and MasterCard. Wheelchair accessible.*

VISTA DEL REY VINEYARDS is really closer to San Miguel than to Paso Robles, and it's the first winery on the west side of US 101 in the Paso Robles area. Take San Marcos Road toward the west off US 101, turn right (north) on Honey Road, and then veer right onto Drake Road to Vista del Rey. If the gate is open, you are welcome at this "mom and pop" winery.

Vista del Rey means "view of the king," a noncoincidental name since David and Carol De Hart–King own the place. Known to some as the "King of Zin," David makes many styles of Zinfandel from his dry-farmed vineyard with spectacular views of the Santa Lucia Mountains. Enjoy gourmet food products, Zinfandel educational materials, and local art with a wine country theme. The

Kings emphasize that their property is a "no-kill farm," where no wild animals, bugs, or even spiders are killed.

Fine points: Featured wines: Zinfandel, Dry Rosé, Barbera, Pinot Blanc. Owners: David and Carol De Hart–King. Winemaker: David King. Cases: 700. Acres: 22.

Vista del Rey Vineyards, 7340 Drake Road, Paso Robles 93446; (805) 467-2138. Open 11:00 a.m.–5:00 p.m. Sunday, by appointment weekdays. Tasting fee: none. Visa and MasterCard. Wheelchair accessible.

WINERIES EAST OF US 101

Now we take you to the wineries out Highway 46 East, and then bring you back on the same road. We do it this way so that you don't crisscross the highway and kill yourself or others. If you don't want to go the whole way, just pick up our tour where you happen to be.

Your first stops east of US 101 on or off Highway 46 East are Rio Seco Vineyard and Penman Springs Vineyard. To get to the wineries, turn right on Union Road; both wineries will be on your right.

RIO SECO VINEYARD specializes in wine and interesting people. Carol Hinkle is a warm and friendly retired teacher, and Tom Hinkle just retired as a western-states scout for the Milwaukee Brewers baseball team. The Hinkles serve tastes of their handcrafted wines at an informal tasting bar in a refurbished barn and consider every day a celebration.

Also try their own olive oils and Wild West ambience.

Fine points: Featured wines: Zinfandel, Cabernet Sauvignon, Syrah, Viognier, Roussane. Owners: Tom and Carol Hinkle. Winemaker: Tom Hinkle. Cases: 4,000. Acres: 31 planted.

Rio Seco Vineyard, 4295 Union Road, Paso Robles 93446; (805) 237-8884; www.riosecowine.com. Open 11:00 a.m.–5:30 p.m. daily. Tasting fee: $5, applied to purchase. Visa and MasterCard. Wheelchair accessible.

FALCON NEST is a slightly funky winery not on any organization's maps, and it's named for the falcons who hang out in the barn. In fact, the local wildlife society releases sparrow hawks here, just because they know the birds will be cared for.

Carolyn and Francesco Grande sell their chickens' eggs, sauces she makes, and pastas, and Carolyn heats pleasant lunches she and Francesco have pre-prepared, and make salads, hoping someday to have a restaurant on-site. They had a very successful restaurant in southern California before Francesco followed his Calabrian roots and went for the wine life.

 Fine points: Featured wines: Zinfandel, Syrah, Merlot (all 100 percent pure varietal), and Cabernet Sauvignon with a slight blend. Owners: Francesco and Carolyn Grande. Winemaker: Francesco Grande. Cases: 5,000. Acres: 55 planted of 150.

Falcon Nest Winery, 5185 Union Road, Paso Robles 93446; (805) 226-0227; www.falconnestwine.com. Open 10:00 a.m.–7:30 p.m. daily. Tasting fee: $5, applies to wine purchase. Visa and American Express.

As you leave Rio Seco, turn right on Union Road to Penman Springs Road, where you turn right to PENMAN SPRINGS VINEYARD, 2 miles from Highway 46 East.

The McCasland family takes great pride in running its artisan wine farm and winery themselves, and they offer you the chance to walk through their new and old vineyards and take in the view of Paso Robles from the top of the rolling hills. The tasting room sits below a white steeple atop the old white-sided building.

 Fine points: Featured wines: Chardonnay, Merlot, Meritage, Cabernet Sauvignon, Syrah, Petite Syrah, Muscat Blanc. Owners: Beth and Carl McCasland. Winemaker: Larry Roberts. Cases: 2,500. Acres: 40.

Penman Springs Vineyard, 1985 Penman Springs Road, Paso Robles 93446; (805) 237-7959 or (805) 237-8960; www.penmansprings.com. Open 11:00 a.m.–5:00. p.m. Friday–Sunday. Tasting fee: none. Visa and MasterCard. Not wheelchair accessible.

CLAUTIÈRE VINEYARD, right down the road from Penman Springs, is definitely the zaniest winery around and a must-visit. Claudine Blackwell and Terry Brady have fun every moment and do very well at making Rhone-style wines. Using an old family farmhouse as the tasting room, Claudine and Terry also converted an old outbuilding into their "House of Wigs and Mirrors," where visitors can try on fifty wigs, worth a belly laugh any time. Their ownership of Santa Monica's The Lobster restaurant shows in the fabulous commercial kitchen here, where you can purchase the best kitchen gadgets recommended by *Cooks Illustrated* magazine. Claudine's outdoor metal sculptures catch the eye everywhere. Claudine describes her tasting room as where "Edward Scissorhands meets the Mad Hatter at the Moulin Rouge."

Clautière's wine club is worth joining for the unusual experiences it entitles you to, including cook-alongs, "bingo and bongos," and on-site theater dinners.

CLAUTIÈRE VINEYARD'S
"HOUSE OF WIGS AND MIRRORS," PASO ROBLES

Fine points: Featured wines: Viognier, Grenache Rosé, Cabernet Sauvignon, Mon Rouge, Syrah, Port. Owners: Claudine Blackwell and Terry Brady. Winemaker: Terry Brady. Cases: 6,500. Acres: 57 planted of 140.

🍇 *Clautière Vineyard, 1340 Penman Springs Road, Paso Robles 93446; (805) 237-3789, fax (805) 237-1730; www.clautiere.com. Open noon–5:00 p.m. daily. Tasting fee: $5. Visa, MasterCard, American Express. Not wheelchair accessible.*

To get to Robert Hall and EOS from Penman Springs and Clautière Vineyards, return west of Union Road, and then turn right (east) on Highway 46 East.

ROBERT HALL WINERY is just off Highway 46 East on Mill Road. Turn right through the gate. If the flag near the winery door is up, they are open. A developer and contractor from Minnesota and Scottsdale, Arizona, Robert Hall searched in France and Napa Valley for his perfect winery site and settled here. Don't let the industrial-looking building put you off—it's much more lively inside.

Winemaker Don Brady graduated from Texas Tech University and made award-winning wines in Texas, some of which were served in the White House to former Presidents Ronald Reagan and George H. W. Bush, as well as to Queen Elizabeth and Prince Charles.

Enjoy the new, splendiferously elegant tasting room with loads of collectibles.

🍂

Fine points: Featured wines: Sauvignon Blanc, Rosé de Robles, Viognier, Chardonnay, Grenache, Merlot, Cabernet Sauvignon, Syrah, Zinfandel, Orange Muscat. Owner: Robert Hall. Winemaker: Don Brady. Cases: 70,000. Acres: 300.

✒ *Robert Hall Winery, 3443 Mill Road, Paso Robles 93446; (805) 239-1616, fax (805) 239-2464; www.roberthallwinery.com. Open 10:00 a.m.–6:00 p.m. daily. Tasting fee: $4, includes logo glass. Visa, MasterCard, American Express, Discover. Wheelchair accessible.*

VIÑA ROBLES winery next door was still under construction at press time.

The European feeling you sense looking at the buildings of EOS ESTATE WINERY at ARCIERO ESTATE WINERY comes from its model, Monte Cassino, a onetime Benedictine monastery built centuries ago near the Arciero family home in Santa Elia Fiumerapido. The Arciero brothers' construction company built the winery. Convenient and smart!

Local winds blow the scent of rose gardens through the air. The 6,000-square-foot tasting room and visitor center has the most comprehensive and elegant gift shop we have seen anywhere. But the real surprise and treat is right around the corner to the right just inside the front door. Even if you aren't a race car fan, you will enjoy the chance to be this close to famous, miraculously fast cars, such as those driven by Arciero Racing Team members Scott Pruett and Cristiano da Matta.

A whole deck of tables facing the vast winery building welcomes you to picnic, and the staff here is extremely well informed and helpful.

Both EOS Estate Winery and Arciero Estate Winery are the creations and dreams of former Indianapolis 500 race car driver Frank Arciero Sr., who more recently has sponsored drivers Phil Hill, Dan Gurney, Al and Bobby Unser, and Michael Andretti.

In 1939 Frank (then fourteen) and his brother Phil (ten) came from Italy, where they had stomped grapes and crushed olives, to join their father and older brother in New York. Neither of them spoke English. The young brothers became ditchdiggers and learned enough to start a paving business. Visiting his Army son at Fort Ord, Frank attended car races at Monterey's Laguna Seca Raceway and fell in love. And he was off to the races! Phil now runs Arciero Brothers concrete construction empire. Now Frank Arciero Jr. (Butch) and his wife, Betty, help with sales and marketing, Butch having worked in his father's construction business and succeeding as Driver of the Year in the Mickey Thompson Off Road Grand Prix Series Unlimited Super 1600 class. Oh yes, you can buy loads of Arciero racing team paraphernalia, from hats to coffee mugs.

EOS AND ARCIERO ESTATE WINERIES, PASO ROBLES

By the way, the Arcieros are making some excellent wines, too. Their 1995 Zinfandel rates equally with several from Napa Valley and costs about half the price. Got your interest now?

Arciero's EOS series, named for the Greek goddess of dawn, focuses on classic, old-world methods and quality. Eos is pictured on labels near the constellation Orion, with whom she supposedly had a dalliance. At EOS the grapes are harvested as near dawn as possible to keep the fruit cool and help retain flavors. According to mythology, Eos gave birth to the four winds—Boreas, Eurusm, Zephyrus, and Notus—after which EOS's four vineyard blocks have been named.

The Vernon Underwood Family, majority owners of Young's Markets, are now partners in EOS Estate Winery and have installed a new well-stocked deli for picnic foods. Enjoy right here!

 Fine points: Featured wines: EOS Chardonnay, Sauvignon Blanc, Fumé Blanc, Zinfandel, Cabernet Sauvignon, Merlot, Moscato; Arciero Arpeggio, Nebbiolo, Sangiovese, Chardonnay, Chenin Blanc, White Zinfandel, Merlot, Cabernet Sauvignon, Petite Sirah, Zinfandel, Merlot, Muscat Canelli; Reserve Chardonnay, Fumé Blanc, Petite Syrah. Owners: EOS: Arciero and Underwood families; Arciero: Arciero family and Kerry Vix. Winemaker: Leslie Felten. Cases: 200,000-plus. Acres: 700-plus.

❧ *EOS* and *Arciero Estate Wineries, 5625 Highway 46 East, P.O. Box 1179, Paso Robles 93447; (800) 249-WINE; www.eosvintage.com. Open 10:00 a.m.–5:00 p.m.*

Monday–Friday, 10:00 a.m.–6:00 p.m. Saturday and Sunday. Tasting fee: $10. Visa, MasterCard, American Express, Discover. Wheelchair accessible.

BIANCHI WINERY is a beautifully designed small winery complete with pond and farmhouse, designed by Pultz, the same architectural firm that designed the new Robert Hall and Viña Robles tasting rooms.

Owner Glenn Bianchi reportedly owns a few Paramount Theatres and the Paramount Swap Meet in southern California.

Look for elegant cheeses and prosciutto to enjoy at outdoor tables (if it isn't too hot), and fun staffers.

Fine points: Featured wines: Pinot Grigio, Sauvignon Blanc, Chardonnay, Zinfandel, Cabernet Franc, Merlot, Cabernet Sauvignon, Petite Sirah. Owner: Glenn Bianchi. Winemaker: Tom Lane. Cases: 5,000. Acres: 40 here, 600 in Fresno County.

❧ *Bianchi Winery, 3380 Branch Road off Highway 46 East, Paso Robles 93446; (805) 226-9922; www.bianchiwine.com. Open 10:00 a.m.–5:00 p.m. daily. Tasting fee: $5. Visa, MasterCard, American Express. Wheelchair accessible.*

BIANCHI WINERY
PASO ROBLES

CHUMEIA VINEYARDS is east of EOS and Arciero on Highway 46 East. This young winery shows environmental sensitivity, initially with a sign and concrete bed over a creek called Chumeia Crossing, with the purpose of helping Kit Fox and other local species cross safely. The sign reads: YOU ARE TRAVELING THROUGH A WILDLIFE CORRIDOR OF 3.1 ACRES DEDICATED TO PRESERVING THE ENVIRONMENT. Chumeia also provides a children's table with crayons and coloring books, as well as Templeton's Olea Farms olive oils.

Chumeia ("koo-may-a") means alchemy in Greek, and the winery club's motto is "It's all Greek to me." Co-owner Lee Nesbitt worked as winemaker at J. Lohr and Meridian wineries. They are off to a quick start, winning a double gold medal at the California State Fair for their Dante Dusi Zinfandel.

Fine points: Featured wines: Viognier, Barbera, Chardonnay, Pinot Noir, Cabernet Sauvignon, Zinfandel. Owners: Lee and Mark Nesbitt, Kristen Nesbitt, Julie Nesbitt, Eric Donniger. Winemaker: Lee Nesbitt. Cases: 15,000. Acres: 2,300.

❧ *Chumeia Vineyards, 8331 Highway 46 East, Paso Robles 93446; (805) 226-0102, fax (805) 226-0104; www.chumeiavineyards.com. Open 10:00 a.m.–5:00 p.m. daily. Tasting fee: none. Visa, MasterCard, American Express, Discover. Wheelchair accessible.*

When you leave Chumeia, turn right (east) and go another few miles to TOBIN JAMES CELLARS, the most hilariously fun winery anywhere. While it's a bit out there, both in distance (12 miles east of Paso Robles) and in ambience, it is actually the first winery you come to if you are coming from Fresno or Bakersfield on Highway 46 East.

As you approach Tobin James on Union Road and Highway 46 East, you first see the peak-roofed, yellow-with-purple-trim Victorian that is Tobin James's little guest house. As you drive into the winery parking lot, you see the two-story wood winery with wagon wheels, palm trees, and all sorts of cowboy and old farm paraphernalia, with the guest house just beyond. Sunbursts are the theme here—they appear on all of Tobin James's labels.

Tobin James Shumrick, unearned Southern accent and all, founded Tobin James after working in a wine shop in Cincinnati, as assistant winemaker at Eberle Winery, and as founding winemaker at Peachy Canyon. Shumrick worked for free at Peachy Canyon, on the condition that he could make his own wine there as well. You will find him outrageous, brilliant, and funny, as we did.

At that Cincinnati wine shop, Gary Eberle walked in one day to promote Estrella River Winery, in which he was then a partner. Toby said he would love to come out to Paso Robles to learn to make wine and would work a harvest crush for free just for the chance. Following his stint as a cellar rat and barrel

In front of the tasting room of
Tobin James Cellars, Paso Robles

room manager, and later in marketing positions at Estrella, Toby followed
Eberle to his own winery, where Eberle offered him the position of assistant
winemaker.

One day at Eberle, a vineyard manager brought six tons of grapes that had
been rejected by another winery as well as by Gary Eberle, and Toby said. "I'll
take 'em." He talked Eberle into letting him make some wine out of them, and
as Toby says, "The medals just started rockin' in." The experience gave him the
courage to go out on his own, and Tobin James is the Wild West result. This is
a guy who knew at age eighteen that he would have his own winery, and it
shows. He's very honest in saying that his Chateau Le Cacheflo (not a French
wine, but a blend of Syrah, Mourvedre, Grenache, and a splash of Zinfandel) is
a "pool, patio, and barbecue wine."

The tasting room is loaded with funk and junque, including a heavy, long
wooden tasting bar Jesse James shot two bullets through and Tobin James
brought here from Missouri, a kids' jail play corner, free video games, and great
music in the background, all of which adds up to feeling like you're in a saloon
and bordello—precisely Toby's goal. Toby also welcomed investor/partner Lance
Silver, who migrated to Paso Robles from Los Angeles (where he developed and
sold an extremely successful clothing company) and now lives over the tasting
room with his family.

The guest house is terrific. We stayed in what's dubbed the penthouse apart-
ment, which felt like the perfect self-sufficient studio to live in for a while and

write a few good (of course) books. The complete kitchen and washer/dryer combination along with the plush feather bed and views make this place heaven.

Fine points: Featured wines: Chardonnay, Chardonnay Radiance, Ballistic Zinfandel, Cabernet Sauvignon, Made in the Shade Merlot, Dream Catcher Muscat, Chateau Le Cacheflo blend, Syrah Bulls Eye, Charisma Dessert Zinfandel, Dessert Sauvignon Blanc Jubilation, Sparkling Wine Dream Weaver. Owners: Tobin James Shumrick, Lance Silver, and Claire Silver. Winemakers: Tobin James Shumrick and Lance Silver. Cases: 40,000. Acres: none, buy locally.

Tobin James Cellars, 8950 Union Road, Paso Robles 93446; (805) 239-2204, fax (805) 239-2204; www.tobinjames.com. Open 10:00 a.m.–6:00 p.m. daily. No tasting fee. Visa and MasterCard. Wheelchair accessible.

As you leave Tobin James, go west on Highway 46 East to MERIDIAN VINEYARDS, on the right side of the highway. The roller-coaster driveway leads you to one of the most beautiful French-like wineries on the central coast, with young tasting-room staffers to match. As you get out of the car and follow the path lined with a tastefully labeled herb garden shaded by 200-year-old oak trees to the natural stone winery, signs announce CAUTION: RATTLESNAKES. PLEASE STAY ON PATH. Believe them. Don't miss the view of Meridian's home vineyards.

You are welcome to enjoy a picnic at Meridian's green umbrellaed tables. If you didn't bring supplies, Meridian is one of the few wineries in the area that has a full and exquisite deli case with goodies such as Dutch and Vermont cheeses, waters, and chocolates, with plenty of crackers available nearby. Be sure to check out the work of Chicago artist Thomas Gathman, who designed the jazzy Meridian labels and whose deal includes Meridian continuing to buy his creations. Hence you get to see a private show whenever you visit. Enjoy!

Original winemaker Chuck Ortman majored in graphic arts at the California College of Arts and Crafts in Oakland, but when a friend gave him some wine he had made in his mother's basement, he was hooked. To his parents' chagrin, in 1968 he

MERIDIAN VINEYARDS'S
TASTING ROOM

got a job dragging hoses (about as low as you can go) in the Napa Valley for Joe Heitz and moved his wife, Sue, and their daughter there.

In the next twenty years, Ortman worked or consulted for Heitz, Spring Mountain, St. Clement, Fisher, Far Niente, St. Andrew's, Shafer, Cain Cellars, and Keenan, during which an Ortman style developed. He was one of the first modern California winemakers to explore barrel fermentation instead of using stainless-steel tanks.

Ortman first bottled an Edna Valley Chardonnay under his own label in 1979, and he changed the name to Meridian at Sue's suggestion to show his love for sailing and because it "means the achievement of an idea." In 1988 Wine World Estates (now Beringer Wine Estates) invested in Meridian and bought this winery (then Estrella River Winery) for Ortman and Meridian to develop. Giant Foster's Wine Group of Australia purchased many of Beringer's properties, including Meridian. Lee Miyamura, a graduate of Sonoma State University with interests in molecular biology and chemistry, started as a lab assistant at Beringer Vineyards in St. Helena and, over twenty years, worked her way to winemaker at Meridian.

 Fine points: Featured wines: Chardonnay, Sauvignon Blanc, Gewürztraminer, Cabernet Blanc, Pinot Noir, Merlot, Syrah, Cabernet Sauvignon, Zinfandel. Owner: Foster's Wine Estates. Winemaker: Lee Miyamura. Cases: won't reveal. Acres: 3,534 of their own, buy from 1,397 of others.

❧ *Meridian Vineyards, 7000 Highway 46 East, P.O. Box 3289, Paso Robles 93447; (805) 237-6000 or (805) 226-7133; www.meridianvineyards.com. Open 10:00 a.m.–5:00 p.m. daily. Tasting fee: $5. Visa, MasterCard, American Express, Discover. Wheelchair accessible.*

As you come out of Meridian, turn right (west) on Highway 46 East for about 5 miles to EBERLE WINERY, which you approach through the high overhead entry gate. The redwood winery, surrounded by poplar trees and flowers, overlooks Eberle's estate vineyards.

Just walking into Eberle is a blood-pressure-lowering experience. Chants waft through the air, guests look as if they're hanging out in a friend's living room, there are loads of known and unusual Jewish and other cookbooks on the shelves, and the staff members are grown-ups. Be sure to walk out the door on the left wall of the tasting room to a platform to view the tanks and smell and hear the winemaking process—a rare experience for visiting tasters.

A native of Pittsburgh, Pennsylvania, Eberle founder Gary Eberle studied biology at Penn State on scholarship while playing defensive lineman on the football team and meeting and marrying Jeanie. After graduation the Eberles moved to

EBERLE WINERY ENTRANCE, PASO ROBLES

Louisiana, where Gary excelled at the study of cellular genetics at Louisiana State University. There he befriended a professor who introduced him to food and fine wines, particularly Bordeaux, and he quickly became fascinated with the Cabernet Sauvignon grape that is the basis of many Bordeaux. Breaking off his genetics studies, Gary visited UC/Davis, where he told the enology department chair that he wanted to be a winemaker, and the chair let him in the program without even requiring him to take the qualifying exam! He ended up with a doctorate in fermentation and enology, rare indeed.

On returning to Louisiana, Gary and Jeanie conferred "for seconds" and decided to move to California. Gary's goal at Davis was to make the best Cabernet Sauvignon possible. He studied the Paso Robles region, saw huge potential, and in 1974 planted 500 acres of vineyards on the Estrella River plains, naming the winery Estrella River and developing it to produce 200,000 cases a year. Estrella River was eventually sold to Wine World Estates, now Beringer Wine Estates, whose Meridian Vineyards now occupies the former Estrella River site. At Eberle Gary focuses on handcrafted limited-quantity wines.

Be sure to ask to see the 15,863 square feet of caves where you can look in on the Wild Boar Room, a one-hundred-seat underground dining facility where guest-chef dinners are held regularly. This is one mailing list to get on! They've won loads of gold medals for Chardonnays and Cabernets. Call ahead to order lunch and enjoy it on Eberle's deck overlooking the vineyards and inquire about their dinner series.

 Fine points: Featured wines: Chardonnay, Syrah, Zinfandel, Roussanne, Cabernet Sauvignon, Cabernet Sauvignon/Syrah blend, Counoise Rosé, Viognier, Barbera, Syrah, Syrah Rosé, Sangiovese, Côtes du Rôbles, Muscat Canelli. Owner and enologist: Gary Eberle. Winemaker: Ben Mayo. Cases: 30,000. Acres: 38 estate and buy locally.

⋆❧ *Eberle Winery, 3.5 miles east of Paso Robles on Highway 46 East, P.O. Box 2459, Paso Robles 93447; (805) 238-9607; www.eberlewinery.com. Open 10:00 a.m.–5:00 p.m. daily, 10:00 a.m.–6:00 p.m. in summer. Tasting fee: none. Visa, MasterCard, American Express, Discover. Wheelchair accessible. Dog friendly.*

When you come out of Eberle's driveway, turn right (west) again and go another 2.8 miles back toward Paso Robles to the remodeled **MARTIN-WEYRICH WINERY.** This puts you just 0.8 mile east of US 101.

In 1998 Mary Martin (not the late actress) and her husband, Dave Weyrich, bought the winery from her brothers, all of whom benefit from the family's Martin Outdoor billboard sign company.

Martin-Weyrich considers itself to be the premier producer of Italian varietals in the United States, attributing many firsts to itself: the only American winery exhibiting at the Italian VinItaly of Verona; first grower and producer of Nebbiolo in the United States in modern times; the largest planting of Nebbiolo in the United States; first U.S. winery to focus solely on Cal-Italia varietals; first and only U.S. producer to age and ferment Chardonnay in chestnut barrels; first U.S. producer to blend Sangiovese with Cabernet Sauvignon; first and only producer to use a "vino di ripasso"; first and only U.S. producer to make traditional Vin Santo from straw-dried Malvasia grapes, then aged in barrels; and first U.S. producer to import all of its glass directly from Italy.

We also happen to like the Italian pottery collection for sale here—nice staff, too! Enjoy the newish tasting room and Italian ambience. You can also get cheese and lunch nibbles here for your picnic. There's also a new Italian-style bed-and-breakfast, Villa Toscana, which is fabulous.

 Fine points: Featured wines: Chardonnay, Pinot Grigio, Sangiovese Il Palio, Nebbiolo, Nebbiolo Vecchio, Cabernet Etrusco, Zinfandel La Primitiva, Insieme blend, Moscato Allegro, Grappa di Aleatico. Owners: Dave and Mary Weyrich. Winemakers: Craig Reed and Alan Kinne. Cases: 45,000. Acres: 350-plus.

⋆❧ *Martin-Weyrich Winery, 2610 Buena Vista, P.O. Box 2599, Paso Robles 93447; (805) 238-2520, fax (805) 238-0887; www.martinweyrich.com.*

Open 10:00 a.m.–5:00 p.m. daily. Tasting fee: $4, reserves $5. Visa, MasterCard, American Express, Discover. Wheelchair accessible.

A little way up Buena Vista Drive from Martin-Weyrich and Highway 46 East is Sylvester Winery, the newish baby of Sylvester Feichtinger. You can get here more directly by turning north from Highway 46 East onto Airport Road and left again onto Buena Vista Drive.

Sylvester bought the ranch in 1962 (a wise move indeed), growing pistachios and grapes since 1989. After his grapes turned into such good wine for others, he decided to make his own wine, with substantial success. Sylvester brought in former Grgich winemaker Craig Effman, and Effman was succeeded by Charles Feaver.

Enjoy the small deli in Sylvester's spacious tasting room, where you can purchase imported meats and cheeses and crackers to snack on around the winery. Don't miss Sylvester's three vintage Rock Island Line train cars.

 Fine points: Featured wines: Chardonnay, Cabernet Sauvignon, Merlot, Sangiovese, Syrah, Zinfandel. Owner: Sylvia Fillipina, daughter of founder. Winemaker: Jac Jacobs. Cases: 50,000. Acres: 200 planted in vineyard, 140 planted in pistachios.

❧ *Sylvester Winery, 5115 Buena Vista Drive, Paso Robles 93446; (805) 227-4000, fax (805) 227-6128; www.sylvesterwinery.com. Open 10:00 a.m.–5:00 p.m. daily; until 6:00 p.m. in the summer. Tasting fee: none. Visa, MasterCard, American Express. Wheelchair accessible.*

Paso Robles Wineries West of US 101

On the west side of US 101 you have to make some choices, and those may depend on the time you have to tour and taste. Or perhaps you want to head for specific wineries. We offer a 50-mile Big Circle Tour (with options) and a 15-mile Little Circle Tour. You could spend a day or two sampling on the Big Circle Tour and make the Little Circle Tour in an afternoon, if you hurry. Of course you can just do part of either tour.

Big Circle Tour

Less than a mile off US 101, Twenty-fourth Street in Paso Robles becomes Nacimiento Lake Drive. As you wind through the hills and almond groves, do not miss Jardine Ranch's Country Nut House, where you can purchase locally grown nuts and fruits (these are not people). If the place looks closed, ring the doorbell and Mary or Bill Jardine will come serve you. Bill's family homesteaded this place in 1889 and has been a real pioneer in nut ranching in these parts.

Just taste the crunchy almonds, fruits, nuts, and candies, and it's easy to convince yourself of the health benefits in the gift packs, including the fat.

🍇 *Country Nut House at Jardine Ranch, 910 Nacimiento Lake Drive, Paso Robles 93446; (805) 238-2365; www.jardineranch.com. Open 9:00 a.m.–6:00 p.m. daily. Visa, MasterCard, American Express, Discover. Wheelchair accessible.*

Take Adelaida Road west off Nacimiento Lake Drive to visit Villicana Winery, Hidden Mountain Ranch, Adelaida Cellars, Le Cuvier Winery, Carmody McKnight, and Tablas Creek Vineyard. Don't let a sign proclaiming Pᴀʀᴋ ᴇɴᴛʀᴀɴᴄᴇ 600 ꜰᴇᴇᴛ get you excited and dreaming of walking in wilderness. It's a mobile-home park.

Vɪʟʟɪᴄᴀɴᴀ Wɪɴᴇʀʏ is the charming and modest creation of Alex and Monica Villicana, who live with their children up the driveway from their new winery. Unusual in this business, the Villicana family dug all the holes, planted their own vines, and now reap the harvest, aiming at low yields of intensely concentrated fruit. Results include a double gold medal and Best of Show for their first vintage estate Merlot at the San Francisco International Wine Competition, and a gold for their Cabernet at the Los Angeles County Fair.

Watch this winery! In their previous young lives, Alex made wine at Alex Trebek's late Creston Vineyards, and Monica worked in marketing for Reebok sporting goods. The tasting corner of their winery is simple and elegant with Oriental rugs. This is a great place to cool off from local summer heat (bring a sweater in winter). The Villicanas are very involved and generous with their time in the Paso Robles community and host charity barbecues and other events in their lovely picnic area.

Fine points: Featured wines: Chardonnay, Dry Vin Rosé, Merlot, Cabernet Sauvignon, Zinfandel. Owners: Alex and Monica Villicana. Winemaker: Alex Villicana. Cases: 2,000. Acres: 10 planted.

🍇 *Villicana Winery, 1715 Adelaida Road, Paso Robles 93446; (805) 239-9456, fax (805) 239-0115; www.villicanawinery.com. Open 11:00 a.m.–5:00 p.m. Saturday and Sunday. Tasting fee: none. Visa, MasterCard. Wheelchair accessible.*

Mᴛ. Oʟɪᴠᴇ Oʀɢᴀɴɪᴄ Fᴀʀᴍ is an organic and health food oasis run by several families of the New Testament Church who farm the land surrounding their store cooperatively. The Ng family bakes bread; makes light meals, sandwiches, and salads to order that guests may eat at tables overlooking the valley; and sells organic herbs, spices, olive tree seedlings, free-range chickens, dried fruits and nuts, organic artichokes, broccoli, and other seasonal vegetables, organic olives (lots of tasting available) and olive oils, yogurt, and healthful drinks. Petting farm.

🌂 *Mt. Olive Organic Farm, 3445 Adelaida Road, Paso Robles 93446; (805) 347-0147; www.mtoliveco.com. Open 10:00 a.m.–7:00 p.m. Thursday–Sunday April–October; closes at 5:00 p.m. November–March. Visa, MasterCard, American Express. Wheelchair accessible.*

WILD COYOTE ESTATE WINERY has the most interesting new winery architecture on the west side of US 101 in the Paso Robles area.

Architect/owner/winemaker Gianni Manucci designed his winery and bed-and-breakfast for his love of Taos, New Mexico. Just arriving at Wild Coyote and walking through its little buildings at 1,800 feet elevation is a moving experience.

Manucci's two labels, Wild Coyote and Coyote Creek, are named for "a little pack of coyote creatures that used to hunt in our land before it became a vineyard," and Manucci's respect for coyote mythology.

WILD COYOTE ESTATE WINERY

While of California Italian background, Manucci does a great job of look-ing Native American with tan skin and long, dark hair hanging in a ponytail down his back.

Fine points: Featured wines: Syrah, Merlot, Zinfandel, Zinfandel Port. Owner and winemaker: Gianni Manucci. Cases: 1,800. Acres: 15.

❧ *Wild Coyote Estate Winery, 3775 Adelaida Road, Paso Robles 93446; (805) 610-1311; www.wildcoyote.biz. Open 11:00 a.m.–5:00 p.m. daily. Tasting fee: $5. Visa, MasterCard, American Express. Wheelchair accessible.*

THUNDERBOLT JUNCTION WINERY is a new name in the winery business and is reached by turning off Adelaida Road onto Hidden Mountain Road. It's the successor to historic Hidden Mountain Ranch, which dates from the late '60s. Founded by Templeton physician Stanley Hoffman, with the advice of famed wine guru André Tchelistcheff, the winery was expanded by the Hoffman family before being sold to a Japanese corporation in the mid-'80s and in turn sold again in 1997 to three individuals.

Richard and Aurora Gumerman purchased the winery and its extensive property in 2005 and gave the enterprise the name Thunderbolt Junction Winery, while they still produce wines under the Hidden Mountain Ranch and HMR labels.

Fine points: Featured wines: Grenache, Merlot, Syrah, Cabernet Sauvignon. Owners: Richard and Aurora Gumerman. Cases: 3,000. Acres: 115.

❧ *Thunderbolt Junction Winery, 2740 Hidden Mountain Road, Paso Robles 93446; (805) 226-9907 (tasting room), (805) 238-7143 (winery), fax (805) 226-9903); www.thunderboltjunction.com. Open 11:00 a.m.–5:00 p.m. Friday–Sunday. Tasting fee: $5. Visa, MasterCard, American Express. Wheelchair accessible.*

As you come out of Thunderbolt Junction Winery, turn left on Adelaida Road for about 0.5 mile, then turn into ADELAIDA CELLARS's road, through Andrew's Curve, and arrive at the winery and tasting room parking lot a mile farther. Adelaida's bold sign on a stucco winery wall is in stark contrast to other winery facades in the neighborhood, and you are indeed in for a different expe-rience. You are just 18 miles east of Hearst Castle and the Pacific Ocean.

As you walk in the door, you will be greeted by owner/partner Elizabeth Van Steenwyk (or another happy and usually funny person), who serves elegant organic sausages and other hors d'oeuvres to prospective wine purchasers along with tastes of wine. Kids of all ages will enjoy the paper and crayons, as well as the apples, bananas, and grapes in a basket at the far end of the tasting bar. The winery's warehouse is to your right, and the barrel room dresses up marvelously for elegant celebration dinners. We also like Adelaida's campaign buttons for designated drivers that proclaim "I'll drink mine later."

Just as many coffee lovers believe in mountain-grown beans, Adelaida believes in mountain-grown grapes, planting the vines close together in the rocky, chalky soil to make them work harder. More than 85 percent of the area's grape harvest is sold to Napa and Sonoma wineries.

It was this legendary fruit and the peaceful lifestyle that first drew John Munch and his wife, Andree, to the west side region, where they purchased ten acres and named the property Adelaida after the old Adelaida schoolhouse built in the 1880s to serve the original mountain community. John made his first bottle of wine under the Adelaida label in 1981, and that Cabernet Sauvignon ranked as one of the top ten Cabs in the country.

In 1990 John met Don and Elizabeth Van Steenwyk and their son, Matt, at a local wine tasting. With a long family history of walnut and almond growing in the Paso Robles area, the Van Steenwyks were interested in diversifying into wine grapes. So John and the Van Steenwyks got together, combined their talents and what they had to give, and created a 500-acre vineyard and winery on the Van Steenwyks' spectacular 1,700-acre ranch. In 1994 the Van Steenwyks purchased sixty acres of vineyards from the neighboring Hoffman Mountain Ranch, originally developed by Dr. Stanley Hoffman with the help of winemaker André Tchelistcheff.

Today John has been joined by winemaker Steven Glossner and assistant winemaker Phil Curnow. Curnow grew up in England and needed to find the perfect place where he could surf and work in the wine business. So he found Adelaida. Elizabeth Van Steenwyk serves as president and CEO of the winery, and John Munch continues as winemaker extraordinaire, vineyard honcho, newsletter scrivener, and raconteur, challenged in the last only slightly by Phil. Don Van Steenwyk oversees his company, Applied Technology, and its main manufacturing plant in Paso Robles.

Fine points: Featured wines: Chardonnay, Chenin Blanc, Zinfandel, Cabernet Sauvignon, Sangiovese, Pinot Noir, Blanc de Blancs sparkling wine. Owners: Don and Elizabeth Van Steenwyk. Winemaker extraordinaire: John Munch. Winemaker: Steven Glossner. Cases: 6,000-plus. Acres: 500.

❧ *Adelaida Cellars, 5805 Adelaida Road, Paso Robles 93446; (805) 239-8980 or (800) 676-1232, fax (805) 239-4671; www.adelaida.com. Tasting fee: $3,* *includes glass. Open 11:00 a.m.–5:00 p.m. daily. Visa and MasterCard. Wheelchair accessible.*

LE CUVIER is the excellent, charming little winery of popular winemaker John Munch and Mary Fox. John was a cofounder of Adelaida and sold his interest in 1998. While his look is ultimate folksy, his background is not. John's father was an engineer for United Fruit, and John graduated from San Francisco State and got his M.A. in England, followed by a wander through Europe, working at a Swiss champagne house. John met and married his late wife in Provence, and visitors will experience a distinct Provençal ambience that capitalizes on the old farmhouse winery and tasting room. Check out the old kitchen utensils and stove in the tasting room, as well as the Provençal pottery.

John and Mary buy all their fruit from small, family producers within 5 to 7 miles of Le Cuvier, which means "washtub" in French. What sets their wines apart, at least partly, is that they age white wines two to three years, age reds four to five years, and Cabernet Franc seven years.

 Fine points: Featured wines: Chardonnay, Chenin Blanc, Cabernet Franc, Cabernet Sauvignon, Zinfandel, Syrah, Sangiovese, and blends. Owners: Mary Fox and John Munch. Winemaker: John Munch. Cases: 3,000. Acres: none.

❧ *Le Cuvier, 9750 Adelaida Road, Paso Robles 93446; (805) 238-5706 or (800) 549-4764, fax (805) 237-0577; www.lcwine.com. Open 11:00 a.m.–5:00 p.m. daily. Tasting fee: $3, $10 for Bordeaux; includes glass. Visa, MasterCard. Barely wheelchair accessible.*

As you get back onto Adelaida Road, turn right (west) and enjoy gorgeous rolling hills, pistachio and almond trees, and lichen hanging from large oak trees. Most of the road is about one and a half lanes with no center line, so be careful!

If you have time, venture a little farther westward to Carmody McKnight Estate Wines, known until 1999 as Silver Canyon Estate Wines. If you don't have time and wish to go directly to Norman Vineyards, about 3.8 miles along Adelaida Road from Adelaida Cellars, turn left (south) on Vineyard Drive. Then follow the directions below (after the section on Carmody McKnight).

To get to Carmody McKnight, follow Adelaida Road past its intersection with Vineyard Drive and turn right (north) on Klau Mine Road to Chimney Rock Road. Turn left on Chimney Rock to Carmody McKnight, which will be on your right, just 17 miles west of US 101.

CARMODY MCKNIGHT ESTATE WINES is well worth the extra time to visit two characters in a marvelous 1860s house. Gary Carmody, an accomplished artist (aka Gary Conway) who uses his own landscape paintings on his labels, starred in the television series *Burke's Law* as a sidekick of Gene Barry and played the part of the commander in *The Land of the Giants* series. As a screenwriter, Gary wrote *American Ninja* and *Woman's Story.*

Marian McKnight, a former Miss America from South Carolina, works in the winery with her husband, so they decided to rename Silver Canyon, which she and Gary have owned since the 1960s, with their own names and not have to explain the relationship anymore.

Gary found the broken-down ranch by looking at it with his Realtor from a helicopter that promptly crashed on the 320-acre property. Gary and the Realtor stumbled out of the whirlybird, and Gary said, "I'll take it!"

Daughter Kathleen Conway, who grew up on what became Conway Vineyards, makes a fabulous Cabernet Franc and manages the day-to-day business of the vineyard and winery.

Kristin Ball, formerly with the highly esteemed Elaine Bell Catering in Napa and Sonoma, runs the tasting room and is extremely knowledgeable about pairing food and wine. Music of the four great tenors—if you count Andrea Bocelli—wafts throughout the tasting room.

Do not miss the art gallery overlooking a lotus pond and Gary's fabulous watercolors, which he blends with his belief in the "art of the vineyard" to make great art and wine. His book *Art of the Vineyard* includes more than a hundred of his brilliant landscapes, which some critics liken to Richard Diebenkorn's work, although Gary uses much brighter colors. Most of Gary's current work is inspired by the surrounding Cambrian hills and Santa Lucia backcountry.

Fine points: Featured wines: Chardonnay, Cadenza Meritage blend, Cabernet Sauvignon, Merlot, Cabernet Franc, Cabernet Sauvignon, and a special late harvest wine called Kathleen Cabernet Franc. Owners: Gary Conway Carmody, Marian McKnight Carmody, Kathleen Conway. Winemaker: Greg Cropper. Cases: 3,500. Acres: 130.

🍂 *Carmody McKnight Estate Wines (Silver Canyon), 11240 Chimney Rock Road, Paso Robles 93446; (805) 238-9392, fax (805) 238-3975; www.carmodymcknight.com. Open 10:00 a.m.–5:00 p.m. daily. Tasting fee: $5, includes glass. Visa, MasterCard, American Express. Wheelchair accessible.*

Justin is the most elegant winery in the Paso Robles area, and includes a large tasting room with stone floors covered by loads of Oriental rugs and a complete restaurant. If you are lucky and get a full tour, you can see the B&B rooms near the carousel-like dining area where wine club members indulge in wood-fire oven pizzas and fine Justin wines. Look forward to warm tongue-wagging greetings from Sunny and Zamboni, winery dogs.

🍂

JUSTIN, PASO ROBLES

Justin offers winery tours ($10), vineyard tours ($10), and a sensory evaluation and barrel tasting tour ($50), all of which are super-educational and interesting. You can also learn by just walking by the educational vineyard.

Rumors are that Justin and Deborah Baldwin traded in his Jaguar to start the winery and now exude success.

Enjoy French and California artisanal cheeses available in a cold case in the tasting room, and dip into Deborah's Room for lunch or dinner. Deborah's menu includes a few salads and entrees of Angus prime filet, pan-seared Hawaiian Escolar with lobster risotto, fettuccini with vegetables, or a pan-roasted free-range chicken breast with three-cheese polenta ($18–$24).

 Fine points: Featured wines: Viognier, Chardonnay, Sauvignon Blanc, Petit Verdot, Syrah, their famous Isosceles, Cabernet Sauvignon, Zinfandel, Malbec. Owners: Justin and Deborah Baldwin. Senior winemaker: Fred Holloway. Cases: 55,000. Acres: 160.

Justin, 11680 Chimney Rock Road, Paso Robles 93446; (805) 238-6932 or (800) 726-0049; www.justinwine.com. Open 10:00 a.m.–5:00 p.m. daily, restaurant later. Visa, MasterCard, American Express. Wheelchair accessible.

TOLO CELLARS is a cozy tiny winery in an 1880s red and white barn where you will undoubtedly get to chat with owner and winemaker Josh Gibson, former assistant winemaker at Le Cuvier Winery, which used to occupy this site and is now farther down the gravel driveway. Indulge in Provençal linens, pottery, and cookbooks.

Fine points: Featured wines: Chardonnay, Zinfandel, Cabernet Sauvignon, Rhone blends. Owner and winemaker: Josh Gibson. Cases: 2,400. Acres: none.

Tolo Cellars, 9750 Adelaida Road, Paso Robles 93446; (805) 226-2282; www.tolocellars.com. Tasting fee: $3. Visa and American Express. Wheelchair accessible.

To get to TABLAS CREEK, retrace your tracks to Adelaida Road. The Perrin family of Château Beaucastel in France, and Robert Haas, founder of Vineyard Brands and president of the Academie Internationale du Vin, selected this location for planting Rhone varietal grapes and creating Châteauneuf-du-Pape–style vineyards in the New World. Pioneers in organic viticulture, the Perrins imported vine material from Beaucastel starting in 1990. Also part of Tablas Creek is winemaker Neil Collins, who has served at Wild Horse and Adelaida Cellars.

WARM GOAT CHEESE AND POTATO SALAD WITH ROASTED PINE NUTS
from Chef Laurent Grangien of Bistro Laurent for Tablas Creek Winery, Paso Robles

---

1½ lbs. potatoes	¼ cup vegetable oil
1 Tbs. Dijon mustard	1 bunch chives, chopped
¼ cup red wine vinegar	10 oz. goat cheese
salt and pepper	3 oz. pine nuts
½ cup olive oil	

Cook potatoes (with skins on) in water with a pinch of salt until they begin to soften (15–20 minutes).

In a salad bowl, combine mustard, vinegar, and salt and pepper. Add oil slowly.

Peel and dice cooked potatoes. Toss potatoes with chives and three-quarters of the dressing. Transfer dressed potatoes into an ovenproof dish, cover with goat cheese, and broil for 5 minutes.

Toast pine nuts in the oven until browned, and scatter on top of potatoes before serving. Toss remaining dressing with lettuce; serve with potato salad. Serves 6. Serve with Tablas Creek Esprit de Beaucastel Blanc.

CRISPY CRAB RISOTTO WITH TOMATO AND TARRAGON COULIS

from Chef Laurent Grangien of Bistro Laurent for Tablas Creek Winery, Paso Robles

FOR THE RISOTTO:

2 oz. onion, chopped

10 oz. arborio rice

3 oz. dry white wine

14 oz. fish stock

1 lb. cooked Dungeness crabmeat

2 oz. butter

2 Tbs. Parmesan cheese

salt and pepper to taste

FOR THE COULIS:

1 lb. tomatoes, peeled and chopped

2 oz. onion, chopped

1 Tbs. tomato paste

1 bunch tarragon

1 cup fish stock

2 oz. butter

FOR THE COULIS: Combine chopped tomatoes, onions, tomato paste, tarragon, and the fish stock in a saucepan and cook slowly for 1 hour. Remove tarragon, blend cooked mixture, strain, and add butter.

FOR THE RISOTTO: Sauté onion in butter over medium heat until golden brown. Add rice and stir, making sure rice is coated in butter. Add white wine and cook 2–3 minutes, until liquid is reduced by half. Add the fish stock and cook 15 minutes, stirring constantly, until there is no more liquid. Add crabmeat, butter, Parmesan cheese, and salt and pepper to taste.

Shape risotto into a disc about 1½ inches thick. Refrigerate for 2 hours.

Fry risotto disc in butter until crispy, approximately 2–3 minutes per side. Serve on a bed of tomato coulis. Serves 6 as appetizer.

After quarantine, the vines were moved to Tablas Creek (a creek that runs through the property), and the owners built a complex of high-tech greenhouses and shadehouses and started to sell Rhone vines to wineries throughout the central coast. (Visitors can buy single-vine plants to take home and plant for just $9.95.)

There's a great collection of cookbooks and French pottery available. This is a must-stop for a new French experience in Paso Robles.

Fine points: Featured wines: Esprit de Beaucastel Blanc, Antithesis, Esprit de Beaucastels, Mourvedre, Counoise, Roussanne, Viognier, Picpoul Blanc, Marsanne, Grenache Noir, Grenache Blanc, Syrah, Blanc. Owners: the Perrin family and Robert Haas. Winemaker: Neil Collins. Cases: 16,000, growing by 2,000 per year. Acres: 100.

🌺 *Tablas Creek, 9339 Adelaida Road, Paso Robles 93446; (805) 237-1231, fax (805) 237-1314; www.tablascreek.com. Open 10:00 a.m.–5:00 p.m. daily. Tasting fee: $5. Visa, MasterCard. Wheelchair accessible.*

HALTER RANCH is a new winery in an 1885 Victorian farmhouse built by Paso Robles pioneer Edwin Smith. Halter's vineyards are planted on steep, south-facing slopes, producing rich wines.

Fine points: Featured wines: Cabernet Sauvignon, Viognier, Syrah, Sauvignon Blanc, Rosé, red blends. Winemaker: Bill Sheffer. Cases: 4,500. Acres: 250.

🌺 *Halter Ranch, 8910 Adelaida Road, Paso Robles 93446; (805) 226-9455 or (888) 367-9977; www.halterranch.com. Open 11:00 a.m.–5:00 p.m. Thursday–Monday. Tasting fee: $3. Visa and MasterCard. Wheelchair accessible.*

Just past Jensen Road is NORMAN VINEYARDS's large stucco building and parking lot. Climb the wooden stairs to the tasting room, which is like a living room with French doors leading to a deck, tile patio, lawn, and then the vineyards. We love the attitude here reflected by "Zinners Wanted" T-shirts, hats, and corkscrews.

Having grown grapes for others since 1971, founders Art Norman and Lei Norman left their

VINEYARD VIEW FROM NORMAN
VINEYARDS, PASO ROBLES

hectic careers as engineer and accountant in southern California's Northridge to make wine and merry to kudos from wine writers Jerry Mead and Robert Parker for their Zinfandel and Cabernet Sauvignon. After Art's death a couple of years ago, Lei has carried on the family's tradition of excellence.

Fine points: Featured wines: Chardonnay, Pinot Grigio, White Zinfandel, Pinot Noir (Cain), Monster and Classic (old vines) Zinfandel, Cabernet Franc, No Nonsense Red, Cabernet Sauvignon, Barbera, Late Harvest Zinfandel. Owner: Lei Norman. Winemaker: Steve Felton. Cases: 25,000. Acres: 70.

❧ **Norman Vineyards,** *7450 Vineyard Drive, Paso Robles 93446; (805) 237-0138; www.normanvineyards.com. Open 11:00 a.m.–5:00 p.m. daily. Tasting fee: none. Visa, MasterCard, American Express, Discover. Wheelchair accessible at hill side of building.*

Also on Vineyard Drive, OPOLO VINEYARDS was created by Rick Quinn and Dave Nichols. The name derives from Quinn's Yugoslavian (Croatian-Serbian) roots on his mother's side and refers to a blended rosé-style wine made from grapes grown on the Dalmatian Coast. Meticulous farmers, Rick and Dave grow grapes on both the east and west sides of US 101 near Paso Robles and sell their fruit to Niebaum Coppola and Hess Collection in the Napa Valley.

While Opolo's winery and tasting room look a little industrial from the outside, they make up for it with all-day barbecues going on weekends, serving yummy, dripping carne asada tacos and whole roasted lambs. Fun is first, well, second here.

Fine points: Featured wines: Chardonnay, Sangiovese, Pinot Noir, Merlot, Cabernet Sauvignon, Viognier, Syrah, Zinfandel. Owners and winemakers: Rick Quinn and Dave Nichols. Cases: 30,000. Acres: 280.

❧ **Opolo Vineyards,** *7110 Vineyard Drive, Paso Robles 93446; (805) 238-9593, fax (805) 238-9594; www.opolo.com. Open 10:00 a.m.–5:00 p.m. daily. Tasting fee: none except for large groups. Visa, MasterCard, American Express. Wheelchair accessible.*

Those of you who have followed us on our Big Circle Tour will arrive at Vineyard Drive and Highway 46 West right across from Mastantuono, which is on our Little Circle tour. You can either cross Highway 46 West directly to Mastantuono and pick up the Little Circle Tour, or you can turn right (west) to Dover Canyon, east of US 101.

DOVER CANYON WINERY specializes in Rhone varietals. The winery tries to emulate those of Europe's Rhone River Valley region, which stretches from the Alps south of Zurich, Switzerland, along the Italian-French border, and into the Mediterranean near Marseilles.

Fine points: Featured wines: Rhone-style wines, Zinfandel. Owner and winemaker: Dan Panico. Cases: 3,000. Acres: none, buy locally.

❧ **Dover Canyon Winery,** *4520 Vineyard Drive, Paso Robles 93446; (805) 237-0101; www.dovercanyon.com. Open 11:00 a.m.–5:00 p.m. Thursday–Sunday. Tasting fee: $3, logo glass $8, one fee waived per bottle purchase. Visa and MasterCard. Wheelchair accessible.*

YORK MOUNTAIN WINERY, TEMPLETON

YORK MOUNTAIN WINERY, west of US 101 off York Mountain Road, is a must-see because it is the oldest winery between San Francisco and Santa Barbara and it has its own appellation, the smallest in California and one of the smallest in the United States. During Prohibition, wine fans could still bring in a jug and get it filled with wine.

Established in 1882 as Ascension Winery by Andrew York on land originally deeded by President Ulysses S. Grant, York Mountain grows its grapes on nonirrigated hillsides up to 1,500 feet. Andrew York and his sons produced about 80,000 gallons of wine annually, shipping it in barrels to San Francisco and the San Joaquin Valley by horse-drawn wagons. Later, when York sons Walter and Silas operated the winery, world-renowned Paso Robles resident, statesman, and pianist Ignace Paderewski brought grapes from his Adelaida Rancho San Ignacio to the Yorks to have them make his personal wine. In 1944 the third generation of Yorks, Wilfrid and Howard, took over the oldest continuously producing winery.

For thirty years York Mountain was owned by physicist-turned-vintner Max Goldman, with son Steve Goldman as winemaster.

In 2001 the winery was purchased by David and Mary Weyrich of the premier Paso Robles winery Martin & Weyrich, whose winemasters Craig Reed and Alan Kinne have maintained the award-winning level of historic York Mountain.

Built with local stone and brick formed on-site, the tasting room has two roaring fireplaces (in winter) and some of the best deli foods, including Stonewall Kitchen sauces and jams, Gil's Gourmet olives, oils, mustards, cheeses, cheese sticks, and a great selection of gifts.

Fine points: Featured wines: Pinot Noir, Cabernet Sauvignon, Zinfandel, Black Muscat, Viognier, Port. Owners: David and Mary Weyrich. Winemasters: Craig Reed and Alan Kinne. Cases: 3,000. Acres: 7 and buy from other York Mountain wineries.

❧ *York Mountain Winery, 7505 York Mountain Road, Templeton 93465; (805) 238-3925, fax (805) 238-0428; www.yorkmountainwinery.com. Open 11:00 a.m.–4:00 p.m. daily. Tasting fee: $4 for five tastes. Visa, MasterCard, Diners. Wheelchair accessible.*

Now you can continue west on Highway 46 West 13 miles to Cambria, or turn left (east) back to continue your wine tour by picking up our Little Circle Tour at Donati Family Vineyard (see page 195).

Little Circle Tour

If your time is limited, you can take this loop beginning at US 101 and visit Midnight Cellars, Dark Star, Grey Wolf, Doce Robles, Windward Vineyard, AJB Vineyards, Dunning Vineyards, Mastantuono, Turley, Wild Horse, Cider Creek cider mill, Bonny Doon and Sycamore Herb Farms, Hunt Cellars, Peachy Canyon, Castoro, and Dover Canyon wineries. (*NOTE:* Wine barrels at a few Templeton-area wineries broke during the December 2003 earthquake. There are still excellent wines to try, however, so be sure to visit.)

You can begin the Little Circle Tour at its southern end on Vineyard Drive off US 101 in Templeton, or at its northern end, where Highway 46 West heads west from US 101 south of the city of Paso Robles. Whew!

The entire Little Circle Tour is thought of as the Templeton area, although the one-street city of Templeton is on the east side of US 101. Be sure to go there.

We begin at the northern end by taking Highway 46 West off US 101. Because we believe in sticking to one side of any highway and then coming back on the other side, DOCE ROBLES (twelve oaks) winery is the first winery you come to west of US 101 on Highway 46 West. Turn right off Highway 46 onto Twelve Oaks Drive, and Doce Robles will be on your right.

Maribeth and Jim Jacobsen welcome you to their new winery to taste their wines and picnic under centuries-old oaks with a panoramic view of area vineyards. You will welcome the trees' shade and some gourmet foods in the gift shop. The Jacobsens' three German shepherds welcome you with wagging tongues and tails.

Fine points: Featured wines: Chardonnay, Merlot, Syrah, Zinfandel, Meritage, Cabernet Sauvignon, Barbera. Owners: Jim and Maribeth Jacobsen. Winemaker: Jim Jacobsen. Cases: 3,000. Acres: 40.

✤ ***Doce Robles,*** *2023 Twelve Oaks Drive, Paso Robles 93446; (805) 227-4766 or (805) 227-6860; www.docerobles.com. Open 10:00 a.m.–5:30 p.m. daily. Tasting fee: $5. Visa, MasterCard, American Express. Wheelchair accessible.*

West of Doce Robles and Twelve Oaks Drive, turn right on Arbor Road at Treana Winery, which is no longer open to the public, then left on Live Oak Road to a fabulous Pinot Noir mecca, WINDWARD VINEYARD.

Marc Goldberg and Maggie D'Ambrosia named their vineyard for the Pacific Ocean winds that blow through Templeton Gap in the Santa Lucia Mountain chain and tell us something of the area's microclimate.

Windward is dedicated solely to the production of fine estate-bottled Burgundian-style Pinot Noir, and to restoring the Paso Robles area's Pinot Noir reputation to what it enjoyed when consultant André Tchelistcheff supervised the Hoffman Mountain Ranch. Windward's wines sell out every year, so skedaddle on over.

Fine points: Featured wines: Pinot Noir. Owners and winemakers: Marc Goldberg and Maggie D'Ambrosia. Cases: 2,000. Acres: 15.

✤ ***Windward Vineyard,*** *1380 Live Oak Road, Paso Robles 93446; (805) 239-2565; fax (805) 239-4005; www.windwardvineyard.com. Open 10:30 a.m.–5:00 p.m. daily. Tasting fee: $5, $10 with glass. Visa, MasterCard, American Express. Wheelchair accessible.*

EAGLE CASTLE is worth the visit just to see what money can buy. In this case, a wine castle, complete with green water moat and armor-clad mannequins. Despite the splendor, much remains mysterious about Eagle Castle. Don't let the blowing dust stop you.

Enjoy good snacks such as La Bella olives, beef jerky, salami, cheeses, crackers, and Mill Road wine grape juice.

Eagle Castle makes Chardonnay, Viognier, Syrah, Syrah Rosé, Merlot, Cabernet Sauvignon, Muscat Canelli, and Zinfandel Port.

Fine points: Featured wines: Chardonnay, Viognier, Syrah Rosé, Merlot, Cabernet Sauvignon, Zinfandel, Petite Syrah, Muscat Canelli, Zinfandel Port. Owners: Marylou and Gary Stempler and partners. Winemakers: Gary Stempler and Patrick Davis. Cases: 5,000. Acres: 750.

EAGLE CASTLE, PASO ROBLES

❧ *Eagle Castle Winery, Highway 46 West and 3090 Anderson Road, Paso Robles 93446; (805) 227-1428; www.eaglecastlewinery.com. Open 10:30 a.m.–5:30 p.m. daily. Tasting fee: $5. Visa, MasterCard, American Express. Wheelchair accessible.*

Next we come to Dark Star and Midnight Cellars, both slightly up Anderson Road from Highway 46 West. Dark Star is 0.3 mile up Anderson Road (2.2 miles from US 101), and Midnight Cellars is right next door. Dark star and midnight? Hmmmm.

Yes, the old barn at DARK STAR CELLARS houses one of the funniest winery experiences around. Hilariously irreverent Dark Star owner Norm Benson left Hollywood to make the best wine possible. For fun he writes his *Star News* for friends of the winery, and the newsletter alone is worth getting on the mailing list.

Since Norm often runs out of his small-lot wines quickly, this is one winery where it really pays to join his club and be sure to get some of his best. The "Normego (Norm's ego) Notes" in the two-sided, one-page newsletter allow him to repeat himself, as well as a few specials, with the admonition: "If you need more wine . . . make it snappy."

Fine points: Featured wines: Chardonnay, Merlot, Cabernet Sauvignon, Ricordati (Bordeaux blend), Syrah, Zinfandel. Owner, winemaker, gardener, and electrician: Norm Benson. Cases: 3,000. Acres: none; buys locally.

✤ *Dark Star Cellars, 2985 Anderson Road, Paso Robles 93446; (805) 237-2389, fax (805) 237-2589; www.darkstarcellars.com. Open 10:30 a.m.–5:00 p.m. Friday–Sunday. Tasting fee: none. Visa, MasterCard, American Express. Wheelchair accessible.*

MIDNIGHT CELLARS is a small and elegant winery owned and run by a bunch of characters who all happen to be related to each other. The Hartenberger family's winery idea began with an offhand remark made in jest on a vacation, and somehow it became their family reality. They bought 150 acres, converted the barn to a winery, and retained winemaker consultant Nick Martin, enabling them to hit the ground running.

What a group! Robert Hartenberger is president, vineyard manager, and legal counsel for the winery, having begun his life in Chicago and continued it as a corporate attorney in Glendale, California, in 1990. In 1995 he left the corporate world to chase his dream, and now he chases gophers and drives his little blue tractor through his vineyard.

Mary Jane Hartenberger is treasurer, head chef, and matriarch of Midnight Cellars. She spends the school year as a librarian at Loyola High School in Los Angeles, commuting to the winery on weekends. Bob and Mary Jane's youngest son, Rich, is now winemaker and marketing director and spends his free time "hacking up area golf courses" with anyone he can find. Mary Jane's oldest son, Mike, helps Bob in the vineyard and with marketing duties, a far cry from his former Chicago job in electronic components sales. What hurt the most was giving up his Bulls season tickets, so do not even try to reach him during Bulls playoff games.

Cool bottled water is available, as is lots of Midnight Cellars logo stuff, including handsome shirts, "grapey" ceramics, candles, pins, earrings, pewter sun catchers, and wine-bottle stoppers.

Fine points: Featured wines: Chardonnay, White Zinfandel, Merlot, Syrah, Cabernet Sauvignon, Zinfandel. Owners: Robert, Mary Jane, Michael, Richard, and Michele Hartenberger. Winemaker: Rich Hartenberger. Cases: 8,000. Acres: 26 of 150.

✤ *Midnight Cellars, 2925 Anderson Road, Paso Robles 93446; (805) 237-9601, tasting room (805) 239-8904, fax (805) 237-0383; www.midnightcellars.com. Open 10:00 a.m.– 5:30 p.m. daily. Tasting fee: $2. Visa, MasterCard, American Express, Discover. Wheelchair accessible.*

Also right along Highway 46 West is GREY WOLF CELLARS, in a 1940s gray farmhouse converted to a small tasting room with the winery in the back in the converted outbuilding. Approach this short driveway carefully because of the deep crevices on this dusty knoll.

After successful careers in construction development in California's central valley, Joe and Shirlene Barton ran a restaurant in Steamboat Springs, Colorado, where they caught the wine bug, and then came west to look for the wine dream. After visiting and looking in the Napa Valley, they settled on the less expensive, more friendly, more community-oriented Paso Robles area, as have many wine folks in these parts.

Grey Wolf Cellars began in August 1994; Joe and Shirlene became partners shortly thereafter, and they purchased full control in January 1996. Tragically, Joe was killed in an automobile accident a couple of years later. Their son Joe Jr., who has studied fruit science and viticulture at California Polytechnic in San Luis Obispo, plays a strong role in the vineyard planting and care and has taken over as winemaker.

Fine points: Featured wines: Viognier, Syrah, Cabernet Blanc, Cabernet Sauvignon, Zinfandel, Merlot, Red Table Wine, Meritage, Alpha Cabernet Sauvignon. Owners: Shirlene and Joe Barton Jr. Winemaker: Joe Barton Jr. Cases: 3,500. Acres: 11.

✤⊱ *Grey Wolf Cellars, 2174 Highway 46 West, Paso Robles 93446; (805) 237-0771; www.grey-wolfcellars.com. Open 11:00 a.m.–5:30 p.m. daily. Tasting fee: $2. Visa and MasterCard. One step into doorway; will help wheelchairs.*

From Grey Wolf Cellars turn west (right) again on Highway 46 West, then right on Oakdale, right again on Las Tablas, and right once more onto Township for AJB VINEYARDS.

Marilyn and A. John Berardo recently founded their vineyards amid the best scenery and vines of the Paso Robles area. Their wines are all estate grown. Your visit may include a stay at the Berardos' Hilltop Hacienda, a two-bedroom vacation rental including a pool and spa right in the vineyards.

Fine points: Featured wines: Estate Sangiovese, Syrah, Viognier, Nebbiolo. Owners: Marilyn and John Berardo. Winemaker: John Berardo. Cases: 3,000. Acres: 12 planted of 44.

✤⊱ *AJB Vineyards, 3280 Township Road, Paso Robles 93446; (805) 239-9432, fax (805) 239-1931; www.ajbvineyards.com. Open noon–5:00 p.m. Saturday and Sunday, by appointment during the week. Tasting fee: none. Visa and MasterCard. Wheelchair accessible.*

After retracing your route down Las Tablas and Oakdale to the junction with Highway 46 West, you can violate our safety principle and turn left (west) across the highway traffic to HUNT CELLARS at the corner of Highway 46 and Oakdale. Founded in the '90s by the remarkable David Hunt, a blind inventor, musician, and real estate developer, the winery was an instant success, scoring numerous ratings above 90, gold medals, and best in class.

Owner and winemaker Hunt has truly refined senses other than sight and has succeeded in his goal to create "memorable wines." Enjoy music, wine, and fresh air on the winery's expansive decks.

Fine points: Featured wines: Rhapsody in Red, Cabernet Sauvignon, Syrah, Merlot. Owner and winemaker: David Hunt. Cases: 7,000. Acres: 550.

❧ *Hunt Cellars, Highway 46 West at Oakdale Road, Paso Robles 93446; (805) 237-1600; www.huntwinecellars.com. Open 10:30 a.m.–5:30 p.m. daily. Tasting fee: $5, $10 for reserves and new releases. Visa, MasterCard, American Express. Wheelchair accessible.*

Just a bit farther on Highway 46 West is CIDER CREEK BAKERY & CIDER TASTING ROOM. The bright green "barn" is a refreshing distraction from wine tasting for little and big kids. Make no mistake, this is a gourmet cider-making establishment and bakery. What a treat! You are now 4.5 miles west of US 101.

Umbrellaed tables outside welcome sweet tooths to stick around a while; inside, the red-and-white tile decor makes you smile immediately. But smell the fresh caramel apples, steaming apple pastries from strudel to pies to turnovers, the cinnamon flips, apple cinnamon bread, and cookies! Even the kids can belly up to the bar to taste three kinds of ciders, all made from apples grown on Ken and Susie Jevec's surrounding property—with no added sugar, water, or preservatives. Cider Creek also sells dried fruits and coffee, along with fruit and apple butters, preserves, jellies, cider vinegar, honey mustard dip/dressing, apple barbecue glaze, baking mixes, syrups, lots of olives and salsas, Vidalia onion products, Fortunes teas, and the most complete selection of apple cookbooks you will ever see. One of our favorites.

❧ *Cider Creek Bakery & Cider Tasting Room, 3760 Highway 46 West, Templeton 93465; (805) 238-5634. Open 8:00 a.m.–5:00 p.m. daily. Visa and MasterCard. Wheelchair accessible.*

ROTTA WINERY, a historic winery originally founded in 1908, was recently re-created by local wine veterans Mike Giubbini (grandson of the Rottas), Steve

Pesenti, and Mark Caporale. The tasting room is currently located on Highway 46 West while the historic winery site is being renovated. (Four Vines, in the same building, is the most irreverent winery anywhere, with labels called Biker, Maverick, and Naked.) Already an award-winner, the actual winery is located at 250 Winery Road, Templeton 93465.

 Fine points: Featured wines: Cabernet Sauvignon, Cabernet Franc, Zinfandel, Merlot, Chardonnay, dessert wine Black Monukka. Owners: Mike Giubbini, Steve Pesenti, and Mark Caporale. Winemaker: Steve Pesenti. Cases: 15,000. Acres: 750.

Rotta Winery, 3750 Highway 46 West, Templeton 93465 (tasting room); (805) 237-0510, fax (805) 434-9623; www.rottawinery.com. Open 11:00 a.m.–5:00 p.m. Sunday–Thursday and 11:00 a.m.–6:00 p.m. Friday–Saturday. Tasting fee: $3 for ten wines. Visa and MasterCard. Wheelchair accessible.

PIPESTONE VINEYARDS is truly a family enterprise led by Jeff Pipes and Florence Wong, whose respect for *feng shui,* peace, and quiet may attract too many humans to join them, their children, and their farm animals along with a picnic. Jeff and Florence carefully combine Eastern and Western traditions in all parts of their lives, including the organic vineyards for good soil and a habitat for beneficial insects.

Pipestone may be the only California winery built according to traditional Chinese *feng shui.* They actually look forward to sharing their "life on the farm."

 Fine points: Featured wines: Handmade estate-grown Syrah, Viognier, Grenache Noir, Mourvedre, Zinfandel. Owners and winemakers: Jeff Pipes and Florence Wong. Cases: 2,000. Acres: 10 planted.

Pipestone Vineyards, 2040 Niderer Road, Paso Robles 93446; (805) 227-6385; www.pipestonevineyards.com. Open 11:00 a.m.–5:00 p.m. Thursday–Monday. Tasting fee: $5. Visa and MasterCard. Wheelchair accessible.

DUNNING VINEYARDS ESTATE WINERY & COUNTRY INN is beyond Pipestone in the hills in another charming old farmhouse amid giant hundred-year-old oak trees.

Originally a home winemaker, Robert Dunning was shy about sharing his wines, won big prizes, and now makes some of the best. A stay in one of their two guest suites includes a personal tour with the winemaker.

Fine points: Featured wines: Chardonnay, Merlot, Cabernet Sauvignon, Cabernet Franc, Syrah, Zinfandel. Owners: the Dunning family. Winemaker: Robert Dunning. Cases: 2,000. Acres: 16 planted of 80.

✤ *Dunning Vineyards Estate Winery & Country Inn, 1953 Niderer Road, Paso Robles 93446; (805) 238-4763; www.dunningwines.com. Open 11:00 a.m.–5:00 p.m. Thursday–Monday. Tasting fee: none. Visa and MasterCard.*

Continue west on Highway 46, and immediately turn left on Oakview Road to reach the DONATI FAMILY VINEYARD winery.

The Donati family completed acquisition of what had been for two decades Mastantuono Winery on February 9, 2007, and after installation of modern equipment, they opened the winery and tasting room April 29. But finding a home for their winery was just the culmination of an effort that began in 1968, when Ron Donati, a CPA and owner of an electronics firm, sold his company and came west looking for a future in California vineyards.

With his son, Matt, then a high school baseball coach, he located a large, long-neglected vineyard in the Palcines area of San Benito County, which he purchased and father and son planted. Their crushes of 2003, 2004, and 2005 vintages were produced at other wineries. Soon they brought in as winemaker Dan Kleck, with experience at several major wineries, who moved to Paso Robles. Kleck introduced the Donatis to French Oak barrels for aging. Ron and Matt developed a special working relationship in which the father handles the business side of the enterprise and the son directs the winemaking from field to decanting. "Matt really runs the show . . . I just provide support," says Ron.

DONATI FAMILY VINEYARD, TEMPLETON

They apparently share dedication to hard work and attention to detail. The Donatis plan to continue to upgrade to make the family winery totally state of the art.

Fine points: Featured wines: Pinot Blanc, Chardonnay, Merlot, Cabernet Sauvignon, Meritage, Syrah. Owners: Ron and Matt Donati and families. Winemaker: Dan Kleck. Cases: 6,500. Acres: 400.

❧ *Donati Family Vineyard, 2720 Oakview Road, Templeton 93465; (805) 238-0676, fax (805) 238-9257; www.donatifamilyvineyard.com. Open 10:00 a.m.–6:00 p.m. in summer, to 5:00 p.m. in winter, daily. Tasting fee: $5–$10, refunded with purchase. Visa, MasterCard, American Express. Wheelchair accessible.*

As you leave Donati Family Vineyard, turn right (east) onto Vineyard Drive. In about 0.5 mile and just around a curve is TURLEY WINE CELLARS, which replaced Pesenti.

The Pesentis were the originals around here, planting their first Zinfandel vineyard in 1923 during Prohibition after clearing the property of oak trees. Frank and Caterina Pesenti raised five children right here; Frank built the house and winery himself.

The first winery building was completed in 1934 after Prohibition's repeal and still follows "the founder's no-frill approach: to offer well-made, award-winning wines at reasonable prices," but still selling lots of grapes to old-timer Italian dairymen. In the early 1940s Frank and Caterina's son, Victor, and son-in-law, Al Nerelli, joined the winery and oversaw additional Zinfandel plantings in 1947 and 1965, all dry-farmed (not irrigated).

Now the winery is owned and named for Larry Turley of Turley Vineyards, who had tried repeatedly to buy grapes from Pesenti and leaped at the chance to buy the property (because of its eighty-year-old Zinfandel vines) when it was just rumored to be available. Now the Turleys focus on Zinfandels, keeping the Pesenti and Nerelli family traditions, including hiring Charity Nerelli (Frank's daughter) to run the tasting room. So you can still get the old family stories right at the counter.

Fine points: Featured wines: Zinfandel, Petit Syrah. Owner: Larry Turley. Winemaker: Ehren Jordan. Cases: won't say. Acres: 78.

❧ *Turley Wine Cellars, 2900 Vineyard Drive, Templeton 93465; (805) 434-1030, fax (805) 434-4279; www.turleywinecellars.com. Open 9:00 a.m.–5:00 p.m. daily. Tasting fee: none for Pesenti labels, $10 for Turley. Visa and MasterCard. Wheelchair accessible.*

As you leave Turley, make an extremely careful left turn onto Vineyard Drive, with special caution because the curves blind your vision of oncoming cars.

Follow Vineyard Drive south and east to Bethel Road. Turn right on Bethel, right again on Santa Rita Road, and left up Raymond to CASA DE CABALLOS VINEYARDS.

Casa de Caballos and Morgan Farms Arabians are well worth the climb up the hill in your vehicle. Sheila and Dr. Tom Morgan, an M.D. in Paso Robles, gradually made their dream come true in the hills west of Templeton.

Tom tried making fruit and berry wines while a resident at Orange County Medical Center, he purchased this property upon graduation, and he and Sheila planted their vineyards with their three sons, all of whom are involved with pruning, fertilizing, hand picking, crushing, bottling, labeling, and marketing.

Sheila manages the farm, which includes English walnuts, and the horses, fulfilling her childhood fantasy. When the Morgans realized they were making more wine than they could drink or give away, they launched Casa de Caballos (House of Horses), combining their interests and artistic expressions to create their "stable of fine wines and horses."

Casa de Caballos's small, rich barrel room is popular for parties and weddings, but watch the road after the reception! Horse fans will love the goodies for sale and on display in the tasting room, which also boasts some of the most clever humor signs we've seen. Many wines are named for their beloved animals.

 Fine points: Featured wines: Pinot Noir, Forgetmenot blend, Merlot, Choclate Lily Cabernet Sauvignon, Lilac Tyme, Fantasy Riesling, Maggie Mae El Nino Red. Owners: Tom and Sheila Morgan. Winemaker: Tom Morgan. Cases: 800. Acres planted: 6.

ॐ *Casa de Caballos Vineyards, 2225 Raymond Avenue, Templeton 93465; (805) 434-1687; www.casadecaballos.com. Open 11:00 a.m.–5:00 p.m. daily. Tasting fee: none. Visa, MasterCard, Discover. Wheelchair accessible.*

To get to WILD HORSE WINERY & VINEYARDS, cross US 101, and continue east on Templeton Road. Go out Templeton Road about 2.75 miles and turn left (north) on Wild Horse Winery Court to reach the winery, thrice voted Best San Luis Obispo County Winery by *New Times* readers.

Wild Horse resides in an elegant but casual-feeling two-story building on a mesa above the Salinas River. White wrought-iron picnic tables with blue umbrellas dot the lush gardens. Its name comes from the wild mustangs that roam east of the estate, descendants of the first Spanish horses brought to California. The mustangs' free and unbridled spirit has been adopted as Wild Horse's approach to winemaking exploration and techniques.

WILD HORSE WINERY & VINEYARDS,
TEMPLETON

The tasting room building, which is surrounded by white ranch fencing, has soft, warm beige walls, Spanish tile floors, Wild Horse tie-dyed kids' shirts, and elegant shirts and caps for grown-ups.

Wild Horse Winery founder, director of winemaking, and president for life Kenneth Q. Volk III is a great guy and third-generation California native from San Marino. Ken first got an associate's degree from Orange Coast Community College, then transferred to Cal Poly in San Luis Obispo, where he graduated in fruit science, intending to manage citrus or avocado groves. The wine bug bit him, though. He made some good wine in his "wine garage," and then got hired to work the 1981 crush at nearby Edna Valley Vineyard. He began to plant Wild Horse Estate vineyards in 1982.

In 1983 Wild Horse Winery & Vineyards launched itself with a Pinot Noir from Santa Maria's Sierra Madre Vineyard and a Cabernet Sauvignon from Paso Robles. March 23, 1986, was a very-big-deal date for Ken: Wild Horse released its first wines, 125 cases of Pinot Noir and 450 cases of Cabernet, and he and Tricia Tartaglione, a Cordon Bleu–trained chef and cooking instructor, were married. Note the order of events on that auspicious day! Now Ken and Tricia live in San Luis Obispo with their two children, Kenny and Valentina.

 Fine points: Featured wines: Chardonnay, Pinot Grigio, Orange Muscat, Roussanne, Pinot Noir, Merlot, Cabernet Sauvignon, Syrah, Valdiguie, Dolcetto, Mourvedre, Negrette. Owners: Ken and Tricia Volk. Winemaker: Jon Priest. Cases: 175,000. Acres: 49 and buy locally.

❧ *Wild Horse Winery & Vineyards, 1437 Wild Horse Winery Court, Templeton 93465; (805) 434-2541, fax (805) 434-3516; www.wildhorsewinery.com. Open 11:00 a.m.–5:00 p.m. daily. Tasting fee: none. Visa, MasterCard, American Express. Wheelchair accessible.*

If you're hungry for lunch, wander into "downtown" Templeton by turning right (west) as you leave Wild Horse and following Templeton Road back to Main Street. Turn right (north) on Main Street and drop into McPhee's Grill (across from the granary) for your restorative. (See "Templeton" in chapter 5.)

Back on the winery trail, cross US 101 once again heading west, and keep going to Bethel Road. Turn right (north) up Bethel Road for a couple of miles to JANKRIS WINERY, which occupies the same cute Victorian home on the Jan & Kris horse ranch that used to house Dover Canyon Winery. The Jendron family sells its wines only in the JanKris tasting room, where you can also purchase gourmet foods and gifts, or enjoy a picnic under huge old oak trees.

Fine points: Featured wines: Chardonnay, White Zinfandel, Merzin, Merlot, Zinfandel, Cabernet Sauvignon, Late Harvest Zinfandel. Owners: the Jendron family. Winemaker: Mark Jendron. Cases: 2,000. Acres: 171.

❧ *JanKris Winery, Bethel Road off Highway 46 West, Route 2, Box 40, Templeton 93465; (805) 434-0319; www.jankriswinery.com. Open 11:00 a.m.–5:00 p.m. daily. Tasting fee: none. Visa and MasterCard. Wheelchair accessible.*

JANKRIS WINERY, TEMPLETON

As you leave JanKris Winery, turn right (north) on Bethel Road to Castoro and Peachy Canyon, across the road from each other and both near the intersection of Bethel Road and Highway 46 West.

CASTORO CELLARS, quite visible from the highway, is a place of beauty, humor, art, and good wine. Niels Udsen, a native of Ventura, California, graduated from Cal Poly in agricultural business management, aiming at the wine business. After getting married, Niels and his wife, Bimmer, looked for winery work in Oregon and Washington to no

CASTORO CELLARS'S PATIO, TEMPLETON

avail, coming back to the Paso Robles area to work the harvest at Estrella River Winery (now Meridian). Niels worked from the cellar floor up at Estrella River over the next five years while creating Castoro Cellars (1983), with Niels making the wine and Bimmer selling it.

Castoro is Italian for "beaver," which was Niels's nickname most of his life. Hence, the Beaver makes "dam fine wine," of course! Even wine critic Dan Berger says, "Inside this charming country tasting room, you'll find some of the best wines in the state."

When you drive into Castoro's parking lot, park between the youngish trees that someday will shade the parking places, a most thoughtful gesture. Walk or roll up the 100-foot-long sloping walkway covered with misty vines and planted with colorful seasonal posies, including hundreds of crocuses. Newish cork trees will offer their own cork harvest in "only twenty years." Don't miss Castoro's animal menageries, including Harley the pot-bellied pig, Simba the cat, Molly the Australian Shepherd, and the just ducky ducks.

Castoro's tasting room and patio feel like a great restaurant and cafe, with soft yellow walls, Mexican tile floors, and a side room featuring regional art shows, a real service to the arts community. We especially enjoy the word block games on the tasting bar, particularly the "Politics of Words." The tasting room offers Ghirardelli chocolate bars for just $1 (great with Zinfandel), canned beaver to "open only with adult supervision," and mouse pads that suggest you "Wine a little. You'll feel better."

Castoro stresses the team approach to winemaking, the team consisting of

Niels, winemaker Tom Myers (who taught Niels at Estrella River), and assistant winemaker Mikel Olsten. Their two vineyards are called Hog Heaven, after the wild hogs that inhabit the area, and Blind Faith, on which Niels and his wife bought it while she was in her native Denmark.

As a result of Castoro's characteristic innovative thinking, Castoro now does a 70,000-case, custom-crush service for other wineries that includes bottling, labeling, pressing, and fermentation. A great place to visit.

Fine points: Featured wines: Fumé Blanc, Chardonnay, Chenin Blanc, Valgiguie Nouveau, Tempranillo (Spanish varietal), Cabernet Sauvignon, Zinfandel, Late Harvest Zinfandel Port, White Zinfandel, Muscat Canelli, Zinfandel grape juice for kids and designated drivers. Owners: Niels and Bimmer Udsen. Winemakers: Niels Udsen, Tom Myers, Mikel Olsten. Cases: 30,000 of their own. Acres: 600.

❧ *Castoro Cellars, 1315 North Bethel Road, Templeton 93465; (888) DAM-FINE, fax (805) 238-2602; www.castorocellars.com. Open 10:00 a.m.–5:30 p.m. daily. Tasting fee: $2 for seven tastes and logo glass. Visa, MasterCard, American Express. Wheelchair accessible.*

Near the intersection of Highway 46 West and Bethel Road is PEACHY CANYON WINERY, nestled amid giant trees in the white, late-1800s Old Schoolhouse Ranch building, which has its original floors. Walk out back to the lush, sprawling lawn with picnic tables and caged roosters right next to the vineyards.

Former southern California schoolteachers Doug and Nancy Beckett moved to Paso Robles in 1981 with their sons, Joshua and Jacob. Doug had also worked in the construction industry, leased shopping centers in San Diego, and co-owned a chain of liquor stores.

The Peachy Canyon Winery building was com-

PEACHY CANYON WINERY, TEMPLETON

pleted in 1987 and opened in 1988 to house the Tobias Vineyards project with Doug and his then partner, Pat Wheeler. Tobias produced a highly regarded local hearty Zinfandel from the Benito Dusi Ranch, and when that partnership dissolved, Doug and Nancy decided to create their own distinct label.

The Becketts always take lots of their wine with them when they travel. It opens all sorts of doors, such as those of the government in China, and it once gave them a chance to pick grapes at a Czechoslovakian castle. As we have heard from many Paso Robles area vintners, Doug always mentions the "unique cama-raderie here in Paso Robles that you just don't find any other place," working with other winemakers such as Niels Udsen of Castoro Cellars, Toby Shumrick of Tobin James Winery, Chris Johnson of HMR (Hidden Mountain Ranch) Vineyard, and Robert Nadeau of Norman Vineyards. Actually, we have also wit-nessed this sharing community feeling in Oregon, Washington, and British Columbia, but rarely anywhere else in California.

Doug is generally credited with inventing the concept of west side and east side (of the Salinas River) for subcultures of Paso Robles grapes.

Fine points: Featured wines: Chardonnay, Zinfandel, Cabernet Sauvignon, Merlot, Port. Owners: Doug and Nancy Beckett. Winemaker: Florence Sarrazin. Cases: 30,000. Acres: 100.

❦ *Peachy Canyon Winery, 1480 North Bethel Road, Templeton 93465; (805) 237-1577, fax (805) 237-2248; www.peachycanyon.com. Open 11:00 a.m.–5:00 p.m. daily. Tasting fee: none for seven tastes, $1 for reserves. Visa and MasterCard. Wheelchair accessible.*

Edna Valley and Arroyo Grande Valley Area

The Edna Valley and Arroyo Grande Valley and their special wine regions run inland south of the city of San Luis Obispo, parallel with Pismo Beach and east of US 101, which at this point heads west to Pismo Beach. Highway 227 cuts right through the appellation and connects to US 101 at both ends.

Here you will find lots of very personal wineries, and a couple of larger cor-porate ones with extremely local passion and management. We take you from San Luis Obispo southward to Cottonwood Canyon, Laverne Vineyards, Windemere, Baileyana, Edna Valley Vineyard, Claiborne & Churchill, Domaine Alfred, Talley Vineyards and Bishop's Peak, and Laetitia Vineyards and Winery, then back on US 101.

From downtown San Luis Obispo, follow Higuera Street south and turn left (east) on Tank Farm Road. From US 101 take the Los Osos or Higuera Street exit and turn north on Higuera on the west side of US 101, work your way back par-allel to the highway north, and turn right (east) on Tank Farm Road.

To get to the COTTONWOOD CANYON WINERY's local tasting room, take Tank Farm Road east and soon turn right (south) on Santa Fe Road to Cottonwood Canyon on the right. This used to be Cottonwood Canyon's wine production facility for Chardonnay, Pinot Noir, Cabernet Sauvignon, and Merlot, but all of their wine is now made at their winery in the Santa Maria Valley, where they also have a tasting room. (See chapter 4.)

🍇 *Cottonwood Canyon Winery, 4330 Santa Fe Road, San Luis Obispo 93401; (805) 549-9463; www.cottonwoodcanyon.com. Open 11:00 a.m.–5:00 p.m. Saturday and Sunday. Visa, MasterCard, American Express. Wheelchair accessible.*

Leaving Cottonwood Canyon, return to Tank Farm Road and turn right (east) and then left (north) on Highway 227 to get to Laverne and Windemere. Turn right (east) on Capitolio Way, and then left on Sacramento Drive. Or just take Broad Street from downtown San Luis Obispo, turn left (east) on Capitolio, and left on Sacramento. The two wineries share a garage door that they roll up to open both wineries.

LAVERNE VINEYARDS co-owner Peter Cron calls his winery's decor "basically a garage gone bad" and "early American auto," and is he right! Laverne is truly a small, family-owned and -operated winery that only makes handcrafted Chardonnay and Cabernet Sauvignon. Peter worked at Estrella River Winery in the 1980s and opened here in 1998. Stop by for fun and a chat with the winemaker/owner.

Fine points: Featured wines: Chardonnay and Cabernet Sauvignon. Owners: Peter and Therese Cron. Winemaker: Peter Cron. Cases: 1,200. Acres: none yet, buys from others.

🍇 *Laverne Vineyards, 3490 Sacramento Drive, Suite E, San Luis Obispo 93401; (805) 547-0616, fax (805) 743-8772. Open noon–4:00 p.m. Saturday and Sunday. Tasting fee: none. Visa and MasterCard. Wheelchair accessible.*

WINDEMERE WINERY/CATHY MACGREGOR WINERY owner and winemaker Cathy MacGregor really means her invitation to "stop by and say hi to the winemaker. That's me." She does everything and ends up winning medals for her limited-edition wines. All her grapes come from the family-owned MacGregor Vineyard, which her father, retired aerospace engineer Andy MacGregor, bought in the 1980s. Andy, the third wine grower here in the Edna Valley, also got the Edna Valley appellation established.

Cathy studied evaluation of food at UC/Davis and worked at the highly respected Grgich winery in the Napa Valley. She runs the whole Windemere operation herself.

Fine points: Featured wines: Chardonnay, Pinot Noir, Cabernet Sauvignon, Zinfandel, Merlot. Owner and winemaker: Cathy MacGregor. Cases: 2,400. Acres: 61.

🍇 *Windemere Winery/Cathy MacGregor Winery, 3536 South*

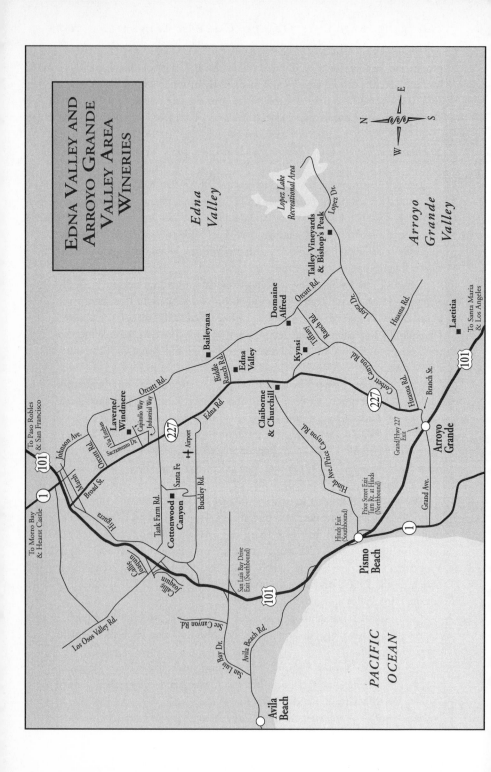

EDNA VALLEY AND
ARROYO GRANDE
VALLEY AREA
WINERIES

Higuera Street, Suite 240-B, San Luis Obispo 93401; (805) 542-0133, fax (805) 545-8080; www.windemerewinery.com. Open 11:30 a.m.–5:00 p.m. Thursday–Sunday. Tasting fee: $2 and keep the glass or take $2 off wine purchase. Visa, MasterCard, American Express. Wheelchair accessible.

As Tank Farm turns into Orcutt and turns south, turn with it and continue for about 3 miles to BAILEYANA WINERY in the charming yellow one-room Independence School building. The little building, built in 1907, was dedicated as a school in 1909 and remained one until 1954, when the Righetti family took it over.

Baileyana is a sister winery to Edna Valley and is located where Seven Peaks's tasting room used to be. Catharine and Jack Niven first planted grapes in the Edna Valley in the early 1970s, and Catharine gets credit for many of the Edna Valley–Baileyana innovations. The name "Baileyana" comes from the neighborhood where Catharine met Jack.

Winemaker Christian Roguenant grew up in Burgundy and got a degree in enology and winemaking from the University of Dijon. After working in Burgundy, Roguenant became head enologist at Champagne Deutz, moving to California initially to run Deutz's California sparkling wine venture, Maison Deutz. Roguenant has bought insulated windows, a new fruit delivery system, small presses, and open-top fermenters to update the winery. You can taste and purchase both Baileyana and Edna Valley Firepeak Vineyard wines here.

BAILEYANA WINERY TASTING ROOM IN OLD
INDEPENDENCE SCHOOL, SAN LUIS OBISPO

Fine points: Featured wines: Sauvignon Blanc, Chardonnay, Pinot Noir, Syrah, Gewürztraminer. Owners: Catharine and Jack Niven. Winemaker: Christian Roguenant. Cases: 20,000. Acres: 1,000.

➳ *Baileyana Winery, 4915 Orcutt Road, San Luis Obispo 93401; (805) 597-8200; www.baileyana.com. Open 10:00 a.m.–5:00 p.m. daily. Tasting fee: $3. Visa, MasterCard, American Express, Discover. Wheelchair accessible.*

As you leave Baileyana, turn left (south) very carefully on Orcutt Road, and continue along this gorgeous terrain at the base of the foothills. If you want to go to Edna Valley Vineyard next, turn right (west) on Biddle Ranch Road. If you prefer to continue south on Orcutt past lovely vineyards and wineries not open to the public, go ahead and visit Talley Vineyards or Domaine Alfred.

When you approach EDNA VALLEY VINEYARD and its tasting room, you might find it difficult to understand what the unusual angular building is doing out here in this blissfully beautiful region. And that is the whole point. Once inside, you see that the nearly 180-degree windows afford spectacular views of Islay Mountain and some of the seven peaks, of Meridian and Paragon vineyards, and of Baileyana's Independence School building against the hills to the east. Breathtaking!

Edna Valley Vineyard is now a joint venture between Paragon Vineyards and Chalone Wine Group, since the latter bought into the winery founded by Jack Niven, who also owns Baileyana and whose son James Niven now runs Paragon. The Niven family owned and sold Purity Stores.

Once inside the Jack Niven Hospitality Center tasting room and gift boutique, you will gasp at the view and want to move right in. Forever. Check out the outstanding book selection, aprons, pot holders, corkscrews, and other gadgetry for wine aficionados. Edna Valley hosts the most stunning cooking classes and guest chef series in central California, ranging from traditional English dinners to vegetarian sushi, cooking with everything from tofu to sausages, and including Provençal cuisine, baking bread, and low-fat grains. Then there's the summer bluegrass concert, an annual barbecue, wine seminars, and a New Year's Eve Explosion for sixty people.

Edna Valley offers terrific hourly behind-the-scenes tours of its production facility, where you can see the whole winemaking process in action from beginning to end, including the demonstration vineyard. Also on the tour is the only truly underground cellar in the Edna Valley, which holds 2,000 cases. These are some of the friendliest tours you will experience, and guides happily explain terms to guests, so please don't be embarrassed to ask.

If you are in the vicinity on a Friday evening and feel frisky, see if you luck into the Friday Evening Wine Down happy hour from 5:00 to 8:00, and winery

VIEW NORTHWARD FROM EDNA VALLEY VINEYARD,
SAN LUIS OBISPO

dinners–call ahead. These treats became so popular with locals that they only hold them occasionally. If you come during the rest of the week, you will get a much better look at the surroundings. Enjoy gourmet foods in the gift shop.

 Fine points: Featured wines: Chardonnay, Pinot Noir Vin Gris, Pinot Gris, Pinot Noir, Syrah. Owners: Diagio and the Niven family. Winemaker: Harry Hampton. Cases: 125,000. Acres: 1,000 producing.

❧ *Edna Valley Vineyard, 2585 Biddle Ranch Road, San Luis Obispo 93401; (805) 544-5855, fax (805) 544-7292; www.ednavalley.com. Open 10:00 a.m.–5:00 p.m. daily, tours hourly 11:00 a.m.–3:00 p.m. weekends. Tasting fee: $5. Visa, MasterCard, American Express. Wheelchair accessible.*

Locals stop at OLD EDNA ANTIQUES AND DELI, a new cafe featuring bready panini, salads that are in the display case but not on the posted menu, the delectable Joseph Schmidt Chocolates, and espresso drinks. It's the only game in town. To get here from Edna Valley Vineyard, turn left onto Biddle Ranch Road, and left again onto Edna Valley Road to Old Price Canyon Road.

❧ *Old Edna Antiques and Deli, 1653 Old Price Canyon Road, San Luis Obispo 93401; (805) 543-1313. Open 8:00 a.m.–5:00 p.m. Monday–Friday, 10:00 a.m.–5:00 p.m. Saturday, 9:00 a.m.–5:00 p.m. Sunday; dinner by reservation Friday–Saturday. No credit cards. Not wheelchair accessible.*

Our next must-stop is tiny CLAIBORNE & CHURCHILL, possibly the most environmentally sound winery building in the country. To get here from Edna Valley Vineyard, come back down Edna Valley's driveway and turn left (west) on Biddle Ranch Road to Highway 227, which is called Edna Valley Road here (going into

**ENTRANCE TO
CLAIBORNE & CHURCHILL,
SAN LUIS OBISPO**

San Luis Obispo it becomes Broad Street; south of Price Canyon Road it is called Carpenter Canyon Road). Turn left (south) on Highway 227. Just past Price Canyon Road, turn quickly into Claiborne & Churchill, right at the corner. Coming from the south, you must alertly make a sharp left into the winery driveway. If you are coming from Old Edna's, go south on Edna Valley Road just across Price Canyon Road. Claiborne (Clay) Thompson and Fredericka Churchill met while teaching at the University of Michigan. Clay, who holds a doctorate in Scandinavian studies from Harvard, was widely recognized as the world's foremost authority on medieval Scandinavian literature, while Fredericka was a lecturer in German language. Seeking a huge change in their lives, the newlyweds moved here in 1981, and Clay soon landed a $6-an-hour cellar-rat job at Edna Valley Vineyard.

Because the staff was small at that time, Clay got to learn all aspects of the winemaking process, and he realized he wanted passionately to make his own fine wine. And he was smart enough to want to do something no one else was doing but something that would work in this environment. Hence, his emphasis on Alsatian wines such as dry Gewürztraminer, dry Riesling, and some late harvest wines.

Claiborne & Churchill's building is interesting in itself. Friends helped erect the winery, the first commercial straw bale building in California. Its 16-inch walls are made of rice straw bales sealed with stucco, resulting in a building that supposedly can't be destroyed by fire or water and whose wine cellar requires no heating or cooling. Be sure to check out the "truth window" inside the tasting room, through which you can see some of the straw, and to look at the collection of photos recording the actual building of architect Marilyn Farmer's design.

Fine points: Featured wines: Dry Riesling, Dry Gewürztraminer, Chardonnay, Pinot Noir, Sweet Orange Muscat (excellent), Dry Muscat, PortObispo California Port, Sparkling Brut Rosé. Owners: Claiborne Thompson and Fredericka Churchill-Thompson. Winemaker: Claiborne Thompson. Cases: 10,000. Acres: buy from Edna Valley, Monterey, and San Luis Obispo and Santa Barbara Counties.

❧ *Claiborne & Churchill, 2649 Carpenter Canyon Road, San Luis Obispo 93401; (805) 544-4066; www.clairbornechurchill.com. Open 11:00 a.m.–5:00 p.m. daily. Tasting fee: $5, refundable with purchase. Groups of ten or more should call for appointment. Visa, MasterCard, American Express. Wheelchair accessible.*

From here we take you back into the foothills, first to Kynsi and Domaine Alfred, and then to Talley Vineyards and its sister, Bishop's Peak. Then we head south to rejoin US 101 to visit Laetitia and travel on southward to Santa Maria and Santa Barbara.

As you come out of Claiborne & Churchill's driveway, turn right, and then almost immediately turn leftish onto Corbett Canyon Road, passing elegant ranches, estates, and vineyards.

Soon you will come to KYNSI WINERY, owned by Don and Gwen Othman, true partners in life and winery. Kynsi ("talon" in Finnish) is a true blue-jeans winery located in a charming 1940s dairy, with the tasting room in the old milk processing room. Kynsi's label features the real-life barn owl that lives in the old barn next to the winery, where she and her mate nest each spring.

Don invented and manufactured the famous "Bulldog Pup" at the Othman's specialty wine tool business, Bulldog Manufacturing, to help handle Pinot Noir grapes. The Othmans keep to their beliefs, working small and toward perfection. Worth the trip!

Fine points: Featured wines: Chardonnay, Pinot Noir, Syrah, Merrah (Merlot and Syrah blend). Owners and winemakers: Don and Gwen Othman. Cases: 3,000. Acres: 30.

❧ *Kynsi Winery, 2212 Corbett Canyon Road, Arroyo Grande 93420; (805) 544-8461; www.kynsi.com. Open 11:00 a.m.–5:00 p.m. Thursday–Monday. Tasting fee: $5. Visa, MasterCard. Wheelchair accessible.*

Also, on Corbett Canyon Road is—you guessed it—the much advertised Corbett Canyon Vineyards, which is not open to the public.

As you leave Kynsi, turn left onto Tiffany Ranch Road, appropriately named for the exquisite neighborhood. Turn left on Orcutt Road to visit Terry Speizer's DOMAINE ALFRED.

Domaine Alfred's Chamizal Vineyard has newly planted vines that should create exciting wines in the fine Edna Valley tradition. Check it out.

Fine points: Featured wines: Chardonnay, Pinot Noir, Syrah. Owner: Terry Speizer. Winemaker: Mike Sinor. Cases: 3,000. Acres: 83.

❧ Domaine Alfred, 7525 Orcutt Road, San Luis Obispo 93401; (805) 541-9463; www.domainealfred.com. Open 10:00 a.m.–5:00 p.m. Friday–Sunday. Tasting fee: $4–$6, includes glass. Visa and MasterCard. Restroom not wheelchair accessible.

Head southeast on Orcutt Road, past Tiffany Ranch Road, and turn left on Lopez Drive. Continue 1 mile to Talley Vineyards. You are now on the northern edge of the Arroyo Grande Valley.

TALLEY VINEYARDS and BISHOP'S PEAK share the Talley family's beautiful historic adobe tasting room on a knoll overlooking Talley's cilantro field. El Rincon Adobe was built beginning in 1837 and grew into a New England–style adobe house where, eventually, Ramón Branch and his bride, Maria Isabella Robbins (a member of the Carillo family), raised eleven children. The Branches were well known for their entertaining and huge barbecues, during which two Chinese cooks helped Isabella. The farm was worked by Chumash Indians, Spaniards, and buccaneers.

The Talley story began in 1948 when Oliver Talley started growing specialty vegetables in the Arroyo Grande Valley. While helping to grow great veggies at Talley Farms, Oliver's son Don grew an interest in the viticulture developing nearby in the Edna Valley and Santa Barbara County. Don convinced himself that Chardonnay and Pinot Noir grapes would do well on the steep loam and clay hillsides, similar to the Côte de Nuits region, and above the produce farm land. So in 1982 he planted a small test plot of five varietals.

TALLEY VINEYARDS AND BISHOP'S PEAK TASTING ROOM IN EL RINCON ADOBE, ARROYO GRANDE

Talley produced its first wine in 1986, in a small winery adjacent to a vegetable cooler. Talley currently uses its 8,500-square-foot state-of-the-art facility featuring a total gravity system for crushing to make sure grapes are handled in the most gentle manner possible. Now Don and Rosemary Talley and their son Brian and his wife, Jonine, all oversee day-to-day operations with winemaker Leslie Meade.

Talley Vineyards's wines are all estate grown, while its Bishop's Peak wines are made from grapes grown by small independent growers in the neighborhood.

 Fine points: Featured wines: Talley Vineyards Chardonnay, Sauvignon Blanc, White Riesling, Pinot Noir, Late Harvest White Riesling, Bishop's Peak Chardonnay, Zinfandel, Dolcetto, Syrah, Cabernet Sauvignon. Owners: Don and Rosemary Talley, Brian and Jonine Talley. Winemaker: Leslie Meade. Cases: Talley, 18,000; Bishop's Peak; 16,000. Acres: 140.

❧ *Talley Vineyards and Bishop's Peak, 3031 Lopez Drive, Arroyo Grande 93420; (805) 489-0446, fax (805) 489-0996; www.talleyvineyards.com. Open 10:30 a.m.–4:30 p.m. daily. Tasting fee: $5 for five wines. Visa and MasterCard. Wheelchair accessible.*

From here we take you on another scenic but somewhat direct route to US 101 and Laetitia Vineyard and Winery. As you leave Talley Vineyards, turn right on Lopez Drive and continue southwest as its name changes to Branch Street. Do not be tempted to turn north on Highway 227 unless you want to stop in Arroyo Grande for lunch. Many winery workers recommend the Back Door Deli or the Branch Street Deli in Arroyo Grande. Otherwise, keep going to US 101 and head south toward Santa Barbara.

Watch very carefully for the sign for LAETITIA VINEYARD & WINERY on the east side of US 101. If you are approaching from the north, get in the left lane and turn into the center strip, get your bearings as traffic races by, watch carefully for a traffic break, and gun it across two lanes of northbound traffic and up Laetitia's driveway.

A visit to Laetitia (lay-TEE-shia), 12 miles south of San Luis Obispo and just 2.5 miles from the Pacific Ocean, can be one of the most pleasant and restful stops on your wine exploration tour. We felt as if we had walked into a friend's bright, sunny kitchen and breakfast room to say hi and have a look at their new books and oils, to say nothing of the wines. We met Julie Fellion, a Rutherford (Napa Valley) native whose mother, Carol, we met at the fabulous Steves' Hardware in St. Helena. We also met San Franciscans who make a couple of trips to Laetitia annually just to visit and pick up their wine.

Formerly Maison Deutz, a proud producer of sparkling wines, Laetitia has joined with BARNWOOD VINEYARDS of Santa Barbara County. In 1998 Laetitia began to focus on still wine production, receiving high ratings and gold medals for its Pinot Noir, Chardonnay, and Pinot Blanc.

Nebil "Bilo" Zarif founded Barnwood Vineyards in 1994, having spent much of his life in France as a collector of Bordeaux wines. He partnered with his longtime friend Selim Zilkha, and now Barnwood is a 2,000-acre estate in the Santa Barbara Highlands (3,200 feet elevation).

Enjoy the elegant sparklers and other fine wines, as well as fig vinegar and a wide range of salad oils. If you call in the morning, Nathan Carlson or Julie will order a picnic basket delivered for lunch to enjoy on the patio. What a nice touch!

 Fine points: Featured wines: Laetitia Chardonnay, Pinot Blanc, Cuvée M, Trio (a Merlot, Cabernet Sauvignon, Syrah blend), Rosé, Viognier, Pinot Noir, Cabernet Sauvignon, Brut Cuvée, Barnwood Sauvignon Blanc, Merlot, Syrah, Orange Muscat Canelli. Owners: Bilo Zarif and Selim Zilkha. Winemakers: Eric Hickey. Cases: 50,000. Acres: 620 planted of nearly 2,000.

❧ *Laetitia Vineyard & Winery* and *Barnwood Vineyards, 453 Deutz Drive, Arroyo Grande 93420; (805) 481-1763 or (805) 481-1772, fax (805) 481-6920; www.laetitiawine.com or www.barnwoodwine.com. Open 11:00 a.m.–5:00 p.m. daily. Tasting fee: $5. Visa, MasterCard, American Express, Discover. Wheelchair accessible.*

From here you can easily go to San Luis Obispo, Pismo Beach, or south to Santa Maria and Santa Barbara.

CHAPTER 8

HISTORY OF CALIFORNIA'S CENTRAL COAST

uan Rodriguez Cabrillo was an intrepid explorer and a courageous commander, but he was unlucky. Although Portuguese, he had been an aide to Spaniard Hernando Cortez in the conquest of Mexico since 1520. On June 27, 1542, the viceroy of New Spain sent him north from the west coast of Mexico to explore the unknown coast of mythical California in two small ships, San Salvador *and* Victoria.

TWO CENTURIES OF NEGLECT

Hugging the coast, Cabrillo discovered San Diego Bay (he named it San Miguel) and San Pedro Bay. In the middle of October, he steered his little flotilla into Santa Barbara Bay. Anchoring off the beach, he was greeted by curious natives who had paddled out in their canoes. Cabrillo was rowed to shore and proclaimed that this land belonged to the king of Spain. He and his men visited the Indian village, where presents were exchanged.

Then Cabrillo sailed away to explore the Channel Islands before again heading north. He spotted and named Morro Bay and Morro Rock. Just as he came in sight of the southern cape to Monterey Bay, the winds drove his ships out to sea. Cabrillo made it to the latitude of San Francisco Bay, but once again the weather forced him away. The storm became so violent that he was knocked down in his ship and broke his arm. He turned back, hoping to spend the winter on one of the Channel Islands. His injured arm did not heal, the break festered, and gangrene set in. By the time he made it to San Miguel Island, he was failing. On January 3, 1543, he died and was buried on the island in a now lost grave. His ships eventually limped back to Central America.

It would be more than fifty years before the Spanish made another serious attempt to explore the west coast north of Baja California. Instead they concentrated on developing trade with the Philippine Islands and other Far East ports, bringing gold, spices, and jewels across the Pacific to Acapulco in scurvy-ridden galleons.

Sir Francis Drake, the English privateer, sailed around Cape Horn into the Pacific in 1577. He pirated Spanish treasure ships and claimed for England the land at Drake's Bay, north of the undiscovered Golden Gate. (There is evidence that in 1579 Drake also stopped at Goleta Beach just west of Santa Barbara to repair his leaky *Golden Hind* and to take on fresh water. In 1891 a sixteenth-century anchor was found in a wooded area near the slough. Then in 1981 five encrusted muzzle-loading cannons were discovered in the water just east of Goleta. These could have been Drake's or from a ship of Sir William Hawkins, another British explorer/pirate.)

Two Spanish crews did touch land on the central coast before the end of the sixteenth century, but really by accident. Under Capt. Pedro de Unamumo, a galleon returning from Manila took shelter in Morro Bay, which de Unamumo claimed for Spain. He sent a landing party inland to explore as far as present-day San Luis Obispo. They were attacked by Indians, two crewmen were killed, and Unamumo lifted anchor. Eight years later, Capt. Sebastian Rodriguez Cermeño foolishly attempted to explore the California coast with a loaded trea-sure ship, the *San Agustin,* on his way back from the Philippines. His ship was smashed on the rocks trying to enter Drake's Bay. In a longboat his crew rowed and sailed back to Mexico, landing for a rest and trade with the natives at San Luis Obispo Bay, where the Indians called them "Christianos"—a word appar-ently learned from Unamumo's men before they were chased off.

In 1602 the Spanish organized a serious expedition to explore the California coast. Under the command of Sebastian Vizcaino, a Spanish Basque, three ships— *San Diego, Santa Tomas,* and *Tres Reyes*—sailed from Acapulco on May 5, 1602. Among the 200 in his command were three Carmelite friars and a cartographer.

The little fleet struggled up the Mexican coast for a half year until November, when it reached Cabrillo's San Miguel Bay, renamed San Diego by Vizcaino. The expedition was in trouble from head winds, leaking water barrels, and the first signs of scurvy. After a rest they picked up speed, and eventually anchored at Santa Catalina Island.

On December 4, 1602, Vizcaino steered his ships around a point on the mainland into a sweeping bay with a wide beach. Carmelite Friar Antonio de la Ascension was in charge of naming new landmarks, and because the date was the anniversary of the death of Santa Barbara, he named the place for that saint. Barbara was an early Roman Christian who had been beheaded by her father, infuriated because she refused to renounce her religion. Immediately thereafter her father was struck dead by a lightning bolt.

Vizcaino did not land, but he invited aboard canoes full of chanting natives, including the local chief. The meetings were friendly, with the chief offering several wives per sailor if they would come ashore, but Vizcaino turned down the offer. What the crew wanted is not known. The Spaniards sailed farther north, anchoring briefly in San Luis Obispo Bay, where they traded with natives who paddled out to the ships.

Vizcaino did land at the broad bay that Cabrillo had only seen before being driven away by a storm. He named the bay Monterey for the count of Monterey, viceroy of New Spain—a politically correct decision—and a nearby river, Rio de Carmelo, for the Carmelites—a religiously correct choice.

Scurvy, the mariner's disease caused by deficiencies of vitamins and other nutrients on long voyages, racked Vizcaino's crew. He put the worst thirty-four cases onto the *Santo Tomas* headed back to Acapulco, after the priests gave many of them last rites. Only nine men survived the return trip. The other two ships made it back to Mexico by late February, but more than forty of their crewmen had died.

Viceroy Monterey was enthusiastic about Vizcaino's discoveries, but he was replaced in 1603. The new viceroy fired Vizcaino and shelved a 1606 order from the king of Spain that he send Vizcaino back to Monterey with colonists. Charges of embezzlement were brought against Vizcaino's able cartographer, Capt. Geronimo Martin de Palacios, who was tried and hanged. The reports of the expedition were ignored. It was more than 160 years before the California coast would be visited again by Europeans.

During the seventeenth century, the Spanish military and religious established only small settlements in Sonora, Mexico, and present-day Arizona. The Jesuits founded five missions in Baja California.

PORTOLA AND SERRA ON THE COAST

In 1765 King Carlos III appointed bright, energetic, and mentally unstable Jose de Galvez as visitor general of New Spain. Exploration and settlement of Alta California (San Diego and north) was high on his list of priorities. He established a port at San Blas, north of Acapulco on the west coast of Mexico, as a shipping base to California. At the same time, the king expelled the Jesuits from all Spanish possessions in reaction to the Jesuit habit of assuming governmental and diplomatic functions. This left the Franciscans as the principal religious order in the Spanish territories.

Galvez named veteran army officer Capt. Gaspar de Portola military governor of Baja California, and he also gave Portola authority as governor of Alta

California, with no constituents, except for Indians. Portola and Galvez met at San Blas to plan an expedition to find Vizcaino's Monterey Bay. Portola would march up the coast, shadowed by two ships to support and supply the marchers at San Diego and Monterey Bay.

Appointed to create and manage an anticipated chain of missions was Father Junipero Serra, a 5-foot-2 Franciscan friar who combined administrative talent with unrelenting religious fervor. He scourged himself to a point of painful ecstasy and limped through life with an ulcer on his leg from an old infected insect bite.

The expedition did not go well. After leaving in late March 1769, the first leg of the trip to San Diego was late because one of the ships went too far out to sea and delayed everyone. Serra, ill with his sporadic leg infection, was lifted onto a mule in Baja and managed to make it to San Diego Bay but could go no farther. He agreed to stay there to direct construction of a mission.

Departing San Diego on July 14, Portola's party included Friar Juan Crespi and another Carmelite priest, twenty-seven soldiers, fifteen Christian Indians, mule drivers, an engineer, and a dozen others, plus cattle for food. They passed through modern-day Los Angeles, San Fernando Valley, Ventura, Santa Barbara, and San Luis Obispo, hacking out a trail as they went. On the narrow plain between today's Ventura and Santa Barbara, Portola counted twenty-one Indian villages, each centered around a large round council house. One of these native towns specialized in making canoes, so Portola's soldiers ignored the saint's name given it by Father Crespi and insisted on calling it Carpinteria— carpenter's shop.

The party slogged through the sand at Pismo Beach, traded with Indians near Price Canyon, and spotted numerous giant bears in what they called Cañada de los Osos ("Valley of the Bears"), a name that lives on. Proceeding past Morro Bay, present-day Cambria, and San Simeon Bay, they prepared to tackle the climb over the Santa Lucia Mountains in search of Monterey Bay.

Eighty-three days after leaving San Diego, Portola and his men reached Punta de los Pinos, at the southern cape of Monterey Bay. Based on Vizcaino's description of Monterey Bay as a sheltered port and not a sweeping crescent of beach, Portola's party did not recognize it. They pushed onward, and when they came to the Salinas River they reckoned it was the Rio Carmelo. Geographically confused, cold, and near starvation, Portola's men pressed on until they discovered San Francisco Bay, unknown until that moment. Portola turned around and led his worn-out troops back the way they had come. Eating the mules one by one, the starving expedition managed to crawl back to San Diego by late January 1770.

Buoyed by the arrival at San Diego of the *San Antonio* with fresh supplies and men from Mexico in late March, the indefatigable Portola organized another expedition to locate Monterey. While Capt. Juan Perez Hernandez sailed up the coast with Father Serra, supplies, and some of the men, Portola retraced his land route northward, again passing through the future Santa Barbara and San Luis Obispo. He made it to Monterey Bay in only thirty-seven days. This time he was convinced this was the "noble harbor" described by Vizcaino. A few days later the ships arrived.

Leaving Father Serra and Pedro Fages as the commandant, Portola boarded the ship *San Antonio* and never returned to Alta California, but he governed from Loreto in Baja. Within a year Serra moved the Monterey Mission to a bluff above the nearby Rio Carmelo, which he named San Carlos Borromeo de Carmelo (Carmel Mission) and where he made his headquarters. In 1771 he inaugurated missions San Antonio de Padua in the Santa Lucia Mountains southwest of King City and San Gabriel Arcangel in the Los Angeles basin.

THE CROSS COMES TO THE VALLEY OF THE BEARS

When the crops failed and a supply ship did not show up, Fages organized a grizzly-bear hunt in the Valley of the Bears. More than 9,000 pounds of bear meat were carted over the hills to save the starving Monterey settlers. This hunt also introduced the soldiers to the attractive and friendly Chumash Indian girls. Known for their good looks, above-average height, artistry, and smarts, the Chumash occupied most of the land from south of Santa Barbara north to the San Luis Obispo Valley. The mutual attraction between soldiers and maidens resulted in numerous assignations and some of the first marriages between natives and settlers.

Determined to force regular supply ship deliveries from San Diego, in August 1772 Father Serra began a mule ride south with Fages. Near the site of the recent bear hunt, Serra halted the pack train beside a flowing creek. There he had the men raise a cross, sang a mass, and left Padre Jose Cavaller to build the mission Serra had christened San Luis Obispo de Tolusa for Saint Louis, bishop of Toulouse (son of the king of Naples). The Chumash name for the place was Tixlini.

Indian labor built a mission chapel and a house, both made of logs and adobe with a roof of dried reeds, and planted crops for the padres and Christianized Indians. On several occasions Indians from non-Chumash tribes shot flaming arrows onto the dry roof, setting the buildings on fire and eventually partially destroying them. In response the mission fathers developed a form to bend clay into interlocking roof tiles, which were dried and fired in a kiln. The fire- and waterproof tiles soon became standard at all California missions.

Four years would pass before Serra would be able to dedicate another mission, much to his almost non-Christian anger. He was in a running feud with three appointed governors of California, Pedro Fages, Fernando Rivera, and Felipe de Neve, and in 1782, Fages again. At the core of the argument was whether the church or the military would control the direction of the colony. Specifically, all of the governors, as military men, felt that presidios should be built to protect the settlers before money and labor were expended on establishing missions.

Capt. Juan Bautista de Anza appeared in Monterey on May 1, 1774, after an amazing trek across the southwest desert to Mission San Gabriel (east of present-day Los Angeles), and then up the old Portola route to Monterey, with a stop at Mission San Luis Obispo. A week later, Father Serra followed, having walked from San Diego in the last leg of a trip back from Mexico City.

Arriving at Monterey, Serra performed weddings for three soldiers and their native brides. Some Indians felt these intermarriages showed Spanish respect for the indigenous people and encouraged natives to become baptized. Serra intended to bring Christianity to the Indians, teach them agriculture and light manufacturing (like making adobe bricks), educate the young women in European-style crafts such as weaving and domestic service, fight the evil of polygamy (actually a privilege of taking three wives accorded only to chiefs of some tribes), and use their labor.

The natives were impressed by the Spaniards' equipment, guns, clothes, glass beads, ships, and other objects, as well as the apparent ability of the priests to commune with their god. Therefore, many Indians came forward to be baptized in this new religion. Soon many of them were working in serflike peonage, their daughters were separated from their families, and the rhythm of their lives, so necessary to hunting, fishing, and gathering, was interrupted forever.

Viceroy Antonio de Bucarelli was very much pro-California and felt Alta California was more attractive than the blistering hot, rock-hard peninsula of Baja California. Bucarelli ordered the provincial capital of the Californias transferred from Loreto in Baja to Monterey. This was accomplished in February 1777. He also OK'd the governor giving deserving soldiers small plots of land.

De Anza came through San Luis Obispo from Arizona again in 1776. This time he led forty soldiers, their wives, children, muleteers, horsemen, and two officers, for a total of 240 headed for Monterey. They had no wagons but drove herds of horses, mules, and cattle.

SERRA AND THE GOVERNORS CLASH

After a four-year hiatus, Serra was permitted to found missions at San Francisco, San Juan Capistrano, and Santa Clara. But in February 1777, Felipe de Neve was named governor of the Californias. When Serra and de Neve met at Monterey, the governor said he agreed that Spanish colonization of the areas of Buenaventura and Santa Barbara was essential to guarantee Spanish domination of Alta California. In February 1782 the governor asked Serra to come south with two padres to head the new missions at both locations. Serra decided he would move to Santa Barbara himself and close out his career there. After dedicating a mission at Buenaventura on March 31, 1782, Serra joined de Neve on the trail to the future Santa Barbara. There the governor was able to convince Yanunali, the local chief, that it would be beneficial to Chumash people if a Spanish settlement were to move in near the village of 500 indigenous folk and a dozen other rancherias that looked to the chief for leadership.

For three weeks de Neve let Father Serra cool his heels while Portola's old scout, Lieut. Jose Francisco de Ortega, started construction of the presidio. Only then did de Neve tell Serra that the founding of the mission would have to wait until the presidio was completed. A dejected Serra took the next passing ship back to Monterey. He returned twice by ship to conduct masses and confirmations at the presidio chapel the following year, but he found the presidio in a constant state of expansion.

While founding the mission was on hold, in 1782 the Spanish government granted 17,826 acres to the pueblo of Santa Barbara. Ranchers, retired military, and other favorites of the governors received "concessions" that allowed them the "use" of large tracts of land, but title to the property technically remained in the government. Neither consulted nor reimbursed were the Indians, who had lived in harmony on the land for several millennia without titles.

Pedro Fages returned for a second stint as governor in 1784 and agreed to let the establishment of the Santa Barbara mission proceed. Fages informed Serra of that decision by letter, but Serra died of cancer within a month. It was two years before a specific Santa Barbara mission site was chosen, after Goleta and Montecito were considered and rejected. Finally Father Fermin Lasuen, the new presidente general of the missions, dedicated the Santa Barbara mission on December 4, 1786.

FOUR NEW MISSIONS

Construction began in the spring of 1787 at the current location west and uphill from the presidio—exactly 1 mile, the distance Serra had prescribed to keep the sex-starved Spanish soldiers away from the Indian maidens living under the protection of the church. The original small structure was soon succeeded by a larger four-room adobe. An even more spacious and sturdy mission building was completed in 1794. Meanwhile the presidio was expanded and reconstructed of stone, lumber shipped from Monterey, and adobe bricks and tiles made by Indian laborers.

That same year, construction of the current mission at San Luis Obispo began. Its arcade was supported by classic Greco-Roman round columns instead of the arches usual in the Spanish-style structures or the frontier post-beam method employed in later missions.

Although the mission fathers brought Christian teachings and some training to the natives in various trades, in the long run the mission system destroyed Indian culture, family life, and self-reliance. European diseases, against which the natives had no immunity, finished the destruction by wiping out entire tribes. Unfortunately the padres believed that baptism and conversion meant signing up for life as wards of the mission. Sending soldiers to chase after "runaways" and the use of the whip, the stocks, and other punishments to keep them in line were standard procedures.

Spain's position as a world power began to shrink in the late 1700s. The British and Spanish came close to war in a dispute over rival outposts on Vancouver Island on the north coast, and Spain had to agree to keep only what it already occupied in the Western Hemisphere. Fearful of British and Russian probes in the north Pacific, the Spanish became desperate to reinforce their control of California.

There followed a period when the missionaries and the military—the cross and the sword—worked in concert to expand colonization. A year after Santa Barbara Mission opened, Padre Lasuen founded La Purisima Concepcion Mission on December 8, 1787, at what is now downtown Lompoc. Santa Cruz and Soledad were established in 1791, but for six years the governors would not authorize new missions without the means to protect them. Eventually, believing the Indians were subdued, three more missions were inaugurated in a four-month period in 1797. One was San Miguel Arcangel, north of San Luis Obispo, at the juncture of the Salinas and Nacimiento Rivers. On dedication day, hundreds of natives showed up, primarily Salinnans, but also some Tulares who came from over the mountains.

Father Esteven Tapis, the latest presidente of the California mission system, wanted to establish a stop north of Santa Barbara that could be reached in a day's walk and could become an agricultural producer. Tapis chose a site in the Santa Ynez Valley at today's Solvang and dedicated the new mission, the nineteenth in California, on September 17, 1804, from an altar under a brushwood shelter. He gave it the name Santa Ines for Saint Agnes, a beautiful and wealthy thirteen-year-old Christian nun of the fourth century who refused to renounce her religion despite horrible threats (from burning to mass rape) by Roman officials and was beheaded.

MISSIONS PROSPER ON INDIAN LABOR

An adobe mission building was quickly built at Santa Ines, and within two years there were 570 native converts, but as a harbinger of what was to come, 118 of them had died, primarily of European diseases. Even such illnesses as measles proved deadly. The cattle and sheep reached 13,000 head, however, and there were substantial crops of wheat, corn, and other agricultural products. Initially there was a shortage of water, which prevented the natives from taking their traditional steam baths.

The same year as the founding of Santa Ines, there were 2,074 baptisms of Indians at San Luis Obispo, but also 1,091 deaths. The mission at San Luis Obispo operated seven sheep ranches, ran tens of thousands of head of cattle, had bumper wheat crops, and raised chickens and vegetables. San Miguel followed suit on almost the same scale. All of this success was due to efforts of the mission Indians, who worked in return for basic foods, blankets, some clothing, and primitive housing.

Because there were no native grapes in California suitable for winemaking, Father Serra had rootstock shipped in so that the missions could make their own sacramental wine. The so-called Mission grapes resulted in a sweetish wine that was passable. Before the close of the eighteenth century, all of the missions on the central coast planted vineyards, as did Santa Barbara Presidio Commandante Felipe de Goycoehea next to what is now De la Vina Street.

La Purisima had two vineyards near the coast, while Santa Ines was successful with three vineyards, but grapes planted next to the mission itself did poorly. None of them matched the production of San Gabriel in the Los Angeles area, which remained the viticulture center of the territory until after statehood. In the early days the crush was performed by barefoot Indians stomping grapes on a steer hide. The juice was fermented in wooden vats.

Santa Barbara's population in the first years scarcely reached more than 250, with almost half of pure Spanish blood, mostly born in Mexico. They were followed in number by mestizos of Spanish-Indian mix, and then variations of mulatto and mestizo combinations. Santa Barbara grew as retired soldiers settled nearby with their families.

RULE OF THE *GENTE DE RAZON*

The social division between those of solely Spanish descent (who modestly called themselves *gente de razon*—people of reason) and those of mixed blood was clear, sharp, and generally immutable. Marriages between one of the *gente de razon* and a mestizo, an Indian, or a person of other mixed blood were virtually nonexistent. The government jobs, the priesthood, the large land grants, the business opportunities, and the marriages to others of the aristocracy were all their monopoly. Even corporals and sergeants could rise to prominence and wealth in frontier society as long as they were of pure Spanish blood.

British explorer Capt. George Vancouver had negotiated with Spanish Adm. Juan Francisco de la Bodega y Quadra for return of British property on Vancouver Island seized by the Spanish. The two men became instant friends, even agreeing the island would be named Quadra and Vancouver (which it remained until the 1840s). The admiral invited the Englishman to visit him in California. When Vancouver landed at Monterey, a four-week fiesta was thrown in his honor. Sailing on to Santa Barbara, Vancouver anchored offshore, and the wary commandante was polite, but he restricted Vancouver's men to the area within sight of the presidio (except for an English botanist, who could explore freely) and insisted they return to their ship at night.

Vancouver sailed away with gifts, sheep, vegetables, water, and lots of information, for he wanted to assess the strength of the Spanish hold on California for possible future expansion by the British. He reported that "Santa Barbara presidio bore the appearance of a far more civilized place than any of the other Spanish settlements in California."

Alta California was officially separated from Baja in 1804, along the line approximately where the American-Mexican border lies today. Monterey remained the capital of Alta. Within a few years cattle ranches around Santa Barbara and Monterey and other coastal valleys were producing thousands of hides, which became the underpinning of the wealth of Alta California. Hide was used for shoes, clothing, saddles, and thongs to bind rafters to posts in construction.

In the early 1800s American ships out of Boston began making regular stops on the California coast to buy hides at docks piled high with the leather. The

Yankees called the hides "Spanish dollars." Otter skins were being taken and shipped to China at the rate of 2,000 a year. The king of Spain arrogantly declared the hunting of otter a Spanish monopoly, however, so they had to be smuggled. High tariffs on importing goods to trade for hides led to further smuggling. American ships would stop at a channel island or in small coves on the coast, unload, and then report only a small cargo to import. Sometimes they would load up away from the main harbor to avoid export taxes. California officials more anxious for trade than taxes (which went to the home country) often winked at such practices, however, and ignored official restrictions on allowing foreign vessels to land.

Fandangos, bullfights, horse races, bearbaiting, music, extravagant weddings, Chinese fireworks, romance, and easy living made this the golden age for the Californio ranchers and their extended families clustered around each central ranch house. Father Lasuen died in 1803, leaving the mission system without a strong leader. The Catalan Volunteers, the seventy-man infantry company at the Monterey presidio, were shipped back to Mexico in 1803 and 1804, as no longer necessary for the protection of the pueblo and mission. In 1804 the commandante of the Santa Barbara presidio, Ramundo Carrillo, outlawed the carrying of knives, which had been commonly tucked in sashes and too often pulled out during arguments.

CHAOS, EARTHQUAKE, AND TIDAL WAVE

In 1806 what started as a roof fire at Mission San Miguel burned down the mission and its large supply of crops, wool, hides, and cloth. It took twelve years to complete construction of a new, larger, and tile-roofed (fireproofed) mission. Most wonderful was the vivid artistry of Esteban Munras, a wealthy ranchero with great design talents, who finished his work in 1821. His murals and decorations have been preserved without being retouched—unique among all California missions.

The home country of Spain was in chaos due to the rampages of Napoleon Bonaparte, who invaded Spain in 1808 and put his brother Joseph on the throne. In the turmoil liberators arose in South America to lead revolts that freed most of the continent. Attempting to emulate their efforts, a Mexican priest, Miguel Hidalgo y Costilla, declared Mexico independent of Spain in 1810. After raising a large army of peasants led by ex-army officers, and meeting early successes, the rebels were defeated when they attacked Mexico City. Hunted down by the Spanish army and betrayed by traitors in his ranks, Father Hidalgo and his top generals were shot in 1811. The result was that Alta California was pretty much on its own.

After a summer of nerve-racking tremors along the Santa Barbara coast, on December 21, 1812, all hell broke loose. Centered under the ocean just off Lompoc, an earthquake equal to the seismic power of the 1906 San Francisco quake occurred. It destroyed the missions at Santa Barbara and Lompoc and substantially damaged the one at Santa Ines. The presidio was left with half standing walls and half rubble. If that were not trouble enough, the quake was followed by a great tsunami triggered by the sudden cleft in the seabed. Ocean water roared seaward—exposing the ocean floor—and then came back in five gigantic tidal waves every quarter of an hour. The fourth was a 50-foot-high wall of water that tore into the coast, splintering wooden buildings and washing away adobes, until it stopped at the steps of the presidio.

The Boston ship *Mercury* under Capt. George Washington Ayres, often suspected of smuggling, was anchored in Refugio Cove. Lifted on the crest of the tidal wave, the ship was carried half a mile inland (to a point just below former President Ronald Reagan's Tip Top Ranch) and just as quickly was sucked back to sea in the outflow. In the hills, little volcanoes spewing sulfur appeared, and offshore of today's Summerland, oil spouted from the ocean floor. A crack 100 feet wide and a fifth of a mile long ripped open Santa Rosa Island, causing the Indians living there to send word they wanted the soldiers to come get them, while others paddled on their own to shore. Soon everyone had left San Miguel Island, except for a forgotten woman who lived there alone for the next twenty years.

In the wake of the devastation, the missionary fathers at Santa Barbara decided it was best to erect a new church. The current large and architecturally attractive "Queen of the Missions," begun in 1815, was built of sandstone with walls 6 feet thick. In charge of designing and building the new mission was Padre Antonio Ripoli, a student and devotee of Greco-Roman architecture. The basic construction was completed in 1820, but add-ons and improvements, including a water aqueduct from the hills, continued to be built for more than a dozen years. The second tower was not erected until the 1830s.

At Santa Ines, reconstruction and some expansion was begun, but even with Indian labor it was slow going. The flattened La Purisima Concepcion (at what is now La Purisima Mission State Park in Lompoc) was abandoned, and a new mission was built in 1815 at its current location farther inland.

DE LA GUERRA TAKES CHARGE

Appointed commandante of the Santa Barbara presidio that year was thirty-six-year-old Jose de la Guerra y Noriega, a Spaniard who had immigrated to Mexico as a teenager. A career officer, he had been a lieutenant at Santa Barbara since 1806 and was married to Maria Antonia, the daughter of previous commandante Carrillo. As his family expanded, he had Casa de la Guerra built to house them. For the next forty years, Captain de la Guerra would be the wealthiest and most influential man in Santa Barbara.

Commandante de la Guerra soon faced a test of nerve. Hippolyte de Bouchard, a French pirate posing as a liberator, sailed down the California coast in 1818 with two ships flying the flag of Buenos Aires, principal province of newly independent Argentina. De Bouchard looted and burned much of Monterey in November and then set sail for Santa Barbara. He anchored at the smugglers' haven, Refugio Cove, but found that the cattle on the Ortega rancho had been herded inland. A squad of Spanish soldiers captured three of his crew by lassoing them like stray horses and took them to Santa Barbara.

On December 8, 1818, a fighting-mad pirate captain and his 300 crewmen dropped anchor in Santa Barbara Bay. A message was delivered to de la Guerra: Release the three men or else. Outnumbered three hundred to fifty, in full view of the pirate ships, de la Guerra marched his scant troops along the beach into a wooded area, where the men changed clothes and marched back. They repeated this maneuver in varied costumes until the buccaneers were convinced he had more men than the invaders. An exchange was arranged, three pirates for one captured Californio, and the pirates sailed away to sack San Juan Capistrano.

While the frustrated pirates were smashing up the deserted Ortega rancho, one of the crew, Joseph Chapman, slipped away. An American sailor who had been shanghaied in Hawaii, Chapman walked to Santa Ines Mission, where the friars gave him sanctuary. De la Guerra agreed to a form of probation because Americans (particularly of pirate crews) were illegal aliens under Spanish law. The condition was that Chapman, an accomplished carpenter, mason, and mechanic, would build a gristmill for San Gabriel Mission near Los Angeles.

After two years Chapman returned to Santa Ines, where he built another gristmill to grind wheat and directed reconstruction of the mission. He also converted to Catholicism (he had been a Baptist), and in 1822 he married Guadalupe Ortega (whose uncle owned the Refugio Rancho). Given amnesty by the governor of California, he and his bride moved to San Fernando for a decade and then returned to Santa Barbara. When he died in 1849, he was the first Yankee permitted burial at the Santa Barbara Mission.

Mexican Independence and the New Californios

The struggle for Mexican independence from Spain had not died with Father Hidalgo. Another parish priest, Father Jose Morelos, led a volunteer army that controlled much of southern Mexico, but in 1815 he was captured by Spanish troops and shot. Leadership of the independence movement passed to guerrilla general Vicente Guerrero. When Agustin Iturbe, the commander of the troops fighting the rebels, switched sides, the Spanish viceroy had to agree to Mexican independence, which was granted on August 24, 1821.

Rumors of independence had circulated from ships up from Baja California as early as January 1822. On April 11, 1822, the official announcement was made to a gathering in the plazas of Monterey and San Luis Obispo, and on April 13 de la Guerra declared independence before a lineup of his soldiers and most of the population of Santa Barbara, numbering about a thousand. Then he personally ran down the Spanish flag, but to his embarrassment there was no Mexican flag to be hoisted. No matter, there followed a weeklong fiesta. Almost everyone joined in taking the oath as citizens of the Mexican empire. The Franciscan fathers waited a week to decide to take the oath, thereby missing the festivities.

One of the first changes under an independent Mexico was legalization of trade with foreign citizens. By the summer of 1822, two partners, Englishman William Hartnell and Scotsman Hugh McCulloch, were importing, selling, and buying for export, with a virtual monopoly in trade with the missions, negotiated by the smooth-talking (in both English and Spanish) Hartnell. He paid a Spanish dollar per hide. They were soon followed by William Gale, representing the Boston trading firm of Bryant and Sturgis, who challenged Hartnell's monopoly by offering two dollars a hide. Other Americans and English were soon on the scene, like Alpheus B. Thompson, a Boston sea captain who managed the Santa Barbara office for Bryant and Sturgis, sea captain Daniel Hill, Alfred Robinson, and Louis F. Burton.

Farther north, William G. Dana, another Boston sea captain, settled outside of San Luis Obispo, turned rancher, and with his wife, Josefa Carrillo from Santa Barbara, raised a large family—twenty-one children, of whom thirteen reached adulthood. The miracle is that Dona Josefa survived. Former British Merchant Marine officer William Benjamin Foxen, who first traded at Santa Barbara in 1818, not only married Eduarda Osuna, daughter of a local official, but also endeared himself to Jose de la Guerra by rebuilding the commandante's schooner lying wrecked at Goleta (which means schooner).

The pattern was usually the same. Find an attractive daughter of one of the prominent pure Spanish families, convert to Catholicism, become a Mexican citizen, and then marry the girl. The usual age for marriage by young women among the Californios was between fourteen and sixteen. The first families were few, the daughters numerous, and the Americans and English gentlemen fit well into the frontier elite society of the *gente de razon*.

Almost all prominent Californios were related by marriage. Trade competitors Hartnell and Robinson wed daughters of de la Guerra. Future Californio leader Mariano G. Vallejo, American settler John Wilson, Alpheus Thompson, and Louis Burton all married Carrillo women, as did William G. Dana, San Luis Obispo's leading American immigrant. And, of course, Señora de la Guerra had been a Carrillo. There were Vallejo sisters who became wives of four prominent merchants, and girls from the Pico, Ortega, and Tapia families married new arrivals. Use of large ranchos, exemptions, and trading rights came easily to them. And when the time came for land grants, family connections counted above all else.

REVOLT OF THE CHUMASH

The Indians became increasingly restive working as near serfs while the soldiers were paid, fed, and clothed at government expense. Their resentment came to a flash point at Santa Ines Mission in February 1824 when a Chumash man was severely flogged by a corporal. Armed only with bows and arrows, young Indians chased the guards and mission padre Francisco Xavier Uria into a building back of the mission and set fire to it. Amazingly, when the fire spread to the roof of the mission itself, the natives ran to put out the flames and save the building. Facing reinforcements by soldiers from Santa Barbara, the Indians headed for the hills, returning only after Uria had guaranteed them amnesty. However, the flames of rebellion had spread to the Santa Barbara and La Purisima Concepcion missions.

At Santa Barbara Indians invaded the mission armory, overwhelmed the three guards, and took an elderly priest hostage. De la Guerra, fearing a massacre, called all local citizens to move within the walls of the presidio. At the same time the Indians sent their women and children into the hills. The presidio soldiers attacked the mission, killing two of the natives, but were beaten back. When de la Guerra's men paused for a strategy session during the noontime siesta, the Indians faded away, and they kept going until they reached the land of the Tulares in the San Joaquin Valley. De la Guerra sent troops to forcibly bring them back, but the Indians evaded them in a dust storm. The commandante did better by sending a priest carrying a proclamation of amnesty along with the next squad of soldiers. In June 1824 the Indians voluntarily trekked back to Santa Barbara.

The same day as the Santa Barbara takeover, natives seized La Purisima Concepcion. They barricaded the gates and fought off a siege by Mexican troops for four weeks. Finally the mission was surrounded by cavalry and the walls were breached by Mexican cannon fire. In the battle one soldier and sixteen Indians were killed before the Indians were convinced to surrender by the mission's padre. Seven Indian leaders were soon executed by Mexican authorities.

A more subtle form of rebellion was the growing use of graffiti in the form of derogatory pictures and symbols surreptitiously painted and carved, often during prayers, on mission walls and benches. The mission fathers were kept scurrying about with whitewash to cover up the signs of resentment. Mission San Miguel Arcangel was the hardest hit, and some irreligious carving can still be seen there.

COMIC OPERA GOVERNMENT

During the remainder of the 1820s, the governments of Mexico and the two Californias were comic opera. In Mexico City General Iturbide created the empire of Mexico and had himself named Agustin the First (he was also the last). He was ousted by a revolt two years later. A republic followed in 1824 with a revolving door of presidents, either by election or rebellion. For the department of California this meant official neglect, nonpayment of soldiers, and repeated changes of governors and policies.

The Mexican central government adopted an anti-Spanish policy, which precluded those born in Spain from holding office in spite of oaths of allegiance to Mexico. Californios generally ignored this policy because many social leaders and respected citizens, including priests (the particular target of the campaign), had been born in Spain. One of these was Commandante Jose de la Guerra. When he was elected a *disputado* (congressman) for California, he sailed for Mexico City via Acapulco. The congress had given his place to his alternate and refused to seat him. Some anti-Spanish zealots were prepared to kill him for his audacity in trying to take his elected position. Disguised as a peasant, he escaped in the middle of the night, with nothing but a passport back to California and a cache of gold coins hidden in a false bottom to his attaché case. Reaching the west coast, de la Guerra bought a schooner. But his ship was wrecked as it entered the slough at Goleta, so the commandante and his crew had to wade ashore.

In 1829 all native Spaniards were ordered by government decree to leave California in thirty days. Commandante de la Guerra received an exemption from the governor. Father Ripoli, designer and builder of the Santa Barbara Mission, and Father José Altimira, founder of the mission at Sonoma, boarded ships for Spain without fanfare.

In November 1829, unpaid, hungry, and ragged soldiers, led by an ex-convict named Joaquin Solis, revolted at Monterey, seized the presidio there, and began marching south with Santa Barbara as their next target. Governor Jose Maria de Echeandia headed north from San Diego to the Santa Barbara presidio. By the time the governor got there, Solis and his rebels were encamped at Santa Ines Mission. Belatedly the governor sent messages to each mission asking them to send able-bodied men and dispatched a courier to Solis, requesting his surrender in return for amnesty. The rebel leader replied with a counterdemand that Echeandia hand over Santa Barbara and began marching toward the town.

The governor sent the older women to safety on a ship in the harbor and urged the rest of the population to seek protection at the presidio. Then he ordered acting Commandante Romualdo Pacheco (de la Guerra was on a trip to Mexico) to take his ninety men and intercept Solis at Rancho Dos Pueblos. When the rebels appeared, Pacheco immediately retreated to the presidio. At what is now Mission and De la Vina Streets, Solis set up a cannon aimed at the presidio 1 mile away, just out of range. For two days the cannons of the presidio and the rebels banged away at each other, doing no damage and causing no casualties. Thirty of the rebels defected, and then Solis's forces ran out of gunpowder. Solis beat a retreat, eventually getting back to Monterey. There he found that the soldiers he had left in charge had been provided a barrel of rum by the foreign merchants, had gotten falling-down drunk, and had been easily jailed. Solis was transported to Mexico in chains and then deported to his native Chile.

One bit of fallout from the soldiers' rebellion was the charge against Padre Luis Martinez, longtime pastor at Mission San Luis Obispo, that he had aided the rebellion by feeding the soldiers when they passed by the mission on their march south. Governor Echeandia demanded the father's arrest and a trial for disloyalty to the government. Held in Santa Barbara, the trial was a stacked deck, with seven "jurors," including the governor and some officers who disliked Martinez. The padre was convicted by a six-to-one vote, put on a ship, and deported to Spain. The underlying reasons were that he was a Spaniard and he had repeatedly made sarcastic comments about the idleness of the soldiers.

SECULARIZATION OF THE MISSIONS

More land was needed to reward friends and pioneers, as well as encourage ranches and businesses. The obvious source was the extensive mission land. Thus, in 1834 the Mexican government decreed "secularization," under which the mission properties would be taken by the government. Actually the zenith of mission success and productivity had been reached by 1830; by 1834 the missions were in decline. In most cases the government took control and legal title. It often sold off much of the land, sometimes renting the property back to the Catholic Church for local chapels. The mission system was over, often leaving bewildered mission Indians to their own devices.

The buildings at Santa Barbara Mission were not secularized by the Mexican government in 1834. It was the only California mission excluded. Father Narciso Duran, by then the father presidente of the California missions, moved his headquarters from Carmel to Santa Barbara.

San Luis Obispo, San Miguel, La Purisima, and Santa Ines were all leased back as parish churches. In 1844 Santa Ines became California's first institution of higher learning, a religious seminary called College of Our Lady de Refugio. This temporarily immunized the mission against sale to private interests.

In September 1835 popular governor Jose Figueroa died of a stroke. The central government replaced him with Mariano Chico, who promptly picked a fight with foreign merchants like Hartnell and flaunted a mistress he called his niece. Then he ordered the arrest and deportation of Santa Barbara's Father Narciso Duran on the grounds that the popular priest was a Spaniard. Actually Chico was angry because the padre would not sing a high mass for the governor because of his mistress/niece. When a squad of soldiers brought Father Duran in a *careta* (a big-wheeled Mexican cart) down to a boat to the departing ship, the women of Santa Barbara linked arms around the *careta* and set up a mournful howl. The captain of the ship, a friend of Duran's, "protested" this interference, so the women said he would have to take them, too. While the soldiers stood by, with the help of two de la Guerra sons, the women "kidnapped" Duran and took him back to the mission as the captive of Santa Barbara's lovelies. Ten days later Governor Chico boarded an outbound ship and never returned. He had been in office only three months.

Nicolas Gutierrez, the next acting governor, was a womanizer who liked to impose himself on young Indian girls. Soon he ordered the arrest of the president of California's house of deputies *(Disputacion)*, Juan Bautista Alvarado, because the deputies had recommended that governors be elected by popular vote. Alvarado and his cousin Jose Castro organized a rebellion against Gutierrez. On November 3, 1836, Castro deployed his handful of men on the ridge above Monterey, where they lit several campfires, beat drums, and sounded trumpets as if they had the Monterey presidio surrounded. The governor's troops began to desert, and Castro demanded that Gutierrez surrender. The governor refused. One cannon shot through the roof of Gutierrez's house (the rebels' only cannonball), and he decided to resign.

ALVARADO AND THE LAND GRANTS

The *Disputacion* promptly chose Alvarado as governor—the first native Californio to hold that position. Mariano Vallejo was named commandante general of California, although he remained headquartered in Sonoma. Although General Castro announced that California was a free state, the rebels settled for a form of autonomy within the Mexican nation.

Richard Henry Dana, a Harvard student from Boston, signed up as a common seaman to recover from eyestrain after a serious bout of measles. In 1835 Dana (a cousin of central coast pioneer William G. Dana) worked loading hides at Santa Barbara as a sailor on the Bryant and Sturgis trading ship *Pilgrim.* In 1840, while a law student, Dana published his story of the trip in his masterfully written *Two Years Before the Mast,* which became a best-seller and is still published. The work stimulated American interest in California.

In bone-chilling detail, Dana described how the sailors had to wade into the surf to load hides and leather sacks of tallow at Santa Barbara because there was no dock. Each time there was stormy weather at Santa Barbara the ship had to hoist sails and head out to sea to avoid being dashed on the shore. Dana noted that the hills above the village were denuded of trees due to a recent forest fire. A lumber shortage was always a problem, and when ships brought lumber down from Monterey it had to be floated ashore because there was no pier.

Dana also provided charming details of the wedding reception for Anita de la Guerra and Alfred Robinson, a local agent for Bryant and Sturgis, including flirtatious games of women breaking perfume-filled "eggs" on the heads of the men and the young swains planting their hats on favored girls, who could reject the man by tossing his hat on the floor. However, his Yankee evaluation of the *gente de razon* was that "The Californians are an idle, thriftless people, and can make nothing for themselves. The country abounds in grapes, yet they buy, at a great price, bad wine made in Boston and brought round [the Horn] by us."

During his six years in office, Alvarado distributed twenty-eight land grants. These included large ranchos in Sonoma and Napa Valleys recommended by his relative, Mariano Vallejo, numerous grants throughout what is now Monterey County, and thousands of acres to Swiss-born John Sutter at the confluence of the Sacramento and American Rivers. In the Santa Barbara area Carrillos and their in-laws were the most favored beneficiaries of grants, including La Purisima Mission property, and a ranch to son-in-law William Hartnell.

The story was much the same in present-day San Luis Obispo County. Carrillo daughter and in-law Dana received 38,000 acres at Nipomo, and Ramona Carrillo, who married sea captain John Wilson, got 49,000 acres. In many cases the grants only confirmed the existing right to use the lands for ranching.

The government named nonclerical administrators of all missions except Santa Barbara, and physical deterioration accelerated. To solve cash flow problems, the padres at Santa Barbara leased out mission buildings (except for the main chapel and cloister) to former American sea captain Daniel Hill and his son-in-law "Doctor" Nicolas A. Den. Den, a Scottish medical school dropout, practiced medicine in Santa Barbara because there were no other physicians. Hill received a grant of Goleta, and Den was given Rancho Dos Pueblos northwest of the city.

In 1840 the pope created a California diocese and named Reverend Francisco Garcia Diego y Moreno of Mexico as bishop. Moreno arrived in January 1842, and the entire town populace, led by Padre Duran, greeted him at the beach and escorted him to the mission as he rode in a carriage pulled by local men. The bishop was so impressed he decided to make Santa Barbara his seat rather than San Diego as originally planned. He had hopes of building a cathedral, but the "pious fund" for such purposes was frozen and used by the government to secularize missions. The bishop died four years later (as did Duran) and was buried at the mission. The seat of church leadership went elsewhere.

Manuel Micheltorena, appointed governor in 1842, tried to maintain control with a company of 300 *cholos,* made up of the dregs released from Mexican prisons. Following a confusing mock war between competing factions, and a revolt by the combined forces of ex-governor Alvarado and southern Californian Pio Pico, Micheltorana resigned in 1844. Pico became governor and moved the capital from Monterey to Los Angeles, leaving General Castro governing as military commander in Monterey. It was all sandbox politics and left California with no coherent government.

POLK COVETS CALIFORNIA

In 1844 James K. Polk, an advocate of western expansion, was elected president of the United States. In 1845 Polk offered Mexico $40 million for California and New Mexico. The proposal was rejected. His appetite for California led him to plan to take the southwest and California one way or another.

U.S. Army captain John C. Frémont, officially the chief of a party of sixty-two topographical engineers, was sent roaming around the northern Sacramento Valley and southern Oregon. He claimed he was searching out trade routes to the west. On March 1, 1846, Frémont and his buckskin-clad, scraggily-bearded, rifle-toting company camped out near Monterey. Three of his men rode over to the ranch of General Castro's uncle and "insulted" his daughters. General Castro immediately sent Frémont a written order to leave California or be arrested. The mercurial Frémont responded by flying an American flag atop Mount Gavilan. Castro raised 200 volunteers. American consul Thomas Larkin convinced Frémont to leave, despite the captain's offer to fight to the death.

Unknown to anyone in California, on May 13, 1846, the U.S. Congress had declared war against Mexico, on the pretext that there was a dispute over the Mexico-Texas border. On June 15, the United States and Great Britain agreed to divide "Oregon Country" at the forty-ninth parallel, but the United States acquiesced to the British desire to keep Fort Victoria on the southern tip of Vancouver Island. This settlement freed the United States from the threat of British naval intervention in its Mexican War.

Frémont returned to Sutter's Fort and encountered a group of Americans from the Sacramento Valley who wanted to throw off Mexican rule. Frémont urged them to intercept a herd of horses Vallejo was sending to Castro at Santa Clara. With fresh mounts, the Americans rode toward Sonoma. In Napa Valley they added more men, and at dawn on June 14, 1846, thirty-three rough-looking men galloped into the Sonoma plaza, arrested Mariano Vallejo, his brother-in-law Jacob Leese, brother Salvador Vallejo, and the general's male secretary. The captives were taken to Sutter's Fort, where Frémont insisted they be kept in prison.

At Sonoma the Americans declared the formation of the California Republic, elected a president by acclamation, and raised a flag featuring a grizzly bear in the shape of a pig with a red stripe cut from a petticoat and a red star. A few days later Frémont showed up and recruited most of the Bear Flaggers into what he called his California battalion.

SLOAT TAKES MONTEREY

On July 2, three American warships under the command of Comm. John D. Sloat anchored in Monterey harbor. Sloat had orders to seize the ports of California if war had been declared, but he had no official report of war. Learning that Frémont was leading a company of 200 to take control of California, war or no war, Sloat landed 250 marines and sailors on July 7 and seized the custom house. The American flag was raised, the Navy band played, and Sloat made a diplomatic speech in which he promised full citizenship rights to the Californios, announced his men would pay for supplies, and said that church properties would be protected.

The locals cheered, for Sloat was preferable to the rude Bear Flaggers who held Vallejo in prison or to Frémont and his California battalion, which had shot and killed three unarmed Californios when they had attempted to surrender near San Rafael.

Sloat sent naval Lieut. Joseph Warren Revere, grandson of Paul Revere, to Yerba Buena and Sonoma to raise the Stars and Stripes. On July 9, Revere pulled down the Bear Flag in Sonoma, thus ending the twenty-five-day regime of the California Republic. Frémont marched south to Monterey.

THE MEXICAN WAR: ROUND ONE

Unsure he had acted legally, Sloat transferred his command to Comm. Robert F. Stockton the first week in August. As his last act Sloat ordered Mariano Vallejo and his compatriots freed from prison and allowed to go home. A few days later an official dispatch reported that a state of war did indeed exist.

Governor Pico moved his headquarters to Santa Barbara and issued a call for all Mexican citizens to take up arms against the Americans. Gen. Jose Castro beat a strategic retreat southward to join Pico, who moved into hiding in the hills south of Los Angeles. Frémont's men invested San Luis Obispo without opposition. Then he took a ship to San Diego with his battalion and occupied that pueblo without a fight. Commodore Stockton sailed from Monterey to Santa Barbara, where his marines raised the American flag. Leaving a few men to occupy Santa Barbara, he then marched into Los Angeles, which he found undefended and virtually deserted.

Believing the battle for California over, Frémont and Stockton returned to Monterey. However, Californio resistance armies were gathering in the countryside outside the towns. Armed with a single brass cannon, Gen. Jose Maria Flores's 400 Mexican guerrillas drove the American soldiers in Los Angeles out to San Pedro harbor, where they holed up on a U.S. ship. Santa Barbara was soon retaken by Flores's little army, which chased the occupying Americans over the mountains into the San Joaquin Valley. San Luis Obispo was recaptured by volunteer civilians.

Stockton and Frémont now had to fight the war over. Stockton sailed to retake San Diego and Los Angeles. Frémont enlarged his battalion, took on a group of Indian scouts from as far away as Walla Walla, and marched south. His 300 horsemen charged into San Luis Obispo at night in a pelting rainstorm and took the town easily. Frémont's men caught an Indian courier carrying a letter signed by ranchero José de Jesus Pico, warning other Californios of Frémont's impending attack. Pico had been taken prisoner when San Luis Obispo had been first occupied, and in exchange for parole had signed a pledge not to take up arms again. Frémont ordered the Indian summarily shot; his stoic bravery facing death becoming the stuff of legend. Then at the mission where his men were drying out, Frémont held a drumhead court-martial of Pico and sentenced him to death for violating his parole.

The next morning Frémont was visited by a delegation of Californio women led by beautiful, aristocratic Ramona Carrillo de Wilson. For more than an hour she talked, playing on Frémont's vanity, his best instincts, and his future in the hearts of Californios. Most of all she was an attractive woman, a Carrillo, courageous and rational, not unlike his own wife, the fabled Jesse Benton Frémont, daughter of Senator Thomas Hart Benton. The mesmerized Frémont relented and pardoned Pico, who had been scheduled to be shot within the hour.

By December 21, 1846, Frémont's ragtag forces had reached Benjamin Foxen's ranch, northeast of Santa Barbara in the hills above Santa Ynez Valley. Onetime English sea captain Foxen, in his twenty-five years around Santa Barbara, had converted to Catholicism, become a Mexican citizen, been befriended by the de la Guerras, and married a local girl. He and his family had not fled from their adobe, choosing to protect their property.

The usual route from the north into Santa Barbara was through Gaviota Pass (now U.S. Highway 101), which could be a death trap because it was a narrow defile between high cliffs. Foxen's wife had heard a rumor that Mexican troops were preparing to ambush the Americans there and push boulders down on them. Frémont was already nervous about trying the pass and asked Foxen if there was another way. Foxen agonized over loyalty to Mexico and the probability that California would become U.S. territory. Eventually Foxen suggested the seldom-used old Indian trail over the Santa Ynez range and the steep San Marcos pass and asked his son to show Frémont the way.

❧

FRÉMONT CAPTURES SANTA BARBARA

Frémont's army made it over the pass (today the often steep Highway 154) in a Christmas deluge. Two hundred of his horses and mules slipped on the wet rocks and fell to their deaths. Luckily, no men were killed. Thus Frémont marched into Santa Barbara out of the hills, from a surprise direction. There were no Mexican soldiers to oppose them; they had been sent to the Los Angeles basin to battle the gringos and were not lying in wait in the rocks above Gaviota Pass. Captain Foxen would pay a price: For a long time he was ostracized by many diehard Californios as a traitor, and his ranch house was later burned by unknown arsonists. His descendants still own much of his ranch.

Meanwhile, in October the California departmental assembly held a special meeting and voted out Governor Pio Pico and replaced Gen. Jose Castro with Manuel Castro, partly because those worthies were south of the border trying to get assistance from the Mexican central government instead of fighting. His removal thwarted Pico's plan to sell the missions.

At the battle of San Pascual (east of San Diego) the Mexicans under Gen. Andres Pico badly bloodied a troop of 175 U.S. Army regulars led by Gen. Stephen Kearny, who had marched from New Mexico. However, the Americans had too great an advantage in numbers, armaments, and military experience. The final victory by Frémont at Cahuenga Pass in San Fernando Valley ended the war in California.

Enter into history another dynamic woman, Bernarda Ruiz, widow of an army officer, owner of the Conejo Ranch, and related by blood or marriage to just about everyone. Fearful that Frémont and Stockton would impose a harsh treaty on the Californios, she asked Jesus Pico (the same man saved by the intervention of Ramona Carrillo) to arrange an interview with Frémont before he left Santa Barbara. He granted her a ceremonial five minutes that turned into two hours. With feminine wiles and playing on his ambitions, she convinced him that "when he became governor" it would be best for him to have thousands of friends gained by a generous and compassionate peace. When the surprisingly generous truce, which gave equality to Californios and Americans, was presented by Frémont, Ramona was present. Andres Pico readily signed on behalf of Mexico. A plaque honoring Señora Ruiz can be found in the new El Paseo on State Street in Santa Barbara.

The Mexican War officially concluded with the Treaty of Guadalupe Hidalgo, signed on February 2, 1848, and soon ratified by both the U.S. Senate and the Mexican government. California, Arizona, New Mexico, and Nevada became

American territory, and U.S. citizenship was granted to all Californios. News of ratification by the Mexican government reached Monterey in August 1848.

THE CONSTITUTIONAL CONVENTION

California was neither a territory nor a state and lacked any official government. In June 1849 military governor Brig. Gen. Bennett Riley ordered an August election of delegates to a constitutional convention in Monterey scheduled for September. Of forty-eight delegates chosen from ten districts, eight were Spanish-speaking Californios, led by General Vallejo, with William Hartnell translating. French-born former *alcalde* Jose Covarrubias was the delegate from Santa Barbara, and Henry A. Tefft, lawyer son-in-law of William G. Dana, represented San Luis Obispo. Also delegates were Pablo de la Guerra and Jose A. Carrillo, whose proposal that Santa Barbara be the state capital was easily defeated. There was only one mestizo delegate. The Constitution and all state laws (until the 1870s) were printed in Spanish as well as English.

The delegates voted to apply to Congress as a state rather than as a mere territory. The proposed constitution prohibited slavery but gave the vote to white males only, which created a crisis because many Californians were of mixed Indian blood. The result was a compromise: The new legislature, when formed, could give the vote to all males of Indian blood.

In November 1849 the new constitution was approved by a popular vote of 12,064 to 811. An interim legislature was elected to meet at San Jose. Even before Congress admitted California as a state on September 9, 1850, this legislature created twenty-seven counties, including San Luis Obispo (population 336) and Santa Barbara, which included what is now Ventura County. Santa Barbara incorporated as a city in 1850 and San Luis Obispo in 1856. Ventura County was split off in 1872.

SAN LUIS OBISPO AND SANTA BARBARA LAID OUT

In 1851 one of the first acts of the San Luis Obispo county government was to authorize a survey and development of a street plan for the town of San Luis Obispo. Santa Barbara's city council did the same. The meandering streets and hazy property descriptions would be replaced by fixed lines. In the case of Santa Barbara, however, the original survey was full of errors, and the wooden survey stakes often broke, rotted, or disappeared. After fences were built these mistakes were obvious. Eventually the council ordered a new survey, which provided grist for decades of real estate litigation.

The American influence on Santa Barbara style was soon evident in the use of wood instead of adobe as the basic building material. Shiploads of lumber from northern California and Oregon Territory were soon being floated onto the beach.

Although the peace treaty had provided for honoring existing rights of Mexican citizens, the great influx of settlers after the discovery of gold in 1848 put the Mexican land grants in jeopardy. The federal Land Claims Commission heard the title disputes, but evidence was hard to produce because title descriptions were vague and almost never based on surveys. Squatters took over sections of ranches, refused to pay rent, and then challenged the title in court. Often the cases dragged on for years—as many as thirty—and legal costs became prohibitive. Although most grant holders won, the rancheros were ordered to pay for surveys that they usually could not afford.

Many of the Californios were land rich and cash poor. Their wealth had been built on Indian labor; the new generation could not afford laborers and was neither physically nor temperamentally prepared to work the land. To get cash they mortgaged parcels of their property to those with ready money at usurious rates as high as 2 percent a month. But even hardworking rancheros were faced with low prices for cattle during the 1850s. The drought of 1863–64 finished off many herds. In Santa Barbara County the number of cattle dropped from 200,000 to 5,000 in that one year. Thus most old rancheros lost their property to foreclosure or distress sales.

Santa Barbara's new government got a scare August 1, 1854, when the Land Claims Commission denied the town's application for confirmation of the Spanish government's 1782 land grant. The decision was appealed to the U.S. Supreme Court, and eighteen years later the occupied 17,826 acres were confirmed as city property.

CRIMINAL GANGS AND FRONTIER JUSTICE

A weak state government with no trained lawmen was trying to manage endless square miles of rugged territory. Thousands of newcomers had arrived looking for gold or other quick riches. Hundreds of dispossessed young Californians roamed the countryside. Given those circumstances, a crime wave in California was a virtual certainty.

Actually, the bloodiest crime occurred before statehood was granted. At San Miguel Mission, an Englishman named William Reed and two Californio friends had bought all but the chapel and priests' quarters and converted the buildings into a home for Reed and his family. Reed was believed to have returned from the goldfields with a stash of gold dust. One day in October 1848 five deserting British sailors stopped by, and then returned at night to murder Reed, his wife (née Maria Antonia Vallejo), a daughter and son-in-law, three younger children, an elderly black servant, and three guests—a total of eleven victims. The killers then tore apart Reed's home in a futile search for the gold. Ranchers John M. Price and Francisco Branch organized a posse and ran down the murderers on the sands of Pismo Beach. The vigilantes tied up their prisoners and heaved them into the ocean to drown.

Gangs preyed on travelers suspected of carrying money, gold, or jewels and invaded the homes of the wealthy. Horse and cattle rustling was a favorite occupation, after which the thieves faded into the countryside. The most infamous was Joaquin Murrieta, whose career began in the late 1840s. With accomplices such as "Three Finger" Jack Garcia (who had stabbed to death two captured Bear Flaggers in 1846), Murrieta often hid in the caves east of Paso Robles after a robbery or a killing. When he was at work near Santa Barbara, he and his gang would hunker down in the hills above the Rincon de la Playa Rancho east of Carpinteria. Years later $13,000 in stolen jewels was found buried there. Although Murrieta was killed in 1853, survivors of his gang were active until the shooting of Abelardo Mendoza while resisting arrest in San Luis Obispo in 1884.

The largest gang was organized by twenty-one-year-old Juan Flores, who had escaped in the mid-fifties from San Quentin's primitive prison, where he was serving a term for horse stealing. He had more than fifty in his organization, which operated from San Luis Obispo to San Juan Capistrano, south of Los Angeles. All too often a robbery or cattle rustling was accompanied by a killing. In a running gun battle in Los Angeles County, the sheriff and two deputies were shot dead. A small army under former Mexican general Andres Pico hunted down the Flores gang, shot some in gun battles, and caught and hanged others after brief "trials." Finally Flores and several of his ring were captured and legally arraigned before a judge, who ordered them tried by the county superior court. A mob, ignoring the new sheriff's protests, took Flores from jail and hanged him and a few others. In some cases those hanged were only young Mexicans who had helped Flores evade capture. One was entirely innocent.

Self-help justice got a bad name around Santa Barbara in August 1859, when the bodies of well-known horse thief Francisco Badillo and his son were found hanged in the woods. Badillo was eighty years old, and his murdered son was only fourteen. Younger Badillo children identified the perpetrators as prominent citizen John Nidever and his son George. A group of Mexican Americans spotted George, beat him up, stabbed him, and shot him for good measure.

Miraculously, he survived. The Nidevers were tried and acquitted, as were those who assaulted young Nidever. Public sentiment demanded a stronger government and appointments to the vacant offices of sheriff and district attorney.

In San Luis Obispo a vigilante committee was organized in May 1858 by community leaders such as William G. Dana and lawyer William Graves. Following the murder of two Frenchmen, the local vigilantes caught the alleged killers, forced them to confess, and then hanged them. After putting a damper on crime in the area, the committee disbanded.

Perhaps this explains that when notorious Jesse James and his brother Frank showed up in Paso Robles while on the lam from Missouri, they were strictly law-abiding. Frank James's signature appears as one of the two surveyors on the first map of Paso Robles.

An unusual bunch of outlaws was the so-called Gang of Five, organized by dashing 6-footer Jack Powers, who had arrived as a nineteen-year-old sergeant in the New York Volunteers when they occupied Santa Barbara in 1847. He had grown up in New York City's Hell's Kitchen, but his smooth manners and glib tongue belied his hard beginnings. He had become a superb horseman in the army and took a job as groom at the de la Guerra stables. At night he was a drinker and gambler, popular with the young town hotshots, and charmer of young women and the Santa Barbara elite. With four old army buddies, Powers secretly created the Gang of Five, which virtually ruled the town by intimidation between 1854 and 1858. Even when suspicion fell on Powers that he and his buddies were night riders stealing cattle and ambushing travelers, the local lawmen were afraid to confront him.

One man who was not afraid of Powers and his bully boys was Dr. Nicolas Den. When Powers's gang tried to rustle cattle from a Den ranch in the Santa Ynez Valley, the doctor's cowboys chased them off. In retaliation Powers invaded Den's other ranch at Dos Pueblos. At Den's urging, Sheriff W. W. Twist called up a 200-man posse. A liquored-up Gang of Five rode into Santa Barbara to face the posse in what shaped up to be a California version of the gunfight at the O.K. Corral. At the corner of Carrillo and Anacapa Streets, in front of Twist's house, the first of the gang rode up and ineffectually stabbed the sheriff, only to be shot dead while still in his saddle. Another shot and it was the Gang of Three. At this point the rest of the posse arrived and faced three leveled rifles from behind a large sycamore tree. The reluctant posse chickened out and decided to go have a drink. Powers retired from the scene, but his days of intimidation were over. When murder charges were brought against him, he hopped a ship for Mexico. Two years later he was stabbed to death in a fight over a woman.

Tiburcio Vasquez was a bandit from a prominent Monterey family who robbed stages and rustled cattle for several years. After most jobs he would hide out in the hills above Paso Robles, much like Murrieta. An acknowledged hater of gringos, he was a Robin Hood to many younger mestizos. He was caught and tried in San Jose for murder. During the trial no witness could identify him, but he gave himself away by joking to one potential witness: "A fine watch you had. I have often regretted I didn't take it." He was hanged on March 19, 1875.

ROUGH ROADS AND COASTAL SHIPPING

For the first sixty years after statehood, the road system along the coast was primitive at best. El Camino Real (the King's highway) was a trail, which was gradually improved enough to serve as a stagecoach route, bumpy, erratic, often steep, and impassable during heavy rains. An underlying problem was that all roads were under local control, either county or a road district. Often ranchers would scrape and cut their own roads to use sweat equity for their road tax, usually without a survey or engineering. Sometimes there was oil and gravel, but most roads were dirt. Although some bridges were of stone, to save money most counties built them of wood.

A stagecoach line between San Francisco and Los Angeles (following the old mission trail) was inaugurated in 1861, running three times a week. A year later it went on a daily schedule with relays of teams of horses stabled along the way. The entire trip took three and a half days. Five years later, once-a-week stages were galloping between San Luis Obispo and the coastal settlements of Cambria and San Simeon. A network of stage routes gradually grew to connect smaller towns with major centers up and down the coast.

Nevertheless, along the coast most farm product delivery and passenger travel was by ship. An enterprising Santa Barbara businessman, Samuel Brinkerhoff, built the first wharf on the Santa Barbara waterfront in 1868. Located at the foot of Chapala Street, the wharf was 500 feet long. It proved a substantial improvement, but it was not long enough to reach deep water and accommodate larger vessels, including lumber ships.

A stagecoach road was completed over the San Marcos pass to Santa Ynez Valley northeast of Santa Barbara that same year, avoiding the roundabout route via Gaviota Pass—heading west to go northeast. The roads from Los Angeles and Ventura were incredibly rough.

As Santa Barbara grew, the supply of water barely kept up. Originally much of the city relied on wells, but the aquifers contained only a finite amount. In 1872 the city made a deal to transfer to the city the mission's right to Mission Creek water, except for enough to service the mission. Metal pipes were installed to deliver the creek water to the city cisterns. Not long thereafter artesian wells were put down to augment the city's water source. In the early 1900s a 4-mile tunnel was built by the city to tap into the Santa Ynez River, and that was followed by a dam across the river to create a reservoir.

John P. Stearns, attorney and lumberyard owner, was determined to get a wharf that would be sturdy and long enough to service all sizes of ships. He obtained a large loan from Col. William Welles Hollister, who had made a fortune in sheep raising in San Benito County and had a financial hand in several Santa Barbara enterprises. Armed with the financing, Stearns convinced the city council to give him a permit to build a 1,900-foot-long wharf at the foot of State Street, and a twenty-year license to operate it. It was completed by the close of 1872. The older Chapala Street wharf was destroyed by a storm in 1878.

Stearns Wharf became the principal conduit of farm products out and needed lumber in. It was also an immediate shot in the arm to the tourist business, particularly from Los Angeles. The problem was that there were not enough places to stay. Some small hotels used horse blankets to provide sleeping places on the floor during the summer. The *Daily Press* campaigned editorially for more hotels.

To meet the need, a group of businessmen headed by Colonel Hollister organized the Seaside Hotel Corporation, which changed its name to Santa Barbara Harbor Company when its members decided to build on State Street in the heart of town, away from the water. Their Arlington Hotel opened in 1874 and was the most elegant tourist hotel in southern California. A mule-powered streetcar carried visitors from Stearns Wharf up State Street to the Arlington. Soon State Street was paved—unusual for the time. Other new hotels followed. In the 1870s lot prices skyrocketed from $100 to $5,000 each.

"DRY" LOMPOC, SANTA BARBARA WINERIES, AND SANTA MARIA'S GUSHER

The town of Lompoc was founded at the original site of Mission La Purisima Concepcion and Mexican land grants to brothers Jose and Joaquin Carrillo, totaling nearly 47,000 acres. In 1874 the land was conveyed to the California Immigrant Union of San Francisco, an organization that settled communities willing to covenant by deed that "No vinous, malt, spirituous, or other intoxicating liquors shall ever be sold or manufactured upon any portion of the Lompoc and Mission Vieja Ranchos." Most of the colonists were ardent prohibitionists.

Twice merchants tried to circumvent the antibooze restriction. A druggist who stocked a supply of liquor was invaded by a crowd of women who began breaking bottles. When he waved a pistol in their direction, the ladies were joined by a group of men who made him put the gun away and watch the destruction. Another man tried to set up a quiet bar in a cottage. It was blown up by a charge of dynamite, set off by unknown parties. The *Lompoc Record* suggested the bomber might have been "a nihilist from Russia."

Santa Barbara wineries and vineyards kept a steady position as fourth in the state, after Napa, Sonoma, and Los Angeles Counties, but did not fall victim to phylloxera in the north or Anaheim's disease in the south. Before statehood the missions were the principal producers of wine, with a little output by individual vineyards. Albert Packard planted an extensive vineyard on the west end of Santa Barbara in the 1850s and built the first large winery, La Bodega, located on West Carrillo Street, in the late 1860s. By the end of the century there were at least seventeen winemakers in the county, some clustered in the Santa Ynez Valley, others close to the sea, plus the large Santa Cruz Island Winery.

Except for the mission fathers, the first serious winemaker in San Luis Obispo County was former French Legionnaire Pierre Dallidet, who came to town in 1853 after trying his hand at gold mining. He built an adobe and planted a sixteen-acre vineyard. Eventually Dallidet had 7,200 vines. His winery continued in operation for a time after his death in 1905. His adobe is now owned by the county historical society.

A notorious Santa Barbara murder occurred in 1880. Clarence Gray was the Republican candidate for district attorney. Noisy and unstable, he had a record of violence, having beaten up an editor and a priest. Theodore Glancey, newly hired editor of the *Press*, wrote an editorial urging "decent Republicans" to vote against Gray. In revenge Gray shot Glancey in the back, killing him. Gray was tried three times: a hung jury in Santa Barbara; a conviction and a twenty-year sentence when the case was transferred to San Mateo County, which was reversed on the claim that the jury had been drinking alcohol; and somehow the third ended in an acquittal. Gray then disappeared.

In 1867 two former Mexican grants in the Santa Maria Valley were voided by court decisions, and the area was opened up for homesteading. Several homesteaders bought land cheap, built houses, and subscribed for a school. In 1875 they laid out the town of Central City on a half square mile set apart by four adjoining landowners. In the early 1880s the name was changed to Santa Maria.

In 1882 the narrow-gauge Pacific Coast Railroad connected Santa Maria with a shipping point at Port Harford to serve local farmers. But it was the discovery of oil in the areas of Los Alamos and Orcutt, followed by the huge Hartnell gusher at Santa Maria in 1904, that stimulated instant growth— tripling Santa Maria's population in the next dozen years. It was soon the second largest city in Santa Barbara County and remains so today.

THE RAILROAD BUILT IN FITS AND STARTS

The settlers of the communities between San Miguel in the north and Carpinteria in the south realized that if they were to prosper and grow, they needed a railroad connection with the outside world. They watched from afar as the transcontinental railroad was completed in 1869. Of more immediate interest to the central coast was the San Francisco & San Jose Railroad, which opened in 1864. A group of San Francisco businessmen bought that railway in August 1868 and changed the name to Southern Pacific. Its president announced the railroad would be extended down the coast all the way to San Diego. He was blowing promotional smoke, for San Jose remained the southern terminus. A year later the Central Pacific bought the Southern Pacific, which eventually gave its name to the entire system.

Both the Central Pacific and the Southern Pacific were owned by the so-called Big Four of Leland Stanford, Charles Crocker, Charles P. Huntington, and Mark Hopkins, who had originally been Sacramento businessmen. With a monopoly on transcontinental rail travel, and thousands of acres of excess property along the rights-of-way, they were now fabulously wealthy. It was also beneficial to the group that Stanford was governor of California between 1862 and 1864.

Their first move after completing the transcontinental railroad was to begin construction of a railroad down the San Joaquin Valley toward Los Angeles, hooking up with Sacramento, Oakland, and San Francisco. The Big Four felt the inland route was a much easier engineering job: Because most of it was flat, there was great agricultural potential, and their land agents had already acquired a right-of-way. It would reach Bakersfield in 1874 and connect with Los Angeles in 1876.

Meanwhile the Southern Pacific had extended the rails to Soledad in Monterey County in 1874. There was no pressure on the company to get tourist business up and down the coast because it owned the steamship line that was carrying passengers to resorts on the shore like Cambria, Morro Bay, Avila Beach, and Pismo Beach, as well as Santa Barbara. The Southern Pacific was more interested in laying rails to Monterey and its massive Del Monte Hotel. When there were complaints from citizens in San Luis Obispo County, the railroad hierarchy hinted that they might just run the line over the mountains at Gilroy or San Miguel, tie in with its San Joaquin route, and forget the rest of the central coast.

Following a decade of inactivity, the Southern Pacific again began to push south along the route of El Camino Real. The rails reached San Miguel in October 1886, Paso Robles in November 1886, Templeton in April 1887, and after a brief hiatus, Santa Margarita on January 3, 1889. Sleepy San Miguel woke up as a center for shipping farm products. A city plan with a grid of streets and a 2-square-block downtown park was laid out for Paso Robles, which was already popular as a resort due to its mineral springs. At an auction in Paso Robles on November 17, 1886, 228 lots were sold. On Spring Street the large Paso Robles Inn, with a fireplace in every room, opened its doors in 1891. Templeton (named for a Big Four son, Templeton Crocker) and Santa Margarita both blossomed as commodity shipping centers.

Then the railroad construction stopped cold just 10 miles north of San Luis Obispo.

Southern Pacific vice president Charles Huntington faced a mass meeting in San Luis Obispo in April 1889 that demanded to know when the railroad would reach the town. Huntington replied that the land titles were so fouled up that the railroad did not want to take the time and money to find the owners and buy the right-of-way. He challenged the town to take care of the problem. The city established a committee, found the owners, and bought the land for the railroad, but it took three years. In return the railroad sent its crews carving out a route over the San Lucia Range, which required seven tunnels, the famous horseshoe curve (where the front cars would actually parallel the last carriages), cuts, fills, and a long steel trestle in a 10-mile stretch.

A Chinatown arose in downtown San Luis Obispo in the 1880s, primarily of railroad laborers. Its leader was Ah Louis (real name Wong On), a labor contractor who started a grocery store and a brickyard. He provided workers for county roads, for flower farms, and for local narrow- and broad-gauge railroads connecting San Luis Obispo, Arroyo Grande, and Avila Bay, as well as a

FIRST TRAIN REACHES SANTA BARBARA, AUGUST 19, 1887

(SANTA BARBARA HISTORICAL SOCIETY)

horse-drawn streetcar line on San Luis Street. His brick store still stands, but the rest of Chinatown was torn down in the 1930s.

On May 5, 1894, the rails reached San Luis Obispo, followed by a county-wide celebration to greet a train full of Southern Pacific officials. Already the railroad had built a luxury hotel, the Ramona, right where the trains would stop. Everything at the Ramona was first-class—electric lights, private baths, tennis courts, fire alarms, even a stage connecting to the ocean at Avila Beach. San Luis Obispo also benefited by installing a skillfully engineered system that separated floodwater runoff from sewage, then a modern innovation.

The Southern Pacific finally began extending its railroad from Los Angeles north toward Santa Barbara in the 1880s. In 1887 the rails reached Santa Paula, Ventura, and Carpinteria in three months. On August 19, 1887, the first train from Los Angeles rolled into Santa Barbara, met by a crowd of more than 1,000. The city declared a holiday—there was a banquet at the Arlington Hotel and a public picnic laid out near the beach. The train's arrival stimulated a land boom with sales at inflated prices, but it soon deflated when the Southern Pacific rails from the south halted at Ellwood, a few miles west of Goleta. However, farm and ranch products, including the increasingly popular

THE SECOND ARLINGTON HOTEL

(SANTA BARBARA HISTORICAL SOCIETY)

lemon crop, found the rails to Los Angeles an easy mode of transport to the consuming world.

Slowly the gap between the railheads was closed, as the railroad extended south one town at a time. A national recession following the panic of 1893 halted the construction a tantalizing 50 miles north of Ellwood. The gap was closed on December 29, 1900. The first southbound train arrived at Santa Barbara on April 3, 1901. Six weeks later President William McKinley rode the train from San Francisco, stopping at San Luis Obispo and Santa Barbara on his way to Los Angeles.

Fire was the implacable enemy of hotels built to accommodate the coast's visitors. Santa Barbara's magnificent Arlington went up in smoke in 1909, and a new version replaced it. The beachside Potter Hotel was destroyed by flames in 1921. During two decades in San Luis Obispo, some seventeen hotels burned down, mostly old wooden structures, but also the plush 112-room Andrews Hotel. Built by banker J. P. Andrews, it opened in October 1885 and burned down seven months later, unfortunately also setting Andrews's bank ablaze. The Southern Pacific's magnificent Ramona burned in 1905. The original Paso Robles Inn met a fiery fate in 1941.

OF COLLEGES AND MISSION RESTORATION

In 1901 the legislature authorized a college for San Luis Obispo: California Polytechnic. Envisioned by its local sponsors as a regional mechanical trade school, Cal Poly was actually established as a statewide school with home economics and agriculture as well as mechanics. Today it is a major California university with popular majors in business, agricultural business, architecture, and engineering. The Santa Barbara Teachers College opened in 1909 and after many years became first Santa Barbara State College and eventually part of the University of California system as UC/Santa Barbara on a seashore campus at Goleta.

The Catholic Church filed a claim for title to the secularized missions before the federal Land Claims Commission. In 1862 the commission ruled in favor of the church, and President Abraham Lincoln agreed that the federal government would not appeal the decision. However, many of the missions were in a state of disrepair, particularly where they had been used for such nonreligious functions as barns, saloons, houses, and stores.

Eventually all the missions on the central coast were restored by the church, through public efforts supported by both small and large donations, or by the government, which was the case with La Purisima Concepcion. Unlike other missions, Santa Barbara was not sold by the Mexican government because an impending sale negotiated by Governor Pio Pico was voided when California became a U.S. territory at the end of the Mexican War. For many years it was also a Catholic educational center. Although damaged in the 1925 Santa Barbara earthquake, the sturdy old building survived in better shape than much of downtown, and within two years the mission was fully retrofitted, including restoration of a collapsed tower.

Title to La Purisima was returned to the Catholic Church in 1874, but the mission was so dilapidated that the church sold it. In 1935 it was acquired by the state of California and restored by 1937, in part through the efforts of young men of the federal Civilian Conservation Corps, who actually made 110,000 adobe bricks and planted gardens of early California plants.

Santa Ines got its property back in 1862, but the buildings were deteriorating. In 1882 the lands surrounding the mission and the seminary were sold off. Under church management between 1904 and 1930 there was a program of gradual improvement of the mission itself. Murals that had been painted over were uncovered. In March 1911 the bell tower—holding five bells dating from the first two decades of the 1800s—collapsed and was replaced by a temporary structure. A proper tower was built in 1949 thanks to a contribution of $500,000 from the Hearst Foundation.

In 1868, in an unbelievable attempt to modernize the buildings, the adobe San Luis Obispo mission was covered with wooden shiplap. Between 1930 and 1934, however, it was restored in the original mission style, once again displaying its inherent beauty. The effect was further enhanced in 1968 when the city council closed Monterey Street in front of the mission.

In the 1860s and 1870s, the long arcade of Mission San Miguel became an early-day strip mall of shops with a popular saloon. The mission buildings were restored to the Catholic Church in 1878, and a gradual rehabilitation of the structures began. In 1928 the Franciscan order again took charge and accelerated the renovation, which returned the mission to its earliest appearance. The only change was the installation of pews for worshipers, since the chapel serves as a parish church. The mission is the most attractive building in the town of San Miguel, now a ghost of its turn-of-the-twentieth-century glory days as a railroad hub.

Not far from the crumbling Santa Ines Mission was a giant bean field owned by the Santa Ynez Valley Development Company. The only building on it was the one-room Santa Ynez School, which served the children of the valley farms. Meanwhile the Danish Lutheran Church Convention, meeting in Michigan, voted to develop a Danish colony and a Danish folk school at a suitable location in the west. In 1911 a committee of three Lutheran leaders found Santa Ynez Valley and bought the 9,000-acre bean field for the Danish-American Colony Corporation. They named the colony Solvang (sunny field).

Within a few months the first wave of Danes arrived. Soon there arose the Solvang Hotel, the Bethania Lutheran Church, several homes, a bank, a bakery, and other shops. The folk school, Attedag ("another day") College, was erected in 1914, and classes on Danish culture and trades for young men were given until 1937. After World War II, Solvang almost spontaneously became a model Danish village and famous tourist destination.

DEVELOPMENTS: MONTECITO TO HEARST CASTLE

The California legislature decided to do something about the state's patchwork road system, and in 1905 authorized a bond issue to fund a system of state highways. Envisioned were two principal highways, just in time for the age of the automobile. One would become US 101, linking cities between San Francisco and Los Angeles on the old El Camino Real route. The other route would be Highway 99, down the center of the state, and also going to Los Angeles. Although it would take about fifteen years to complete the highway system, by the early 1920s California would have one of the best in the country, with a concrete two-lane highway passing through Paso Robles, San Luis Obispo, Santa Maria, Buellton, Santa Barbara, and Carpinteria. In the 1930s scenic Highway 1 would give thousands of tourists easy access to coastline towns not reached directly by US 101.

Santa Barbara became a popular destination for the wealthy in the first decades of the 1900s. West of the city, the 2,000-acre Hope Ranch had been purchased in 1887 by the Pacific Improvement Company, owned by Southern Pacific's Big Four, and subdivided into extra-large lots. Montecito, with its oak-studded rolling hills southeast of the center of town, became an enclave of large mansions with views of the ocean. Charlie Chaplin, the nation's number one movie star at the time, built the luxurious Montecito Hotel in 1928. Other stars, such as Mary Pickford, found Santa Barbara a handy escape from the spotlight. Debonair actor Ronald Colman and Alvin Weingand purchased the upscale San Ysidro Ranch in 1935 to cater to their Hollywood friends.

Not only was Santa Barbara a retreat for cinema luminaries, it was also popular as a place to make movies in the silent film era, with its variety of outdoor scenery—hills, canyons, and beaches—with historic buildings as backdrops. Between 1910 and 1920 the American Film Company's Flying A Studio, located at the corner of State and Mission Streets, cranked out more than a thousand movies.

Journalist Thomas Storke bought the failing *Daily News* for $1,500 in 1913. Then he purchased another moribund paper, the *Independent*, for a mere $2,500, merging them as the *Daily News and Independent*. For years he competed with the venerable *Morning Press*. In 1932, in the heart of the Depression, he was able to buy his rival cheap, and in 1937 he combined them as the *News-Press*. His legend and fame went national in 1962 when the *News-Press* won a Pulitzer Prize for its articles on the ultraright John Birch Society. For more than fifty years Storke's views helped shape Santa Barbara. He lived to be ninety-five, dying in 1971. The *News-Press* became part of the *New York Times* chain and then was sold to a local woman whose disputes with the paper's journalists are ongoing.

In 1919 media mogul William Randolph Hearst began building his castle on the family ranch above the village of San Simeon, which was also Hearst's. Designed by Julia Morgan, California's leading female architect, the palace grew year after year with classic statuary, giant swimming pools indoors and out, a medieval-looking dining hall, tennis courts, apartments, offices, and art galleries, all furnished with antiques from Europe. The most influential newspaper publisher in the country until his death in 1951, Hearst presided over his empire from the castle, sending out directives simply signed "The Chief" and entertaining friends, topflight columnists, and his mistress, movie actress Marion Davies. Eventually the Hearst Foundation conveyed the Hearst Castle to the state of California.

Prohibition (1920–33) made the manufacture and sale of alcoholic beverages illegal. As a tourist destination and a resort of the prominent who thought that limitations on lifestyle were meant for others, Santa Barbarans tended to find Prohibition unpopular and something of a joke. Throughout the twenties, liquor

HOTEL CALIFORNIAN AFTER THE 1925 EARTHQUAKE
(SANTA BARBARA HISTORICAL SOCIETY)

smuggling became a game of cops and robbers. The coves, inlets, and islands that had been smugglers' lairs in Spanish and Mexican times now sheltered high-speed boats and trucks with dimmed lights rumbling through the night. Canadian rumrunners would land on the Channel Islands and deposit their liquid cargo, and then local motorboats would load up and usually evade revenue cutters, local deputies, and federal revenuers. A tank truck painted exactly like a Richfield Oil truck regularly drove through Santa Barbara filled with liquor until a deputy sheriff spotted it where there were no gas stations.

Grape production was not diminished by Prohibition. The law allowed production of 200 gallons a year for "personal use." Grape juice was shipped across the country for home winemakers, often with the warning not to add yeast lest it cause "illegal fermentation." Professional wineries were history, however, except for a few elsewhere in California licensed to make wine for "sacramental purposes."

NATURE AND PEARL CHASE SHAKE UP SANTA BARBARA

As Santa Barbarans were waking up on June 29, 1925, the city was rocked by the most violent earthquake since 1812, a 6.3 on the Richter scale. The town had become a hodgepodge of style, intermixed with some old buildings covered with unfortunate facades. It was what one writer called "a wasteland of western junk." The earthquake splintered the wooden buildings, and the masonry structures collapsed in clouds of powdered plaster. Some 618 buildings were destroyed or substantially damaged. State Street was a total mess. Thirteen people in the area were killed.

After the initial cleanup, a wonderful thing happened. Led by Pearl Chase, a dynamic woman with an indefatigable zeal for civic beauty and public responsibility, Santa Barbarans realized they had a real chance to rebuild the city with

PEARL CHASE
(SANTA BARBARA HISTORICAL SOCIETY)

harmonious designs. Miss Chase, who had graduated from the University of California at age nineteen, pushed, reasoned, and intimidated civic leaders for fifty years as chair of the city's Plans and Planting Committee. She also founded the Santa Barbara Trust for Historic Preservation and the California Conservation Council. Pearl was honored as "Woman of the Year" by the *Los Angeles Times* (1952) and the City of Santa Barbara (1956).

Height limitations and other controls were adopted by the city government. New stores, office buildings, commercial courtyards, theaters, and even service stations were built in compatible Mediterranean, Colonial Spanish, Mission Revival, and related styles.

The earthquake saved Santa Barbara from mediocrity. Fortunately there was local wealth and money earned from tourism to fund the reconstruction and tasteful development. Years later, after a major oil eruption from offshore wells, the city's response was much the same. Take advantage of disaster: They shut down the wells in the name of good ecological sense valued over taxes and profits.

The highlight of the new Santa Barbara was the courthouse completed in 1929, designed by architect William Moser in Spanish Moorish style. Surviving historic adobes blended in well with the new structures. Two warm, artfully developed State Street commercial courtyards—El Paseo and La Arcada—not only employed quality design but also helped keep business downtown.

BEAUTIFICATION OF SAN LUIS OBISPO

In 1949 San Luis Obispo was an ugly town dominated by train yards. There was no central park, and few trees lined the streets. Its historical centerpiece, the mission, faced a line of parking meters along Monterey Street. The first seeds of change were planted in 1949 by three students in the art class of Margaret Maxwell at San Luis Obispo Junior College working on a project to "apply art to the community." They came up with the concept of "Mission Gardens" in front of the Mission, which would require closing Monterey Street. The city council was not interested.

Cal Poly professor of architecture Kenneth Schwartz also had students tackle the problem of developing a downtown park. They too thought the only answer was closing Monterey Street and incorporating the open space across the street into a public park. Agreeing with them were the planning commission, a landscape consultant hired by the city, and the new planning director. But losing parking spaces was anathema to the council.

In 1967 three Cal Poly seniors were given a matching fund grant by the council to suggest ways to beautify downtown, as long as they presented a plan that did not include closing Monterey Street. At a standing-room-only council meeting, the students had the nerve to present two plans, the first of which recommended closing the street. The spectators were enthralled, but the meeting grew raucous when the mayor barked that they had violated their mandate and should pay back their grant.

The result of the uproar was an initiative to adopt a city park plan closing Monterey Street. Drafted by former city attorney George Andre, the measure passed by a popular vote of two to one. A tree planting program was accelerated. Monterey Street was closed. In 1970 architectural professor Schwartz was elected mayor for the first of five two-year terms, along with a pro-planning slate of three council candidates. The park was built, the art museum added, and private citizens planted flowers, shrubs, and trees at no cost. Eventually another block was added to the park. Across the creek, business owners granted an access easement in perpetuity and donated brickwork to make a walkway. The park now hosts concerts, the Mozart Festival is held in the mission, and in September 1999 the "Creek Walk" was completed along the park side of the creek.

The Downtown Association, the Chamber of Commerce, the city council, and the people of San Luis Obispo caught the spirit of the movement. There are sign ordinances prohibiting the garish and glaring, and more and more trees have been planted. San Luis Obispo is ugly no more.

Although UC/Davis enology professors had long contended that the central coast could be a prime wine-producing region, it took two Davis grads, Uriel Nielson and Bill DeMartini, to kick-start the wine renaissance in Santa Barbara County. Their initial success with their 1968 Santa Maria Valley planting evoked a rush of interest and attention to some of the existing wineries. Dozens of newcomers to the wine business were encouraged to establish wineries and plant vines. Paso Robles, San Luis Obispo, and Edna Valley were not far behind. The number of vines, wineries, cases of wine, medals, and higher ratings have grown every year in the past decade.

The history of California's central coast is a story of delayed discovery. The Spanish dallied for two centuries, the Mexican government treated it like a stepchild, many of the first Americans were primarily exploiters, the railroad barons put it at the bottom of their schedule, the wine gurus ignored its obvious potential, and Mother Nature was often unkind. Tourists hurried past its beauty on the way to somewhere else. In response, the people of Santa Barbara and San Luis Obispo Counties have struggled to improve not only image but also reality. In great measure they have gotten it right. Now it is up to you to discover the central coast.

ANNUAL EVENTS

(Calling ahead is highly recommended for all these events. Dates often change yearly, as do locations. Ticketed events are often sold out early.)

Santa Barbara County

January

New Year's Day Hang Gliding and Paragliding Festival, south side of Elings Park, Cliff Drive; (805) 965-3733

February

Santa Barbara International Film Festival, various locations near State Street; (805) 963-0023

March

International Orchid Show, Earl Warren Showgrounds, U.S. Highway 101 at Las Positas; (805) 969-5746

Santa Barbara Whale Festival, third Saturday and Sunday, 10:00 a.m. to 5:00 p.m., Stearns Wharf; (805) 969-5244

April

Presidio Days, El Presidio de Santa Barbara, 123 East Canon Perdido Street; (805) 966-6719

Santa Barbara County Vintners' Festival, April 19, 2008, River Park, Lompoc; (805) 688-0881

Santa Barbara Fair and Expo, starts third week, Wednesday–Sunday, terrific entertainment, Earl Warren Showgrounds, US 101 and Las Positas; (805) 687-0766

Harbor Festival, end of State Street, Stearns Wharf; (805) 563-0003

June

Summer Solstice Celebration, nearest Saturday to summer solstice (approximately June 21), parade from waterfront up State Street, attracts as many as 100,000, floats and fun, starts at noon; (805) 965-3396

Santa Barbara Jazz Festival, Leadbetter Beach; (805) 480-FEST

July

French Festival, Oak Park, 300 West Alamar Avenue; (805) 564-5418

Independence Day, July 4, State Street parade starting 1:00 p.m., symphony at courthouse, fireworks at 9:00 p.m., also in Solvang

August

Old Spanish Days, starts first Wednesday of month, several locations; (805) 962-8101

Old Mission Santa Ines Fiesta, second three-day weekend, Santa Ines Mission in Solvang; (805) 688-4815

September

Danish Days, third three-day weekend, Solvang; (805) 688-6144 or (800) 468-6765

Mexican Independence Day, second full weekend; (805) 925-8824

October

California Avocado Festival, Linden Avenue, Carpinteria; (805) 684-0038

Santa Barbara Festival of Art, second three-day weekend; art, music, food, wine; Court House Sunken Garden, at Anapamu and Anacapa Streets; (805) 884-1881 or (800) 538-1881

Goleta Lemon Festival, third Saturday and Sunday, Stow House, Goleta; (805) 967-4618

December

Folk and Tribal Arts Marketplace, Santa Barbara Museum of Natural History, 2559 Puesta del Sol; (805) 682-4711

Parade of Lights, Waterfront off Stearns Wharf; (805) 564-5520

San Luis Obispo County

March

Central Coast Orchid Show, first Friday and Saturday, South County Regional Center, Arroyo Grande; (805) 929-1791

May

Paso Robles Wine Festival, second three-day weekend, a major event for wine lovers; (805) 239-8463

West Coast Kustom Car Show, last Friday through Sunday, concert and show, in City Park

June

Great Americana Festival and Parade, last Saturday in June, 10:00 a.m.–1:00 p.m., City Park

July and August

Central Coast Shakespeare Festival, mid-July to mid-August, 1401 San Luis Bay Drive, Avila Beach; (805) 546-2881

San Luis Obispo Mozart Festival, starting in late July for four weeks, at various venues including wineries and centers; (805) 756-2787; www.mozart festival.com

October

Paso Robles Harvest Wine Affair, second three-day weekend; (805) 239-8463; www.pasowine.com

PLACES TO STAY

(Cities are listed south to north. Be sure to ask if there are discounts such as AAA, AARP, military, seniors, or corporate.)

Carpinteria

Best Western Carpinteria Inn, 4558 Carpinteria Avenue, Carpinteria 93013; (805) 684-0473 or (800) 528-1234, fax (805) 684-4015; www.bestwestern .com; $125–$200; 145 units, pool, continental breakfast, restaurant, pets okay

Holiday Inn Express Hotel, 5606 Carpinteria Avenue, Carpinteria 93013; (805) 566-9499 or (888) 409-8300, fax (805) 566-9433; www.carpinteria express.com; $125 and up; 108 units, pool, continental breakfast, pets okay

Santa Barbara

Motels

Sandpiper Lodge, 3525 State Street, Santa Barbara 93105; (805) 687-5326; www.sandpiperlodge.com; $125 and up; 74 units, pool, continental breakfast

Best Western Pepper Tree Inn, 3850 State Street, Santa Barbara 93105; (805) 687-5511 or (800) 338-0030, fax (805) 682-2410; www.shotels.com; $250 and up; 150 units in Spanish style, two pools, sauna, whirlpools, restaurant, no pets.

Ramada Limited, 4770 Calle Real, Santa Barbara 93110; (805) 964-3511, fax (805) 964-0075; $110–$150, with larger suites up to $215; pool, whirlpool, continental breakfast, use of athletic facility, no pets.

Resorts

Bacara Resort and Spa, 8301 Hollister Avenue, Santa Barbara 93117; (805) 968-0100, fax (805) 968-1800; www.bacararesort.com; $395–$2,200, penthouse $2,500, presidential suite $5,000; some ocean views, balconies, Internet access, facilities for disabled, pets under 25 pounds with $125 fee

San Ysidro Ranch, 900 San Ysidro Lane, Santa Barbara 93108; (805) 969-5046 or (800) 368-6788; studios and one-bedroom $899, large house $4,100, 20 cottages $1,375–$1,475, and the "Kennedy Suite," at $1,875, where John

and Jacqueline spent their honeymoon; 500 acres, restaurants, Plow and
Angel bistro, ocean views

Montecito area

Coast Village Inn, 1188 Coast Village Road, Santa Barbara 93108; (805) 969-
3266, fax (805) 969-7117; $115–$165, suites $185–$395; pool, smoke
free, continental breakfast, children free, no pets, trolley tour of Santa
Barbara available

Four Seasons Biltmore, 1260 Channel Drive, Santa Barbara 93108; (805) 969-
2261, fax (805) 969-4682; $395–$660 (some midweek lower rates if available); waterfront resort, AAA four diamonds, pool, tennis courts, pets okay
in cottages

Montecito Inn, 1295 Coast Village Road, Santa Barbara 93108; (805) 969-
7854, fax (805) 969-0623; $205–$350; fully restored 1928 60-room retreat
built by Charlie Chaplin as hideaway for Hollywood figures; pool, sauna,
some fireplaces, handicapped-equipped rooms, fitness center, French
Provincial furnishings, restaurant, cafe, free breakfast, no pets

Close to Water/Cabrillo Boulevard

Brisas Del Mar Inn at The Beach, 223 Castillo Street, Santa Barbara 93101;
(805) 966-2219 or (800) 468-1988, fax (805) 962-9428; www.sbhotels
.com; $125 and up; 31 units, pool, kitchenettes, pets okay

Country Inn by the Sea, 128 Castillo Street, Santa Barbara 93101; (805) 963-
4471 or (800) 455-4647, fax (805) 962-2633;www.countryinnbythesea
.com; $89 and up; 45 units, patios or balconies, small pool, sauna, conti-
nental breakfast, no pets

Fess Parker's Doubletree Resort, 633 East Cabrillo Boulevard, Santa Barbara
93103; (805) 564-4333, (805) 893-0892 for reservations, fax (805) 564-
4964; www.FPDTR.com; rates are flexible starting at $200; 360 units in
waterfront parklike setting, patios, balconies, pool, tennis courts, restaurant,
coffee shop, bar; pets with deposit

Harbor View Inn, 28 West Cabrillo Boulevard, Santa Barbara 93101; (805)
963-0780, fax (805) 963-7967; www.harborviewinnsb.com; $250–$750;
115 units, pool, whirlpool, restaurant with ocean view; excellent service,
layout, AAA four diamonds; no pets

Hotel Mar Monte, 1111 East Cabrillo Boulevard, Santa Barbara 93101; (805)
963-0744 or (800) 643-1994, fax (805) 962-0985; www.hotelmarmonte
.com; $125 and up; 173 units, pool, fitness center, pets okay

Hotel Oceana, 202 West Cabrillo Boulevard, Santa Barbara 93101; (805)
965-4577 or (805) 966-9133, fax (805) 965-9937; www.hoteloceanasanta
barbara.com; summer $180–$350, winter $130–$250; 122 units overlooking ocean, small pool, continental breakfast, no pets.

Inn by the Harbor, 433 West Montecito Street, Santa Barbara 93101; (805) 963-7851 or (800) 626-1986, fax (805) 962-9428; www.shotels.com; $125–$200; pool, continental breakfast

Marina Beach Motel, 21 Bath Street, Santa Barbara 93101; (805) 963-9311, fax (805) 564-4102; www.marinabeachmotel.com; $119–$259; 32 units, continental breakfast, kitchenettes, pets okay

Santa Barbara Inn, 901 East Cabrillo Boulevard, Santa Barbara 93103; (805) 966-2285 or (800) 231-0431, fax (805) 966-6584; www.santabarbara inn.com; $279–$369; 71 units, pool, whirlpool, sundeck, French restaurant, pets with fee

Downtown/State Street

El Prado Inn, 1601 State Street, Santa Barbara 93101; (805) 966-0807 or (800) 669-8979, fax (805) 966-6502; www.elprado.com; $125 on up; 68 units, pool, continental breakfast

Hotel Santa Barbara, 533 State Street, Santa Barbara 93101; (805) 957-9300 or (888) 259-7700, fax (805) 962-2412; www.hotelsantabarbara.com; $129–$219; 75 units, restored historic hotel in heart of downtown, continental breakfast, valet parking

Upham Hotel, 1404 De La Vina Street, Santa Barbara 93101; (805) 962-0058 or (800) 727-0876; www.uphamhotel.com; $150–$400; 50 units divided between 1871 Victorian and cottages on beautiful grounds, complimentary breakfast, antiques, restaurant, beer/wine, no pets

Goleta

Best Western South Coast Inn, 5620 Calle Real, Goleta 93117; (805) 967-3200, fax (805) 683-4466; $106–$169; pool, whirlpool, continental breakfast, poolside patio, no pets

Holiday Inn–Santa Barbara/Goleta, 5650 Calle Real, Goleta 93117; (805) 964-6241, fax (805) 964-8467; $119–$155; pool, restaurant, use of health center, pets okay

Solvang

Alisal Guest Ranch, 1054 Alisal Road, Solvang 93463; (805) 688-3053; $335–$415; 10,000 acres, 73 cottages, 2 golf courses, tennis courts, riding, boating, dining, bar

Best Western–King Frederik Motel, 1617 Copenhagen Drive, Solvang 93463; (805) 688-5515, fax (805) 688-2067; $79–$129; pool, whirlpool, continental breakfast, no pets

𝓑ED-AND-BREAKFASTS

A surprising number of Santa Barbara area bed-and-breakfasts are historic buildings dating back well over a century. Simpson House Inn (805-963-7067), an 1878 Italianate Victorian, has been awarded a remarkable five diamonds by AAA and has fourteen units. Bath Street Inn (805-682-9680) is an 1890 Queen Anne Victorian, and the Cheshire Cat (805-569-1610) is an 1880 Queen Anne Victorian. The Mary May Inn (805-569-3398) includes a Queen Anne Victorian and a Federal-style house, both built in the 1880s. The Parsonage (805-962-9336) is an 1892 Victorian and is smoke free. Tiffany Inn (805-963-2283) is in Colonial Revival style built in 1898, and one house of Blue Dolphin Inn (805-965-2333) dates from 1860, making it one of the city's oldest occupied structures. The Glenborough Inn (805-966-0589) includes a portion built in the 1880s, while Olive House Inn (805-962-4902) is a California Craftsman erected in 1904. Early-twentieth-century structures include Old Yacht Club Inn (805-962-1277) and the Secret Garden & Cottages (805-687-2300). Even if you are not a devotee of historic architecture, you can enjoy the hospitality of the hosts and hostesses who have developed the amenities in these grand old buildings.

Best Western Kronborg Inn, 1440 Mission Drive, Solvang 93463; (805) 688-2383, fax (805) 688-1821; www.kronborginn.com; $139 and up; whirlpool

Petersen Village Inn, 1576 Mission Drive, Solvang 93463; (805) 688-3121, fax (805) 688-5732; www.peterseninn.com; $199–$340 including 3-course dinner and buffet breakfast; villagelike complex of cafes, bakery, conference facilities, Internet access, smoke free, AAA four diamonds, no pets

Royal Copenhagen Inn, 1579 Mission Drive, Solvang 93463; (805) 688-5561, fax (805) 688-7029; www.royalcopenhageninn.com; $65–$209; pool, free breakfast, pets okay in certain pet-friendly rooms, free wine tasting

Royal Scandinavian Inn, 400 Alisal Road (mail to P.O. Box 30), Solvang 93463; (805) 688-8000, fax (805) 688-0761; www.solvangrsi.com; $186 and up; some patios or balconies, pool, whirlpool, restaurant, on-sale license, continental breakfast, completely renovated in 2001, no pets

Solvang Inn and Cottages, 1518 Mission Drive, Solvang 93463; (805) 688-4702, fax (805) 688-6907; $45–$215; 6 cottages and 35 other units, beautifully landscaped, some Jacuzzis, pool, continental breakfast, no pets

Svendsgaard's Danish Lodge, 1711 Mission Drive, Solvang 93463; (805) 688-3277, fax (805) 686-5616; www.bestvalueinn.com; $55–$145, with no higher rates on holidays and "Danish Days" ("we do not gouge"); many fireplaces, pool, spa, continental breakfast, no pets

Bed-and-breakfast: Story Book Inn (805-688-1703; www.solvangstory book.com)

Ballard

Ballard Inn, 2436 Baseline Avenue, Ballard 93463; (805) 688-7770, fax (805) 688-9560; www.ballardinn.com; $195–$275; 15 units, AAA four diamonds, wine tasting in evening, full breakfast, no pets

Santa Ynez

Santa Ynez Inn, 3627 Sagunto Street (3 blocks off Highway 246), Santa Ynez 93460; (805) 688-5588 or (800) 643-5774, fax (805) 686-4294; www .santaynezinn.com; call for rates; luxury inn completed late 2001; 14 individually designed suites furnished with European antiques selected by owners, whirlpools, steam showers, dataports, spa services, restaurant

Los Olivos

Fess Parker's Wine Country Inn, 2860 Grand Avenue (mail to P.O. Box 849), Los Olivos 93441; (805) 688-7788, fax (805) 688-1942; www.fessparker .com; $260–$360, one suite at $450; some rooms with gas fireplaces, dining, pool, whirlpool, full breakfast, pets okay with $50 fee

Buellton

Best Western Pea Soup Andersen's Inn, 51 East Highway 246, Buellton 93427; (805) 688-3216 or (800) PEASOUP; www.peasoupandersens.com; $80–$109; 97 units, pool, whirlpool, continental breakfast, no pets

Days Inn Windmill, 114 East Highway 246, Buellton 93463; (805) 688-8448 or (800) 946-3406; www.daysinn-solvang.com; $80–$150; 108 units, pool, bar, pets okay

Santa Ynez Valley Marriott, 555 McMurray Road, Buellton 93427; (805) 688-1000 or (800) 638-8882; www.santaynezhotels.com; $81–$150; 149 units, pool, tennis courts, whirlpool, pets okay

Lompoc

Best Western O'Cairns Inn, 940 East Ocean Avenue, Lompoc 93436; (805) 735-7731, fax (805) 737-0012; $138 average; 83 units, pool, sauna, whirlpool, continental breakfast, small pets (10 lbs.) okay with $20 fee

Embassy Suites Hotel of Lompoc, 1117 North H Street, Lompoc 93436; (805) 735-8311, fax (805) 735-8459; $185 and up; 155 units, Internet access, pool, no pets

Holiday Inn Express, 1417 North H Street, Lompoc 93436; (805) 736-2391, fax (805) 736-6410; www.ichotelsgroup.com; $204 average; pool, whirlpool, continental breakfast, no pets

Quality Inn and Executive Suites, 1621 North H Street, Lompoc 93436; (805) 735-8555, fax (805) 735-8566; $144 average; 218 units, pool, spa, breakfast buffet, pets okay with $25 fee

Super 8 Motor Inn, 1020 East Ocean Avenue, Lompoc 93436; (805) 735-6444, fax (805) 735-5558; $91 and up; 53 units, sauna, whirlpool, continental breakfast, pets okay with $10 fee

Santa Maria

Best Western Big America, 1725 North Broadway, Santa Maria 93454; (805) 922-5200, fax (805) 922-9865; $124 and up; 106 units, pool, whirlpool, restaurant, continental breakfast, pets okay if under 30 lbs. and attended

Comfort Inn, 210 South Nicholson Avenue, Santa Maria 93454; (805) 922-5891, fax (805) 928-9222; $135 and up; 64 units, pool, spa, continental breakfast, small pets with $10 fee

Holiday Inn Hotel and Suites, 2100 North Broadway, Santa Maria 93454; (805) 928-6000, fax (805) 928-0356; $132 and up; pool, whirlpool, restaurant, on-sale license, no pets

Santa Maria Inn, 801 South Broadway, Santa Maria 93454; (805) 928-7777, fax (805) 928-5690; $140 and up; 164 units, pool, spa, restaurant, lounge, no pets

Arroyo Grande

Best Western Casa Grande Resort and Suites, 850 Oak Park Road, Arroyo Grande 93420; (805) 481-7398, fax (805) 481-4859; www.casa-grande.com; $125 average; 114 units, pool, sauna, whirlpool, restaurant, lounge, continental breakfast, no pets

Grover Beach

Holiday Inn Express Grover Beach, 775 North Oak Park Boulevard, Grover
Beach 93433; (805) 481-4448, fax (805) 473-3609; $62–$141; 78 units,
pool, whirlpool, steak house and saloon next door, continental breakfast, no
pets

Pismo Beach
Note: Price Street accommodations are on bluff overlooking surf.

Best Western Shelter Cove Lodge, 2651 Price Street, Pismo Beach 93449; (805)
773-3511, fax (805) 773-3511; www.bwsheltercove.com; $148–$288 (winter somewhat less); pool and spa, continental breakfast, no pets

Best Western Shore Cliff Lodge, 2555 Price Street, Pismo Beach 93449; (805)
773-4671, fax (805) 773-2341; www.shorecliff.com; $69–$299; pool,
sauna, whirlpool, balconies, restaurant, lounge, continental breakfast, no pets

Cottage Inn by the Sea, 2351 Price Street, Pismo Beach 93449; (805) 773-4617;
www.cottage-inn.com; $203–$369; pool, spa, free Internet connection,
continental breakfast, pets with $10 fee

Kon Tiki Inn, 1621 Price Street, Pismo Beach 93449; (805) 773-4833, fax
(805) 773-6541; www.kontikiinn.com; $125 average; 86 units, pool, sauna,
whirlpools, racquetball and tennis courts, restaurant, on-sale license, no pets

Oxford Suites Resort, 651 Five Cities Drive, Pismo Beach 93449; (805) 773-3773,
fax (805) 773-5177; $114 average; 133 units, pool, whirlpool, buffet break-
fast, pets okay with $5 fee

Sandcastle Inn, 100 Stimson Avenue, Pismo Beach 93449; (805) 773-2422, fax
(805) 773-0771; www.sandcastleinn.com; $131 and up (ocean view); 75
units, whirlpool, sundeck, no pets

SeaVenture Resort, 100 Ocean View Avenue, Pismo Beach 93449; (805) 773-
4994, fax (805) 773-0924; www.seaventure.com; $281 average (ocean view);
50 units, large spa, continental breakfast, no pets

Spyglass Inn, 2705 Spyglass Drive, Pismo Beach 93449; (805) 773-4855, fax
(805) 773-5298; www.spyglassinn.com; $89–$220; pool, whirlpool, large
Jacuzzi, restaurant, on-sale license, no pets

Also, Beachcomber Inn in the center of town (805-773-5505); Pismo
Lighthouse Suites (800-454-6835); and modestly priced motels including
Edgewater (805-773-4811), Ocean Palms (805-773-4669), Rose Garden
Inn (805-773-1841), Sea Crest Resort (805-773-4608), Sea Gypsy (805-
773-1801), and Shell Beach (805-773-4373)

Avila Beach

Avila La Fonda Hotel, 101 San Miguel Street, Avila Beach 93424; (805) 595-1700, fax (805) 773-8606; www.avilalafondahotel.com; $377 average; 33 units, a post-city restoration hotel with many luxury amenities, daily wine and barbecue, big-screen suite available, Internet access, DVD library

Avila Lighthouse Suites, 550 Front Street, Avila Beach 93424; (805) 627-1900 or (800) 372-8452, fax (805) 627-1909; www.avilalighthousesuites.com; $260 average; 54 two-room suites, next to beach, fireplaces, heated outdoor pool, spa, fitness room, Internet access, complimentary breakfast

Inn at Avila Beach, 256 Front Street, Avila Beach 93424; (805) 595-2300, fax (805) 773-8606; www.avilabeachca.com; $211 average; 31 units, 4 Jacuzzis, no pets. Oldest inn in Avila Beach dating back to late 1800s when it reputedly was a house of ill repute, then site of most social events when Avila was important port, Shore Patrol headquarters during WW II, '60s hippie commune, then refurbished as tourist haven, and in 1997 purchased by Micheal "Captain" Kidd and Kevin Thornton, who re-created the inn in Mediterranean, Mexican, Key West style (Jimmy Buffett music in the background) for beachcombers

San Luis Obispo

Apple Farm Inn and Apple Farm Trellis Court, 2015 Monterey Street, San Luis Obispo 93401; (805) 544-2040, fax (805) 544-9495; Inn: $149–$269; AAA four diamonds; Trellis Court: $231 average; 104 units, shared pool, whirlpool, restaurant, no pets

Best Western Royal Oak Hotel, 214 Madonna Road, San Luis Obispo 93405; (805) 544-4410, fax (805) 544-3026; $117 average; 99 units, pool, whirlpool, free breakfast, small pets okay with $10 fee

Best Western Somerset Manor, 1895 Monterey Street, San Luis Obispo 93405; (805) 544-0973, fax (805) 541-2805; $114 average (includes full breakfast); 40 units, pool, whirlpool, coffee shop, children twelve and under free, no pets

Embassy Suites, 333 Madonna Road, San Luis Obispo 93405; (805) 549-0800, fax (805) 543-5273; $218 average; 193 units, indoor pool, outdoor spa, deck whirlpools, restaurant, bar, Internet access, no pets

Garden Street Inn, 1212 Garden Street, San Luis Obispo 93401; (805) 945-9802; $140–$200; restored historic 1887 Queen Anne with 13 guest rooms and suites, decks, some Jacuzzis and fireplaces, library, wine reception, close to mission, no pets

Holiday Inn Express, 1800 Monterey Street, San Luis Obispo 93401; (805) 544-8600, fax (805) 541-4698; $179 average; 100 units, pool, spa, restaurant with bar, free breakfast, no pets

La Cuesta Motor Inn, 2074 Monterey Street, San Luis Obispo 93401; (805) 543-2777, fax (805) 544-0696; www.lacuestainn.com; $158 average; 72 units, first inn from north, attractive design, pool, whirlpool, balconies, continental breakfast, no pets

Madonna Inn, 100 Madonna Road, San Luis Obispo 93405; (805) 543-3000, fax (805) 643-1800; $137–$238, plus larger suites; dining room, lounge, shops, wine shop, coffee shop, bakery, spectacular lobby, smoke free, no pets

Peach Tree Inn, 2001 Monterey Street, San Luis Obispo 93401; (805) 543-3170 or (800) 227-6396, fax (805) 543-7673; www.peachtreeinn.com; $69–$170; bright, friendly family-run 31-room motel, continental breakfast, no pets

Quality Suites, 1631 Monterey Street, San Luis Obispo 93401; (805) 541-5001, fax (805) 546-9475; $169 average; 138 units, all suites; pool, spa, cooked to order breakfast, Internet access, library, no pets

Sands Suites and Motel, 1930 Monterey Street, San Luis Obispo 93401; (805) 544-0500, fax (805) 544-3529; $79–$189; 70 units, pool, whirlpool, on-site deli and liquor store, continental breakfast, pets okay with $10 fee

Los Osos

Best Western Sea Pines Golf Resort, 1945 Solano Street, Los Osos 93402; (805) 528-5252, fax (805) 528-8231; www.seapinesgolfresort.com; $99–$169; nine-hole golf course, two driving ranges, bar and grill, no pets

Morro Bay

Ascot Suites, 260 Morro Bay Boulevard, Morro Bay 93442; (805) 772-4437, fax (805) 772-8860; www.ascotinn.com; $229 average; most 31 rooms with whirlpools, pool, spa, restaurant, continental breakfast, wine and cheese at sunset, no pets. Historic Ascot Inn at same address; (805) 772-4437; $59–$179

Best Western San Marcos Inn, 250 Pacific Street, Morro Bay 93442; (805) 772-2248, fax (805) 772-6844; $192 average; 32 units, complimentary wine and cheese, continental breakfast, balconies, 50 percent have ocean views, no pets

Embarcadero Inn, 456 Embarcadero, Morro Bay 93442; (805) 772-2700, fax (805) 772-1060; www.embarcaderoinn.com; $142 average; 30 units, Internet access in rooms, many balconies and fireplaces, whirlpools, no pets

Inn at Morro Bay, 60 State Park Road, Morro Bay 93442; (805) 772-5651, fax
   (805) 772-4779; www.innatmorrobay.com; $203 average; 98 units, honey-
   moon cottage $400–$600; many rooms with fireplaces or balconies, pool,
   some bay views, restaurant, bar and grill, smoke free, no pets

La Serena Inn, 99 Morro Avenue (mail to P.O. Box 1711), Morro Bay 93442;
   (805) 772-5665 (phone and fax); www.laserenainn.com; $154 average,
   from $119; sauna, cider and cookies in evening, continental breakfast, no
   pets

Sunset Travelodge, 1080 Market Avenue, Morro Bay 93442; (805) 772-1259,
   fax (805) 772-8967; $174 average; 31 units, pool, continental breakfast,
   smoke free, no pets

Other decent lodgings, some with bay views: Bay View Lodge (805-772-2771), Best
   Western El Rancho (805-772-2212), Best Western Tradewinds (805-772-7376),
   Blue Sail Inn (805-772-7132), Breakers Motel (805-772-7317), Days Inn (805-
   772-2711), EconoLodge (805-772-5609), El Morro Lodge (805-772-5633),
   Keystone Inn (805-772-7503), Morro Crest Inn (805-772-7740), Sundown
   Motel (805-772-7381), Twin Dolphin (805-772-4483), Villager Motel (805-
   772-1235)

Cayucos

Beachwalker Inn, 501 South Ocean Avenue, Cayucos 93430; (805) 995-2133,
   fax (805) 995-3139; $80–$190; continental breakfast, upper-level rooms
   have view of ocean, no pets

Also four modest motels: Cypress Tree Motel (805-995-3917), Dolphin Inn
   (805-995-3810), Estero Bay Motel (805-995-3614), and Shoreline Inn
   (805-995-3681)

Atascadero

Best Western Colony Inn, 3600 El Camino Real, Atascadero 93422; (805) 466-
   4449, fax (805) 466-2119; www.pasoroblesgogrape.com; $130 average; 67
   units, pool, saunas, whirlpool, continental breakfast, no pets

Paso Robles

Adelaide Inn, 1215 Ysabel Avenue, Paso Robles 93446; (805) 238-2770, fax
   (805) 238-3497; www.adelaideinn.com; $64–$86; pool, sauna, whirlpool,
   no pets

Best Western Black Oak Motor Lodge, 1135 Twenty-fourth Street, Paso Robles 93446; (805) 238-4740, fax (805) 238-0726; $102 average; 110 units, pool, sauna, whirlpool, playground, coffee shop, no pets

Holiday Inn Express Hotel and Suites, 2525 Riverside Avenue, Paso Robles 93446; (805) 238-6500; $120 average; 44 units, indoor pool, no pets

La Bellasera Hotel and Suites, 705 Alexis Court, Paso Robles 93446; (805) 238-2834 or (866) 782-9669 or (866) STAYNOW, fax (805) 238-2826; www.labellasera.com; four levels of suites, about $300 average; 60 units, fireplaces, patios, kitchenettes, wireless access, pool, whirlpool, fitness center, restaurant, bar; opened July 13, 2007; via Highway 46 West, Theatre Drive

Paso Robles Inn, 1103 Spring Street, Paso Robles 93446; (805) 238-2660, fax (850) 238-4707; $95–$235; 100 units in historic, charming inn; pool, restaurant, lounge, no pets

Paso Robles Travelodge, 2701 Spring Street, Paso Robles 93446; (805) 238-0078, fax (805) 238-0822; $79 average; 31 units, pool, pets with $10 fee

Cambria

Best Western Fireside Inn by the Sea, 6700 Moonstone Beach Drive, Cambria 93428; (805) 927-8661, fax (805) 927-8584; $109–$239; 45 units, pool, whirlpool, continental breakfast, no pets

Blue Dolphin Inn, 6470 Moonstone Beach Drive, Cambria 93428; (805) 927-3300, fax (805) 927-7311; $159 average; 18 units, continental breakfast, no pets

Cambria Landing on Moonstone Beach, 6530 Moonstone Beach Drive, Cambria 93428; (805) 927-1619; $95–$225; most rooms face ocean with fireplaces and Jacuzzis, breakfast in bed, whirlpools, no pets

Fog Catcher Inn, 6400 Moonstone Beach Drive, Cambria 93428; (805) 927-1400, fax (805) 927-0204; $149–$169; 60 units, English country style, pool, whirlpool, buffet breakfast, no pets

Pelican Cove Inn, 6316 Moonstone Beach Drive, Cambria 93428; (805) 927-1500, fax (805) 927-3249; $239 average; 24 units, pool, continental breakfast, no pets

San Simeon Pines Seaside Resort, 7200 Moonstone Beach Drive, Cambria 93428 (mail to P.O. Box 117, San Simeon 93452); (805) 927-4648 or (866) 927-4648; $100–$175; nine-hole golf, pool, croquet, cottages, no pets or children

Sea Otter Inn, 6656 Moonstone Beach Drive, Cambria 93428; (805) 927-5888, fax (805) 927-0204; www.seaotterinn.com; $226 average; 25 units, pool, whirlpool, continental breakfast, no pets

Also (along Moonstone Beach Drive): Sand Pebbles Inn (805-927-5600), Captain's Cove Inn (805-927-8581), White Water Inn (805-927-1066), Cypress Cove Inn (805-927-2600), Cambria Shores Inn (805-927-8644), Castle Inn by the Sea (805-927-8605), Mariners Inn (805-927-4624); (downtown) Creekside Inn (805-927-4624), and Burton Inn (805-927-5125)

Bed-and-breakfasts: Blue Whale Inn B&B (805-927-4647, AAA four diamonds), J. Patrick House (805-927-3812), Olallieberry Inn (805-927-3222), Squibb House (805-927-9600), and Beach House (805-927-9850, not wheelchair accessible)

San Simeon

Best Western Cavalier Ocean Front Resort, 9415 Hearst Drive, San Simeon 93452; (805) 927-4688, fax (805) 927-6472; www.cavalierresort.com; $210 average; 60 rooms, many oceanfront, 4 ADA-compliant rooms, Internet access, pools, restaurant, bar, bonfire on bluff at sunset, pets okay

California Seacoast Lodge, 9215 Hearst Drive, San Simeon 93452; (805) 927-3878, fax (805) 927-1781; $79–$175; pool, whirlpool, continental breakfast, no pets

Also Inns of California, San Simeon (805-927-8659), San Simeon Lodge (805-927-4601), Silver Surf Motel (805-927-4661), Motel 6 Premier (805-927-8691), Sands Motel (805-927-3243), El Rey Garden Inn (805-927-3998)

San Miguel

One small, modestly priced motel: Western States Inn (805-467-3674)

GOLF COURSES

(All eighteen-hole, unless otherwise specified)

Santa Barbara County

Santa Barbara

Rancho San Marcos Golf Course, 4600 Highway 154, Santa Barbara; may need one-month reservation; (805) 688-6334

Santa Barbara Golf Club, Las Positas Road and McCaw Avenue, Santa Barbara; par 70; need one-week reservation; (805) 687-7087

Goleta

Glen Annie Golf Course, 405 Glen Annie Road, Goleta; par 71; need one-week reservation; (805) 968-6400

Hidden Oaks Golf Course, 4760 Calle Camarada, Goleta; nine holes, par 3; (805) 967-3493

Ocean Meadows Golf Course, 6925 Whittier Drive, Goleta; nine holes, par 3; (805) 968-6814

Sandpiper Golf Course, 7925 Hollister Avenue, Goleta; par 72; need one-week reservation; (805) 968-1541

Twin Lakes Golf Course, 6034 Hollister Avenue, Goleta; nine holes, par 29; (805) 964-1414

Vandenberg Air Force Base

Marshallia Ranch Golf Course (semiprivate), Vandenberg Air Force Base; par 72; (805) 734-4764

Lompoc

La Purisima Golf Course, 3455 East Highway 246, Lompoc; need one-week reservation; (805) 735-8395

Buellton

Zaca Creek Golf Course, 223 Shadow Mountain Drive, Buellton; nine holes, par 29; (805) 688-2575

Solvang
River Course at the Alisal, 150 Alisal Road, Solvang; par 72; (805) 688-6042

Nipomo
Black Lake Golf Resort, 1490 Golf Course Lane, Nipomo; par 72; (805) 343-1214

Santa Maria
Sunset Ridge Golf Course, 1425 Fairway Avenue, Santa Maria; nine holes, par 29; (805) 347-1070

San Luis Obispo County

Grover Beach
Pismo State Beach Golf Course, 25 Grand Avenue, Grover Beach; nine holes, par 29; (805) 481-5215

Avila Beach
Avila Beach Golf Resort, Avila Beach Drive, Avila Beach; par 71; (805) 595-4000 (ext. 510)

San Luis Obispo
Laguna Lake Golf Course, 11175 Los Osos Valley Road, San Luis Obispo; nine holes, par 31; (805) 781-7309

Los Osos
Sea Pines Golf Resort, 250 Howard Avenue, Los Osos; nine holes, par 28; (805) 528-1788

Morro Bay
Morro Bay Golf Course, 101 State Park Road, Morro Bay; par 71; (805) 772-4560

Paso Robles
Hunter Ranch Golf Course, 4041 Highway 46 East, Paso Robles; par 72; (805) 237-7444

Paso Robles Golf and Country Club (semiprivate), 1600 Country Club Drive, Paso Robles; par 71; (805) 238-4710

Atascadero
Chalk Mountain Golf Course, 10000 El Bordo Avenue, Atascadero; par 72; (805) 466-8848

MISSIONS OF THE CENTRAL COAST

Five of the chain of twenty-one missions founded in California by the Franciscan fathers were built in what is now Santa Barbara and San Luis Obispo Counties between 1772 and 1804. They are, in order from south to north:

Mission Santa Barbara, 2201 Laguna Street, Santa Barbara 93105; (805) 682-4713

La Purisima Concepcion, in La Purisima Mission State Historic Park, 2295 Purisima Road, Lompoc 93436; (805) 733-3713

Mission Santa Ines, 1760 Mission Drive, Solvang 93463; (805) 688-4815

Mission San Luis Obispo de Tolosa, 751 Palm Street at Monterey Street, San Luis Obispo 93401; (805) 543-6850

Mission San Miguel Arcangel, 775 Mission Street, San Miguel 93451; (805) 467-3256

MUSEUMS

Santa Barbara Museum of Art, 1130 State Street, Santa Barbara; (805) 963-4364

Carriage and Western Arts Museum, 129 Castillo Street, Santa Barbara; (805) 962-2353

Karpeles Manuscript Library Museum, 21 West Anapamu Street, Santa Barbara; (805) 962-5322

Santa Barbara Historical Museum, 136 East De la Guerra Street, Santa Barbara; (805) 966-1601

Santa Barbara Museum of Natural History, 2559 Puesta del Sol Road, Santa Barbara; (805) 682-4711

South Coast Railroad Museum, 300 North Los Carneros Road, Goleta; (805) 964-3540

Lompoc Museum, 200 South H Street, Lompoc; (805) 736-3888

Santa Maria Museum of Flight, 3015 Airpark Drive, Santa Maria; (805) 922-8758

Santa Maria Valley Historical Society Museum, 616 South Broadway, Santa Maria; (805) 922-3130

Museum Art Center, near Cook and Pine Streets, Santa Maria; (805) 346-1855

Elverhoj Museum of History and Art, 1624 Elverhoj Way, Solvang; (805) 686-1211

Santa Ynez Valley Historical Museum, 3596 Sagunto Street, Santa Ynez; (805) 688-7889

San Luis Obispo Art Center, 1010 Broad Street, San Luis Obispo; (805) 543-8562

San Luis Obispo County Historical Museum, 696 Monterey Street, San Luis Obispo; (805) 543-0638

San Luis Obispo Children's Museum, 1010 Nipomo Street, San Luis Obispo; (805) 544-5437

Saint-Onge Museum of Natural History, Thirteenth and Spring Streets, Paso Robles; (805) 467-3710

Veterans Memorial Museum, 801 Grand Avvenue, San Luis Obispo; (805) 543-1763

FACTORY STORES

Santa Barbara is known for its companies' factory stores. Here are the larger ones.

Italian Pottery Outlet, 19 Helena Street, between State and Anacapa Streets, Santa Barbara 93101; (805) 564-7655. Open 10:00 a.m.–6:00 p.m. Monday–Saturday, 10:00 a.m.–5:00 p.m. Sunday. Visa, MasterCard. Wheelchair accessible. The largest selection of Italian ceramics in the West, including seconds and firsts from classics to glass, jewelry, and garden fun.

Jandd Mountaineering, 30 Calle Cesar Chavez, Santa Barbara 93103; (805) 882-1195. Open 9:00 a.m.–7:00 p.m. Monday–Saturday, 11:00 a.m.–5:00 p.m. Sunday. Visa, MasterCard, Discover. Wheelchair accessible. Great independent source for outdoor and adventure gear, firsts and seconds in travel and book packs and luggage, fly-fishing, hiking, mountaineering equipment. Fun place and people.

Magellan's Catalog Retail Outlet Store, 110 West Sola Street, next to the Upham Hotel, Santa Barbara 93101; (805) 568-5400. Open 9:00 a.m.–5:30 p.m. Monday–Saturday. Visa, MasterCard. Partly wheelchair accessible. One of the country's largest mail-order travel stores for hats, clocks, outerwear, bags, walking sticks.

Santa Barbara Ceramic Design Factory Store, 436 East Gutierrez Street, Santa Barbara 93101; (805) 966-3883. Open 10:00 a.m.–5:00 p.m. daily. Visa, MasterCard. Wheelchair accessible. Irregulars, overstock, discontinued and experimental pottery, as well as seconds from Mary Engelbreit, Nancy Thomas, Classic Pooh, Judy Buswell, Carol Endres, and others.

Teddy Bear Outlet, 4185-1 Carpinteria Avenue, Carpinteria 93013; (805) 566-4883, fax (805) 684-5536. Open 10:00 a.m.–5:00 p.m. Monday–Saturday, noon–5:00 p.m. Sunday. Visa, MasterCard, American Express. Wheelchair accessible. More than 50,000 collector Steiff, Gund, Applause, Cooperstown, Raikes, Boyds, Russ Berrie, and artist teddy bears.

Territory Ahead Outlet Store, 419 State Street, Santa Barbara 93101; (805) 962-5558. Open 10:00 a.m.–6:00 p.m. Monday–Saturday, 11:00 a.m.–5:00 p.m. Sunday. Visa, MasterCard, American Express, Discover. Wheelchair accessible. Same great outdoor equipment and clothing as in its retail store 1 block up State Street, but here everything is maybe one season old and a lot less expensive. Great people both places.

INDEX

ABOUT THE AUTHORS

*K*athleen and Gerald Hill have written more than twenty books together, including six Hill Guides on the U.S. West Coast, as well as political and legal dictionaries.

Fourth-generation Californians, the Hills live in the heart of northern California's wine country. They also spend time in Victoria, British Columbia, where they taught U.S. politics and government at the University of British Columbia and at the University of Victoria. They currently teach at Sonoma State University.

The Hills each host weekly radio shows and are regular columnists for the *Sonoma Valley Sun,* where Kathleen serves as Food & Wine Editor.

The Hills's four children are scattered from British Columbia to Los Angeles, providing a great excuse to travel and sample the food and wine of every region along the West Coast.